Living as the Beloved:

One Day at a Time

Living as the Beloved: One Day at a Time

Sandra L. Bochonok

2004
Chi Rho Press, Inc.
Gaithersburg, Maryland, USA

Unless otherwise noted, all Bible translations used are from the *New Revised Standard Version*, Copyright of the New Revised Standard Version, 1989 by the Division of Christian Education of the National Council of the Churches of Christ in the United States of America.

Chi Rho Press, Inc.
P.O. Box 7864
Gaithersburg, MD 20898, USA
301/926-1208 phone/fax
Orders@ChiRhoPress.com e-mail
http://www.ChiRhoPress.com Web site

Dedication

To you, the reader
Cherish your belovedness

About the Author

Writer, retreat leader, labyrinth facilitator, former nurse and Navy Chaplain, Rev. Dr. Sandra Bochonok is the founding pastor of http://soulfoodministry.org, a special ministry of the Metropolitan Community Church of Washington, D.C. Originally ordained in the Evangelical Covenant Church of America, she transferred her clergy credentials into the Universal Fellowship of Metropolitan Community Churches in 1996.

She holds a Diploma in Nursing (Cook County School of Nursing in Chicago), BSHSA (University of Phoenix), Master of Divinity (Trinity Evangelical Divinity School in Illinois), four units of Clinical Pastoral Education, a certificate in Group Spiritual Direction (Shalem Institute for Spiritual Formation in Bethesda, Maryland), and Doctor of Ministry (Wesley Theological Seminary in Washington, D.C.). In her spare time she enjoys clogging, gardening, birding, lighthouses, hiking, cross-country skiing, and sailing in the Pacific Northwest.

Acknowledgements

There have been so many people instrumental in my life and the development of this book. Without their encouragement and assistance, contributions, and inspiration, this book would never have been written. I thank God for each person.

I am especially grateful to Adam DeBaugh, my publisher and friend at Chi Rho Press. Adam encouraged me to write for publication several years before this book was even a conscious thought in my head.

Then two retreat opportunities facilitated by the Reverend Ann Dean at Dayspring Retreat Center forever transformed my understanding of belovedness and ministry. I am indebted to her wisdom, compassion, humor, spiritual direction, and friendship.

How do I begin to express my deep appreciation and gratitude to Jenny Glenn and Geraldine Wright? Their friendship, encouragement, generosity, and dedication to the multilingual work at the ministry of http://soulfoodminstry.org are my constant source of blessing and joy. I thank God for these two wonderful women and their enthusiastic "mischief making" and unflagging support for this book.

Special recognition goes to my editor, Kevin Stone Fries. His numerous questions and devoted work helped create a better book, and matured my writing. And my most sincere thanks to artist Craig Arnold – his marvelous painting graces the cover of this book.

Heartfelt appreciation to Metropolitan Community Church of Washington, DC and their dynamic senior pastor, my dear friend and MCC mentor, the Reverend Candace Shultis. As a very busy pastor of a large urban church, she always had time to offer constructive feedback and comments in the early days of my devotional writing.

Thanks to my excellent writing mentor and friend from Australia, "God's Gnome." You inspire me with every e-mail and long distance telephone conversation.

Finally, I bless and thank family and friends who loved me unconditionally throughout the years involved in writing this book.

The Rev. Dr. Sandra L. Bochonok
January 2004

Publisher's Note

This remarkable book is a labor of love, dedication, and patience. The Rev. Dr. Sandra Bochonok has poured her immense spirit, her steadfast faith, her great learning, and her gentle, loving presence into each of these 366 daily meditations.

Living as the Beloved features a Scripture reading, a devotion based on it, and prayer for every day of the year. Dr. Bochonok's meditations are poignant, wise, and amazingly pastoral. Her many years of ministry as a military chaplain and pastor, and now as an Internet pastor, shine through her every word. Her meditations are simple, basic Christian teaching; yet glow with power, grace, and beauty. These are devotions that will light your days for many years to come.

Dr. Bochonok's beloved grandmother is the inspiration for many of the daily devotions found in *Living as the Beloved*. Her familiar saying, "One day at a time, dear Lord, one day at a time" is reflected from time to time throughout the book. Dr. Bochonok has expressed her hope that through this book, she will help people reclaim their belovedness.

We are sure you will agree that Dr. Bochonok has fulfilled her goal of "helping people reclaim their belovedness" with this wonderful new book.

The author's dedication to her ministry has been joined by the dedicated work of Kevin Stone Fries, who served as Editor of Chi Rho Press during much of the time we were preparing this book for publication. His editorial skills and dogged determination are reflected in every page.

And patience has also been required since it has taken far too long to get the book you now hold into your hands. We are grateful to the author for her patience with our sometimes cumbersome and glacially slow process, and to our readers who have waited patiently for this book. We believe it is worth the wait!

We want also to acknowledge the talent and skill of Craig Arnold, who painted the cover art for this book. The Rev. Clay H. Witt, a loyal and hard working member of the Chi Rho Press board of directors, served as a strong supporter of this book, a reader, and a guide throughout this process and continues to be a strong, steady, and faithful presence in Chi Rho Press.

I would be remiss if I did not acknowledge some amazing people who have invested financially in the life and ministry of Chi Rho Press and especially in this book. They choose to remain anonymous, but they know our thanks and prayers are with them.

Enjoy, learn from, and be blessed by this book! You are beloved!

R. Adam DeBaugh
Director, Chi Rho Press
http://www.ChiRhoPress.com

Living as the Beloved: One Day at a Time
†   Foreword   †

My beloved grandmother blessed me with a rich spiritual legacy that I wish to pass on to the next generation. Her faith was deep and simple. She prayed every day of her adult life and would often croon, "One day at a time, dear Lord, one day at a time." "One day at a time" became her mantra for living when life was difficult. She loved reading the Bible and she loved her church. I wish to honor her blessed memory and faithful life with the title of this book.

Several years after her death, my life and ministry was transformed when I first read the late Henri J. M. Nouwen's devotional book, *Life of the Beloved: Spiritual Living in a Secular World.* Belovedness was something I desperately needed, as I left the denomination that originally ordained me and found a ministry in the Universal Fellowship of Metropolitan Community Churches (UFMCC). My spiritual director at the time facilitated guided, silent, contemplative retreats at Dayspring Retreat Center in Germantown, Maryland. I read Nouwen's book numerous times and eventually co-facilitated the first Beloved Retreat specifically for gay, lesbian, bisexual, and transgendered people throughout the UFMCC's Mid-Atlantic District. Those on the retreat were deeply touched by their experiences and I became determined to spend the remainder of my life helping people reclaim their belovedness, especially among those the traditional mainstream churches often rejected because of their sexual orientation.

Though I was myself a technically challenged pastor, I had been researching the Internet as a spirituality tool for my doctor of ministry project in 1997 and 1998. A technically gifted and generous Web manager provided the expertise to begin online outreach, distributing my written reflections.

As a result, the gracious ministry of www.soulfoodministry.org began in August 1998. From the very beginning, I felt called to write materials that would help people pray and read the Gospel for the first time. I have attempted to write respectfully for an international readership while affirming all sexual orientations.

I remember reading in the national news the surprising statistic that one out of every five North Americans now uses the Internet as a spirituality resource.[1] Over the past two years, these reflections have been enjoyed by cyber-readers from more than eighty countries. Some of these devotional thoughts have been translated into Spanish, French, Portuguese, and Russian. My gratitude is boundless for all who have provided time, prayers, talents, and skills to empower this growing multilingual outreach. Yet not everyone is online. About half of America's adults choose not to use the Internet, and experts say it may take a generation for that attitude to change. They are called "America's Netless by choice,"[2] and they represent approximately 31 million Americans.

Living As the Beloved is not only for those who might miss my online ministry, but also for all readers on a spiritual journey of their own. I have written these reflections to help meet the three major needs of those people I have encountered during my ministry. Throughout my years of ordained ministry, I have heard two questions over and over again. Those questions have been, "Can you help me pray?" and "Just what is a gospel?" Many of these reflections address those two needs. Many people in the twenty-first century are unfamiliar with the gospel stories, therefore the daily reflections for several months are provided to help readers linger in the gospel of Matthew.

Why Matthew's gospel? The name "Matthew" means "God's gift." He was initially despised by many of his peers and society until Jesus brought him into the inner circle of disciples, mentoring him into spiritual greatness and leadership. As an ordained MCC minister, I serve within a growing Christian global movement that affirms and welcomes people of all sexual orientations. Some people unfortunately experience a lack of acceptance in homophobic churches, their families, and societies. I believe Matthew's perspective as one who is no longer despised, but beloved by Jesus, offers these readers profound insights for spiritual empowerment. Matthew is a great teacher. He brings us into the classroom of Christ where all are welcomed at the table of God.

The third universally shared need is to receive personal blessings. We often live in a world full of cursing and negative messages. Cursing is destructive while blessing empowers. Thus, the reflections for the entire

---

[1] Barna, George. "New Study Predicts a Cyberchurch," *Internet for Christians Newsletter.* Issue 57, 12 May 1998.

[2] Jesdanum, Anick. "Working Netless…by Choice." *The Sun.* 22 September 2000, p. A8.

month of March are dedicated to reclaiming and sharing our blessedness and belovedness.

Internet readers have commented on how much they have appreciated and enjoyed an unhurried daily reading in Matthew. Some were surprised to learn that reading the Bible could be so interesting. Others noted that the contemplative reading helped them become more alert and open to God's loving presence in their daily lives.

Many have asked me why I initially wrote these reflections under the Internet penname, "Surprised by Joy." I have been surprised by God and surprised by life. My initial ordained ministry was serving as an active duty Navy chaplain through a conservative evangelical church. When I left that ministry to serve more fully in an inclusive Christian denomination (MCC), my spirit felt crushed with doubt and despair. One day I needed a pen name to write a brief devotional for a local MCC congregation. All the pastors and seminarians from that worshipping congregation wrote their devotional contributions under various pen names. As I wrote that short meditation, I realized I had been "surprised by joy." I have written under that pen name since 1997. Names are deeply significant and "Surprised by Joy" has been a great blessing and encouragement to many readers in cyberspace.

Now it is time to be known by my real name as an ordained Christian minister.

May the peace of Christ and all the blessings of God be with you. May your *Living as the Beloved: One Day at a Time* experience be one of wonder and ever growing love. May the kindness of God meet you and bless you. I hope and pray God will surprise each of you with joy throughout the journey.

Rev. Dr. Sandra L. Bochonok

† How to use *Living as the Beloved: One Day at a time* †

This is a daily devotional for your spiritual empowerment and enjoyment. Each day contains a scripture reading with an appropriate reflection and closing prayer. The reflections are contemplative in nature, inviting readers to experience a new and fresh experience in God. They are meant to broaden your sacred reading with carefully selected nourishing words to savor and enjoy.

Many people start the year with plans to diet and exercise. Here is a fresh diet of sacred words with easy to learn spiritual exercises and practices. The daily devotionals offer a wide variety of Bible readings.

Now the key to keeping any New Year's resolution is to stick with it until the resolution becomes a routine. Holy habits take time, patience, perseverance, and a willingness to experience God in new and deeper ways. So find the time of the day that works best for your reading and reflections. Some of us are energized by morning habits. Others find the afternoon or evening more conducive for personal reading. The key to success is to make your reading time a habit.

Jim Ryan was a famous American track athlete who understood the power of daily practices that strengthen winning habits. He often motivated himself and others by saying motivation is what gets us started, but habit is what keeps us going.

How do we develop the habit of living as the beloved on a daily basis? So many doubt their belovedness. This deeply influences our view of others and ourselves. These doubts deeply affect our self-worth and sense of well being. They can actually lead us to self-rejection and inner self-loathing. Lingering with these uncomplicated reflections can begin and encourage deep inner healing, self-acceptance, and wholeness.

This daily devotional invites all readers to live as the beloved on a daily basis. Belovedness is our common calling. Refuse to settle for anything less in your spiritual life with God.

†   Daily scripture readings   †

This is a book for readers who may perhaps be new to daily Bible reading and prayer. But it is also written for people who are spiritually fatigued, discouraged, and disillusioned with religion in general. This book is also for those well acquainted with sacred words from various spiritual traditions. Sometimes these inspirational words are so familiar that they become common, stale, and trite. And others are even afraid of reading sacred words of any kind.

A good daily devotional can help move us from dull religiosity to a vibrant spirituality, from being scared to enjoying sacred readings. Enjoy these reflections and experience spiritual sanctuary, hospitality, generosity, and abundance as you engage in many conversations with your Divine center.

Daily scripture readings are provided with each meditation. Sometimes entire passages will be listed. At other times you will find there is only a phrase or single verse used for that day's reflection. Certain meditations tell a story or retell a parable of Jesus in common terms. It is often empowering and healing as we hear the stories in more depth and detail, learning to retell these stories in our own words. In doing so, we find our own place in them and our lives are transformed in the process.

In other reflections, only a word or phrase is needed to become more focused and intentional in your quiet time. In the contemplative tradition sometimes less is best. Our spiritual skills improve as we use these simple centering prayer practices daily. Reclaiming inner strength through intentional moments of silence, stillness, solitude, and lingering with a sacred word or phrase encourage and strengthen the growth and nurture of the portable chapels of our hearts.

Many traditions encourage the lighting of a candle while engaging in spiritual readings. God's light in each of us is generous. Often through lingering by a candle, we can become more intentionally centered and grounded. We can symbolically breathe in the light while breathing out our inner darkness, while seeking more spiritual understanding, healing, and wholeness.

Certain themes are emphasized to empower inner growth. Be encouraged and use this devotional every day. Reading the Bible is a worthy spiritual discipline to learn. Take it one page or chapter at a time and trust the process of daily tending your soul with sacred words.

We read for many reasons. We read for information, knowledge, inspiration, and pleasure. The Bible is a valuable resource. The teachings of Jesus offer words of love and wisdom worth reclaiming for every generation. They have a universal appeal. Originally these daily devotionals were posted at http://www.soulfoodministry.org. Readers from 83 countries enjoyed them. Some were actually surprised when they realized that they were reading the Bible. They were amazed at how culturally relevant and helpful it was. Others noted that the slower pace of devotional reading actually enhanced their awareness and openness to the powerful words of scripture.

There have been times in my own life when large amounts of Bible reading have fed my soul. But there are other times when less is best. You will notice certain readings encourage very old, cherished, and simple devotional practices. *Lectio divina* is one such trusted practice of holy reading and rereading until a word or phrase lingers in your heart with special awareness and grace. Sometimes you will be encouraged to imagine yourself in the Bible story using your senses of smell, taste, sight, and touch. Scripture memorization is yet another practice with which to experiment. Reading holy words aloud again and again can be a powerful and transforming experience. Try them all and find what blesses you. These nourishing sacred words will come back to help you during moments of your greatest needs. These profoundly simple practices cannot be rushed. They help us hear our heartbeat and listen to our breathing, while experiencing loving holy Presence.

So be open to the reflections and inner movement of the Spirit. Read them with an open heart and mind. Let the words sink into your heart and being. Respond to the scripture with an awareness of your own history, actions, desires, and needs. Dialogue with the scripture with your mind, emotions, and heart. Read the scripture as a personal love letter from God to you. It is helpful to ask questions while reading. What are these readings telling you about God and yourself? What meaning do they have? Where and how is God moving in your life? Can you discern new movement of the Spirit?

This daily devotional is simply a guide. It will guide you through a variety of Bible readings, including the gospel of Matthew, the lovely story of Ruth, generous sections of Philippians, and a variety of Psalms to enhance the prayers of your heart. In these pages you will experience the journey to Christmas, Jesus as a great spirituality teacher, the pilgrimage to the cross, and the victorious Easter story.

You might find yourself considering the purchase of your first Bible while reading these reflections. If so, congratulations. Reading the Bible can be one of the most pleasurable experiences in your life. Buying one is a significant investment. Reading it will transform your life. So before buying your first Bible, take the time to experience a variety of translations. Find a translation that speaks deeply to your heart and that is easy to read and understand. Many public libraries have a variety of Bibles in their reference sections. Consider experimenting with the amazing variety of free Internet Bibles. These will enhance your reading experiences with this daily devotional.

† Prayer †

We each talk with God in our own way. There are many valuable and sometimes confusing prayer practices, methods, and formulas. Some are more helpful and speak more deeply to our hearts than others. Most involve many words and some may even feel like you are presenting a grocery list of needs to God. We can be so busy talking to and about God that we neglect to listen deeply to God in the silence. And most cultures and lifestyles are noisy, busy, and hectic. As a result, we often pray on the run as we commute to work, activities, and social events.

But prayer is often learned best by praying in quiet and privacy. There are many simple yet profound daily practices that can help us become more attentive and available to God. These practices can help us discern God's loving holy presence throughout the day, wherever we go. Many of these daily devotionals are focused on prayer, especially with selected teachings and prayer habits of Jesus.

Prayer resources are within each of us. Praying helps us experience God nearer than our hands and feet. Prayer helps us experience God being closer than our breathing. We pray when God seems silent and when our feelings are too deep for words. The Bible is full of hundreds of great prayers, offering many teaching and contemplative, centering prayers. Prayer is a great gift from God.

Jesus believed in prayer. He prayed and lived greatly. Prayer helped him die without fear, anger, hatred, or despair. Prayer helped him die with dignity and courage, experiencing great inner peace within him and with God. Jesus was and remains the world's greatest prayer master. The gospels never mention the disciples asking Jesus for a preaching or teaching class. Instead, they noted his deep spiritual power and asked for prayer lessons. The Lord's Prayer is the result of their request and you will find a number of reflections devoted to this great prayer.

Daily prayers help us carry inner altars of our hearts everywhere we go. Each daily devotional concludes with a very brief prayer. Feel free to expand those prayers. Jot down specific prayers that come to your heart and mind. Date and sign them. You will find this to be a source of great spiritual blessing and a reminder of God's continual, gracious care and intervention in your life. Prayer changes us, world history in the making, and others. History actually belongs to the intercessors.

So be open to some of the prayer suggestions in the devotional readings. Find quiet and uninterrupted places for your prayer closet. Linger in conversations with God throughout the day. Search for intimate, tender names for the Holy. Let God speak to you through stillness, silence, a word, a repetitive prayer mantra, or an image. Consider practicing prayer through meaningful repetition, such as repeating the Lord's Prayer morning, noon, and night as you interact with the devotional materials.

Pray the daily scripture reading. Ask God for understanding, specific help for your day, and for others. Consider closing your prayers in the name of Jesus. Praying in the name of Jesus Christ has been a source of great power and comfort for millions. Many are amazed at their answered prayers when they keep a periodic prayer journal and notebook. Write some letters to God and ask for even more understanding and insights.

Expect miracles of grace in your life. But pray until you pray. Expect to meet God. Expect transforming moments. Be open to new ideas. Open minds mean open doors to God. Some of the prayer devotionals mention exterior prayer tools such as prayer rugs and Tibetan prayer bowls. There is something to be learned with such simple and universal practices from other faiths.

There are many breath prayers throughout this book. We are what we breathe. Breathing with God helps us center and find inner resources. Other reflections in this book encourage the use of body prayers. Simple symbolic movements can bring holy and delightful changes into our prayer lives. Through sitting, walking, standing, kneeling, moving our bodies, we can experience loving holy presence in many new ways.

Yes, there are many ways to pray. Two essential conditions to nurture your conversations with God are moments of silence and solitude. Money cannot buy what the silence will bring you. This is a book dedicated to helping you experience silence, solitude, inner quiet, and stillness with and without journal writing. There are many reasons why these ancient and universal prayer practices have lasted throughout the centuries.

Our prayers can also be strengthened by times of fasting. Fasting helps us enter our private prayer closets with more intention and attentiveness to God. Through fasting, we give up something very important to us in order that our prayer time for others can be empowered. Whether you fast or feast during your daily reading, find a quiet place to linger in prayers of the heart.

Silence, stillness, solitude, journal writing, spiritual readings, prayer, and meditation all require a daily discipline that many of us lack. Ask God for help. But also ask your family members, friends, and roommates to honor your quiet times and not interrupt you. I have found it helpful to have special areas in the house to pray and read. While reading these reflections, remove your pagers and turn off the alarm on your watch. Let your telephone voice mail or answering machine take your calls.

Honor your quiet time. Your body and spirit will benefit from a few daily minutes of stillness and quiet. Rich moments of such simple soul care can bring deepening awareness of loving, holy Presence. Even thirty seconds to two minutes a day can bring amazing benefits into your life. Experiment and schedule times of prayer at a local park or use an indoor or outdoor labyrinth. An increasing number of people are finding the labyrinth and other forms of walking meditation energizing and helpful. Going to a special place is a pilgrimage that every reader can enjoy.

✝ Conclusion ✝

This book begins with a centering prayer suggestion using the word "beloved." Belovedness is our spiritual heritage. It is to be our lifestyle. We are called to live as the beloved and not as the despised. God is passionately in love with you. Be loved in word, thought, and deed. Expect to be loved in every day of your reading and prayer. Belovedness is God's gift to us. So be loved, beloved reader. Prepare for an adventure with God as you read this book.

As with all spiritual practices, we can only make the effort. The next step is up to God. Expect God to honor your spiritual readings and practices. Expect to be surprised by God, by life, and with moments of great joy when you least expect them as you practice the presence of God in your life through these readings. Accept the blessings with great gratitude. Share your experiences with others. Spiritual empowerment is as close as your hands and feet, nearer than your breathing.

God bless you.

Rev. Dr. Sandra L. Bochonok

Living as the Beloved:

One Day at a Time

Sandra L. Bochonok

† January 1 – New Year's Day †

Beloved

1 John 4:7

Welcome to a new year with all its promise and potential. If I could give you only one word for the year, it would be "beloved." The late Henri Nouwen wrote, "Being the Beloved expresses the core truth of our existence."[3] But how do we live as the Beloved? I think my grandmother might have had an answer.

If I listed the ten people who have most influenced my life, my grandmother would be at the top of that list. It was Voltaire who noted that common sense is not so common. Common sense was my grandmother's great virtue, in addition to her hearty sense of humor. Her favorite saying was "One day at a time, dear Lord, one day at a time." She would often remind me to "keep looking up!" Her spiritual wisdom and common sense have stayed with me for more than forty years.

Grandma was a courageous woman who came to North America from Norway with her family during the Great Depression. She never had the opportunity to finish grammar school. She was well acquainted with sorrow, having buried her first-born on her first Christmas Day in a new country. Grandma's marriage lasted seventy-two years. When she prayed, God listened!

I lived with her and Grandpa during my early seminary career. Together we cared for my mother as she struggled with breast cancer. We also cared for Grandpa during this difficult time. He was both speechless and paralyzed from a series of strokes. Every evening Grandma would prepare him for bed. Before sleeping, she would sit at his bedside, hold his hand and pray for all her family by name. And she would softly sing, "One day at a time, dear Lord, one day at a time. Help me keep looking up." She was living as the Beloved.

Usually New Year's resolutions are broken or forgotten within days. But if you want this year to be different from all others, commit yourself to an experiment with God for the next 365 days. Use the word "beloved" as your centering breath prayer and mantra. Let this word grow into two words, quietly breathing in the word "be," while exhaling the word "loved." Invite these words to become your daily prayer. Do this and your life will be transformed. And keep looking up.

---

[3] Nouwen, Henri. *Life of the Beloved: Spiritual Living in a Secular World*, p. 28.

God, bless me as your beloved child. Help me be loved this year with every breath. Amen.

† **January 2** †

Love

1 Corinthians 13:4-7

The older I get, the more grateful I am for love. On my home re-frigerator hangs a magnet that reads, "To love and be loved is the greatest gift." Another magnet reads, "Kindness - a language deaf people can hear and blind people see." My favorite phrase, however, comes from the Bible and is engraved on my favorite coffee cup, "Most of all, let love guide your life" (Colossians 3:14 TLB).

Many people are surprised to learn the Bible is a wonderful love story. We can find our place in the Bible story by simply reading the Gos-pel accounts of Matthew, Mark, Luke, and John. The storybook uses many different words for love. Those words describe erotic love, platonic friendship, and God's enormous and unconditional love for us in all its fullness and beauty. Love is the greatest force in the universe and, I be-lieve, it is our greatest blessing.

The Bible tells two great truths about God. The first is summed up in three words, "God is love" (1 John 4:16b). Evidence that shows God and love are one is found throughout all the stories, dramas, parables, and ancient Biblical narratives.

The second astonishing truth is that the God of Creation is deeply and passionately in love with us (John 3:16 and 1 John 4:10). No matter how unlovable we feel, God loves us. God's love for us is boundless and deeper than any ocean, higher than any mountain. We can never fully un-derstand the depth and commitment of God's love for us. God's love is a free gift and great mystery. Gratitude can be our only response.

What is love? Love is God. Love is patient and kind; never arro-gant or rude or irritable or resentful. God's love never ends. We are God's beloved and called to live loving lives. Being in love with God is our highest calling.

The New Year awaits us with all its wonders and uncertainties. May our love grow deeper with every passing day for God, others, and ourselves.

Give us more love, dear God. Overflow our hearts. Help us love. Amen.

† January 3 †
Friends with God
John 13:23b

"I want what you have," explained a lesbian friend as we walked and talked one wintry afternoon. "You have something I need. Do I get it by being in spiritual direction?" I marveled at her intensity as I struggled to explain what spiritual direction was.

"Perhaps," I gently suggested, "before beginning spiritual direction, you might consider reading the Gospel stories about Jesus found in Matthew, Mark, Luke, and John and try praying with the Psalms. Try a few minutes of daily quiet prayer, spiritual reading, and simply rest in God. This has been my way of becoming friends with Jesus while learning to trust God."

God and I have been in this ongoing, growing relationship for more than forty years. Relationships take time, effort, intention, and openness.

I know of many people who are afraid to trust God. When we are afraid to trust, it is difficult to love. Numerous sexual minorities have been tragically Bible-bashed by well-intentioned people of faith. But after years of study, I believe these well-intentioned people are misguided in their Biblical understanding on this issue.

Jesus is totally non-homophobic and is quite open to human diversity. Many believe John to be the disciple "whom Jesus loved" (John 13:23; 19:26; 20:2; 21:7, 20, 24). John's Gospel is written as by a close and intimate friend of Jesus. John's Gospel is a love letter. He and Jesus were soul friends. Their love was as intense as David and Jonathan's in the Hebrew Scriptures.

When others betrayed, deserted, denied, and persecuted Jesus, only the beloved disciple John actively tried to protect his dear friend. He bravely stood at the cross with the courageous women as his dearest friend was brutally crucified. As a result, John's best and dearest friend's dying trust was for John to care for his mother. We see God honoring families of choice. Jesus entrusted his mother to his beloved John.

Beloved John offers us many insights on friendship. He knew how to linger with his beloved friend. They enjoyed spending time together. Deep, intimate friendship grows this way. Contemplative friendship is often like prayer. It is companionship without words. Friendship with God is like two dear friends sitting together who do not need words to share their feelings.

God invites us into personal friendship with the remarkable person of Jesus Christ. Through Christ, we find God is wonderful. God is in love with us. People are not required to earn God's love by attempting to change their sexual orientation. John and Jesus offer people of all sexual orientations a place in the love story.

Take a chance with God. Become dear, cherished, beloved friends with God through Jesus Christ. Spend some daily time together in prayer, spiritual readings, and beloved community.

Dearest God, help us trust and love you as John trusted and loved Jesus. Amen.

† January 4 †

Words of strength and power

Luke 21:33

I wrote this reflection some time ago in honor of my beloved grandmother's birthday. She was wise and full of love for her family and God though she never had the opportunity to attend school when she came to America. As she and Grandpa had children, they learned English when the children began attending school. She literally taught herself to read and write a new language in a new country. I admire her persistence. As she wrote letters in her elder years, sometimes she would forget the English words and begin inserting Norwegian words from her childhood. She still managed to convey her meaning and I treasure those faded, dear letters, painstakingly written with her arthritic hands.

She would often read her English Bible to improve her language skills. Grandma never went to bed until she had done some kind of spiritual reading. One of her favorite devotionals was by the Reverend Billy Graham. When she died, I inherited her Bible and that well-worn devotional. I treasure those books!

Grandma clearly understood heaven and earth would someday pass away. She revered "the Good Book" and she treasured the "words in red" [4] found in the Gospel accounts of Matthew, Mark, Luke, and John. So she would frequently memorize scripture and would carry those words in her heart throughout the day.

It has been years since I have memorized scripture. It is almost a lost art these days. Yet, memorizing a word, a phrase, a sentence is spiritually empowering. When Grandma's eyes dimmed with age and cataracts, as she cared for a sick and dying husband of seventy-two years she could remember sacred words that nourished her soul.

Will you consider memorizing empowering sacred words this year? The quiet task is a form of soul food that brings rich moments of soul care. Try it, it is simple. "Heaven and earth will pass away, but my words will not pass away," Luke reports Jesus as saying. Repeat those words again and again in meaningful repetition. Let them linger deep in your heart. World history may come to an end, but the words of Christ endure throughout eternity. Let the "words in red" dwell in your spirit and nourish your soul.

Thank you, God, for these "words in red." Bless these words as they linger deep in our hearts. Bring them to our awareness in times of need. Amen.

---

[4] Many Gospel editions print Jesus' words in red. Often called "Red Letter Editions" these highlight the words historically recorded by the Gospel writers as having been spoken by Jesus.

† January 5 †

A beloved nurse and her dusty Bible

1 John 3:2a

I worked as a registered nurse (RN) for more than sixteen years before becoming an ordained minister. People often ask why I changed professions. Sometimes I will smilingly mention I emptied and cleaned bedpans for years until I read that Jesus washed feet instead of other body parts. That's when I asked for a new calling!

Competent nurses are in constant demand. This caring profession taught me how to look, listen, feel, assess, plan, and understand people, health, and wellness issues, sickness, death, and dying realities. I am a wiser person for all those years in the classrooms of numerous hospital wards and emergency rooms. Nursing has deeply influenced my understanding and practice of pastoral care.

I worked as an RN while earning my Master of Divinity degree. Over the months, certain nursing floors began to specifically request me by name for shift work when the patient census increased, or nursing staff took vacation time or called in sick.

One nurse in particular seemed both fascinated and sarcastic about my studies. One evening she approached me with a surprising question. "Can you come over after work? I want to talk to you about something." "Of course," was my response. The shift was extremely busy that day. There was too much to do, and not enough hands to get the job done. With relief, I headed to the parking lot only to remember our scheduled meeting.

She greeted me with eagerness at the door. In the bedroom, she opened a cedar chest and began emptying it. A dusty Bible lay at the bottom. She unsuccessfully tried to blow off the thick layer of dust on its cover. Embarrassed, she wiped the Bible clean with her shirtsleeve.

To my utter amazement, she asked me to help her begin reading it. It had been years since she had opened her Bible and she didn't know where to begin. "Oh God," I inwardly prayed, "Help!" Slowly I opened the Bible to the letter (epistle) of 1 John, whom many believe was written by the disciple "whom Jesus loved" (John 13: 23). Beloved John was writing to his beloved friends in the church about his beloved Jesus. For some reason, it seemed important to read about belovedness. Quietly reading aloud, I began in chapter one until all five chapters were read. My nursing colleague quietly wept throughout the entire reading. "Thank you," she murmured. We have since gone our separate ways, but I remember her every time I read 1 John and come to the endearing name, "Beloved." I wonder how she is and pray for her. She is a dear child of God.

Let us live as the Beloved and blow the dust off our Bibles! Truly, as Mother Frances Dominica has said, "You will find the living God in the pages of the Bible. You will find him also just exactly where you are." [5]

God, help us live as your beloved children. Amen.

✝   January 6 – Epiphany   ✝

Spiritual stress busters
Jeremiah 31:25

Stress can be physically, emotionally, and yes, even spiritually exhausting. Commuting tensions, work pressures, family worries can make us want to howl with frustration and anxiety. By now many of our New Year's resolutions have already been broken, leading to feelings of guilt and personal failure. Many of us have not exercised or dieted. Others may have sworn off cigarettes, alcohol, or drugs with the best of intentions and have miserable results after a week. Or perhaps we had a fight with someone and feel terrible about it.

People need healthy stress busters. Releasing constant worries and tensions from our bodies might prevent early strokes and heart attacks, nervous breakdowns, migraine headaches, and ulcers. Ignoring our bodies often results in physical and emotional symptoms that persistently cry out for our attention. When feeling frantic, slow down and take a mental health break before your stress breaks you.

Human beings also need the spiritual stress busters of rest, unscheduled time, and rejuvenating sleep. North American society and culture hurries us on the inside and the outside. We need God's sense of time to prevent spiritual fatigue. We need moments of holy leisure. We need moments where we literally refrain from productive activity to rest. Perhaps we need to remember that sleep is sacred. Rest is a holy word. The

---

[5] Job, Rueben P. and Norman Shawchuck. *A Guide to Prayer for Ministers and Other Servants*, p. 15

words of an ancient Jewish prophet invite us into God's rest, "I will satisfy the weary, and all who are faint, I will replenish" (Jeremiah 31:25).

Consider making time for adequate sleep and taking naps throughout the year as part of your spiritual stress buster strategy. Listen to your body and honor your spirit. Rest securely in the presence of God. Let yourself be inwardly replenished with healing rest and you will find your stress levels significantly reduced.

May our sleep be healing and restoring, dear God. Amen.

† **January 7** †

Breath prayers

Colossians 4:2

Today I feel spiritually exhausted. I am weary of "doing prayer." Too many words feel like a grocery list to God. Why can I not simply be in holy presence without words? The ancients understood "God is closer than our breathing, nearer than our hands and feet." [6] Perhaps answers are found in simple breath prayers of the heart. Sometimes all we can do is breathe. When life is chaotic, confusing, and painful, anything else is too difficult.

I have heard it said that there is no such thing as a little prayer. Oh God, teach me to pray! I sometimes wonder if God hears and if prayers make a difference. I wonder how to pray, for often I feel so inadequate even though I own dozens of books about prayer. The Internet also offers many spirituality Web sites eager to tell me how to pray. Why must prayer be so confusing? How can it be simplified? I think the answer is through breath prayers.

We must breathe everywhere we go. Breath prayers can travel with us everywhere, and help create an awareness of the inner chapel of our hearts. Through breathing, we can invite the Spirit to go deeper and help us in our prayers. By paying attention to our bodies through breath-

---

[6] Wuellner, Flora Slosson. *Prayer and Our Bodies*, p. 36. Wuellner describes this as "beautiful words of an old prayer." She does not attribute the phrase to any particular person.

ing, the healing breath of life from God can enter with each inhalation. Breath prayers help us hear our hearts beating with God.

Meister Eckhart has been credited with saying, "If the only prayer we ever pray is thank you, that would be enough." Perhaps the secret of devoting ourselves to prayer with an attitude of thanksgiving is found through a breath meditation used by Thich Nhat Hanh when he is with little children. Wherever they go, he teaches them to breathe in the words, "Yes, yes, yes." And to breathe out, "Thanks, thanks, thanks." [7] He believes this prayer helps them respond to life, to society, and to the earth in a positive way.

Yes, yes, yes. Thanks, thanks, thanks. Amen.

† January 8 †

Contemplative activists

Micah 6:8

Sometimes I am surprised when people ask my opinion. I am even more surprised when people act on it. Such was the case one sunny afternoon when two Christian lesbians questioned me for about six hours about potential workshops to be offered at an international justice conference for gay, lesbian, bisexual, and transgendered people.

A number of workshops were being suggested on economic and political justice issues, but there was a notable lack of spirituality topics. I asked, why? Their answer should grieve the ecumenical Church at large. It seemed that these particular people were hesitant to offer spirituality resources to such a "Bible bashed" community. The committee had considered a welcoming and affirming Bible and homosexuality workshop at one point but then backed off. The conference was to focus on social justice issues instead. Social justice issues were considered safer than spiritual issues.

Yet it seemed to me an important trilogy is found in the Micah 6:8 verse. Justice without mercy is harsh. Mercy untempered with justice can actually encourage lawless and violent behavior. Working for justice and

---

[7] Hanh, Thich Nhat. *The Long Road Turns to Joy: A Guide to Walking Meditations*, p. 36.

mercy without a personal spiritual life is difficult if not impossible. We are called to a humble walk with a higher power.

It seemed unethical to me to train and motivate activists of any kind, without offering spiritual resources to empower them. Some will be jailed for their beliefs. Others will experience the consequences of living in a world that often rejects and ridicules the justice seeker. Many people in the world are eager to repress the basic human rights of sexual minorities. Potential martyrs and change agents need spiritual empowerment.

"So," I said thoughtfully, "this justice conference is based on the nonviolent teachings of Gandhi, the late Dr. Martin Luther King, Jr., and Jesus Christ in the Gospels. These three world leaders are what I would call contemplative activists. Each leader had spiritual practices, which sustained them as they lived and died in their prophetic roles. A workshop on spiritual empowerment needs to be offered to conference attendees."

"Fine," came the instant response. "Will you do it?"

"Yes," was my reply.

When that particular conference was finished, the spiritual empowerment workshop had been one of the most popularly attended events. People hungered for spiritual resources as they worked for justice and full inclusion into society and their various religious institutions.

Higher Power, bless us with spiritual empowerment. Amen.

† January 9 †

Changed hearts

Matthew 7:3

"I don't understand what you mean," I asked, "Who are 'trash people?'"

The angry response came immediately. To this man, just about everyone except himself was a "trash person." One of his sons married a "trash person." What made her "trash" in this man's opinion was her skin color. "Trash people" included all the minimum wage employees who cared for his aging mother, along with gays and lesbians, and people from different ethnic backgrounds. It sounded as if the only non-trash person on the face of the earth was this angry, embittered man. My heart felt sick as I listened and felt deep grief for his children's spouses. This angry man felt none of them were good enough for his sons. His disapproval distanced them from his life.

"Do you have any pictures of your grandchildren?" I asked. He seemed surprised at this question and stopped his tirade for the moment. "No," he replied slowly, "I've never seen them. Their mother is 'trash.' Why would I want to spend time with her and her children?"

The Psalmist writes, "When I look at your heavens, the work of your fingers, the moon and the stars that you have established; what are human beings that you are mindful of them, mortals that you care for them?" (Psalm 8:3-4). We are made in the divine image and are not trash. We are fearfully and wonderfully made in our human diversity. God is an artist, making human beings with many beautiful skin colors with the capacity to love deeply. God must be sorely grieved by our prejudices.

Madeleine L'Engle shares this insight about Jesus, the storyteller. Jesus tells the story of a person who had a huge plank of wood in his eye, yet did not hesitate a moment to severely criticize another for having a wee bit of dust in his eye (Matthew 7:1-5). The word Jesus used was "hypocrite." L'Engle writes, "The parable is … a true story about our unwillingness to see our own enormous faults, and our eagerness to point out much smaller faults in other people." [8]

It is easy to see other people's prejudices and not our own. I wonder what people see in me? I wonder what hidden prejudices are deep within me? Where do I need to have a new heart to see people with God's eyes? Søren Kierkegaard (1813-1855), a famous Danish theologian, clearly understood that while prayer did not change God's unchangeable character and attributes, it could transform the one praying with a new divinely inspired perspective. [9]

Months after my first encounter with the man who thought of people as trash, I had the privilege of attending church with him again. He had experienced a dramatic moment with God and was truly reborn in his inner spirit. My mouth dropped to the floor as I saw him embracing people of color. I rejoiced at seeing him with his daughter-in-law. His grandchildren delighted in their new and wonderful relationship with their grandfather. His son was profoundly grateful to have a relationship with

---

[8] L'Engle, Madeleine and Carole F. Chase. *Glimpses of Grace: Daily Thoughts and Reflections*, p. 320.

[9] Bretall, Robert, editor. *A Kierkegaard Anthology*, p. 470.

his father again. The son's mother joyously shared with me that she had been praying for her husband's attitudes for the past twenty-five years.

It was a moment of self-realization for me. Quite honestly, I had not been actively praying for this family. Fortunately God worked a miracle in spite of my prayerlessness. Truly, God can change the hardest of hearts. God is alive and well, still in the miracle business of transforming lives. Prayer changes things, beginning with the one who is praying. Perhaps all of us can learn from my experience. Are there people for whom you should and could be praying?

God, change the hardness of my own heart, before I so eagerly pray for others to have a change of heart. Help me see the planks of wood in my own eye, before the perceived dust in the eyes of others. Let any needed inner change begin with me. Amen.

† January 10 †
Justice and the Shower of Stoles
Ezekiel 34:16

Once I had the opportunity to see the Shower of Stoles Project, which made a lasting impression on me. It is a collection of hundreds of liturgical stoles worn by sexual minority ordained clergy, elders, deacons, missionaries, and other gifted people who have been barred from serving their faith communities only because of their sexual orientation. The stoles are a powerful symbol of the huge loss to the church of exceptionally able leadership, representing Methodists, Lutherans, Baptists, Catholics, Episcopalians, Presbyterians, and many other denominations from at least three continents. Their voices have been silenced in their beloved churches and they cry out for justice and vindication.

The Hebrew word *mishpat* is often translated as "justice," meaning a biblical attribute associated with holiness (Micah 6:8). The word "justice" occurs 115 times in the Old Testament. Sometimes *mishpat* is translated as judgment. The concepts of "fair play" and "legal equality" are always associated with *mishpat*. According to the Good Book, *mishpat* is the moral standard by which God measures human conduct. One commentary suggests "justice" could be described as "divine pity, love, and grace."

• Scripture reveals that God admonishes the ancient spiritual shepherds for violating the trust of their followers (Ezekiel 34:1-10). They had, as an entire nation, become spirituality abusive to the people entrusted to their care. Rather than tend their flock, they cared first for themselves. The ancient text reads, "You have not strengthened the weak or healed the sick or bound up the injured. You have not brought back the strays or searched for the lost. You have ruled them harshly and brutally. . . . They were scattered over the whole earth, and no one searched or looked for them" (Ezekiel 34:4-6 NIV). The chapter continues with God saying, "I myself will search for my sheep and look after them" (verse 11). "I will provide for them . . . and they will no longer . . . bear the scorn of the nations" (verse 29).

The thirty-fourth chapter of Ezekiel should be a warning for all twenty-first century spiritual leaders as we shepherd our flocks. Homophobic citizens all over the world silence, brutalize, and murder sexual minorities simply for being alive. Many Christian churches are often silent as they refuse to recognize these hate crime victims as sheep dearly loved by God, the Tender Shepherd. The Church will also face holy judgment for rejecting from ministry so many dedicated, devoted, gifted, and called Christian leaders.

To be just requires us to be careful and to pray thoughtfully as we read the Bible. Too easily, readers pull a scriptural verse or word out of context. The lessons learned by students who have gone before us can help us be just in our reading and in our lives. Karl Barth (1886-1968), a leading European theologian wrote, "I take the Bible far too seriously to take it literally." [10] Madeleine L'Engle, a contemporary spirituality writer, makes this important comment, "It is terrifying to realize that we can prove almost anything we want to prove if we take fragments of the Bible out of context. Those who believe in the righteousness of apartheid believe that this is scriptural. I turn to the Bible in fear and trembling, trying to see it whole, not using it for my own purposes, but letting its ongoing message of love direct me." [11]

The Shower of Stoles is a powerful reminder to me to cry out for justice. Be encouraged. God is just. God sees. God cares. Justice will prevail in God's timing.

---

[10] L'Engle, Madeleine and Carole F. Chase. *Glimpses of Grace: Daily Thoughts and Reflections*, p. 316
[11] ibid., p. 317

God, hurry up with your mishpat *for all your people! Amen.*

For more information about the Shower of Stoles project, contact: Director, Shower of Stoles Project, 57 Upton Ave. S., Minneapolis, MN (USA) 55405. Phone: (612) 377-8792. E-mail: stoleproj@aol.com. See their Web site at http://www.showerofstoles.com.

---

†   **January 11**   †

Breathing with God

Psalm 62:1

Beware of the barrenness of a busy life.
~ Corrie ten Boom

"I miss God," confided a friend. As she continued talking, it quickly became evident she was spiritually fragmented and exhausted by ministry demands. How could she find the time to be with God when her workday began at 5 A.M. and did not finish until after evening classes? Bible school homework and limited financial resources contributed to her inner tension. She also came in to the office on her days off and holidays. It was never enough. The poor were always coming in through the doors, needing emergency food and shelter. There were never enough hands around to share the responsibility. Life felt overwhelming.

Realistically her finances were not going to improve. She would grit her teeth and stay up all night, if need be, to do her homework. The ministry was in its busiest time of the year and would not slow down for another month or so. There would be no additional help. Her most dependable helper was about to leave for long overdue and much needed surgery. My friend did not need more to do. She was already on overload. Did I have any suggestions, she asked?

Yes, I did. She needed to stop and just be with God for a breather. I gave her a votive candle and suggested she begin her morning breathing with God in the candlelight. Simply breathe in holy presence for several minutes a day. Don't read or write anything. Just breathe with God and slow down for a minute or so before the demands of your day begin.

A month later my friend returned and shared her experience, "I began to sit in the light. I'd bring the candle to work and light it for a minute or so, between clients and job demands. When the votive burned down, I saved the wick as a reminder to sit and breathe with God."

Martin Luther (1483-1546), the great German reformer, often declared that he had to hurry all day to get time to pray. Realistically, most of us are too tired at the end of our days to pray as he did. He sometimes prayed four hours a day. But each of us can try and take a breather with God for a few minutes every day. Let it be a moment of personal spiritual empowerment. Our souls need moments of holy leisure for renewal. See if it makes a difference for you.

Many people find lighting a candle the simplest way to begin developing a sense of sacred space. Whether we are Christian, Buddhist, Hindu, Muslim, Jewish, Wiccan, or of another faith, all of us can experience spiritual awareness and centering in the light. Light is generous in all traditions.

God, slow us down and let us be aware of your loving Presence with every breath. Help us rest in the calming light of a centering candle, the soft glow of a sunset or sunrise, and be renewed. Amen.

† January 12 †

Spiritual power

Psalm 138:2b-3

What is spiritual power? How do we get it? Where do we look for it? One answer is that we can experience spiritual power through our breathing. How and what we breathe is significant for our inner well being.

A centering breath prayer and meditation on an intimate, tender name for God provides enormous power. Gandhi used different sacred names for God, as he understood the divine through his Hindu tradition. Gandhi highly recommended breath prayers and meditation spiritual practice to his followers, although he did not require it of them.

Anthony De Mello writes about this practice in his book *Sadhana: A Way to God.* Many devout Hindus take the trouble to learn this practice. There are a thousand names for God in Sanskrit and each name has a full meaning that reveals some aspect of the divinity. Many Hindus recite these names lovingly in time of prayer. De Mello suggests we take the time and trouble to invent a thousand names for our own spiritual practice. Imagine a loving and caring presence or higher power. Or if that is offensive to you, imagine a thousand loving names for your inner spirit that gives you life. Use your creativity from a heart "full of love." [12]

If we are nervous and anxious, angry and fearful, we may be breathing rapid, shallow breaths. If we would only slow our breathing a little with awareness and a centering word or phrase, we would become more empowered. Attending to our breath increases the strength of our souls. We can find inner strength with nonreligious words such as "love," "peace," "yes," "thanks," and many others. If we have a preferred and trusted religious or spiritual tradition that offers sacred names for Divine Presence, those can also be empowering and calming to our interior center and bring us a sense of healing, wholeness, and inner peace.

If this practice was empowering for Gandhi, it is worth trying. These breath meditations can be done anywhere. We can center ourselves and become more empowered while in our cars, on the bus, as we wait in a doctor's clinic, ride the elevator, and commute to work. We can center with a word while doing household chores and even while having dental work done.

We need some intentional spiritual formation to help us become contemplative activists. Sacred names and words are power sources worth reclaiming. The ancient Psalms have helped people be empowered in their cries to God as they suffered in life and for their beliefs. They can help us today.

Oh God, give me a word and a trusted sacred name to increase the strength of my soul. Amen.

---

[12] De Mello, Anthony. *Sadhana, A Way to God: Christian Exercises in Eastern Form*, p. 118.

† January 13 †

Beloved community

1 John 1:1

A mile walked with a friend contains only a hundred steps.
~ Russian Proverb [13]

I have a dear friend who loves to walk and talk. Whenever possible, we try to either have a cup of coffee or walk every week. This is not easy to do with her schedule. She is a single mom and full-time graduate student with a rigorous commuting schedule. She is a great walker and a good talker too. My friend also knows how to listen. We can walk miles, and it feels like only a hundred steps.

One afternoon she was excitedly describing classes, books, and new classmates. She paused a moment and asked if I had ever heard the expression "beloved community?" She had read about this idea in a recent homework assignment and was intrigued by its meaning. "Oh yes," was my instant reply, "the Bible has many writings on beloved community." My friend was amazed. Where were they?

My favorite biblical description of beloved community is found in the love letter known as 1 John. These five brief chapters help define beloved community and community living. I find most North Americans are amazed when they learn this radical and biblical concept of beloved community exists. We so often live as a nation that respects and elevates rugged individualism, but the Bible contains a collection of books on beloved community living. When one looks at the original Greek language used in John's writings, it is always in the plural form.

In the USA we often think and live for "me, myself, and I." But we are called to live as a beloved community. We are called to live as "we, us, and you (plural form)." It is significant to realize that social justice involves living in community and not isolation.

John writes, "That which was from the beginning, which we have heard, which we have seen with our eyes, which we have looked at and our hands have touched – this we proclaim concerning the Word of life" (1 John 1:1, NIV). He speaks and writes from the perspective of beloved

---

[13] Davis, Kathy. *Proverbs from Around the World: A Mile Walked with a Friend Contains Only a Hundred Steps. Volume 2.*

community and describes how to balance justice, mercy, and spirituality as explained in Micah 6:8.

Without beloved community, it is hard to live. We need beloved community to experience the fullness of life. It is essential for spiritual empowerment, and it is good for our souls. Unfortunately, many people lack beloved community. Some people have been rejected by families of origin, or harassed by neighbors or even their governments. Perhaps religious institutions have treated you as the non-beloved and exiled you from a community.

The Internet is often a helpful place to find Web sites of spiritual safety and hospitality that can sometimes lead to local beloved communities. Seek affirming community with all your heart and you will be deeply blessed. Remember that God loves you. God wants to bring you into beloved community. Take a chance with God and step out in faith. A Chinese proverb might provide helpful wisdom to begin a journey toward spiritual empowerment within a beloved community, "The journey of a thousand miles starts with a single step." [14]

God, please bring me into beloved community. Amen.

† January 14 †

Spiritual empowerment and our human bodies

1 Corinthians 3:16a

How we relate to our bodies profoundly influences our spirituality, our inner wellness. Our bodies affect how we live and how we relate to one another. Spiritual empowerment involves living with our bodies one day at a time. We are embodied beings in need of sacred space. We have many emotions that are part of our body experience. For wholeness, our deep feelings need to be acknowledged, honored, and heard with loving discernment. When our feelings are too deep for words, they can help us pray. When we are teased, rejected, criticized, stressed, and exhausted, our bodies show symptoms and reflect a spiritual concern.

---

[14] ibid., Davis, p. 48.

As a minister in the United States, most people that I encounter, young and old, sick or well, rich or poor, gay or straight, male or female, single or married, do not love their bodies. This is a significant spiritual concern. Our bodies are a sacred trust, but negative self-images often lead to subtle and overt acts of self-hatred. Our bodies need loving care and attention. We need to cherish and nurture our bodies physically, mentally, emotionally, and spiritually in order to thrive and live up to our fullest human potential. Our bodies are God's gift to us. In sickness and in health, they help us pray. It is in God that we live and move and have our being. Our bodies require responsible stewardship for they are our portable chapels. Our bodies reflect a sacred trust. We are God's temples. God's Spirit lives in each of us. Try praying today about your body and your many feelings.

Many people do not realize that learning to live peacefully with our imperfect bodies can help us grow in inner wellness and personal empowerment. Often our first memories and awareness involve our bodies with feelings of pleasure, shame, or other emotions. We were never meant to live as disembodied people. Our bodies can help us get grounded and centered.

"Don't you know that you yourselves are God's temple and that God's Spirit lives in you?" (1 Corinthians 3:16a).

God, help us love and nurture our bodies as precious gifts from you. Help us experience spiritual empowerment as embodied people. Amen.

† January 15 †

Till death do us part

Ruth 1:16–17

The legacy of Ruth and Naomi lives on wherever women struggle to survive in patriarchal societies where men hold the power of life and death. Perhaps their most significant legacy, however, is found in their powerful commitment towards each other in the face of bereavement, hunger, and poverty. These courageous women chose to become a nontraditional family based on loving choice, when the odds were against their survival.

Today's Bible verses are famous and popularly used for heterosexual marriage vows. But originally the spoken words of commitment were between these two remarkable women. Their ancient love story was lived thousands of years ago, yet it offers us timeless insights about love and devotion for any millennium. God blessed their love and so did their local community and neighbors. Devoted couples from all sexual orientations can express their love, fidelity, and devotion through these cherished words of commitment.

Ruth and Naomi bless us with their family values. Their loving words and actions are a standard I would like for my own family. Two hearts beating as one. Through sickness and in health, for better or worse, in riches or poverty, till death do us part. Hate was not their family value. Love was their priority and guided everything they did. Their love came from God and was repeatedly blessed and publicly affirmed.

The Bible tells us "there is nothing new under the sun" (Ecclesiastes 1:9c). Over the centuries people have loved deeply. Some people love through "traditional" marriages and others in "nontraditional" marriages. Love is a beautiful part of life. The apostle Paul reminds us that "the best is love" (1 Corinthians 13:13).

Could Ruth and Naomi be a lesbian couple? I doubt it, although some would disagree. Yet the scriptures offer a blessed sacred ambiguity inviting seekers of all sexual orientations to find a place at the table of God through Ruth's timeless words of loving commitment.

God, bless us all with the love and commitment, loyalty and faithfulness of Ruth and Naomi. Amen.

† January 16 †

Worry and 911

Matthew 6: 27

I read somewhere that "worrying is worth two days work." How true, I thought while waiting to hear about my father's condition as he underwent emergency surgery. I had been with Dad as he convalesced after emergency open-heart surgery. He had been well on the road to recovery, but overexerted himself one day. He collapsed in a grocery store parking lot. I was a complete and total stranger in town. As I rushed to Dad's side, a kind stranger called the emergency phone number 911. More concerned strangers gathered, providing first aid to him and then emotional support to me. I feared he was dying. The ambulance arrived within minutes. Competent emergency medical personal whisked him away. Another anonymous stranger rode to the hospital with me and graciously waited until my father was out of danger.

One of the paramedics got me a cup of coffee in the waiting room. She gently noticed I seemed to need a word of prayer. She offered to pray for me and I gratefully bowed my head. For many years I had prayed for others in crisis while serving as a military chaplain. Now I needed spiritual help. God provided. God always does in our moments of need.

As the paramedic prayed, I realized all my worrying would not add a moment to my father's life. All I could do was commit him to God's loving presence while I waited and prayed. The paramedic went back to her duties, but her simple prayer strengthened me. She helped me remember that the God who clothes the grass of the field, which is alive today and is gone tomorrow, will take care of both of us.

God is enough. There is no such thing as a little prayer. Praying empowered me. I was not alone. God was with me. God has big shoulders and an eager ear to hear our concerns and worries. God cares.

What are you worried about today? Can you share it with God in prayer? Jesus gives us good advice on spiritual empowerment in Matthew 6:25–34.

Caring God, hear our prayers today. Take our worries. Be closer than our breathing, nearer than our hands and feet. Amen.

† January 17 †

God is enough

Matthew 6:34

I have been reading the Bible for more than forty years. Yet sometimes I feel I am reading it for the very first time. These words of Jesus touch my heartstrings today. Do not worry about tomorrow. Tomorrow will bring it's own worries. Today's trouble is enough. Jesus' wisdom is always profoundly simple. Perhaps this is why his words have lingered throughout millennia.

Yes, my Dad needs medical tests. He is in surgery while I write this reflection. I worry about him for today, tomorrow, next week, and beyond. But God is enough for today's concerns.

My beloved grandmother would often croon throughout her day, "One day at a time, dear Lord, one day at a time." This had been her litany for many years. Now it has become my mantra. Oh God, help me not worry about tomorrow. Help me stay with today's troubles with a faith as strong as my grandmother's. She understood God was big enough for all our problems.

Each of us can find God through the pages of scripture. These words are universally empowering. God is enough for today. God is enough for tomorrow. God has been enough in the past and will be enough for tomorrow's concerns. We may not know what the future holds, but we know the Loving One who holds the future. Simply breathe in God's peace, be still a moment and know that the Caring One is with you.

God, you are enough for all our concerns and anxieties. You are enough for my sick father in the hospital. You are enough for every reader. Thank you for being more than enough yesterday, today, and tomorrow. Amen.

†   **January 18**   †

Trust God

Psalm 25:2a

"I think I believe in God," confided a gay man, "but I don't trust God." I listened prayerfully as he continued to share painful experiences from past "Bible bashing" by well-intentioned, homophobic Christians. The Bible had been frequently used as a weapon against him. He was reluctant to use it as a spiritual resource. His spiritual injuries were soul deep.

Many people have spiritual injuries. Perhaps we were abused as children or adults. Many of us have been betrayed, disappointed, and disillusioned by life. Life is difficult and sometimes enormously unfair. But it can also be incredibly beautiful, fulfilling, and wonderful.

Whatever our life situation or sexual orientation may be, the Psalms are prayers that have stood the test of time. They are good for our souls and full of soul food. They give us the language of prayer. The Psalms empower our prayer life, equipping and energizing our honest heart to heart conversations with God. The Psalms help us with words when we are speechless and have feelings too deep for words.

The Psalms are completely non-homophobic. The primary author was King David. David was passionately in love with a man named Jonathan. He loved Jonathan with a depth and passion that surpassed the love of women. These written prayers are safe for all people. Praying them can help us begin our own conversations with God. As we linger in conversation, trust will gradually grow. As trust grows, love will deepen. We can both trust and love God with all our hearts and souls, secret dreams and hopes, hurts and disappointments.

The Psalms give us prayers from the heart. People from all walks of life have found in the Psalms words of faith, hope, and love as they struggled to pray. If you have never read the Psalms before, consider an adventure with God in the year ahead. There are 150 Psalms that give us words for prayer, words of praise, lament, anger, and confession of sin and great statements of faith. Try reading one a day. Before the year is half over, you will have read the entire prayer collection. In praying them, you will find God is enough. God is trustworthy. God is faithful. God is with us everywhere. God knows when we sit, stand, speak, and are silent. God cares. God helps. God rescues.

God, help us trust you anew this year. Help us have many wonderful conversations with you. Amen.

† January 19 †

Noisy contemplation

Mark 3:20

A great book for busy people to read is *Noisy Contemplation: Deep Prayer for Busy People,* written by William R. Callahan. Callahan insists that noisy contemplation is "street spirituality." He expresses his conviction that ordinary people can experience deep prayer and learn to pray in a world of noise and conflict. He suggests that we get away to a place of quiet when we can, but that we learn to pray "noisy contemplation" when getting away is impossible.

Callahan encourages his readers to pray like Jesus, "Jesus prayed throughout a busy 'activist' ministry . . . Jesus engaged in noisy contemplation and so can we." [15] We can find moments apart, to learn how to pray constantly and pray during the busiest moments of our lives. We can pray like Jesus. He saw people and events through God's eyes and prayed for them while they interacted. But he also sought quiet places apart from friends and the crowds when he could. He believed in prayer and welcomed opportunities to pray and rest both privately and publicly. Two impressive examples: Jesus prayed alone (Luke 9:18), but he also intentionally took his disciples with him as he went away to rest and pray (Mark 6:31).

Jesus was a contemplative activist. His quiet time restored him so he could return to work and ministry. We would be wise to heed his words to, "Come away to a deserted place by yourselves and rest a while" (Mark 6:31). Because of these spiritual practices, he could experience deep prayer during hectic, chaotic, busy moments of "noisy contemplation."

God, teach us "noisy contemplation." Help us pray like Jesus. Amen.

---

[15] Callahan, William R. *Noisy Contemplation: Deep Prayer for Busy People.* p. 2.

†   January 20   †

The beatitudes of holy leisure
Psalm 46:10a

Time is a precious four-letter word. We never seem to have enough of it in our busy lives for personal moments of holy leisure. We often refer to time as "slipping through our fingers." Sometimes we "waste or kill time." Then we try to "buy" and/or "recapture time." We frequently "run out of time." Periodically we take "time-outs" to review our strategy. We rush about with things to do, places to go, and people to see. Participants in North American culture worship activity and denigrate stillness, rest, and moments of holy leisure.

One very busy mother of two teenagers came to me years ago with such a need. She could not seem to find a moment to catch her breath. She began scheduling thirty seconds a day of stillness and quiet and eventually achieved several minutes a day. God, she said, began meeting her with moments of quiet refreshment. Once she even found herself quietly at rest for twenty minutes. She was surprised and delighted with God's quiet presence.

A very busy man once invited me to facilitate a retreat for a very busy church full of young families and youngsters. The retreat theme was holy leisure: spirituality for daily life. The retreat schedule had hourly and sometimes multiple concurrent events. We had a wonderful time. There was something for everyone of every age. Holy leisure was a luxury many of those tired parents did not have at home. Childcare was provided at the retreat, so tired parents who needed a nap could rest without worry. Sleep, stillness, and moments of quiet are truly sacred. Our souls will be restored with these simple practices.

After the retreat, I found myself reflecting in more depth on holy leisure. We need to be still and rest, if even for two minutes a day. So I wrote the following beatitudes of holy leisure, modeled after Jesus' Sermon on the Mount (Matthew 5:1-11).

- ✞ **Blessed** are those who live daily moments of holy leisure, for they shall be refreshed in God.

- ✞ **Blessed** are those who linger with God, for they shall experience a profound sense of God's blessing.

✟ **Blessed** are those who carry the chapel of their hearts everywhere, for they shall know God is nearer than their breathing, closer than their hands and feet.

✟ **Blessed** are those who hunger and thirst for holy leisure, for they shall experience Sabbath rest.

✟ **Blessed** are those who seek wonder-filled moments with God, for they shall be satisfied.

✟ **Blessed** are those who insist on moments of stillness, for they shall find ordinary life beautiful.

✟ **Blessed** are they whose hearts yearn for stillness, for they shall know God.

✟ **Blessed** are the contemplatives, for they shall be instruments of peace in a troubled world.

✟ **Blessed** are those who are ridiculed for their insistence on holy leisure, for they shall be friends with God.

✟ **Blessed** are those who experience "noisy contemplation," [16] for they shall see people with new eyes and hearts.

✟ **Blessed** are they who seek thirty seconds daily of stillness, silence, and solitude, for they shall be fulfilled in their souls.

The following year I was invited to return as a retreat leader for this very busy church community of faith. The retreat planning committee unanimously agreed they wanted a less busy and exhausting retreat. Together we decided less was best and planned a very different retreat experience. Ample time was provided for retreat participants to rest, relax, nap, and quietly enjoy nature and leisured beloved community.

God, bless us with many unexpected moments of holy leisure. Amen.

---

[16] Callahan, William R. *Noisy Contemplation: Deep Prayer for Busy People*, p. 1.

†   January 21   †

Leisure

Mark 6:30–32

Today's verses are the only place in the entire Bible where we find the word "leisure." It is a story some of us might not be familiar with, yet all busy people can relate to it. Crowds of people are coming and going. They are eager to experience and hear a famed speaker. They need healing and want to see miracles. They are hoping to get something they need, even if they cannot put their needs into words.

The apostles are deeply involved with the demands from the noisy and needy crowds. The apostles were people deeply committed to Jesus and his message of faith, love, and hope. They are more frequently called "disciples" in other Bible stories. They "followed" Jesus and hungrily sought his teachings. In this story, Jesus sees his apostles are exhausted and hungry. They had no leisure to even eat. So he takes them away to a deserted place to rest a short while.

Welcome to a moment of leisure. Webster's dictionary defines leisure as having freedom from responsibilities and duties. How often are we too busy with duties and responsibilities that we cannot pause to eat? Do we need to come and rest awhile in a quiet place? Let us take time to slow down today. In North America, we live in a culture of fast foods and drive-ins. Many of us eat on the run, in the car, and while continuing our work and play.

Where are you in this story?

God, bring us a few leisure moments today. Amen.

†   January 22   †

No time to eat – an experience in holy reading

Mark 6:30-32

I know we have already read these verses in yesterday's reflection. But I personally need to linger with this story through an ancient, cherished, and trusted form of contemplative reading known as *lectio divina*. Perhaps this will be helpful for your spiritual journey today. It is simple enough for a child yet challenging for most people in a hurry. *Lectio divina* is a form of holy reading. One slowly reads and rereads sacred words until a word, a phrase, or perhaps a sentence lingers in our heart and nourishes our prayer. Allow rich moments of silence to punctuate your sacred reading. These are words worth lingering with – for there are times when we are too busy to eat and both our bodies and souls become malnourished.

Lectio divina helps us slow down in nourishing moments of holy leisure spirituality. And I need this in my own life. It is far too easy to become over committed with activities and projects. People often tell me that I have a tendency to take on too much. Because I work out of a home office, I am never truly away from my work. This has led to some bad work and personal habits. It is very easy to stop exercising and gulp down fast foods. Sometimes I get so involved with my work, that I do not even take time to eat at a table. I will eat on the run, or at the computer, or even while standing over the kitchen sink while eating out of my cooking pot.

An Irish proverb reminds us that God made time and plenty of it. How can that be? Sometimes I feel I am living life at seventy miles an hour, but need to see God at three miles an hour. How do I slow down and experience moments of leisure?

Perhaps lingering with the Jesus stories in the gospels is a good place to start. His life has a great deal to teach us as busy people. He knew how to rest, play, laugh, and manage his time. Sometimes he intentionally left the crowds to take care of his personal needs for privacy, solitude, and quiet.

God, teach me how to slow down to three miles an hour today. I need moments of daily leisure. Amen.

† January 23 †

Seeing God in slow motion

Mark 6:31

As a concept, holy leisure experienced through *lectio divina* intrigues me because many of us experience life on the run. We become weary and worn out. We need quiet moments of retreat and rest for reflection and renewal.

A dear friend gave me a glimmer of what it means to see God in slow motion while mushroom picking. Peg had been picking mushrooms for decades. "Take the day off," she urged, "Come pick mushrooms with me for a few hours." The day was a revelation. Rather than drive seventy miles an hour and see the scenery flash by, she brought me into the forest and taught me how to walk slowly, perhaps seventy yards an hour. Rather than gaze through the forest from a speeding car, she taught me to pause, look at all the beauty available at my feet, and deeply breathe in my surroundings. She helped me see God in slow motion.

The forest was thick with trees. Sunlight streamed through the branches and leaves. Birds sang. There were no car noises. The ground smelled pungent. The layers of pine needles muffled our steps. At first I did not see any mushrooms. I had to stand still. One had to look closely at the ground to see the mushrooms. As we searched for mushrooms, we wandered off in different directions. From time to time, my friend would blow on her whistle. This kept us together and kept me from getting lost! I felt quite safe with her. The forest felt like a soothing balm to my soul. The forest had become a cathedral of holy leisure. It was a day of slow motions. God was everywhere.

You do not need to go mushroom picking to experience God in slow motion. But we all need moments of slow motion throughout the day. Samuel Chadwick said, "Hurry is the death of prayer." Try an experiment with God during your busy day. Stop. Pause. Pray. Then continue on with your chores and other activities. Meaningful moments of God-awareness can dramatically change our perspective and provide renewal for our journeys.

God, help us see you in moments of slow deliberate motion today. Amen.

† January 24 †

God's sense of time

Ecclesiastes 3:1-2a

There are times when we need moments of holy leisure. They are good for our souls. We also need moments of meaningful activity, holy work, and availability to others. Sometimes we must honor the clock and respect chronological time restraints and limitations. We may not feel our task has been accomplished but the allotted time is gone and we must go on to other things.

But there are also moments in life that are divinely inspired. They might appear as moments frozen in time and etched into our memories forever. Perhaps they have a translucent quality, clearly luminous and holy. Or it may be only with hindsight that we realize they were special God moments. Then we interpret these as either divine appointments or divine interruptions. Through them, we can more fully experience God's presence in our lives.

The Bible offers a variety of Greek and Hebrew words for time. The words and illustrations used by the ancient prophets and teachers offer important clues to understanding God's sense of time through their contextual perspectives. Today's verses are timeless in their wisdom and insight.

There is a time to be born and a time to die. There is a time to laugh and a time to weep. There is a time to mourn and a time to dance. There is a time to search and a time to give up, a time to love and a time to hate, a time for war and a time for peace. Some might call these moments fate, destiny, or chance, but they often represent important decisive crossroads in life. I suggest these moments are divinely ordained and we are most fully blessed, energized, and empowered when we are aware of God in our midst.

God, teach us about your sense of time. Bring us into a deeper awareness of your presence in the midst of our busy lives. Amen.

† January 25 †

Baptized in the name of Jesus Christ

Acts 10:47

Baptism can be a controversial subject in many Christian churches. As a child, I was taught that only believers could be baptized. While in seminary, however, I changed denominations and was rather shocked to learn my new church affirmed and honored the practice of infant baptism. Clearly I had a great deal to learn and learn quickly. Over the years I have come to cherish these baptismal opportunities.

As my ministerial understanding grew and deepened, I realized God blesses Christian baptism for gay, lesbian, bisexual, and transgendered people of faith too. But not all Christian churches or denominations would agree with this understanding. As a result, it is sometimes more difficult for these pilgrims to become church members and receive baptism for themselves and their children. And so once again, I found myself changing to a Christian denomination that would allow me to baptize them in the name of Jesus Christ.

I clearly remember one lesbian couple and their search for a welcoming church after they adopted a beautiful baby boy in a small town in Virginia. I had been invited to preach at a Metropolitan Community Church (MCC) in their town. This small church had faithfully struggled without a pastor for the past two years and was using a variety of visiting pastors like me.

This young family had recently discovered this MCC and wished to have their infant son baptized. They wanted to have him grow up in the church, hearing the wonderful Bible stories and experiencing the community of faith. They had been searching for a church home and for a pastor to baptize and bless their child. The church called and asked if I would consider baptizing the child. The mother and I then began a series of telephone conversations about infant baptism and church membership.

God chose us to come together for a divine appointment. God honored this faithful small church with a child needing baptism. They were now entrusted with the next generation. It was obvious to me that the Holy Spirit was active in the lives of these eager parents. I felt honored to bless, baptize, and welcome this child and his parents into the Christian church.

The Internet can often be a very helpful place to locate gay friendly churches and spirituality resources. Three helpful Web sites to begin your search and to learn more about this growing, global movement are www.wow2k.org, www.mcchurch.org, and www.christianlesbians.com.

Come Holy Spirit. Linger in our hearts and teach us about this growing, global voice of faith among gay, lesbian, bisexual, and transgendered Christians. Guide our prayers today. Amen.

† January 26 †

Chosen by Christ for extraordinary living

John 15:16a

God loves to use ordinary people in extraordinary ways. The remainder of that verse reads, *"And I appointed you to go and bear fruit, fruit that will last."* We are called by a power higher than ourselves. God calls us to a purposeful life.

Years ago Mother Teresa was questioned in an interview about her own response to God's call to live a meaningful life. The interviewer was blunt and to the point, asking, "Mother Teresa, you are surrounded by so much poverty and need. Do you ever get discouraged? Do you ever feel like a drop of water in the ocean of human need?" [17]

Her answer encouraged me and brought divine perspective. Her response was simple, "Yes, I am like a drop in the ocean, but if my drop were missing, it would be greatly missed."

We exist to make a difference in the world. If we were not here, we would be missed. The world needs what Jesus Christ has called and appointed us to offer. Realistically, most of us are not going to serve as Mother Teresa did in India. But we can live faithfully where we are. Extraordinary living begins with simple acts of kindness and beauty where we live, work, play, rest, worship, and interact with others.

---

[17] Muggeridge, Malcolm. *Something Beautiful for God,* p. 119.

A total stranger recently commented to me in a parking lot, "I like your bumper sticker!" The bumper sticker invites us to commit random acts of kindness and senseless acts of beauty. I thanked her, but said I thought it should read differently. Why not "commit intentional acts of kindness and purposeful acts of beauty?" This is extraordinary living everyone can offer. Simple acts of kindness and beauty can transform lives, bring hope, and empower friends, family members, and total strangers in moments of great need. God will use us in the simplest ways. We too, are like drops of water in the great ocean of life. We can make a difference, as did Mother Teresa. If we do not act in our moments of opportunity, our contributions will be greatly missed.

If your inner being prompts you to pause, smile, act kindly, and offer a moment of beauty through your hands, act on your impulse. It could be a divine appointment Jesus Christ has chosen you to perform. The ripple effects of your obedience will be a blessing to someone, somewhere, somehow, in some way.

God, empower us to make a difference in our world. Amen.

† January 27 †

Encouragement

Psalm 146:8b

Several years ago I enjoyed a brisk, invigorating morning run with a dear friend and her puppy. The sunrise was glorious. A dusting of snow lay on the ground. It was her birthday. "Yes," she said, "somehow I'm just not real excited about this year or my birthday. It's been difficult. I've been surviving. This year can only be an improvement." Surviving is a good thing. Her world turned upside down when someone outed her as a lesbian. The past year had been horrific with loss of income, retirement benefits, and economic security.

Others I know struggle to simply survive with illnesses such as AIDS and breast cancer. For many it has been a time of multiple losses. Another friend wrote a letter, saying, "If you want a happy New Year, stop reading here." My friend went on to describe the year's losses of home, job, a beloved partner's deteriorating health due to AIDS, and the death of a parent. He ended his letter saying, "I know God is in this somehow. I am simply trying to survive."

My beloved grandmother outlived all her children. She also attended the funerals of many of her family members and friends. Her husband suffered over a dozen strokes and she nursed him devotedly around the clock for years. Every day she would say, "One day at a time, dear Lord, one day at a time." Every night she would sit on Grandpa's bed and hold his hand. The strokes had taken his speech away, so Grandma prayed aloud for both of them. She would pray for those gone and those remaining. She prayed for her friends and family, thanked the good Lord for getting her through one more day, prayed for the church and missionaries around the world, gave thanks for the day's food, shelter, health, and medicine. She was a great woman of faith and courage. She knew how to bow down before God with her burdens. And God always lifted her up.

So whatever your circumstances, please be encouraged. God sees. God cares. God will help you one day at a time. God will help you one moment at a time when the day feels overwhelming.

One day at a time, dear Lord, one day at a time. Bless us with faith, hope, joy, courage, endurance, and love. Help us keep looking up. Amen.

† January 28 †

Praise

Psalm 146:2b

My spiritual director once asked what my spiritual resolutions were for the new year. I piously pondered and responded, "Years ago I used to read ten chapters of scripture a day. I haven't done that for years. I'd like to resume that spiritual discipline." Her eyes twinkled as she laughed. "Ten chapters of scripture a day?" She gasped with glee. "You need to sit with ten words of scripture a day. Try praying a few words or phrases. Hold them in your heart and enjoy God."

How on earth can any of us truly enjoy God? Praise through singing is one good place to begin. When I baptized a little boy several years ago, I invited both his family and the church to teach this young child to sing before he got old enough to be self-conscious and worried about what other people think. Then we sang the beautiful hymn, "Jesus loves me, this I know, for the Bible tells me so. Little ones to him belong. They are weak but he is strong. Yes, Jesus loves me. Yes, Jesus loves me. Yes, Jesus loves me. The Bible tells me so." [18]

The apostle Paul reminded the first century Colossian church, "with gratitude in your hearts sing psalms, hymns, and spiritual songs to God" (Colossians 3:16c). Singing praises helps us pray more fully. I have often heard it said that those who sing pray twice.

Any songs coming from our hearts are music to God's ears. Many enjoy singing scripture as a wonderful way to pray. So sing! Make up your own melodies. Sing in the shower. Sing in your car. Sing while cleaning bathrooms. Sing praises to God with gusto. God loves our joyful sounds. Sing for the rest of your precious lives. Enjoy God.

God, let psalms, hymns, and spiritual songs make beautiful music in my heart. Bless each reader with many songs of joy, gratitude, love, and peace. Amen.

†   January 29   †

Costly discipleship

Mark 1:17

I have a confession. As a minister I have not always practiced what I preach. There have been times in my life when I have been very human, bemoaning financial concerns. Once a friend cared enough to reprimand me as I voiced these concerns. "What's wrong with you? Are you in the ministry to make money and a comfortable living? If so, you are in the wrong business! If I read the text correctly, Jesus said, 'Follow me.' The disciples who dropped their nets and livelihood did not ask for a compensation package!" My friend mused, "Isn't there a story about a widow giving a penny or two? Didn't Jesus say she gave more than the millionaires?"

---

[18] Osbeck, Kenneth W. *Amazing Grace: 366 Inspiring Hymn Stories for Daily Devotions,* p. 73. The author quotes Anna Warner's hymn, "Jesus Loves Me," written in 1860.

My spiritual lapse reminds me of the time when my family and I attended the play *Fiddler on the Roof.* It is about a very poor Russian peasant family. During the play, a question is asked, "Lord, I know there is nothing wrong in being a poor man. But would it spoil a vast eternal plan if I were a wealthy man?"

I was stricken. I had forgotten a basic reality about costly discipleship. Spiritual rebirth costs nothing. Discipleship, that is, following Jesus, sometimes calls us to sacrificial service. My calling is to be a faithful and devoted follower of Jesus Christ. I was not called to riches. Christ came in poverty. Who am I to demand comfort, security, and affluence? My first love for God had become tainted with envy for money, comfort, status, and job security. I confess these things. God has always provided generously. I have food, shelter, health, and people who cherish me. I can be secure in knowing people do not love me for my money or income earning potential!

The apostle Paul had something to say about true wealth, "For you know the generous act of our Lord Jesus Christ, that though he was rich, yet for your sakes he became poor, so that by his poverty you might become rich" (2 Corinthians 8:9). I need to ponder this verse. For my sake, Christ became very poor, so that I may become very rich in God. You have heard my story. What does this mean in your life?

Help me, dear God, to count my blessings today and be thankful for your simple abundance and care. Amen.

✝ January 30 ✝

Pray at all times

Ephesians 6:18

Today's scripture reminds us to pray in the power of the Holy Spirit at all times. I need to be alert and pray with perseverance for all the saints. I understand this intellectually, but I need help to practice this in my prayer life. Sometimes I simply do not know how or for what to pray. I also get lazy in prayer. My mind wanders. My attention span is fitful.

My associate pastor knows the benefits of spiritual vigilance and has successfully helped church members benefit from it in daily life. Several years ago, my church organized a twenty-four hour prayer vigil for the new year. People signed up around the clock and the church was filled with people praying. The preacher called people to leave their baggage of the past year behind. A new year had new baggage for them to carry. Let the old go and take up the new. Several saints felt called to give up smoking during their prayer vigils. One had smoked cigarettes for more than forty years. She had been told if she does not give up the nicotine, the nicotine would have her life in five years or less. Another had been a heavy smoker for twenty-four years. She cannot remember being a non-smoker. Both quit cold turkey at midnight. They stepped out in faith to leave old self-destructive habits behind. Both have resumed smoking and feel spiritually defeated. They struggle daily with nicotine addiction.

I sympathize because I used to be a heavy smoker. It took years before I eventually was able to stop smoking. Even after fifteen years of nonsmoking, I resolve each and every day to be smoke free one day at a time. Just as many struggle with drugs and alcohol, I struggled with cigarettes. I sometimes wonder how many people patiently and quietly prayed for me during the years I struggled with my nicotine addiction. I will never know. But I do know this – if people had not prayed for me, I would still be smoking today.

Never underestimate the power of your prayers. Pray often for others. Pray with alertness, compassion, patience, and perseverance. Pray with Holy Spirit power. You may save someone's life through your prayers.

God, hear the cries and struggles of our hearts. Teach us to pray constantly in the Spirit and in our spirits, with renewed alertness, dedication, and perseverance for others and ourselves. Amen.

† January 31 †

Be in spiritual community

Philippians 2:1-2

Sometimes we need friends. We need spiritual community in order to thrive and to get through life when the unexpected happens. Even the strong and independent among us need loving support, encouragement, consolation, compassion, and sympathy when our dreams burst and loved ones die.

I recently was invited to preach at a local church. During the sermon, I invited people to be in spiritual community. I shared an example of a young missionary family in Peru. The Peruvian government mistakenly identified their small plane as a drug trafficking aircraft and shot them down. The young mother and her infant child died in the resulting crash. The local church lovingly embraced and cared for the grief stricken husband. Many family members and friends from their church denomination assisted in the funeral and continued to love and comfort the young widower. I shared during the sermon that this bereaved man was being uplifted and supported by his spiritual community.

We need the encouragement of community. We need people. We need to gather together for moments of fellowship, community, and worship. When we feel numbed by grief, discouraged, and disappointed in our lives – caring community can be a great source of blessing. Caring community energizes, equips, empowers, and encourages us.

After the sermon, we had time for sharing our concerns for community prayer. Various people raised their hands and shared prayer needs and requests, joys, and concerns. A man in the back hesitantly lifted up his arm. Very quietly he said, "I just found out an hour ago that my brother died in a car accident. I didn't know what else to do and so I came to church."

We prayed for him and his family. Caring people surrounded him after the service, offering their help and hugs. They helped him with travel arrangements and got him to the airport. A number of people called and e-mailed their love and support. They sent sympathy cards and flowers for the funeral. His pastors stayed in close contact. Through this church, a grief stricken brother experienced the comfort, consolation, loving compassion, and caring of Christ through people.

Find a spiritual community this year. It is part of living as the beloved, one day at a time. Worship regularly in the good times and the bad. You will be energized, empowered, and equipped for everything that life brings your way. You will also be a blessing and source of strength to others in their moments of deepest need.

Caring God of comfort, consolation, compassion, and love – bless us with such a spiritual community. Amen.

†   February 1   †

What is a Gospel?

Mark 1:1

One Sunday after I had just preached, a member of the church board of directors quietly approached me with a question. "Excuse me," he said, obviously embarrassed. "But what is a Gospel?" I had referred to the Gospel a number of times during my sermon. He had no idea what I meant. Could I please explain?

I suddenly realized if he had this profound question, so did many others. He was a well-respected leader in the church. He was extremely well informed regarding human rights and other justice issues, but he did not know what the Gospel was, despite serving in a key church leadership position.

Like many other ministers, I had made some assumptions based on years of experience in the ordained ministry. I assumed listeners in church would know what the word "Gospel" meant. I was wrong in my assumptions. About half of the adult population in the USA also do not know the answer. They have never heard of the Sermon on the Mount and do not understand what Christians celebrate on Easter. [19] The Bible stories in the Gospels of Matthew, Mark, Luke, and John are unknown treasures. The citation "John 3:16" means nothing to them.

The word "Gospel" comes from the Greek word *evangel*. It means "good news." The Gospels bring us good news in a world often full of bad news. They have amazing spiritual power. Reading them can help us begin to love and trust God. They are full of stories about spiritual hospitality and generosity. These stories offer us wonderful words of life.

Try a ninety-day adventure with God in the months ahead. Consider reading a chapter per day in the Gospels. By doing this, you can easily read them in their entirety in eighty-nine days. They are full of stories about love and hate, trust and betrayal, life and death, miracles and more. "Come and see" (John 1: 39) for yourself. God will bless your readings. On the ninetieth day, consider taking a personal retreat day. Reflect on how the Gospels have helped your spiritual life and enhanced your understanding of God. Consider reading other books in the Bible. They will change your life with words of spiritual empowerment.

---

[19] Hunter III, George G. *How to Reach Secular People*, pp 44-45.

God, it would be great to have some good news in a world so full of bad news. Help us be spiritually empowered by reading these amazing Gospel stories. Amen.

✝   February 2   ✝

Great courage

Luke 4:18-19 (Jesus is quoting from Isaiah 61:1-2 and 58:6)

Discipleship is joy.
~ Rev. Dietrich Bonhoeffer [20]

If we take the words of Jesus seriously, we quickly realize great courage is required if one chooses to follow his leadership. His teachings comfort the afflicted and afflict the comfortable. Jesus' liberation theology and his preaching about the realm of God challenge the status quo and our assumptions. Jesus Christ is for the poor, imprisoned, battered, burdened, and disempowered. Following Jesus demands that we pursue justice for all. As I understand the justice and compassion principles of Jesus, this would include sexual minorities who suffer locally and globally at the hands of homophobic families, religious institutions, and societies.

Fortunately growing numbers of courageous people are making a difference as they work for justice with the principles of nonviolence as taught by Gandhi. Civil rights heroes used them to train brave people who were willing to be involved in lunch counter sit-ins and freedom rides, which eventually led to the end of legal segregation in the United States in the 1960s.

Some of those heroes now have joined the struggle to bring justice to sexual minorities. They are courageous role models for all of us. The Rev. Dr. James Lawson, a distinguished African American United Methodist clergyman who trained the Rev. Dr. Martin Luther King Jr., is one such example. The Rev. Dr. Mel White, a gay Christian activist, once remarked, "Dr. Lawson's decision to support our GLBT struggle for justice is a gift from God." But Dr. Lawson bluntly shared this observation from his 70 years of wisdom with Dr. White, "Your struggle for civil rights is

---

[20] Dietrich Bonhoeffer, *Cost of Discipleship.* Page 41.

harder than ours. . . . We had our families and our churches on our side. . . You have neither."

But here is the good news. The number of supportive churches is growing. According to the Universal Fellowship of Metropolitan Community Churches (UFMCC), Christian churches in at least twenty-one countries have opened their doors and communion tables to sexual minorities. These churches baptize and bless loving families of choice, recognizing that they are worthy of respect, recognition, and divine blessing from both civil and religious institutions. Many people are surprised when they learn about this growing, global, inclusive voice of Christian faith.

A careful and humble reading of history reveals that the ecumenical Church has not always been correct on controversial issues. The martyred Rev. Dietrich Bonhoeffer recognized this when his beloved Lutheran denomination failed to stand against the gross evil of Hitler. Bonhoeffer lived his convictions as a devoted follower of Jesus Christ. He was eventually imprisoned and executed by the Nazis. He understood that "a Christian is someone who shares the suffering of God in the world" and that bold "discipleship is joy."

As we daringly identify with and share the suffering of others, we can also experience the joy of courageous discipleship. We can make a difference and help the world become a better place. Jesus expects no less.

God, give us the joyful bravery to confront injustice and evil. May our lives make a difference! Amen.

†   February 3   †

The best prayers
Psalm 10:1

The best prayers have often more groans than words.
~ John Bunyan [21]

The question most frequently asked me as a minister and chaplain is this, "Would you teach me how to pray?" This seems to be a universal heart cry from people of all sexual orientations. I have heard this again and again, while on U.S. Navy ships, in inner-city hospices and hospital emergency rooms, as well as in prisons. Perhaps this is why we are seeing such a proliferation of Internet prayer chapels and prayer ministries. People have universally struggled for words to connect with the divine, wondering if God hears or cares. Often we do not know how to pray for ourselves, those we love, our enemies, and the world we live in.

Please be encouraged and reclaim your prayer birthright. Our common spiritual heritage is prayer. Through the cries of our hearts and the groaning of our innermost being, we can experience God's loving heartbeat. Prayer, as I understand it, is simply conversation with God through a tender and intimate relationship. Sometimes our feelings are just too deep for words. Prayer is as simple as breathing our feelings to God!

Other times written prayers can be spiritually empowering. They have stood the test of time for good reason. The Gospel stories are a good place to begin learning about prayer, especially if we have experienced toxic and abusive religion and Bible concussions. Jesus spoke against such spiritual injustice and brought a new and revolutionary understanding of what God's reign on earth can look like. We find this summed up in the revolutionary Lord's Prayer located in two Gospels (Matthew 6:9-13 and Luke 11:1-4).

The most important heart cry to God might be, "teach me to pray!" Consider reclaiming the Lord's Prayer from meaningless repetition to meaningful repetition. The Lord's Prayer can change the world, cause spiritual and physical revolutions, transform lives, bring hope, and usher in the Reign of God. Its boldness can also change us. There is a reason why

---

[21] Bunyan, John. From his 1662 sermon, "I Will Pray With The Spirit ... A Discourse Touching Prayer."

John Wesley cried out, "O give me that book! At any price, give me the book of God!" [22]

God, teach us to pray. Amen.

† February 4 †
The Lord's Prayer and lectio divina
Matthew 6:9-13

Do not pray by heart, but with the heart.
~ Anonymous

Jonathan Edwards, the Puritan theologian said, "Many pray with their lips for that for which their hearts have no desire." The Lord's Prayer is often prayed this way by many. When our hearts are not in our prayers, they lack spiritual power. One ancient way to experience spiritual empowerment is to reclaim sacred words that have become common. Many of us have memorized this prayer and can probably recite it by heart in sixty seconds. We can recite it without appreciating its full meaning.

Every element of worship is found here. We are also given six simple prayer requests to change the world the way God wishes it to be. We experience worship, intercession, thanksgiving, and penitence. The Lord's Prayer is a spiritual heritage worthy of reclaiming for the new century. It will last throughout eternity.

During the Middle Ages, monks used to practice a spiritual discipline called *lectio divina.* [23] It is one form of holy reading. They would read a passage of scripture slowly to savor the nourishing words. Then they would reread it with pauses of silence between readings. Sometimes a word or phrase would glimmer and catch a reader's attention. The reader would nurture that word throughout the day in the reader's heart and let it linger in the soul.

---

[22] Quoted in Job, Rueben P. and Norman Shawchuck. *A Guide to Prayer for Ministers and Other Servants,* p. 34.

[23] Hall, Thelma. *Too Deep for Words: Rediscovering* Lectio Divina *with 500 Scripture Texts for Prayer,* p. 7.

Thoughtfully linger over these beautiful words from the Lord's Prayer. Reclaim your spiritual heritage with every sentence or perhaps just one sentence at a time.

God, teach us to pray from our hearts. Amen.

† **February 5** †

God will use your prayers
Romans 8:26

Those who pray always are necessary to those who never pray.
~ Victor Hugo, *Les Miserables*

Just the other day, a friend mentioned she is reluctant to bother God with her little requests when the world needs God's attention with the big problems. Yet God is eager for us to pray. There is no such thing as a little prayer and this prayer thing is something with which we all struggle.

As an Internet minister, I receive e-mail prayer requests from people around the world. People from Australia to Zimbabwe ask for prayers in war and peace, when in safety or in danger, for sick and dying loved ones, employment and educational needs, sharing deeply personal concerns for their children and for themselves.

Prayer changes things. God listens when we pray. "Those who pray always are necessary to those who never pray," said Victor Hugo, and I add for those afraid to pray. But how do we get started? And for what should we be praying? When do we know when God hears and answers our prayers?

Just as some people have personal trainers for physical fitness, God has given us the Holy Spirit as a personal trainer for our prayer lives. When we are unable to articulate our needs and burdens for others and ourselves, God's gracious Spirit intercedes for us with feelings so deep that words are unnecessary. Our prayers have amazing power when we allow the Spirit to guide us.

It is good to bring the big world concerns to God. I often pray while listening to local and world news and when reading the newspaper and ministry e-mail. God is concerned about world hunger, tensions in the Middle East, and nuclear weapons. We are called to intercede on a global scale.

It is also good to bring the neighborhood concerns to the Almighty such as the unemployed migrant workers on the corner who are waiting for sporadic employment, the nearby food bank, homeless runaway teens, drug dealers in the area, and for local victims of domestic violence. We need to pray for those who prey on others. Sometimes our prayers can even lead to civic involvement and action.

It is also appropriate to pray for the little things that concern us too. I pray for kittens and puppies, for small issues and situations in my personal life and home, for daily blessings and divine protection for those I love.

God is interested in the details of the day-to-day events in life. God delights in our small talk as well as our heartfelt intercessions for the world. The Spirit of God will honor our desire and willingness to pray. Just care enough to make the effort and you will sense when it is time to stop. God will use your prayers in amazing ways.

Spirit of God, guide our prayers when we are weak and strong, with and without words. Amen.

† February 6 †
Be sensitive to your life experiences
Psalm 5:1

Prayer is learned by praying.

Reclaiming a tender, loving, intimate, and sacred name for God in our prayers often brings spiritual empowerment. For Jesus, his favorite name for God was "Father." His use of this name is mentioned more than 240 times in the Gospels. Once would have been significant. God was his dearest, beloved, and loving heavenly parent. But the Psalmist in today's

Bible verse would have found that to be a revolutionary and radical way to pray.

Some twenty-first century people find both "Father" and "LORD" highly offensive sacred names. They prefer more inclusive and less patriarchal names for God. Yet others love to use one or both names in their prayers and refuse to use any others.

Both public and private prayers call for sensitivity to life experiences. As a professional minister, I have a responsibility to pray publicly with the greatest of care. Far too many children have experienced a history of physical or emotional abuse, rejection, or incest usually by a male parent, neighbor, adult friend, or relative. I know a number of children who have been abandoned by their fathers. One of my young friends had a father who committed suicide. For them, our American celebration of Father's Day is often a day of pain and anger rather than of appreciation and gratitude. To insist that any of them pray to God as a father figure seems cruel and insensitive. Forcing them to do so could actually hinder and hurt their prayers and cause deep spiritual damage and resentment.

Ancient wisdom reminds us that we can only pray as we can. When I visit people in hospitals as a chaplain, many ask for prayer. Before praying, I usually ask what their favorite or preferred name for God is. This shows respect and as a result our shared prayer time is more effective and strengthening.

So if "LORD" or "Father" is offensive and painful, find other sacred names to empower your prayers. Consider searching for new tender names for the Holy. I know many use alternative names such as "Dearest," "Beloved," "Tender One," "Loving Healer," and "Mother-God." God has many names and delights in hearing them spoken by us in prayer.

A saying reminds us that prayer is learned by praying. If traditional names for God block your prayers, then experiment with new ones with holy boldness. Ask God for your own uniquely personal sacred name for your prayer life. Search with all your strength for an intimate, loving, and cherished name for God and your prayers will be enormously empowered. You may even find yourself surprised with joy.

Holy One, bless our prayers as we try out new names for you. Amen.

† February 7 †

Lack words for prayer?

Psalm 5:2a

God can pick sense out of a confused prayer.
~ Richard Sibbes (1577-1635), *The Bruised Reed* (1630)

Do you struggle to honestly pray your feelings of suffering and spiritual anguish? Do you lack words for prayer? Are you searching for a prayer book? Do you struggle to find words for praise, lament, hatred, revenge, repentance, and other feelings?

Try praying the Psalms. Christ often prayed them, memorized them, and quoted them in times of crisis and danger in his life. They are spiritually empowering and have withstood the test of time by countless generations of spiritually hurting and rejoicing humanity.

The Psalms address a range of prayer needs.

Are you discouraged? Then be encouraged. Lament is the back-bone of many of the Psalms. A taste of lament can be found in Psalms 13, 22, 39, 88, and 130. These are truly the cries from our hearts.

Are you angry and yearn for vengeance? You are in good company and can find such voiced prayers recorded in Psalms 10, 58, 69, 109, and 137.

Confession has always been good for our souls. Consider browsing Psalms 6, 32, 38, 51, 102, 130, and 143 for starters!

Many people struggle with praising and thanking God. Some famous Psalms of praise are found in Psalms 111 – 118. Magnificent doxologies (hymns of praise to God) await us in Psalms 145 – 150.

One Psalmist declared, "I will pray morning, noon, and night" (Psalm 55:17). Whatever our moods and emotions, life circumstances, time of the day or night, we will find words of spiritual empowerment in the Psalms. Whatever your mood is, pray. Remember, "God can pick sense out of a confused prayer."

God, help us be spiritually empowered morning, noon, and night through prayer. Amen.

✝   **February 8** ✝

Power of praise

Isaiah 25:1, 4

Spiritual empowerment can be experienced through moments of praise, as we weep with God and cry out for justice and assistance. Many ancient Biblical writers knew this. Isaiah gives us a word of hope when life is very difficult. He gives us words of praise and comfort and reminds us that God is God. God is worthy of praise. God is doing wonderful things. God has a plan for us. God is our refuge in moments of need. God cares. God is with us.

Isaiah gives us some of the most beloved words of spiritual strength and comfort in the Hebrew Testament. Yet, his own people turned against him and the message God gave him to share. Church historians believe he may have been sawn in two as a result of his prophetic words.

Sometimes following God is costly. Those who work for spiritual and social justice need Isaiah's strengthening insights as they too live their convictions. Perhaps this is why Theodore Roosevelt said, "Pray not for lighter burdens but for stronger backs."

God, I will praise your name in the hard times of my life. Amen.

✝   **February 9** ✝

God has plans for us

Jeremiah 29:11

During my late twenties I lived in Miami, Florida, and attended a large Southern Baptist church. A friend was going through a very difficult time in her life and was once able to exchange a few words with the senior pastor between worship services one Sunday. I remember overhearing her tearfully share her despair and discouragement. The pastor kindly asked what she was reading in the Bible and she mentioned Jeremiah. "Oh my dear," he exclaimed, "try reading the Psalms instead. Jeremiah is difficult

48

to read in the best of times. He can be very difficult in the worst of times." That pastor was very wise. When we are stressed and feeling chaotic and exhausted, reading Jeremiah may very likely feel overwhelming and futile.

Yet God speaks to us in amazing ways in our moments of need. I know of many people who have found great comfort while reading Jeremiah in the direst of circumstances. With this in mind, perhaps it is misleading to encourage reading the book of Jeremiah only when life is good.

Jeremiah understood adversity and loneliness. His was a very difficult calling from God. Jeremiah was called to be faithful, not necessarily successful or popular. And he clearly understood God was faithful in the good and the bad times. Jeremiah experienced grief and despair, as well as joy and exultation. He found God safe to cry with and shed so many tears that we now call him the weeping prophet.

Through his extraordinary faithfulness, he came to realize God has plans for every individual. Plans for good and not for evil. Plans to give us a future with hope. That is a mighty powerful understanding of God.

Life is sometimes quite difficult and can seem bleak. Discouragement, disillusionment, and despair can overpower the best of us. We worry about our present and future. These strong feelings can cause a person to wonder if life is worth living. Like Jeremiah, we can cry with God and find hope for the moment and strength for the day.

Remember that God has good plans for your life. God wishes to bless you with a future full of hope. Just take it one day at a time and cling to your belovedness. Never, ever give up your hope. God will give you strength for the day when life feels overwhelming.

God, give us strength and courage to live your good plan for our lives. Even if we can not understand what is happening, give us enough hope to get through today. Amen.

✝   **February 10**   ✝

What is good?
Micah 6:8

"I just want to be a good person," explained a lesbian friend, "but I don't know how or what to do." We continued our blustery winter walk and discussion at some length. My dear friend was frustrated. Where was God? What did God want from her? How was she to live her life? The Bible was a strange and confusing book. What was she to do? Her questions became my questions.

What is good? Micah, who despite his important insights is sometimes considered a minor prophet, gives modern students guidance. Goodness is three things. It is a lifestyle of being and doing. They are hard to separate and can only be done with God's help. Secondly, to be good is to act justly. Be fair in all dealings with others. Finally, goodness is mercy. Justice with mercy is to be done without arrogance. This can only be done while humbly walking with our Higher Power. One commentary explains, "Doing justice is a way of loving mercy, which is a way of walking modestly with God."

Our new millennium is not much different from previous ones. We have modern technology, but people are basically the same. In Micah's time in history, his society was not living justly (Micah 2:1-2; 3:1-3; 6:11). People were not loving (Micah 2:8-9; 3:10-11; 6:12). Their attitude was arrogant (Micah 2:3). Their society and time in history sound uncomfortably like ours in the twenty-first century. What difference can one average person like me make? What difference can any one of us make? We can make a significant difference in our world if we live the good life.

God, help us live the good life! Help us create and be part of good communities. Amen.

†   February 11   †

Requirements of true religion
Micah 6:8b

I often feel I fall far short of God's requirements. Micah shows us how our hearts should respond to God. We are taught what is good and required from Torah (Old Testament law). Rather than be rigidly legalistic and dogmatic in matters of organized religion and social concerns, we are to live Torah from our hearts.

Jesus certainly made this clear to the religious leaders of his day who erred on the side of legalism, not compassion. "Woe to you, teachers of the law . . . you hypocrites! You give a tenth of your spices – mint, dill, and cumin. But you have neglected the more important matters of the law – justice, mercy, and faithfulness . . ." (Matthew 23:23 NIV).

God requires we do justice as our ethical response to community living. Our actions have social consequences. We are to love *chesed*, which is the beautiful Hebrew word that translates as "mercy." We are to freely and willingly show kindness and mercy to others. All this is humanly impossible without spiritual humility. Mercy can change the world.

James, believed to have been one of Jesus' brothers, wrote a New Testament passage found in the epistle of James that scholars think of as linked to the words of Micah. In his letter, James emphasizes a vital spirituality that is characterized by good deeds and faith. He summarizes his brother's teachings with the statement, "[F]aith by itself, if it is not accompanied by action, is dead" (James 2:17 NIV). If the Hebrew Testament prophets are difficult to read and understand, consider reading the five short chapters in James. James learned true religion from his big brother, Jesus Christ. James gives us an example of what true religion should be by emphasizing the importance of both words and actions.

I often hear people say of others, "Oh, s/he is very religious." What does that mean? Do they mean those individuals act justly, freely show mercy to others, and humbly walk with their Higher Power?

James writes a great deal about religion. "Religion that God our Father accepts as pure and faultless is this: to look after orphans and widows in their distress and to keep oneself from being polluted by the world" (James 1:27 NIV).

God, help me be just, kind, merciful, and humble in word and deed. Amen.

†   **February 12**   †

Our bodies have a spiritual vocabulary

John 1:14

The most popularly used Greek word for body is *soma,* which re-fers to the whole human being of body, emotions, intelligence, and will. *Soma* means all our feelings, personalities, spirit, and physical experiences of hunger, thirst, sexual desires, fatigue, pain, pleasure, and joy. Tasting, feeling, seeing, and hearing is part of our *soma* vocabulary. If we are feel-ing tired, we probably are in need of rest. Exhaustion and fatigue are often precursors of illness and emotional breakdowns. Sleep is not only a time for healing our body, but a time for healing our spirit. Sometimes our moods may be telling us to pay attention to our bodies.

How we relate to our bodies profoundly influences our inner well-ness, our spirituality, how we relate to one another, and how we live. If we have contempt for even one part of our body, it is deeply damaging to the whole. We can gain great insights by simply observing our own body language.

Jesus came to earth in human form. He taught many wonderful spiritual truths, but we frequently forget what he modeled for us. Our bod-ies have a vocabulary, which can help or hinder our spiritual wellness. We are embodied creatures just like Jesus. He laughed and cried, rested and played, worked and slept. He still lives among us today, showing us the fullness of God's grace and truth.

God, thank you for my body. Show me how my body vocabulary helps or hinders my prayer life. Amen.

† February 13 †

Inner wellness and empowerment

Acts 17:28a

We can experience empowering inner wellness by practicing simple symbolic body movements enjoyed over the centuries by followers of many spiritual traditions. All of us can do these ordinary movements. Touching a tree, taking a walk, lying in the grass, and even dancing can help us experience a sense of wellness. Body empowerment and wellness can be experienced through carefully planned periods of fasting or eating.

Our bodies help us be more open and available to our interior center. Attention to our bodies is integral to our spiritual lives. Posture, breath, movement, gestures, clothing, and diet all affect our inner being and spirit.

Even when our bodies betray us through illness, physical suffering, and aging, they can help us live gracefully, peacefully, and joyfully. One recent article in a *Spiritual Directors'* magazine caught my attention. The author shared the insight that even our diseases help our prayers.[24] Quietly repeat the name of your illness. Let it become your prayer. Meditate on what this means for you, and where you discern God's loving, holy presence. Consider writing your prayers. Our bodies help us pray as we age and experience health, illness, and trauma.

God, even if my body is aging and failing me, help me pray with the body I have. Amen.

---

[24] Earle, Mary. "Reading the Text of an Illness." *Presence: The Journal of Spiritual Directors International*, 6:1 (2000) pp. 7-11.

†   **February 14**   †

Stillness before God

Psalm 46:10a

Soul food can be best experienced in simple stillness, something we often fear. Stillness, silence, and solitude are counter-cultural, at least where I live in North America. We are so busy. Our world is full of noises and intrusions. Stillness helps us know God.

We can develop a growing spiritual awareness with simple daily practices of stationary postures. Standing, sitting, kneeling, and lying down on a carpet or in the grass helps us to pray. Taking off our shoes or using a corner in our homes for personal meditation and journal writing can help us focus our spiritual life. For sustained meditation, sitting is often best. By sitting straight, not tense, with our feet flat on the ground in a comfortable chair or using a meditation bench can help us remain alert and attentive to our spirit.

Sitting meditation is a lost art. Movement can be distracting. Learning to sit motionless yet relaxed is an ancient and trusted contemplative practice cherished by many different traditions. Tilden Edwards, founder and former executive director of the Shalem Institute for Spiritual Formation in Bethesda, Maryland, teaches that "a still body invites a still, receptive mind." [25]

For your spiritual practice today, consider sitting still for thirty seconds to two full minutes. Listen to your breathing and heartbeat. Let the rhythm of your breath and pulse strengthen your awareness of God's loving presence.

God, help us be still and know that you are God. Amen.

---

[25] Edwards, Tilden. *Living in the Presence: Spiritual Exercises to Open Our Lives to the Awareness of God*, p. 35.

† February 15 †

Body prayers

Psalm 5:7

We stretch for exercise, and prayer is no different. Easy movements help us warm up and stretch our praying muscles. We can move our bodies through space in simple, symbolic movements that enhance rather than hinder our awareness of the Holy.

Try walking with several intentional slow and deliberate steps. Stand in your bare feet for a few minutes in a prayer corner or on a prayer rug. Take some easy, deeper, and slower than usual breaths while sitting comfortably. By taking several minutes during our busy days for prayerful movements, we can center and relax our spirits. Prayerful movements can help us live in the moment gratefully aware of our bodies. If we feel a tense part of our body, stop a moment and acknowledge it. Relax those muscles. Tense, breathe, and relax several times.

Consider using meaningful gestures such as touching, bowing, smiling, genuflecting, handshaking, or lighting a candle to help center your spirit and focus. Simple hand postures can greatly assist us. Try sitting with your hands and arms open, resting your hands palms up on your upper thighs or lap. These simple practices help us unite our mind and body. They help us be holy and wholly present to our spiritual center.

Consider placing your hands together in the universal prayer posture. Breathe quietly in stillness for a full minute. Listen to your body at rest.

Teach me how to pray with my body, O God, beginning with the miracle of every breath. Grace my prayers today with unexpected moments of stillness and body awareness. Amen.

† February 16 †

Take a breather!

Genesis 2:7

All of us can experience spiritual wellness and healing through breathing. Contemplative people from many different religious and non-religious traditions can breathe in life with every breath. All of us can breathe slowly, breathe a little more deeply, and breathe in a centering word to symbolize our desire to meditate, reflect, relax, and reclaim inner empowerment. Each spiritual tradition has cherished words of centering prayer, phrases to enhance breathing practices.

A story is told of a spiritual seeker who desired instruction in the art of prayer from a Hindu guru. The guru said, "Concentrate on your breathing." After about five minutes, the guru said, "The air you breathe is God. You are breathing God in and out. Become aware of that, and stay with that awareness." [26] People throughout the ages have discovered spiritual empowerment by examining their awareness of their breath.

Another ancient prayer reminds us that God is "as close to us as our breathing, nearer than our hands and feet." [27] Breathing is the simplest way to center, focus, and be inwardly quiet and still. Breathing helps us listen to our bodies. We can breathe, feel, and listen to our heartbeat. By sitting silently, in stillness, quiet breath meditations can connect us with our hidden, buried feelings and help us become truer to ourselves. Breathing can help us come into inner healing and transformation.

Try to concentrate on your breathing for the next five minutes.

God, help me become aware of you with my breathing. Amen

---

[26] De Mello, Anthony. *Sadhana. A Way to God: Christian Exercises in Eastern Form*, pp. 7-8.
[27] Wuellner, Flora Slosson. *Prayer and Our Bodies*, p. 36.

†   February 17   †

Peaceful moments

John 20:19a

Listen to your body. Breathe. Sit. Feel. Listen. Relax. If you do this every day, you will experience amazing inner wellness and self-improvement. Consider a small smile while breathing.

Thich Nhat Hanh is a remarkable Vietnamese Buddhist monk who was recommended for the Nobel Peace Prize years ago by the Rev. Dr. Martin Luther King, Jr. Thich Nhat Hanh modeled great spiritual leadership for us through his refusal to take sides during the Vietnam War. His inaction lead to his own exile, but he worked diligently to bring peace by teaching people how to "be peace" [28] to all they encountered. He suggests we look at our neighbors and smile gently at one another. Smile your peace at friends and strangers while breathing gently in a relaxed manner. You will be tremendously empowered.

Be careful how you use this breathing meditation. It will change your life and the lives of others. Try it for thirty seconds to two minutes daily. These moments can be costly, however, as they were for Thich Nhat Hanh. Peaceful moments are within us, but others may not be receptive to our non-violent smiling. Know that the benefits of peaceful moments are worth the cost.

Be spiritually empowered. Smile peacefully at all you meet today, including your enemies.

God, teach us to smile peacefully today. Amen.

---

[28] Hanh, Thich Nhat. *The Long Road Turns to Joy: A Guide to Walking Meditation*, p. 9.

† **February 18** †

Powerful words

Colossians 4:6

The other day while in town doing errands, I had my hair cut. I had made an appointment. While waiting my turn, a friendly stranger exchanged a moment of pleasant conversation. My name was called and I went to the stylist assigned to me. As she began to cut my hair, the previously pleasant stranger began complaining loudly with increasing bursts of profanity. His anger caused everyone to stop conversation and look at him. He finished his angry outburst to the store manager while calling her a number of obscenities. He was totally rude, profane, inappropriate, and intentionally hurtful. The manager treated this customer with the utmost respect and courtesy. The customer stormed out of the store while continuing to vent his frustration and anger, breathing threats to get her fired. A stunned silence followed his exit. I found myself silently breathing prayers for the angry man, and all who were unfortunate enough to meet him in his fit of rage.

While paying my bill, I gave the manager my business card. I offered to be a reference for her in this situation if the angry man made an official complaint. While preparing to leave, I thanked her for her professionalism and courtesy. Then I said, "God bless you. I hope you have a wonderful day."

Our spoken words have enormous power to harm or to heal. Chose them prayerfully when irritated or annoyed. When encountering vile language, verbal abuse, hate-filled rhetoric, and words spoken in a fit of rage, make every effort to respond courteously even to the rude, the crude, and the offensive. In doing so, your words will never return to haunt you with feelings of shame and regret. When in doubt, always err on the side of gracious speech.

God, guard my tongue and protect me from uttering hasty or thoughtless words. Help me think twice before speaking in anger. Give me new ears to hear the power of words. When I hear others responding with words of rage and hate, remind me to privately pray for them. When I speak, may my words always be seasoned with your Spirit. Amen.

† February 19 †

Sound and silence

Psalm 46:10a

Sound and silence can help guide us into stillness and rest. Sound shapes and guides life. Drums, bells, and musical instruments have been used as meditation tools for a long time. Beethoven is credited with saying, "Music is a fuller way to God than words." [29] A friend's favorite saying is, "The key to maintaining the rhythm of life is resting at the right time." Sound and silence can help us rest and develop inner empowerment. Music, with its mixture of sound and silence, can inspire us to journal or create our own spiritually empowering practices.

We also experience the power of vibrations in nature through wind, rain, and the sounds of birds and animals. Many spiritual communities in both the Eastern and Western worlds use chant for meaningful and powerful experiences.

Simple resonant words are especially effective in guiding us from sound into silence. Often they have "ah" and "om" sounds. Words such as *shalom, om a hum, Abba, Amma, Yeshua, Adoni,* "holy," "amen," and "alleluia" are simple words that are easy to use in chant and centering meditation.

Meditating on different names for the sacred can be an important step toward claiming spiritual empowerment. Gandhi was famous for using this spiritual technique and recommended it highly to his followers as he worked for justice using nonviolent principles.

God, give me a word today for centering prayer. Bring me from sound into silence. Amen.

---

[29] Edwards, Tilden. *Living in the Presence.* p. 34.

† **February 20** †

Body prayer

Psalm 16:1

Today I want to teach you a body prayer I learned several years ago at the Shalem Institute for Spiritual Formation. I began teaching it in contemplative prayer workshops and churches and sometimes used it while inviting people to the communion table. I have seen many people responding to its power in interfaith groups. Perhaps it will be a blessing for you today. As you move and breathe, feel free to adapt it however you are most comfortable. It can be helpful for crisis, stress, and times of inner chaos and confusion.

The body movements are simple. Find a quiet and private place where you will not be interrupted. Either stand or sit in a comfortable position. Relax and prepare yourself with simply breathing in the word "love" and then breathing out the word "peace." When you are ready, gently place your hands together in the universal prayer position. Raise your arms up to the sky with all your spoken and unspoken questions and feelings. Slowly open your arms and your spirit to the answers you will receive in your interior center. Linger as long as you are comfortable. When you wish to move on, quietly and tenderly hug yourself in a spirit of gentleness and kindness. Quietly open your hands to be more available and attentive to your spirit. Repeat these simple body movements for wordless meditation several times. Rest. Be. Wait. Enjoy your quiet inner spirit. Perhaps journal a word, a phrase, a sentence of what happened in your prayer.

God, bless this simple body prayer beyond our expectations. Amen.

† **February 21** †

Shhh

Psalm 59:9

The great mystery of silence can draw us deeper into reality, stillness, openness, gentleness, and awareness of our inner spirit and a Higher

Power. Many of us are actually afraid of silence, so we become very noisy inside to compensate. Modern fax machines, beepers, boom boxes, cellular phones, and other electronic interruptions distract us from developing our still interior. Sometimes we need to intentionally leave those distractions behind us to be more available for times of silence. This requires some inner discipline.

While facilitating a number of guided silent retreats, I saw this dramatically demonstrated one weekend. Participants were encouraged to leave their cellular phones and electronic pagers in their cars to most fully experience the quiet times. I was astonished to see how many raced to their cars during a period of free time to see if anyone had called. Upon questioning them, none expected urgent or critical business. Several retreat participants began to realize they had become addicted to electronic interruptions. By being so available to everyone and anyone, they were losing precious time for reflection, rest, and mediation.

The same people who had raced to their phones and pagers had traveled a great distance at some expense to get interrupted by a casual caller. Those who showed restraint and discipline were able to refrain from the temptation to carry their electronic equipment during their prayer walk and experienced a deeper sense of inner stillness, peacefulness, and joy. They had greater focus and undisturbed inner awareness.

Many contemplative traditions encourage us to trust silence. Psalm 46:10 tells us to "be still" as a form of spiritual meditation.

God, help us enjoy blessed moments of silence and stillness today. Amen.

† February 22 †

Start with 30 seconds

Ecclesiastes 3:7

Silence is the great revelation.
~ Lao-tse

Attaining silence is not easy. Anthony De Mello writes about the riches of silence in his book *Sadhana: A Way to God*. He suggests ten full minutes of pure silence are needed to experience profound insight. Many people discover to their amazement that they are not accustomed to inner silence. No matter what we do, it is hard to still the wanderings of our mind or quiet the emotional turmoil inside. Others might panic with inner silence. Do not be discouraged or frightened. Even our wandering thoughts are a revelation. If remaining silent for ten minutes is too difficult, start with thirty seconds. Build a foundation.

Even two minutes of daily silence can help us build and grow into increased self-awareness. Silence reveals our very self to us. Money cannot buy what the silence will reveal. Wisdom, serenity, joy, and perhaps even a sense of the sacred will be ours.

Silence takes work. We must have a comfortable posture. Close your eyes. Do not expect anything sensational. Do not seek anything at all. Simply observe and take in everything that comes to your awareness, no matter how trite and ordinary. The important thing is to be aware. As we become accustomed to silence, the quality of our silence will improve and our silence will deepen. Revelation is a mysterious power that can transform us.

God, give me golden moments of silence today. Amen.

†   **February 23**   †

Spiritual geography

Psalm 84:3

Kathleen Norris writes about "spiritual geography" in her wonderful book *Dakota*. She writes about places where our spirits and souls feel at home. There is a sense of belonging where we can be real and authentic. Our spirits feel big and at one with our surroundings. Some may call it sanctuary. Whatever we do call it, we need safe places to be for our sense of wellness and to enjoy some unhurried time for personal reflection.

We need beautiful, quiet areas of sanctuary in our homes and workplaces. They provide places of tranquility and peace. Consider creating a corner in your home for personal reflection and quiet time.

A comfortable chair, a prayer bench or prayer rug, a rock, a vase with a flower can enhance our spirituality and sense of wholeness. There is a saying that "spirituality is participation." We can participate in our spiritual awareness and inner wholeness by intentionally seeking, making, and finding quiet places to breathe, rest, relax, retreat, and revitalize.

God, help us find and create places of spiritual geography in our homes, offices, and lives where we can be real and authentic. Amen.

† February 24 †

Solitude and community

Luke 6:12

Solitude is inner fulfillment.
~ Richard Foster [30]

Solitude and loneliness are not the same. Loneliness is inner emptiness, but solitude is inner fulfillment. In his book *Celebration of Discipline*, Richard Foster writes that solitude "is more a state of mind and heart than it is a place." [30] Solitude can be maintained in crowds or while alone. It is an inner attentiveness. Foster calls this our "portable sanctuary of the heart."

Many spiritual leaders have lived outward manifestations of this inward solitude. Jesus Christ is one example. He spent days fasting and praying in the wilderness. Sometimes he went to mountains and other lonely places for meditation and prayer. He returned to people with a renewed sense of mission and purpose.

Thomas Merton has said, "It is in deep solitude and silence that I find the gentleness with which I can truly love my brother and sister." It was also his life experience that while in solitude he discovered his need and desire to contribute something to a community.

Solitude without welcoming and affirming community leads to a lack of wholeness in our lives.

[30] Foster, Richard J. *Celebration of Discipline. The Path to Spiritual Growth*, pp. 96, 108.

God, help us find the inner fulfillment of solitude. Bring us into a beloved community where we can love our brothers and sisters. Amen.

†   **February 25**   †

Spiritual success

Mark 1:35

Without silence, there is no solitude.
~ Richard Foster

Dietrich Bonhoeffer was a famous Lutheran pastor who lived in Nazi Germany during World War Two. He actively worked with the underground resistance in an effort to remove Hitler from power. He passionately believed we need both solitude and community for spiritual success. Both are essential.

There is an inseparable connection between inner silence and inner solitude. Masters of the interior life have often written of this profound truth. The purpose of silence and solitude is to be able to see and hear. They are powerful inner disciplines and help us know when to speak and when to refrain from words. There "is a time to keep silence and a time to speak" (Ecclesiastes 3:7). "A word fitly spoken is like apples of gold in a setting of silver" (Proverbs 25:11).

God, give us spiritual success through silence and wise speech, solitude, and community. Amen.

†   February 26   †

A source of blessing and healing
Romans 15:33

The palest ink is better than the best memory.
~ Chinese proverb

Journal expert Anne Broyles tells the story of a young girl who breaks her leg and faces a summer in bed. Her Grandma gives her a journal and tells her this, "It's a journal . . . a special place for you to put down all the special things you think or see or dream, anytime you want. When you are in a rotten mood and your brain is full of cobwebs, or when life is so marvelous you feel like you're soaring in a balloon, you can put it all down . . . you can go through your own looking glass . . . all kinds of things happen during the day, but sometimes you don't notice them because you aren't paying attention. Writing in your journal helps you see things you never thought about before . . . soon each day seems full of small marvels you must write down." [31]

When we keep a journal, we discover things about ourselves. Journals can help us reach life-goals, examine our feelings, and see personal growth or the lack of it. Many people have found journal writing rewarding and enriching. Try an experiment with God and consider journal writing over the next few weeks. See if it is rewarding for you and may the God of peace be with you.

Your life has a story. A journal is a good place to relive your story as a spiritual discipline. When we record our words, it can be a source of healing and blessing. Journal writing is one way to experience spiritual empowerment.

God, our lives do have a story. Perhaps it is too painful to share with others, but it can be safe to share with you through a private journal. Give us courage and strength to begin writing our stories. Amen.

---

[31] Broyles, Anne. *Journaling. A Spirit Journey*, p. 11.

† February 27 †

Who am I?

Mark 10:51

The major difference between journal writing and keeping a diary is that a diary only records the daily events in our life. A journal may begin there, but in it is a record of much more. In journals, writers record how those events affect them. Journal writing helps us sort through feelings about daily life, our relationships, and the events in the world around us. Journals help us to talk with ourselves. Journals reflect back to us, in ink or pencil, what we see, what our minds think and our hearts feel.

Anne Broyles suggests journal writing is greatly helped by asking the following questions, "Who am I? What am I doing and why? How do I feel about my life and my world? In what ways am I changing or growing?" [32]

Many people find this kind of writing a helpful spiritual discipline. Sacred writings from different religious traditions can be a powerful starting place. Other writers respond to personal meditation walks or are inspired to write after a time of silence. We can jot down daily events and reflect more deeply.

Many people have found keeping a gratitude journal a profound life changing and empowering discipline. This kind of journal can be a simple list, made at the end of the day, of several things that we are grateful for. We can give thanks for experiences as simple as breathing, seeing, hearing, and tasting, a kind touch, a gentle breeze, and a moment of rest.

Imagine how impoverished we would be if our favorite spiritual writers did not journal their struggles, prayers, inner reflections, and outward lives. We are likewise impoverished when we do not journal our own. After all, "every life has a story" (*Biography* magazine's motto). Story telling helps us figure out who we are and whose we are.

God, who am I? What am I doing and why? How am I changing or growing? Amen.

---

[32] Broyles, Anne. *Journaling. A Spirit Journey*, p. 24.

✝ February 28 ✝

Forgotten feelings, memories, and unresolved issues
Psalm 61:1-2

Many writers like you and me have journaled their dreams to find added meaning during our waking hours. In recording the most mundane events in our lives, we may be deeply touched in our spirits. Daily reading of newspapers, magazines, and books might catch our attention and spirit. Conversations among friends, strangers, business colleagues, and family may spark a journal entry. Ordinary conversations may suddenly not seem so ordinary.

Journal writing may often bring up forgotten feelings, memories, and unresolved issues. Rather than be frightened, use these for reclaiming and working for your inner wellness. Sometimes deep feelings and emotions may rise to the surface and surprise us with their intensity.

When we are in distress, sickness, adversity, betrayal, abandonment, brokenness, guilt, or experiencing slander, false accusation, persecution, and oppression, we have feelings that affect our inner wholeness and wellness. The silence, stillness, and rest a journal provides may be healing for some seekers.

Life is full of emotional and physical suffering. Many prayer books in different traditions are wet with tears as people struggle with mistakes, disappointments, heartaches, and feelings of revenge, injustice, and complaint.

Be honest with yourself in your journal about your feelings. Pour your emotions out on paper. Do not let them cause bitterness or unresolved pain. Journal writing can be enormously healing. Perhaps a counselor or therapist would be helpful in resolving painful memories. Seek your wholeness with all your heart. God will honor your journey.

God, hear my cry today and honor my feelings. Amen.

†   February 29   †

Tears are part of life
Psalm 88:1-2

We all need to cry out with our complaints and calls for divine help when we feel helpless and hurt. Sometimes we feel desperate. These feelings may be hard to understand, but understanding progresses with journal writing, talking with trusted counselors and therapists, friends and family members.

Sacred literature from different traditions can empower us to write in our journals or take other action to help ourselves. In the Judeo-Christian tradition for example, we find sacred writings full of crying. A few examples are found in Job 16:20, Jeremiah 9:1, Isaiah 16:9, and certainly in the strong voices of lament in Psalms 13, 22, 35, 88, and 130. Even Jesus wept with loud cries and tears (Hebrews 5:7 and Matthew 23:37). "Blessed are those who mourn, for they will be comforted" (Matthew 5:4).

To experience inner healing, wholeness, and rest, we need to acknowledge our feelings and give them words and time for self-examination. We need to honestly describe our physical and emotional suffering to reach inner joy and peace. Journal writing in stillness and silence, while allowing several minutes or longer to rest from your feelings, can lead to inner empowerment and self-improvement in many difficult circumstances. By giving words to what we feel, we begin to identify problems and joys more clearly. We find answers within ourselves. We learn what we need to do and be for our wellness.

God, tears are part of life and reflect our feelings too deep for words. Thank you for their healing power. Help us give words to our feelings in prayer for strength and comfort. Amen.

† **March 1** †

God bless you

Genesis 1:28a

Many people are surprised to learn that the first chapter of the Bible offers a number of creation blessings (Genesis 1:22, 28). While many debate the creation versus evolution theory, the opening chapter in Genesis simply reads, "In the beginning . . . God created . . . and it was very good" (Genesis 1:31). By the power of the spoken Word, chaos became order and the formless void evolved into a beautiful and perfect creation.

God has a wonderful, creative, and playful mind and imagination. God was enormously pleased with creation. We read again and again that "God saw that it was good." [33] The earth was full of diversity and unlimited variety of living things.

At the end of creation, God decided to create people in the divine image with meaningful work as stewards of the earth. And God blessed them. The first chapter about the first days closes with this statement, "God saw everything that had been made, and indeed, it was very good" (Genesis 1:31). I personally believe this blessing is for people of all sexual orientations. No one is excluded. The divine blessing embraces all races and all people.

Blessing is a widespread biblical practice. Its most basic meaning is to speak well of someone with praise and happiness. Blessing is actually mentioned 640 times in the Bible, most commonly found in Genesis, Deuteronomy, and the Psalms. The Old Testament teaches us the language of blessing.

Blessing is empowerment. Cursing is destructive. The ancients understood this. We, as modern twenty-first century people, would be wise to learn from their wisdom.

God, please renew our personal sense of blessing. Amen.

---

[33] Genesis 1:4, 10, 12, 18, 21, 25, 31.

† March 2 †

Blessed rest

Genesis 2:1-3

God worked six days and then set an astonishing universal precedent of holy rest for humanity. As human beings made in the divine image, we likewise need a rhythm of work and rest. Work and rest are good for our souls. As a North American, I realize this concept is countercultural. My society worships activity. Realistically, many must work longer hours to pay their bills in a troubled economy.

But a dramatic biblical story beautifully illustrates a common need for Sabbath rest. The people of Israel were slaves without rest.

Think about this. Rest dignifies and restores creativity. People need rest or they become enslaved by work. Consider your own life. Where are you in need of blessed rest? Are you enslaved by unhealthy and exhausting work rhythms? How and where can you make changes to enjoy a rhythm of sacred rest?

Rest is a vital part of the creation mandate. Reclaim blessed rest and you will feel like a new person, renewed and refreshed in a hectic, often exhausting world.

God, please bring us into moments of blessed rest and renewal as part of our soul care. Amen.

† March 3 †

Holy breathing

Exodus 20:8-10a

Sabbath rest is mentioned in a number of places in the Bible. Sabbath is about holy leisure for people of all races, cultures, and spiritual traditions. We are to keep Sabbath because God kept it (Exodus 20:8-11). God wants us to rest. Rest is our spiritual heritage. We need meaningful work with regular rhythms of meaningful rest.

Tilden Edwards suggests the Hebrew meaning of Sabbath is found in the word, *menuchah*. *Menuchah* translates as "rest" and has the basic principle of abstaining from any kind of productive activity. In his insightful book, *Sabbath Time*, Edwards writes, "Harvey Cox notes that the Hebrew word for God's resting used in the fourth commandment literally means, 'to catch one's breath.'" [34] Resting with God is as simple as breathing.

How is God speaking in our personal lives today about our need for rest? Where can we "catch our breath" with God throughout the day? Where can we seek Sabbath moments of rest throughout our busy week?

God, bless us with many moments of menuchah. Amen.

† March 4 †

Blessed rest with Jesus
Matthew 11:28

Certainly Jesus understands our needs for rest. He invites all of us to enter his rest through some of the most cherished words in the Scriptures. A spiritually empowering meditation can be experienced through the ancient, cherished practice called *lectio divina*. *Lectio*, as it is more commonly called, is a simple form of holy reading. Sacred words are slowly read with pauses of silence. Read these words again and again until a word or phrase lingers in your heart. Simply breathe with it and let it become the prayer of your heart. "Come to me, all you that are weary and are carrying heavy burdens, and I will give you rest" (Matthew 11:28, NRSV).

Are you feeling tired today? Is there some inner burden that is exhausting you? Can you share that sense of burden with God? Consider writing down your feelings and whatever comes to mind in the silence. List your heavy loads and concerns. Ask God for rest and strength for the day.

---

[34] Edwards, Tilden. *Sabbath Time*, p. 19.

*God, help us come into your blessed rest. Carry our burdens today.
Amen.*

†   **March 5**   †

God's rest

Hebrews 4:9-11a

Sometimes we need to slow down to hear God during moments of rest. "If God speaks anywhere, it is into our personal lives that [God] speaks . . . we sleep and dream. We wake. We work. We remember and forget. We have fun and are depressed. And into the thick of it, or out of the thick of it, at moments of even the most humdrum of our days, God speaks," [35] writes Frederick Beuchner, an expert in daily meditation.

What is God saying to us about rest? God says that we need it. Why are we not making every effort to enter that blessed rest? Rest is a blessing for all the people of God.

At times in my life rest was not always humanly possible. Too many responsibilities, activities, and commitments in the day's schedule often lead to exhaustion. Money cannot buy what rest brings us. Rest is our most basic spiritual birthright.

As we close our meditation, let the Spirit be in our breathing to-day. Breathe with God. Breathe slowly, breathe deeply, and breathe in quiet moments of rest throughout the day's activities. Breathe with God one step at a time. One moment at a time. Breathe in God's rest while breathing out whatever is not restful in you today.

God, bless us with moments of sacred rest and renewal this day. Amen.

---

[35] Beuchner, Frederick. *Listening to Your Life: Daily Meditations with Frederick Beuchner*, p. 2.

†   **March 6**   †

Our power to bless

James 3:10

We can only bless others when we learn to bless ourselves. People want to be blessed and actually yearn for it. Many spend a lifetime in search of the blessing. Henri Nouwen suggests to us that "blessing is a true sign of the Beloved." [36] We need blessing to live well. Blessing is an ancient, cherished tradition found in many cultures and is worth reclaiming for the twenty-first century.

Every one of us has been given the power to bless or curse ourselves and others. The power to bless is as close as our fingertips, as close as the words in our mouths. A future without blessing is bleak indeed. Blessings say "yes" to our belovedness. Blessing helps us find inner strength and empowerment, and to achieve our fullest potential.

Cursing is destructive. It brings much harm and creates deep spiritual injuries. Cursing ridicules, demeans, rejects the other's belovedness, limits their potential, and accelerates negative and self-defeating behavior.

What happens if we do not get blessing from those we love? It is intensely heart wrenching when we are either denied a blessing or we lose it through deeply personal words from those we love. Families that withhold or deny blessings hurt their children. Rejection and ridicule can be bitter pills to swallow.

I once preached a sermon on today's verse. An engaged couple was in the congregation. They were so impressed with the power of blessing that they chose to include blessings as part of their wedding vows. I now include blessing materials in all my premarital and holy union counseling. Blessings beget blessing. Cursing begets cursing.

Which will be your legacy? Blessing or cursing?

God, watch my mouth today. Teach me how to bless others and myself. Amen.

---

[36] Nouwen, Henri. *Life of the Beloved: Spiritual Living in a Secular World*, p. 56.

† March 7 †

The power of blessing

Genesis 12:3

God blessed Abraham, an individual of enormous faith and courage with these famous words, "I will bless those who bless you and whoever curses you I will curse, and all peoples on the earth will be blessed through you" (Genesis 12:3 NRSV). Abraham's faith was enormous for he believed nothing was impossible with God. He was even willing to leave his birthplace, kinfolk, and country in joyful obedience to follow God's specific call in his life. As a result, God blessed this faithful pioneer and promised to make Abraham and his descendants into a great nation.

This sacred blessing is not limited to Abraham and the nation of Israel. Gay or straight, we can have the faith and blessing of Abraham too. None are excluded from Divine blessing for other verses also show that God's blessing is for all people.[37] Dr. Ralph Blair, noted psychotherapist and founder of Evangelicals Concerned (a national organization dedicated to assisting lesbians and gay men and churches better understand homosexuality and the Good News of God's grace and peace)[38] reinforces this understanding of divine love, blessing, and inclusion.

Experience the power of your blessing and with Abraham as your example, journey with God as someone divinely blessed. Your blessing is irrevocable and can never be removed. Once blessed, always blessed. Memorize Genesis 12:3 and whenever you doubt your blessedness, recite it as a prayer of gratitude. In doing so, you will be strengthened and encouraged through the power of your blessing.

God, bless me as you blessed faithful Abraham. Bless my journey through life. Amen.

---

[37] Genesis 12:3, 18:18, Galatians 3:8, and Acts 3:25.
[38] Blair, Ralph. "Dr. Ralph Blair's Remarks to Parents & Friends of Lesbians & Gays at St. Bartholomew's Church in New York City, September 8, 2002." www.ecinc.org

† March 8 †

The last page in the Bible
Revelations 22:3

The Bible concludes with the promise from God that "no longer will there be any curse." Someday there will be a new heaven and a new earth. There will be no more death, or mourning, or crying, or pain. All the broken, sin-twisted creation will have passed away (Revelations 21:4).

It seems to me that blessing is good and a gift from God. Blessing, not cursing, is spiritually empowering for healing and wholeness. The origin and source of all blessings comes from God. Someday, there will be a new heaven and new earth full of blessing. There will be no destructive and despairing effects of sin and death. It will be heaven on earth. Never, ever again will the damaging power of any curse harm you and those you love.

God, help me live my blessing now! Remind me to keep looking up. Amen.

† March 9 †

What is a blessing?
Genesis 27:27-29

"OK, just what is a 'blessing?'" asked a dear, irreverent bowling friend. Her gay son echoed the question, "I don't understand what you are talking about!" The air was thick with cigarette smoke as people laughed, drank, and joked around us in the noisy bowling lanes. How, I wondered, do I explain blessing during scattered moments while people are bowling? I struggled to explain between loud cheers and groans from the neighboring team as they bowled in a local tournament.

We often use words without understanding their meaning and power. Without thinking, we might say "God bless you" when someone sneezes. Or perhaps someone mentions, "You're a blessing." What does blessing really mean? In some Bible versions, the translators have even removed the word "blessing" and substituted "happy" in an effort to be culturally relevant.

Henri Nouwen puts it this way, "In Latin, to bless is *benedicere*. The word 'benediction' that is used in many churches means literally: speaking (*dictio*) well (*bene*) or saying good of someone. . . . I need to hear good things said of me, and I know how much you have the same need. Nowadays we often say: 'We have to affirm each other.' Without affirmation, it is hard to live well. To give someone a blessing is the most significant affirmation we can offer. It is more than a word of praise or appreciation; it is more than pointing out someone's talents or good deeds; it is more than putting someone in the light. To give a blessing is to affirm, to say 'yes' to a person's Belovedness. And more than that: to give a blessing creates the reality of which it speaks" [39].

Blessing goes beyond mutual admiration. A blessing touches our original goodness and equips, energizes, and encourages us to live our belovedness and our full human potential.

God wishes to bless us beyond our deepest hopes and yearnings, if we would only ask. Blessing helps us live stronger lives of faith, defeating the spiritual enemy of self-rejection. Blessing can transform us.

Once blessed, always blessed. But we can always be blessed again and again. It was Mae West who said, "Too much of a good thing can be wonderful!" Blessings are always wonderful as they bring us joy in living.

God, we need blessing and belovedness. Bless us today. Amen.

† **March 10** †

Claim your blessing

1 Chronicles 4:10

We need to be blessed as children by our parents. Parents need blessing from their children. We all need each other's blessings. This in-

---

[39] Nouwen, Henri. *Life of the Beloved: Spiritual Living in a Secular World.* p. 56.

cludes all our personal and professional relationships. We need ongoing blessings to help us hear that we are guided by love every step of our lives.

Our busy lives make it difficult to hear God's blessing, God's guidance. Perhaps some of us have been told we were not wanted or are not good enough. Perhaps we have been denied blessing all our lives. But perhaps we are being blessed without realizing it. Slow down and begin noticing every day what blessings are coming our way. Slow down and be less busy. Notice when we are being blessed and affirmed. Stop. Listen. Pay attention to our lives. Receive gracefully what affirmation people are giving us.

Be gratefully aware of every moment in life. When I achieve a moment of better understanding through prayers of thanks, I call those instances "gratitude moments." Gratitude is something all of us can give and receive. Appreciate people in your life and what they give you in friendship and love. Bless them with a word of thanks.

Giving a blessing is the most important affirmation we can give someone, and this helps him or her experience their belovedness. It helps us experience ours in return. Try blessing others as a thirty-day experiment. See what happens. Lives will be profoundly transformed. Perhaps even your own.

God, help me reclaim my blessing and belovedness through many moments of grateful awareness. Amen.

† March 11 †

When blessing is denied

Genesis 27:36d

The concept of blessing is ancient and found in many cultures. We can learn and appropriate the Jewish tradition of blessing for our own use in modern Western cultural contexts. If we get a blessing from our parents, we can be a source of blessing to others and ourselves. Families that withhold or deny blessings are very hurtful to their children.

Blessing is well documented in the Middle East. In ancient Jewish culture, blessing was part of daily and weekly life. Before children could walk, they received blessings from their parents, on the Sabbath, and other holy days. It was actually the duty of parents to bless their children. It was then the duty of the rabbis to bless the children on Sabbath, feast, and other holy days. A family blessing is important to communicate a sense of identity, meaning, love, and acceptance. Many orthodox Jewish families give their children a weekly blessing by candlelight. They speak special words of love and acceptance for each child.

I have listened to many people over the years when their families reject them. I wonder if parents truly understand the pain caused when a blessing is denied their children. People are denied parental blessing for many reasons. Perhaps a desperate woman had an abortion, or another has taken drugs. Many parents from abusive homes never received a blessing themselves and pass on their destructive behaviors to the next generation. Denied blessing can lead to desperate and destructive behaviors as people look for love in all the wrong places.

The six most healing words in the world are "God bless you" and "I love you." When was the last time we spoke those words to someone in our family? When was the last time we shared these words with friends? Have we denied someone their blessing through our words or actions?

God, even if others may have denied me a blessing, help me bless them. Amen.

✝ March 12   ✝

The most famous blessing in the Bible
Numbers 6:24-26

Today's blessing is as old as Moses and has stood the test of time. It is the most famous blessing in the Bible, and it applies to everyone. It is one of the most beloved blessings in the world. It is my favorite and is worth memorizing for the new millennium.

Many people are surprised upon learning the Old Testament teaches us the language of blessing. The Old Testament teaches five basic elements of blessing. Gary Smalley and John Trent write about them in their lovely book *The Blessing*. The five biblical elements of blessing consist of a spoken message, words with high value, meaningful touch, a message that pictures a special future for the one being blessed, and an active commitment to fulfill the blessing. [40]

Sometimes silence needs to be broken with spoken words of blessing. Words have great power to heal, empower, and encourage. Words can also hurt, destroy, and devastate. Choose them carefully. People need words of love and acceptance to bloom and grow in life.

Blessing is as good as it gets! God bless you.

God, bless and keep us and bring us peace. Amen.

†   March 13   †

God blesses human beings
Genesis 1:27-28

In the midst of all the drama, monotony, old stories, and proverbs there is a consistent theme in the Old Testament: God blesses human beings. The Old Testament is sometimes a strange and confusing book full of ancient customs and foreign sounding names. Full of Jewish religious rules and regulations, its pages are full of patriarchal language and male heroes while mentioning few strong female spiritual leaders. Human beings are shown at their best and worst. The Bible is full of human trickery and schemes for power, prestige, and safety. There are many things I do not understand or relate to in these sections as a twenty-first century, North American, female, Protestant minister. Yet I seek to understand God's blessing for me in the many biblical stories that tell of God's blessing women and men. (An interesting blessing sampler can be found in Genesis 27:27; Exodus 23:25; Deuteronomy 7:13 and 28:12; Job 1:10; Psalm 65:11, and Jeremiah 31:23.)

God's blessing is so precious that people will steal, lie, and cheat to get it, but once spoken, it cannot be revoked, according to the ancients' understanding. Blessings consist of high value words that show respect, awe, reverence, and help people feel they are valuable. They give a loved one a sense of security and confidence to serve God and others in the future. These high value words convey powerful images and we see our-

---

[40] Smalley, Gary and John Trent. *The Blessing*, p. 24.

selves in them. A future without divine blessing is bleak indeed. All Old Testament blessings recognize God as the source of all blessings past, present, and future.

It is possible, of course, to offer blessings without recognizing God as the powerful source of all blessedness. From time to time I have been specifically asked to perform weddings and funerals without any spiritual or religious component. For me, those ceremonies lack power and dignity. While, I respect those wishes, is not life difficult enough without depriving oneself of such a source of divine strength and comfort? God delights in blessing human beings. Why live without your blessing?

God bless you.

Bless us too, dear God, as only You can. Give us a future with hope. Amen.

†   March 14   †

How to bless
Luke 24:50

Blessing is a widespread Biblical practice not limited to the Old Testament. Jesus fully understood the power of blessing and in this passage blesses his people as he leaves them. He equips them with divine power and confidence for a great life work through his blessing.

The simplest formula for performing a blessing is "blessed are you!" It often comes with simple actions with symbolic significance. The one blessing raises the right hand (Genesis 48:13ff), or raises both arms and hands (Exodus 17:11). People kiss or embrace as a blessing without embarrassment (Genesis 48:10) or sexual intent or seduction. Often the one who is to give the blessing eats a special meal before bestowing it (Genesis 27:4). The patriarchs in Genesis chapters 12 through 36 demonstrate performing blessings in a variety of ways.

For Christians, often blessing is spoken with the right hand raised, making the sign of the cross. It is the pronouncement of God's gracious favor and given on the authority of scripture to faithful believers. Christians are assured of God's grace, love, and spirit in us.

We do not have to be Jesus to bless people we love. We can bless with simple, symbolic body movements such as raising our arms and careful touch. Meaningful touch can be healing when done well. Be careful with this however! In today's world, many have been assaulted or sexually molested. While touch was essential in Old Testament blessing, use caution and discretion in our twenty-first century world. When touch is acceptable and appropriate, it can convey warmth, personal acceptance, and even physical health. In the Bible, people kissed and hugged gently, and lovingly laid on hands while performing a blessing.

God, give me a blessing today and help me pass the blessing on to others. Amen.

†   March 15   †

Valued, precious, needed, loved

Philippians 1:3

We need blessing to be spiritually empowered for healing and wholeness. We need on-going blessing that helps us hear we are guided by love every step of our lives. Blessing is something all of us can give and receive. Giving a blessing is the most important affirmation we can give someone. It helps people experience their belovedness.

Years ago I struggled with my own sense of belovedness and a kind friend heard of my despair and disillusionment. She sent me a card that simply said, "Remember these things – you are valued, you are precious, you are needed, you are loved. Sometimes we just need someone to tell us, so I'm telling you – and I mean it with all my heart."

Those gentle and affirming words greatly encouraged me. I have saved that thoughtful card and display it where it is easy to see. As a Japanese proverb says, "One kind word can warm three winter months." Her words blessed me and gave me inner strength that continues through today. Perhaps they can also bless you.

God, help us remember we are valued, precious, needed, and loved by you. Amen.

† March 16 †

How to bless others

Ruth 2:4

Have you ever wondered how you could bless another person? The Book of Ruth in the Bible offers every element of blessing in four brief pages. The blessings are spoken with an active commitment to see the blessing come to pass. The blessings include moments of meaningful touch and spoken words of high value with a clear message that pictures a special future for the individual being blessed. Imagine what a difference our world might be if we dared to bless each other.

Blessing one another is good for our souls. The Ruth story is full of examples of people blessing others. Boaz blesses his employees and they bless him in return. Naomi blesses Boaz and Ruth. Boaz blesses Ruth and she returns a blessing. The entire town blesses Ruth, Naomi, and Boaz. Blessings begat blessing. Their ripple effect can change lives and world history.

Perhaps there is someone in your life that you wish to bless. Consider writing a blessing for them on a card or in a letter. This is easy to do with a bit of practice. You may find the spoken blessings in Ruth helpful. Try lingering with spoken blessings found in Ruth 2:4, 19 and 20, and 3:10.

God, teach us how to bless others. Amen.

† March 17 †

The blessing of friendship

Proverbs 17:17a

"May you be blessed with good friends. May you learn to be a good friend to yourself." [41]

---

[41] John O'Donohue, *Anam Cara: A Book of Celtic Wisdom*, p. 36.

How do you understand friendship? When times are good and money is plentiful, the world seems full of friends. But when the money is gone and the times are hard, our real friends quickly become known.

Friendship can be tested through bereavement, poverty, and danger. Sometimes friends may even leave biological families of origin, birth countries, and religions to journey with a friend. A friend is a great gift from God. Friends can speak the truth in love and their words reach our souls. There are times when dear friends need no spoken words. It is enough to simply be together. A good friend truly loves at all times.

The story of Ruth offers both men and women important lessons about real friendship. In Hebrew, the name Ruth means friend, companion. She is responsible when others are irresponsible. She lived during a time of bloody civil war, great corruption, and famine. She was not born in ancient Israel, yet her deep friendship characterized by tender, fierce loyalty to her friend Naomi earns her a place as one of the most significant women in Israel.

If you have never read this old, old story, consider it. It will change your understanding of friendship forever.

Dear God, bless us with good friends. Teach us how to be a good friend to others. Help us learn to be good friends even to ourselves. Amen.

†   March 18   †
When life goes bad
Ruth 1:5

What does it mean to go from joy to bitterness? From fullness to emptiness? What does it mean to leave our families of origin to seek a new life with a family of choice? How do we survive multiple bereavements, setbacks, crushing disappointments, and broken dreams? Where is God in all this pain? How do we experience the blessings of God when life goes terribly bad?

If you have ever asked these questions yourself, keep reading. Even when the unthinkable happens, we can experience blessing empowerment while grieving and rebuilding our lives.

But how? The remarkable and timeless story of Naomi can show us the way. Life had dealt her the worst that could happen. First, her husband died. Subsequent tragedy then took the lives of both her adult sons. In her extreme grief, Naomi decided to return to her birth country and family of origin for survival. Ruth, one of her beloved daughters-in-law insisted on accompanying her. Ruth's deep love, friendship, and devotion would become an ongoing source of blessing for Naomi in the days ahead.

Reflect upon your own life. How have friends strengthened and encouraged you in the past? Through their love and faithfulness, how did you experience God's loving presence through it all? Try to make the effort to thank friends for their encouraging words and many acts of kindness during times of deep personal grief and loss. Thank God for the countless blessings of friendship. Pray for cherished friends even when your own heart is throbbing with anguish. Such heartfelt prayers tap into an unlimited source of divine strength and loving encouragement. Remember to keep looking up and when you are feeling fragile, treat yourself gently. Take it one day at a time.

God, help us grow in strength and wisdom through Naomi's story. Bless us with good friends and help us be a blessed friend ourselves. Amen.

✝   March 19   ✝

Love and bitterness
Ruth 1:20-21

Naomi teaches us the blessing of being brutally honest with her feelings and perceptions of what God as done in her life, valuable lessons for today. And people listened to her story of grief with respect. They blessed her with holy listening. They heard her with compassion.

Listen to me, said Naomi. My life is no longer pleasant, but bitter. I left this country with my husband with wonderful dreams and hopes. And now look at me. My life is empty and barren. God has dealt harshly with me and brought calamity after calamity.

Poor Ruth. Her friendship and commitment to Naomi is being sorely tested. Her mother-in-law is so steeped in her own grief that she cannot see beyond her pain. Ruth has sacrificed her own happiness and physical security to remain with Naomi in her vulnerability. Now all Ruth has to show for her steadfast love is a living situation with a bitter, unhappy, and depressed relative.

Love and bitterness, bitterness and love. Have you ever experienced these feelings? What does today's story mean to you? Pour out your honest feelings to God through prayer. May God bless you in your prayers.

God, bring us from bitterness into love, from barrenness to fullness, from sorrow to joy, from pain to rejoicing. Amen.

† March 20 †

The healing power of blessing
Ruth 2:12

The second chapter of Ruth begins with a conversation between Naomi and Ruth about finding daily food. Naomi had a relative on her husband's side who owned some fields. It was the beginning of the barley harvest, and Ruth saw an opportunity to work for food by gleaning the field. They discussed the possibility, and then Naomi sent her to the field. As Ruth worked behind the field hands, Boaz, the owner of the field, was supervising the work. Boaz blessed his reapers and noticed Ruth at work. He asked a servant who she was. Boaz was informed that she had worked all day without rest or food.

Boaz spoke kindly to her saying, "Listen to me. Stay in my fields where you will be safe. I have personally ordered the young men not to bother you. Drink my water and eat my food while you work."

Ruth prostrated herself in gratitude and relief. Boaz had heard of her many acts of kindness for her mother-in-law in their common bereavement and of her great sacrifices to help Naomi, and he decided to help her.

Boaz then blessed Ruth for the first time, but Boaz's blessing was not only verbal. He fed her from his own lunch and quietly instructed his workers to leave extra food for her to glean.

Ruth came home with an armful of food. Her mother-in-law asked in astonishment where she got so much. Earlier Naomi had expressed her inner feelings of God's perceived harshness in her life. Now she is able to bless someone's act of kindness and give God thanks. Upon hearing Ruth's story, *Mara* (bitterness) began her recovery as *Naomi* (pleasant) with a spoken blessing. "Blessed be he by the LORD, whose kindness has not forsaken the living or the dead!" (Ruth 2:20)

Ruth's story illustrates the powerful healing that blessing makes possible.

God, help me bless someone for an act of kindness in my life. Help me see the blessing with eyes like Naomi's. Amen.

✝   March 21   ✝

Security, risk taking, and blessing

Ruth 3:10

Naomi is now able to think beyond her own anguish of bereavement and begin to show concern for her beloved daughter-in-law, Ruth. A practical and spiritual woman, Naomi needs, like we do, more than just food. She says to Ruth, "My daughter, I need to seek some security for you, so that it may be well with you" (Ruth 3:1). Naomi shares a plan with Ruth to get some security and protection through a male benefactor. It is calculated risk taking for both women. Ruth agrees and does what her mother-in-law suggests. She washes and dresses with care, then quietly goes to the threshing floor after darkness to lay with Boaz in bed. He awakens, startled to find a young woman in bed with him. She asks his protection as next-of-kin and he agrees to do so.

Boaz blesses Ruth's courage for approaching him for security. "May you be blessed by the LORD . . . this last instance of your loyalty is better than the first . . . do not be afraid, I will do for you all that you ask, for all the assembly of my people know that you are a worthy woman" (Ruth 3:10-12).

We have just read the fifth blessing in Ruth's story (2:4, 12, 19, 20, and 3:10). Ruth and Naomi, and now Boaz and Ruth demonstrate committed responsible relationships. A common thread of *chesed*, that is, of kindness, love, and loyalty, permeates this lovely story (Ruth 1:8; 2:20; 3:10). Blessing requires an active commitment to see the blessing fulfilled in another's life. Talk is cheap without action. Ruth and Boaz "walked the talk" of *chesed* commitment.

When was the last time we blessed someone for his or her courage and commitment to another's welfare? What does it really mean to bless another person? What does it mean to love someone with *chesed*? How can we bless someone with security if they are an outsider? What is in this story for us?

God, what do I need to learn about security, risk taking, and blessing from today's story? Empower my understanding. Equip me with new insights and energize my faith through blessing others. Amen.

†   March 22   †

Community blessings

Ruth 4:11

I love stories with a happy ending. The book of Ruth ends with two magnificent community blessings. The village elders speak first as they bless the future of Ruth and Boaz. The village elders bless Boaz and Ruth with divine blessing for children as they marry. "May the LORD make this woman who is coming into your house like Rachel and Leah . . . may you produce children . . ." (Ruth 4:11). Ruth conceives and bears a son.

The second blessing is by the village women who bless Naomi, for God is giving her new life and family. Naomi takes the child in her arms with the women's blessings. "Blessed be the LORD, who has not left you this day without next-of-kin . . . [this child] shall be to you a restorer of life and a nourisher of your old age; for your daughter-in-law who loves you, who is more to you than seven sons, has borne him" (Ruth 4:14b-15).

Through the power of blessings, Naomi has lost her bitterness and regained her life full of loving relationships, in family and community. Through the power of blessing, Ruth who was formerly an outsider and foreigner has become an insider and a vital part of the community.

What does this mean for us? I suggest we need community blessings in our personal relationships. We need what is called beloved community. Dietrich Bonhoeffer is credited with saying that we need both solitude and community for spiritual success.

Ruth's story also teaches us how to pray. Real needs by real people are uttered throughout the pages (Ruth 1:8-9; 2:12; 4:11-12). Ruth teaches us how to pray with different names for God, with real life needs, with a growing awareness of God's constant activity in the darkest of times. It is also a book of blessing and commitment in responsible relationships. It is a story about kindness, love, and loyalty. We need the spiritual lessons from the Book of Ruth in our twenty-first century world.

God, thank you for the spiritual richness of Ruth and Naomi's story. Bless us as you have blessed her. Bring us also into beloved community for spiritual success. Amen.

† March 23 †

Centering and contemplative prayer ideas
Ruth 4:13-22

It is easy to read Ruth again and again. People of all sexual orientations can be blessed by this lovely story. The Book of Ruth's profound words are meditations on commitment, love, and loyalty.

Consider writing blessings for yourself and those you love from the blessings found in this love story. Another valuable experience might be found in rewriting the prayers for help found in these four chapters. By rewriting prayers in our own words, we find ourselves in new conversations with God and aware of God's loving presence in our lives.

Where are you in this love story? Where is God in your life? What does it mean to be a soul friend in a Ruth and Naomi relationship? Are you considering a Holy Union or marriage? Perhaps Ruth's words of commitment might be appropriate for your ceremony and vows. Or perhaps you are in a relationship where the love and commitment are gone. Perhaps lingering with Ruth may offer some profound and life-changing insights for your relationship. Or writing your answers to these questions in a journal might be spiritually empowering for you.

Consider centering prayer with one of the sacred names for God used by Ruth. Ruth gives us several names for God that we can use in prayer. "LORD" (*Yahweh*) is used 17 times. "God" (*Elohim*) is used three times and "Almighty" (*el Shaddai*) is used twice.

God's activity is mentioned numerous times (Ruth 1:13, 20-21; 2:20; 4:12, 14). Prayers are prayed by people with immediate needs in life (Ruth 1:8, 9; 2:12; 4:11, 12). Responsible relationships are seen in Ruth 1:17 and Ruth 3:13. Redemption is a key concept in the book of Ruth with the Hebrew word emphasized through the use of twenty-three various forms of the word "redeem," "redemption," and "kinsman-redeemer." Why is this important? Ruth is an ancestress of Jesus (Matthew 1:1, 5) and ultimately her story prepares us to experience Jesus as the long awaited and eagerly anticipated divine redeemer/Christ in the New Testament. Linger with these verses in prayer and expect God to bless your spiritual reading and meditation.

The bottom line in Ruth, however, is that the story teaches us how to bless one another with spoken words of high value, meaningful touch, and commitment to see the blessing fulfilled (Ruth 2:4, 19 and 20, and 3:10). It is a story about *chesed*, the Hebrew word for love, kindness, and loyalty that is often demonstrated by God towards humans. We are to share our *chesed* with others through intentional acts of kindness, love, and loyalty in our community and personal relationships.[42]

May all the blessings of chesed *living be yours, and for those you love. Amen.*

<h1 style="text-align:center">†   March 24   †</h1>

Let joy be part of your blessing today

Acts 8:36

I once attended a marvelous retreat hosted by a Seattle church consisting of mostly gay and lesbian parishioners and seekers. The facility had an outdoor hot tub and the retreat concluded with the minister offering Christian baptism to anyone who believed in Jesus Christ. As the retreat

---

[42] The lovely word *chesed* is found in these verses, Ruth 1:8; 2:20, and 3:10.

participants joyously sang a cherished hymn, "Shall we gather at the river," there was a spontaneous change in phraseology, to "Shall we gather at the hot tub." Several came forward and made their confession of faith before being immersed in the waters of baptism. Truly, this was a day of rejoicing.

Gay or straight, the New Testament story of Philip and the Ethiopian eunuch (whom some contemporary scholars believe to be a gay man) offers every reader an invitation to Christian baptism. As the eunuch experienced new faith in God, he asked Philip a soul searching question, Is there anything to stop me from being baptized?

Homophobic churches often cause gay, lesbian, bisexual, and transgendered seekers to feel unloved and unacceptable to the very core of their being. Some have been tragically refused Christian baptism because their sexual orientation was known and condemned. As a result, many carry deep spiritual wounds of guilt, shame, violence, anger, and bewilderment to the world's hatred, violence, rejection, and humiliation.

But the Ethiopian eunuch shows us how the good news of Jesus Christ embraces all seekers, and he demonstrates how to experience the message of God's inclusive love with gratitude, acceptance, and joy. Immediately ready to receive the blessing of baptism as a new believer in Christ, the Jesus story became more than a mental image for him. It went to his heart and became action.

I thank God for the growing numbers of welcoming churches who proclaim a non-homophobic gospel message of divine grace, love, and inclusion. They can be easily found through Internet search engines by typing in key words such as "gay and Christian." These represent a growing global voice of faith worth investigating with an open heart and mind.

Learn to love your life and accept yourself as precious to God. Begin sitting with sacred words as the Ethiopian eunuch did. If you have never been baptized, consider it. Ask the Spirit for understanding and guidance. Let joy become part of your spiritual blessing today. Is there anything to stop you from receiving your blessing today? [43]

God, give me heartfelt joy today and the understanding of the Ethiopian eunuch. Amen.

---

[43] Hinson, E. Glenn. Editor. *Spirituality in Ecumenical Perspective*, p. 190.

†   March 25   †

A blessing word

2 Chronicles 6:13b

The most commonly used Hebrew word for blessing in the Old Testament is *barak.* It is used hundreds of times. It means to kneel, bless, praise, and salute. Some feel there is an association between kneeling and receiving a blessing (2 Chronicles 6:13; Psalm 95:6; Genesis 24:11). One theological dictionary summarized the use of *barak* in Old Testament blessings in this way, "To bless in the Old Testament means to endure with power for success, prosperity, fecundity, longevity." [44]

In general, it seems that blessings are bestowed from the greater to the lesser such as from a father to a son (Genesis 49), brother to a sister (Genesis 24:6), or a King to his subjects (1 Kings 8:14). Blessings are given for special occasions, departures, and introductions (2 Chronicles 6:3; Genesis 47:7, 10). But the main function of blessing seems to confer abundant and effective life upon something or someone (Genesis 2:3; 27:27ff; Genesis 49; 1 Samuel 9:13; Isaiah 66:3). Blessing can be a formalized way of expressing thanks and praise to a person for life's abundance. It can offer futuristic power for living in a person.

However *barak* may be used, it is used with the knowledge that God is the only source of blessing. God controls blessing. Only God's presence can bring true blessing and God's name is the heart of all blessing. Those wrongly related to God cannot bless or be blessed (Deuteronomy 10:8; Malachi 2:2).

Barak blessings are for people of all sexual orientations. So consider an experiment with God today.

Take a moment and kneel in your hearts. Spread out your hands toward heaven. Ask God for moments of *barak* blessed awareness as you go about your day. Count your blessings with gratitude and joy. You will be amazed at how many come your way.

God, you are our ultimate source of blessing. Energize us with your presence and power. Give us a special blessing today. Amen.

---

[44] Harris, R. Laird, Gleason L. Archer, Jr., and Bruce K. Waltke. *Theological Wordbook of the Old Testament.* Volume 1, p. 132

† March 26 †

Blessedness of faith

Psalm 34:8b

Everyone believes in something. We live our beliefs in action through faith at work, at play, and in how we interact with friend and foe, neighbor and family member. Faith is the centerpiece of spiritual empowerment. It is our lifeline when life is raw, ugly, painful, and tragic. Faith also brings us into great moments of hope and love. Through faith, we can pray to a power greater than ourselves. Through faith, we find it safe to cry, laugh, rage, and rejoice with the Holy One.

The ancient Psalms quickly reveal that trust in God is essential for living. Faith is a great blessing. It is an attribute pleasing to the Creator and influences lifestyle choices. Wisdom is found in trusting God while foolishness is found by trusting only in ourselves. Throughout the Psalms, blessed faith is usually expressed by words such as "believe," "trust," and "hope." This kind of faith brings great happiness in God.

The bottom line is this – only God is truly worthy of our fullest trust. God is our rock, salvation, refuge, deliverer, shield, and stronghold. The Psalms are full of rather ordinary and sometimes dysfunctional people of great faith. Through their faith, they also experienced their greatest joy and happiness.

Would you like to be happy in God? Then consider praying the Psalms. If you have never read them before, they are worth reading. They help us talk with God. We learn prayer by praying them. The Psalms are not always easy, but understanding comes with use. God will bless you with true happiness.

Bless us with great moments of inner happiness, O Holy One. Be our refuge, our rock, our protector, and our guide this day, we pray.

† **March 27** †

Blessed by God

Psalm 119:1b

Would you like to be blessed by God? Then Psalm 119 is worth reading again and again. Our souls do love to stroll and it is easy to wander through these lovely verses. As we travel through Psalm 119 with eyes of faith, we are empowered and blessed by God. These sacred words help us experience the holy in extraordinary moments of renewal.

Many people enjoy prayer walks. Long walks, short walks, morning walks, or evening walks – they are good for us. The philosopher Søren Kierkegaard said, "Above all, do not lose your desire to walk: every day I walk myself into a state of well being and walk away from every illness. I have walked myself into my best thoughts." Friedrich Nietzsche remarked, "Never trust a thought that didn't come by walking."

Take a moment today and browse through some of the verses in Psalm 119. Stroll with God in a brief prayer walk. Reflect on what it means in your own life to walk in the ways of God. You will be blessed.

God, we ask you for greater understanding and guidance. Teach us to love you more dearly. Bless us with a changed heart and new spiritual eyes to love your ways, decrees, laws, and commands. Amen.

† **March 28** †

Blessing God

Psalm 66:8-9

God has created us to be a divine blessing. We are created to bless, that is, to extol God's majesty, greatness, and goodness to all of creation. We are created to worship God with every fiber of our being and the Psalms give us wonderful words of praise. "Bless the LORD, O my soul, and all that is within me, bless God's holy name" (Psalm 103:1, inclusive). We are created for praise and blessing, for God is good. God is gracious. God is great. God is God. God is. Blessed be the Lord of all creation who is involved in our lives! Praise the name of the Holy One with every breath of our being.

The more we bless God on earth, the better our praise will be in heaven. So learn to be a blessing and source of praise to our Maker. Consider this an investment in your heavenly future! Someday we will bless God with the angels and all other heavenly hosts, along with the great crowd of witnesses who have gone before us, and it will be glorious. Bless our God, O peoples. Let the sounds of praises be heard from our lips, for God has kept us among the living and has not let our feet slip. Blessed be the LORD.

God, I bless your holy name with all that is within me. Amen.

✝   **March 29**   ✝

God's blessing cup

Psalm 23:5

Psalm 23 is the most beloved psalm. It never ceases to amaze me in hospitals and hospices, to feel these powerful and comforting words as someone is dying. Even those who have never attended a religious institution of any kind seem to know the words. But Psalm 23 is also for the living! Psalm 23 is for all the days of our lives, the good, the bad, the beautiful, and the difficult. Psalm 23 is a great confession of faith when we wonder where God is.

I will always remember preaching a sermon based on Psalm 23 the Sunday after the 1999 massacre at Columbine High School. Two students had shot, killed, and maimed a number of their classmates without warning earlier that week. That Sunday, people needed to hear these words and be reminded of God's blessing cup during moments of danger, fear, and despair. During the worship service, I passed a blessing cup with oil for personal anointing during the sermon. People dipped their fingers into the cup, and touched their hearts and foreheads with the sign of the cross. Parents even anointed their little children.

We are invited to the Shepherd's table to live as beloved and anointed people. We are offered God's blessing cup of healing oil. The cup offers us simple abundance, goodness, and mercy all the days of our lives. God is actually eager to provide for us and lavish us with spiritual hospitality and generosity. God delights to provide for us when we are surrounded by those who wish us harm. Even in impending danger, our Shepherd Host spreads out a table for us. Our anointing oil is refreshing, soothing, and harmonizing with the gracious host hospitality of ancient times. We are welcomed into the home of God. The cup is a blessing offered to everyone.

One of the most empowering things we can do in our life is to claim our blessing and bless others. Will you allow yourself a moment for God's blessing today? Have you ever considered anointing yourself while using a blessing cup? It is easy to do and can become a cherished family tradition. If you have never been blessed by your family, blessing yourself may begin deep spiritual healing. You are God's blessing to the world. You are of high value. Your life is important. God yearns to bless you, even if your families were unable to bless you.

God, give me your blessing. Help me live as your anointed one. Amen.

†   **March 30**   †

God's love and mercy is our blessing

Psalm 23:6a

Psalm 23 is good for our souls. God's love and mercy will go with us everywhere in life. We will dwell in the house of the LORD forever. In reclaiming our place at the Shepherd's banquet table, we can live with personal confidence, joy, and triumph from beginning to end. God wishes to bless each of us with goodness and mercy all the days of our lives. This is our blessing.

I love Psalm 23. It is worth memorizing for times of need. Consider rewriting it in your own words in a paraphrase. Every sentence is a blessing. For today's meditation, read it again and again. Try and hear it as if for the first time. Write your thoughts and prayers in response to these gracious words. Sometimes it is helpful to read familiar words in a different translation for fresh power and insights:

"Because the LORD is my Shepherd, I have everything I need! He lets me rest in the meadow grass and leads me beside the quiet streams.

He gives me new strength. He helps me do what honors him the most. Even when walking through the dark valley of death I will not be afraid, for you are close beside me, guarding, guiding all the way. You provide delicious food for me in the presence of my enemies. You have welcomed me as your guest; blessings overflow! Your goodness and unfailing kindness shall be with me all of my life, and afterwards I will live with you forever in your home." (Source of paraphrase unknown.)

Reading Psalm 23 is better than winning the lottery. In this psalm, we find a tender and intimate holy name for the sacred and are brought into a state of rest, quiet, and stillness. The psalm itself is a great confession of faith in the Shepherd of our souls. Our souls are restored without any frantic activity being required of us.

This great confession of faith encourages us to let love guide our lives. These beloved words help us journey with courage through the valley of shadows and of death, but without fear. In today's unsettling and scary world, our growing faith can comfort and equip us for whatever lies ahead. The twenty-third psalm is a reminder that through it all, God is enough. God is with us. God is closer than our breathing. We can trust the Shepherd.

God, may your goodness and mercy be ours all the days of our lives. Amen.

†   **March 31**   †

May God continue to bless us

Psalm 67

I once had the privilege of facilitating a virtual book study-retreat over a ten-week period. It was a closed group experience dedicated to female sexual minority Christians, seekers, skeptics, and doubters. It was an outreach ministry that lovingly respected, accepted, and affirmed all people in the Christian faith with an attitude of hospitality, sanctuary, and generosity. The majority of participants were lesbians, although a number of women identified as bisexual. Everyone was welcomed. There was always room for one more in the study. Through the power of the Internet, we gathered in virtual community from several continents. We chose to study the late Henri Nouwen's book, *Life of the Beloved: Spiritual Living in a Secular World.*

It quickly became apparent that some struggled to accept their belovedness in God, for so often the messages of their societies, families, and churches had been extremely negative. As the weeks continued, we lingered in "The Book," as it came to be called. We discussed what it meant to be chosen, broken, blessed, and sent into the world as the Beloved. Every week I would post a summary of the reading and closed with a brief written prayer.

One of our favorite breath prayers came from the word, "beloved." Sometimes people would use "beloved" as their centering word for the day's prayer. At other times, we prayed it as two words, "be loved." The power of belovedness graced each woman. Lives were transformed, faith was strengthened and explored, and all were helped. Some were able to reconcile their sexuality and spirituality with humor and peace of mind. Deep blessing, caring, and nurture characterized the entire experience.

Today's psalm reminds me of that wonderful international virtual beloved community. May this psalm be our blessing prayer for readers of all sexual orientations. May God continue to bless us one day at a time. Live as God's beloved. Be loved all the days of your lives.

God, help us be a blessing to our families, friends, work colleagues, neighbors, and even our enemies. Amen.

† April 1 †

Reading a Gospel for the first time

Luke 1:1-3

One of the questions most frequently asked of me is, "Just what is a Gospel?" Millions of people throughout world history have asked that important question. Gospels are the Jesus stories that have brought hope to people throughout the centuries. Each Gospel lesson teaches spiritual empowerment. One does not have to be a Christian to read them or live by these life-nourishing principles.

The Gospel writers are Matthew, Mark, Luke, and John. None attended formal seminary, yet each individual writer brings his unique perspective and understanding of the amazing spiritual leader named Jesus Christ. Quite frankly, Jesus turned their earthly world upside down and they had to share these adventures with God. So they wrote about his birth, life, ministry, death, and amazing return from the dead. These stories have transformed lives in every culture, language, and country over the past two millennia. People have joyously gone to their deaths as martyrs of the Jesus faith rather than betray or deny this amazing teacher, healer, preacher, friend, beloved companion, and prophet.

All the Gospels are good reading. Matthew writes from an orthodox Jewish perspective and includes many of the major teachings of Jesus. Mark's Gospel is shorter and written for people without a Jewish background. Luke is a non-Jewish physician who carefully researched the Jesus stories for a two-part series. The Gospel of Luke is written to describe Jesus as the Great Physician while the book of Acts, also attributed to Luke, is an adventure account of the early church. John's Gospel is written from the heart about beloved Jesus.

The Greek meaning of the word *gospel* means "good news." Gospels are written accounts by four writers who shared what they knew about Jesus' teaching, about the Jesus way of life. The Gospels are a carefully gathered selection of stories and teachings by people, called disciples, who followed Jesus. Disciples are spiritual apprentices who study the teachings and life of their spiritual leader. They share these teachings and lifestyles with others. Christian discipleship begins with two simple words uttered by Jesus, "Follow me."

God, help us be spiritual apprentices as we begin our reading adventure with you! Begin a spiritual revolution in our lives today. Show us what it means to follow Jesus. Amen.

† April 2 †

Getting started

John 1:1

Once it was my privilege and challenge to present five spiritually centered sessions over the course of a weekend retreat. It was a retreat specifically offered to sexual minorities and their friends. The program emphasized the theme "relinquish, reclaim, and renew." Many had felt isolated and condemned by their experiences with mainline religious organizations. We wrestled with what to relinquish and reclaim for inner renewal as God's beloved people. This was radical information for some retreat attendees who had only experienced the Bible as a weapon used against them. The only books we used were the Gospel of John and *Life of the Beloved* by Henri Nouwen. It was a remarkable weekend of spiritual empowerment as many took a risk with God and reclaimed their belovedness.

I will always remember the exuberance of one woman who attended this retreat. This particular woman eagerly went to a bookstore after the retreat to buy her very first Bible. We happened to meet by chance in the parking lot. We hugged and chatted about the weekend. Then she asked me, "Now how do I get started in reading this book?" She was a brilliant executive and dynamic leader, but the Bible was strange and unfamiliar to her. How do we begin reading the Bible?

An old Chinese proverb wisely tells us the journey of a thousand miles begins with a single step. Our spiritual journey begins with opening the book for the first time. Be open to its message. Ask yourself what prejudices or experiences may need to be relinquished so you may enjoy spiritual openness to these new words. Take a chance with God and ask to claim or reclaim an insight, a centering word, or strengthening thought for your day. Expect inner renewal. You will find spiritual nourishment in the Gospels for yourself, those you love, and those you do not.

God, help us relinquish whatever is spiritually negative in our lives. Help us reclaim truth and strength for the day. Let us experience deep spiritual renewal through our readings. Amen.

† April 3 †

The radical genealogy of Jesus

Matthew 1:1

Genealogy defines us. We yearn to know where we have come from. I certainly do and find most people both want and need to know the answers to the following questions: Who am I? Where did I come from? What were my ancestors like? Why am I the way I am? What are the traditions, strengths, and weaknesses in my family tree?

The Gospel of Matthew intentionally opens with the genealogy of Jesus Christ. Because so many modern readers are unaccustomed to the foreign sounding names, it is easy to skim through the first seventeen verses and miss the significant inclusion of four women found in verses 3, 5, and 6.

The lives of Tamar (Genesis 38), Rahab (Joshua 2:1-21), Ruth (The Book of Ruth), and Bathsheba who was "the wife of Uriah" (2 Samuel 11-12) offer important insights and a unique perspective for our reading adventure through Matthew's Gospel. Women were rarely highlighted as spiritual leaders in the Old Testament. Females were not highly valued in that culture. They had no rights and could not own property. Their culture was completely patriarchal.

Yet the radical genealogy of Jesus Christ recognizes these women. By including their names in the genealogy, they are no longer invisible. Their lives bring us contemporary and relevant insights through their spiritual sensitivity, leadership, courage, and obedience to God, although their lives were incredibly difficult.

Matthew is making a significant theological point by naming them. There is a place in this Gospel for both men and women. I personally find this refreshing. So much of church history has been written from a patriarchal perspective, automatically excluding many great women of faith. Tamar, Rahab, Ruth, and the wife of Uriah help us better understand the family tree of Jesus the Messiah, the son of David, the son of Abraham.

Perhaps we have excluded others through our own willingness to support societal traditions. Yet the genealogy of Jesus Christ helps us see people through holy eyes.

God, teach us remarkable truths about Jesus in this genealogy so frequently overlooked. Bless us with contemporary and relevant insights for living through our own genealogy. Teach us to value the men and women in our lives. Amen.

† April 4 †

Christmas in April

Matthew 1:18

Usually we hear this famous story only at Christmas time. But if you have ever felt pregnant with holy longings, this great story is relevant any day of the year. Mary risked everything by agreeing to this divine impregnation. Her culture could have demanded the death penalty by stoning for her perceived illegitimate pregnancy.

Joseph reminds me of many young unmarried men today who have pregnant girlfriends. This was not his biological baby, and quite frankly, Mary's explanation about how the Holy Spirit impregnated her sounded farfetched and impossible. He wrestled with her story and almost left her. But he sensed God in a powerful dream, which told him to stay with Mary and the remarkable child.

And unknown to Mary and Joseph during the tumultuous pregnancy, the Magi, often called wise men or three kings in popular Christmas carols, were traveling many arduous and dangerous miles to worship this amazing child. Their holy pilgrimage innocently contributed to the destruction of many male infants. In order to protect his throne, King Herod willingly slaughtered young children, hoping to do away with the newborn "king of the Jews." Mary and Joseph fled for their lives with the newborn child to another country and sought refuge until God again spoke to them through a dream.

If you have never read the entire Christmas story in this Gospel (Matthew 1:18 –2:15), it is a real thriller. Mary, Joseph, and the Magi were ordinary people willing to be used in extraordinary ways for God. They were holy dreamers and remarkably sensitive to God. Their faith can be our faith as we search for what is reliable and trustworthy in the great mystery of God through our own holy readings and journey.

God, help us be as spiritually sensitive and courageous as these holy dreamers. Bring us into new faith and help us find a place in these Gospel stories. Amen.

† April 5 †
The Baptism of Jesus
Matthew 3:16-17

We are given a picture of the spiritual humility of Jesus. Jesus insisted John baptize him as a symbol of consecration to God, thus beginning his public ministry. Immediately after being baptized, the Holy Spirit landed on Jesus in the form of a dove. A voice from heaven called out, "This is my Son, the Beloved, with whom I am well pleased."

John was a prophet, sent to prepare the way for his cousin, Jesus. He called people to confess their sins and then be baptized. Many seekers, including Pharisees and Sadducees, came to where John was baptizing. According to Matthew's Gospel, John the Baptist was baptizing in the river Jordan. John was preaching a message of repentance. John spoke bluntly and let it be clearly known that someone listening to him was God's greatest spiritual leader. John understood he was not worthy to even loosen the sandals of Jesus. John would only baptize with water, but taught that Jesus would baptize with the Holy Spirit and with fire.

Now people may disagree on the fine points of baptism. Some would baptize infants and children. Other churches may refuse to do this while insisting on "believers baptism" only. Certain churches insist on a number of baptism classes and issue a certificate afterwards. Others will baptize you on the spot during a church service. Each claims the authority of scripture as the basis of their practice. Welcome to the great diversity in the Christian church. Jesus was baptized as an adult. Later on in the book of Acts, we see entire families baptized. Both in my opinion are fine and worthy of divine blessing.

If you have never been baptized as a Christian, consider it. Jesus did it. It will be a source of blessing for you. Or perhaps you have been baptized as a child and do not remember it. Consider reaffirming your baptism through your local church. Whether infant, child, adult, immersed, or sprinkled, baptism is a spiritual sacrament for us to consider. Baptism is part of discipleship.

God, help me consecrate my life to you anew this day. Amen.

† April 6 †

Temptation

Matthew 4:1

Who has not been tempted? Who has not struggled with the enticements of this world? Life is full of temptation and those who tempt. It is very easy to quote sacred writings to justify our longing to satisfy desires. Resisting temptation can be very difficult. Temptation takes many subtle and not so subtle forms. Sex, prestige, comfort, money, power, food, success, and a desire for fame are just a few things that often tempt us.

Jesus was tempted throughout his life and ministry career. Let us linger in the story of Jesus' great temptation for the next few days (Matthew 4:1-11). Jesus has just been baptized in public consecration to God in the previous chapter. The Holy Spirit immediately leads him into a desert wasteland for a time of prayer, fasting, and meditation. Through these spiritual disciplines, he was able to discern his ministry and life priorities. Read scripture to learn what the Spirit says to you about these spiritual disciplines. Perhaps, like Jesus, you will better know your own ministry.

We have much to learn about being led by the Spirit and going somewhere special to pray. When have you felt "led" to go somewhere for a special time of prayer and possibly fasting? One does not have to go to a desert to experience solitude for spiritual growth and moments of discernment. Perhaps it would be good to reflect today on what tempts us into areas harmful for our lives and loved ones.

God, lead us by your Spirit into special moments for prayer today. As we linger with this story for the next few days, teach us about temptation, prayer, fasting, solitude, and scripture. Amen.

✝   **April 7**   ✝

Temptation and fasting

Matthew 4:2

The pastor of St. Michael's Church of Hamburg, Germany, Helmut Thielicke reminds us that Christ experienced severe hunger, his stomach growled. [45] His intestines were twisted into knots, his abdomen became bloated, and his head throbbed with pain. Jesus Christ felt weak and faint. This was an extreme situation. Jesus was famished. He was extremely vulnerable to temptation in this physical state of weakness.

We have much to learn about prayer and fasting. We know that going without food for forty days and forty nights is medically dangerous. Fasting for forty days is not safe and I do not recommended it. At the same time, Jesus teaches that fasting is part of spiritual life. In just a page or two, Jesus assumes we will fast (Matthew 6:16-18) and teaches his disciples how to fast in moderation. There are times and seasons in our lives when we need fasting for spiritual growth, maturing, and discernment.

Many in the world do not have the luxury of going to bed with a full stomach. Jesus identifies fully with those without adequate daily food. He hungered. He was actually starving. Consider scheduling a prayer fast for the spiritual experience of identifying with those who hunger. If you are under a physician's care, ask your doctor if fasting would affect your health. Missing one meal a month for prayer purposes is a realistic place to start. List special concerns for prayer. Select scriptures or special readings in advance. If possible, plan on a specific place for your prayer. Put it on your calendar. It will transform your prayer life. Fasting and prayer refines our faith, strengthens and matures us. It helps us identify with those who are actually famished and in desperate need.

---

[45] Quoted in Blackmore, James H. *Reflections on the Temptations of Christ*, p. 14.

God, bring your compassion on those who hunger physically and spiritually this day. Amen.

†   **April 8**   †

When the tempter comes

Matthew 4:3

Certainly all of us are tempted throughout life. The English word "temptation" comes from the Latin word *temptare*. It has two basic meanings. The first is to try or test. The second is to entice to evil. Jesus experienced both. He was tried and tested as well as enticed to do what was evil. He overcame the tempter, who is also known as the evil one. Jesus overcame his temptation, freeing himself to help those who are experiencing temptation.

An anonymous New Testament author writes, "Because he himself suffered when he was tempted, he is able to help those who are being tempted" (Hebrews 2:18 NIV). "Therefore, since we have a great high priest who has gone through the heavens, Jesus the Son of God, let us hold firmly to the faith we profess. For we do not have a high priest who is unable to sympathize with our weaknesses, but we have one who has been tempted in every way, just as we are, yet without sin. Let us then approach the throne of grace with confidence, so that we may receive mercy and find grace to help us in our time of need" (Hebrews 4:15-16 NIV).

I personally find it comforting to realize Jesus Christ has been tempted and understands my human weakness. I can approach him through prayer with great confidence in my most vulnerable moments.

God, help us realize when the tempter is tempting us. Help us remember to pray and find grace to help us in our times of need. Amen.

† April 9 †

Temptation and holy words
Matthew 4:4

Food for the body is not enough to satisfy the deepest longings of our souls. We all hunger for meaning, purpose in living, and a sense of value. We hunger for God. Christ refused to use his power for self-service. He chose to experience hunger, one of the keenest pains human-kind experiences. He chose to identify with those who suffer. He gave himself completely to serving God. "Seek first the Kingdom (Reign) of God and God's righteousness, and all these things shall be added to you" (Matthew 6:33 NIV). Food is not our only concern in this life. We need soul food that sustains us when we are physically and spiritually starving. Sacred words in scripture are one form of soul food, which will endure forever.

Jesus knew the words of scripture and quoted Deuteronomy 8:3 to his tempter. Jesus is exhausted, starving, and vulnerable to evil. Yet he is inwardly sustained by a word of holy scripture. His Bible was the Old Testament. He had committed himself to memorizing large portions of it since childhood. In his moment of need, he had spiritual food for his jour-ney. He carried scripture in his heart. Jesus did not have a copy of a writ-ten Bible with him. He had it engraved in his heart.

Holy words nourish us in difficult times. We also need to carry them in our hearts. We would be wise to memorize nourishing words for our times of need. Perhaps you have never before memorized scripture. It is a spiritual discipline that has encouraged people in danger and safety, health and sickness, from birth to death.

Jesus is later recorded as saying, "I am the bread of life. Whoever comes to me will never be hungry, and whoever believes in me will never be thirsty" (John 6:35). The One who hungered is now bread for the world.

God, help us carry nourishing words in our hearts for our times of need. Amen.

✝   **April 10**   ✝

Scriptural duels and temptation

Matthew 4:5-7

Jesus is involved in a scriptural duel. He and the devil are battling with Bible texts. Jesus is quoting scripture always in context. The devil, however, is using them out of context in a dangerous manner intended for harm. The devil uses scripture to tempt Christ. There is always enormous danger in isolating scripture out of context. It can be quoted correctly but with the wrong intent, with a hidden or not-so-hidden agenda.

We see Jesus using scripture in context to accurately reveal God's truth. He did not "proof-text," that is using a word, a sentence, and even a paragraph out of context to prove our cherished point of view. Often this harms people who do not hold the same opinions. We are to follow Christ's example of interpreting scripture with scripture in context. This is often easier said than done.

C. J. G. Montefiore, a noted Jewish scholar, writes that the wilderness temptations are written in the ancient rabbinical forms. "Jesus at each temptation overcomes the devil by a quotation from scripture, exactly in the rabbinical manner." [46] We do not have to be noted scholars to use scripture quotations accurately. It takes a humble heart and lifetime of reading, prayer, discernment, study, and maturing. We will make mistakes. It is part of being human. Reading all the Gospels again and again as part of our spiritual reading will help us grow up in God.

God, the Bible is a very big book. Teach us to read it through the eyes and understanding of Jesus. Amen.

---

[46] Quoted in Blackmore, James H. *Reflections on the Temptations of Christ*, p. 6.

†   April 11   †

The temptation to do good through evil
Matthew 4:8-11

How tempting it must have been for Jesus to consider the easy way out for power. The cross would not be necessary. He would not have to suffer and die a shameful death. He would use his power for good. Compromise beckoned. Life is full of compromises.

Christ was tempted to satisfy himself and put God to a test. The devil tempted him to do good by evil means and to bask in popularity. Jesus was being tempted to act rashly and conform to popular demand. How tempting it must have been to consider compromising truth for favor. It must have been a great temptation to stay on the mountaintop and look after number one. It would have been easy for Christ to compromise God's idea and let others dictate his actions. He was being offered all the power in the world.

James H. Blackmore makes a profound insight for us in his book *Reflections on the Temptations of Christ,* "Because the Savior was tempted as we . . . he understands." [47] What kept him from this enormous temptation to use evil for good? In a word, worship. He lived, breathed, and let God be the center of his life. He knew who he was and whose he was. He communed with God every day of his life, privately and regularly in public worship according to his religious tradition. Once again he quoted an Old Testament verse (Deuteronomy 6:13). Only God is to be worshiped and served. Go away, Satan! You are not wanted here. Jesus dismissed Satan with scripture.

The biblical text tells us the devil was defeated and left. Yet another Gospel account tells us the evil one simply went away for a short time (Luke 4:13). He would be back at some of the most vulnerable times in Christ's life. These spiritual battles would be fought again and again.

We have so much to learn from this. It is human nature to linger with temptation and let it have too much power in our lives. We too, can dismiss significant evil temptations in our lives by being grounded and centered in worship and scripture. We should also realize that life is a battle of good and evil. If the tempter returned again and again to tempt Jesus, we can expect the same in our lives. This is why we need spiritual accountability, community, and strengthening through private and corpo-

---

[47] Blackmore, James H. *Reflections on the Temptations of Christ,* p. 6.

rate worship, bible study, and prayer. We can be spiritually empowered through worship as we encounter the daily temptations of life.

God, help us to worship and serve only you. Amen.

† April 12 †

Repentance

Matthew 4:17a

Immediately after Jesus finished his great temptation experience in the wilderness, he received some bad news. His cousin, John the Baptist had been put in prison. John's message was a powerful one which called both the religious and irreligious to the repentance of sins, and for changed lives. He was blunt and spoke his truth boldly. He called crowds of people to prepare for Jesus, God's called and special One who would save people from their sins. John deeply offended many powerful people as he named their sins. He was jailed for his words and would later be executed for them. John refused to compromise his message from God.

I find it interesting that Jesus immediately began preaching a message of repentance. Repentance has always been dangerous and unpopular. It takes courage to look within and be honest with God. We need to come to God for mercy. God is righteous and utterly good. Sin is the opposite of God's goodness, love, and mercy. As we continue reading the gospels, we will find Jesus is a friend of sinners. He offers us divine forgiveness. Jesus traces sin to the human heart and challenges us on the sins of neglect, good left undone, and our unused talents; our insensitivities and lack of compassion towards others, and all the sins against love. Sin is also anything that will not let us trust God's goodness, or revere God's name, or love God wholly.

A Prayer of Confession: *"Forgive them all, O Lord: our sins of omission and our sins of commission; the sins of our youth and the sins of our riper years; the sins of our souls and the sins of our bodies; our secret and our more open sins; our sins of ignorance and surprise, and our more deliberate and presumptuous sins; the sins we have done to please others; the sins we know and remember, and the sins we have forgotten; the sins we*

*have striven to hide from others and the sins by which we have made oth-
ers offend; forgive them, O Lord, forgive them all." Amen.*

(Attributed to John Wesley.)

†   **April 13**   †

Heaven is near

Matthew 4:17b

The kingdom of heaven means a spiritual revolution, yet Jesus'
words about it are the teachings we most frequently overlook. This phrase
is mentioned thirty-three times in the Gospel of Matthew. The kingdom
(reign) of God is mentioned a total of ninety-nine times in all the combined Gospels and twenty-five more times throughout the remainder of the
New Testament. God's kingdom is the major focus of the good news of
Jesus Christ. The reign of God is the most holistic spiritual message heard
in world history.

Why do we so quickly focus on other teachings? Often people settle for a plan of salvation rather than the full teachings of Jesus. The
Kingdom of God is near. It is within and around us. God's *shalom*
(peace) is available through Jesus Christ. All are welcome in this kingdom
that dignifies, arouses human conscience to injustice and the roots of sin,
and liberates the hearts of all people. Jesus is teaching us radical discipleship.

What exactly is the kingdom of heaven? The Lord's Prayer gives
us some amazing insights in six short petitions.

*Our Father [Mother] in heaven, hallowed be your name, your kingdom
come, your will be done on earth as it is in heaven. Give us today our
daily bread. Forgive us our debts as we also have forgiven our debtors.
And lead us not into temptation, but deliver us from the evil one. Amen.*

(Matthew 6:9-13, NIV Inclusive.)

111

† April 14 †

Ordinary people willing to be extraordinary
Matthew 4:19-20

The disciples are all ordinary people willing to be extraordinary. The brothers Peter and Andrew immediately leave their careers to follow Jesus. Jesus continues on and calls two other brothers, James and John. They also immediately leave their livelihood and aging father to follow this amazing teacher. These four men soon become key members of the inner circle known as the twelve disciples. The remainder of Matthew's Gospel describes the next three years of their lives as Jesus carefully prepares them to become spiritual revolutionaries.

The disciples are willing to take a chance with God. I have often wondered what I would have done in their situation. Their response seems so impulsive and I am much more cautious by nature. But did you know that these four brothers had known Jesus before this call to ministry?

These ordinary people had been following the prophet known as John the Baptist. After Jesus had been baptized, the Baptizer immediately pointed his followers to Christ. As a result, a small number of his dedicated disciples sensed in Jesus someone remarkable. They left their fishing nets without hesitation when Jesus called them by name with the imperative to follow him.

Their response to Jesus' call was based on an earlier relationship with him (John 1:35-42). They had lingered, asked questions, searched their souls, and discussed among themselves what they heard. They trusted Jesus enough to risk their security and status quo. These early followers understood Jesus offered a new way to live with God. And they wanted what Jesus had.

God, help us be spiritually extraordinary people and follow you. Amen.

† April 15 †

When God calls you by name
Matthew 4:21-22

How do you know when God is calling you by name? Sometimes God calls when we least expect it. For James and John their workday began uneventfully. They arose and went to their family business. There was nothing unusual as they sat on the beach with their father, Zebedee, mending the worn fishing nets.

Then suddenly everything changed forever as God surprised them. Jesus appeared out of nowhere and stood quietly before them. And he called them by name. "James and John, come follow me!" I would imagine Zebedee blustered about how this would ruin the family business, but the brothers responded without a second thought. For months they had been carefully listening to Jesus and discussing among themselves what he taught. Their revered and charismatic spiritual leader, John the Baptist had pointed Jesus out as God's special messenger to planet earth.

And here Jesus was on the beach by the boats, calling them by name to come and follow him in an adventure with God. The brothers acted without hesitation and their father threw up his hands towards heaven in frustration. He would have to fish alone that day without his strong sons by his side.

So the question begs asking. How do we know when God is calling us by name? For me, this kind of discernment has grown over the years with experience, memories, and even training. Discerning God's call reminds me of the Hindu parable about six blind men trying to describe their elephant. But none of the blind men had the big picture, only their limited human experiences. They did the best they could with what they had. And with each shared experience, they grew in understanding of the entire elephant. [48]

And so it is with us as we attempt to discern God's calling in our lives. There is wisdom to be learned in seeking the counsel of others in the faith. Talk with your pastor, spiritual director, a pastoral counselor, and other friends in God. Describing your experience helps define it to yourself and others. Then step out in faith with the knowledge you have and take the next step into the unknown. If you feast your eyes on Jesus, you can trust the path before you. And sometimes those divine interruptions

---

[48] Huston, Sterling W. *Crusade Evangelism and the Local Church*, p. 62.

are really our divine callings. But we will never know until we take the first step.

God, interrupt our day as you did so long ago with James and John on the beach. Help us discern the call of Jesus in our day-to-day lives. As we take steps of faith in the direction of your call, guide us day by day. Amen.

✝ April 16 ✝

Large crowds came

Matthew 4:23, 25

Many people are surprised to realize that Jesus quickly became a famous international teacher, preacher, and healer. People came in their neediness from great distances, often on foot. He spoke with an authority that had never before been heard. He reinterpreted God in fresh, new, and exciting ways. Every known disease and sickness was healed by either his touch or spoken word. Large crowds flocked from many cities when they heard Jesus was in the area. News about him spread quickly through word of mouth.

People would throng around Jesus and press close. They would actually interfere with his meals and rest in their eagerness to be with him. He was wonderful to be with. Jesus preached a message that comforted the afflicted and afflicted the comfortable. Sometimes we forget how popular Jesus was in his early preaching, teaching, and healing career.

God, help me see Jesus with new eyes, hear him with new ears, and respond to him with a new heart. Amen.

† April 17 †

Blessed attitudes

Matthew 5:1-3a

The Sermon on the Mount, as described by Matthew, is one of Jesus' most famous teachings. People from many different faith backgrounds have found it transforming and life-changing. I know of a Unitarian minister who loves to read it from time to time. Although she is not Christian, she marvels at the Sermon on the Mount's amazing power and on occasion will teach and preach it to her religiously diverse congregation.

The first twelve verses in this marvelous chapter are known more commonly as the Beatitudes. The actual Greek root word translates as "blessed, fortunate, and happy." The Beatitudes are literally blessed attitudes that energize, empower, equip, and encourage us in day-to-day living. Through them, we can also rest and retreat, relax and revitalize, refocus and renew our spiritual lives. The Beatitudes help us experience stepping stones and not stumbling blocks to God. They help us experience divine breakthroughs and not breakdowns. So all this is to say, if you would like to be happy and live a better life, then these concise teachings of Jesus are as good as it gets. The Beatitudes help us live as God's beloved, one day at time.

We carry our attitudes with us everywhere we go. Attitudes affect how we perceive and interact with life. Perception is everything. Our attitudes can bring us peace, joy, comfort, courage, and endurance. Or they can destroy our sense of well being with unease, depression, fear, and the inability to commit to anything or anyone. Our attitudes can even change the world. And we ourselves are changed and the world becomes a better place. Blessed attitudes help us experience a little bit of heaven on earth.

So come and be blessed through the Beatitudes. Consider meditating on one per day. Do a little journal writing. Ask yourself how each Beatitude can help and improve your life. Then ask God for strength for the day as you let these lovely words become part of your prayer life. You will be glad you did.

God, give me these energizing, empowering, equipping, and encouraging attitudes for life. Amen.

†   April 18   †

Blessed are the poor in spirit
Matthew 5:3

The Beatitudes teach us about spiritual joy when life is difficult. One does not have to be a Christian to learn from them. If the Beatitudes are the only part of the Bible you read, you will be well equipped for life. The Sermon on the Mount is about countercultural living and a radical way of being with God. These words are for everyone. They take a lifetime of living to understand, and they are well worth pondering again and again. When life is difficult, read the Beatitudes.

What does it mean to be "poor in spirit?" One commentary suggests contrasting poor in spirit with those who are spiritually proud and self-sufficient.

What do the words "theirs is the kingdom of heaven" mean? Earlier Jesus was preaching that the kingdom of heaven was near (Matthew 4:17). Now he is teaching it is here within us when we are broken and needy.

When have we been broken and needy? Are we not all broken at times in our lives with tragedy and disappointment? Have there not been times when our strength and abilities were completely powerless and inadequate? Then ours is the kingdom of heaven. The Amplified Bible puts the verse this way, "Blessed (happy, to be envied, and spiritually prosperous – with life – joy and satisfaction in God's favor and salvation, regardless of their outward conditions) are the poor in spirit (the humble, who rate themselves insignificant), for theirs is the kingdom of heaven!" (Matthew 5:3)

When we are at our lowest, the kingdom of heaven is ours. God is closer than our breathing, nearer than our hands and feet. Sometimes we need to be poor in spirit to realize God is near. God cares. Pray for strength. God hears and will provide. Ask for your blessing today.

God, let these words linger in my heart all day. I want the kingdom of heaven in my life. Let me not be arrogant or proud in your eyes. Amen.

† April 19 †

Blessed are those who mourn
Matthew 5:4

Years ago when I was a young woman away at nursing school, our beloved family dog Lu Lu Belle died. The cherished pet died during my final exams. My parents wisely chose to tell me after those exams were completed. They understood I loved Lu Lu Belle deeply. She had been part of my life for more than seventeen years. Since Lu Lu Belle's passing, I have cried over the deaths of many beloved friends and family members. Now years later, as a chaplain, I have cried with many people as their loved ones have died.

We all cry and cannot escape grief. There is a time to rejoice and a time to weep. Sad things happen. We lose loved ones, jobs, security, our health, and sometimes our dreams. In North America we sometimes trivialize our grief and minimize it. Often we will say, "Oh, I should be over him/her by now." We often hide our grief and pretend to others that we feel strong and well.

The ancients were wise about mourning. They often wore mourning clothes as a visible sign of their grief so people would respect their feelings of loss. They would remember their loved ones in memorials and through days of remembrances. They understood good grief takes time. Grief work cannot be rushed. Sometimes we need to slow down and acknowledge our grief. Sitting with those feelings can bring us comfort and healing.

Please know that you can cry with God. Jesus was a man well acquainted with grief and sorrow. He also wept and grieved when loved ones died. Tears by people of faith have wet the pages of the Bible over the centuries. Jesus is our wonderful counselor and comforter. Do not let your hearts be troubled. Know that your grief is blessed and that you will receive comfort in your moments of need. [49]

God, help us mourn, comforted by you. Amen.

---

[49] A good resource for those who are grieving is *My Memory Book: A Journal for Grieving Children*, by Gretchen Gaines Lane. Gaithersburg, MD: Chi Rho Press, 1995. Though prepared for children who have lost a beloved family member or friend, *My Memory Book* is used by adults as well to create a very special and personal memorial of the one who has died, helping the bereaved through his or her grief process. (www.ChiRhoPress.com)

† April 20 †

Blessed are the meek

Matthew 5:5

While writing this reflection, my country is actively waging war against international and domestic terrorism. The horrific September 11, 2001 attacks on America changed the world forever. American military forces are bombing terrorist camps overseas in retribution, while I write this.

I find myself asking as you might be asking, just how can the meek be blessed? How can the humble and powerless inherit the earth in a world full of such raw evil and hatred? A popular saying of President Teddy Roosevelt's was, "Speak softly and carry a big stick." Even with the big stick of military power, America was caught off guard and thousands of innocent men, women, and even children were killed by religious Islamic extremists on that dreadful day. How do the meek inherit the earth in war and peace? I do not have those answers. Welcome to sacred ambiguity.

It is good to remember that God's ways and thoughts are not ours. These words from Jesus so long ago illustrate that God's definition of power is much different from societal norms and national might. One commentator suggests this Beatitude is not so much an attitude towards people but an attitude before God. To be meek, according to the Bible, is to be humble and even powerless in the divine presence.

Sacred words have different meanings for each person. I can only wonder what today's verse might mean for the women suffering under Islamic terrorism in Afghanistan and those who have suffered greatly from terror in my own country.

But I do know what this tension means in my own life. While might is not always right, it is a force to be reckoned with. Power speaks and can be a great force in the world for good or evil. Yet in God's reign, humility, and powerlessness will one day inherit the earth. Truly, God's ways and thoughts are not ours. They are certainly not always mine.

God, you will have to guide my thoughts and inner attitudes today as I wrestle with meekness in a world at war against terrorism. I am also limited in my finite understanding of meekness and how that is reflected in my own life. Yet I want this blessed attitude from you. Hear my prayer. Amen.

† April 21 †

Blessed are those who hunger and thirst for righteousness
Matthew 5:6, 10

Righteousness is not a popularly used expression among the people I live and work with. It often carries a negative connotation. Frequently we hear it used as criticism, "Oh don't be so smug and righteous!" It is often associated with hypocritical, legalistic, religiously judgmental attitudes towards life and people.

Yet the Biblical word is worth reclaiming. Righteousness is a positive attribute of God. We too, are to be righteous and just. We are to be faithful and truthful. This is pleasing to God and is not burdensome. Righteousness condemns evil. Jesus often uses this word throughout the Gospels as a good attribute that conforms us positively to the will of God.

It can be helpful to use other English Bible translations for added insights for our spiritual readings. I feel blessed with the Amplified Bible's interpretation with this verse, "Blessed and fortunate and happy and spiritually prosperous (in that state in which the born-again child of God enjoys [God's] favor and salvation) are those who hunger and thirst for righteousness (uprightness and right standing with God), for they shall be completely satisfied." I need to hear this, for I had read ahead and discovered to my dismay that those who hunger and thirst for righteousness will experience persecution! This persecution is considered a spiritual blessing.

Righteousness is used three times in this chapter, in verses 6, 10, and 20. Meditate on both the positive and negative sense of the word. Watch how Jesus uses it. Righteousness is a blessing from God, but will bring us persecution. If we are not careful, we can become hypocritical, negative and legalistic, judgmental religious hypocrites.

God, dare I ask for you to fill me with a sense of your holy righteousness? Will you bless me with an ongoing awareness of righteousness through the life of Jesus? Will you help me not be a negative, pompous, and legalistic religious hypocrite? Protect me from a "holier than thou" attitude. Let my righteousness be a blessing for many. That is the best I can pray today. Amen.

✝   April 22   ✝

Blessed are the merciful

Matthew 5:7

Jesus taught a great deal about mercy (Matthew 9:13, 27; 12:7; 15:22; 17:15; 18:21-35; 20:30, 31). God is known as being "rich in mercy" (Ephesians 2:4). Jesus was a real person, a famous teacher who taught people to be merciful towards each other.

Righteousness and mercy go hand-in-hand. We need them both. Perhaps being merciful is the key to avoiding a "holier than thou" reputation as a religious hypocrite.

Just what is mercy, and what does it mean to be merciful? Mercy is compassion, kindness. In my kitchen hangs a saying, "Kindness, a language the blind can see and the deaf can hear." In being merciful we sympathize with someone else's feeling miserable. Our sympathy leads to involvement. Jesus was often moved to compassion and action.

The opposite of mercy is vengeance and punishment. A television evening news program caught my attention the other day with a report about a remarkable event somewhere in the Middle East. A young man had murdered, and the authorities had caught him. According to Islamic law, he was sentenced to die by hanging in a public event. The murderer wept like a baby as the noose was hung around his neck. Thousands in the crowd began to cry out for mercy. The victim's father had the power of life or death. It was his decision. He hesitated and with emotion gave life to his son's murderer. The crowd erupted into ecstatic cries of "praise be to Allah the merciful."

Mercy had occurred at significant emotional cost. We can only be merciful with the help of God who is rich in mercy.

God, have mercy on me, a sinner. Amen.

†   April 23   †

Blessed are the pure in heart
Matthew 5:8

One of the most genuinely pure in heart people I have known died far too young. Keith was a sailor in the United States Navy, a gentle and hard working man with a dream. He wanted to become a nurse and help people. Keith would frequently go out of his way to befriend sailors who were new and lonely, often away from their homes for the first time. He was a spiritually sensitive person who was only in his twenties when the unthinkable happened. And it happened unexpectedly. I was the ship's chaplain and was often the first to know of unfortunate events. I will always remember the phone call.

A simple routine visit to the dentist had revealed this young man had some unusual swelling of the neck. The dentist insisted on an x-ray. The x-ray revealed a massive tumor surrounding the heart. Emergency surgery began. Keith's mother had flown in to be with her son as he underwent surgery. The sailor died several hours later.

I met with this grieving mother several times. She insisted I preach a memorial message for Keith's Navy friends with, "Blessed are the pure in heart, for they will see God." She clearly understood her son. She also knew that our hearts are the center of our being, including our minds, will, and emotions. During the memorial service, dozens of his friends wept openly – the tears being a fitting offering in honor of Keith's life.

God, sometimes we forget our lives reflect your Presence in our hearts. Purify our hearts, so we may see you more clearly. Give us your heart. Amen.

†   April 24   †

Blessed are the peacemakers
Matthew 5:9

Peace is within you, child of God. Share your peace with others at home, at work, with those you love, and the stranger on the street. In a world full of conflict and conflict mediation specialists, we are to be peacemakers and children of God. What in heaven's name does this mean? It means each one of us can share the message of peace on earth where we live today. It is not easy to be a peacemaker in a world of violence, hatred, and mistrust.

The word "peacemaker" comes from the two Greek words, *eirene* (peace) and *poieo* (to make). *Eirene* is found in every New Testament book with the exception of 1 John and Acts. *The New International Dictonary of New Testament Theology* describes peace as the "harmonious relationships between people and nations" and signifies friendship and freedom from molestation. Some would define peace as order and quiet. Peace for others is a sense of rest and contentment. Living out one's own definition of peace is one of the signs of a healthy spiritual life (Galatians 5:22).

God is known as a God of peace. We find this title in many places (Romans 15:33; 16:20; Philippians 4:9; 1 Thessalonians 5:23; Hebrews 13:20). The prophet Isaiah described Jesus as "Prince of Peace" (Isaiah 9:6). We are promised peace with God through Jesus Christ (Romans 5:1). Jesus has a great deal to say about peace as we continue reading the Gospels. Peace with God is God's greatest gift for us.

Thich Nhat Hanh, a Buddhist monk and peace activist, teaches people to "be peace" by smiling our peace at all we encounter. He suggests we smile a small half smile whether we feel like smiling or not. Perhaps we could smile our peace at the people we live, work, and play with today. Peacemaking is within us, as close as a small smile on our lips.

God, bless our small smiles today. Let us be your peacemakers. Amen.

† April 25 †

Blessed are the persecuted, insulted, and slandered
Matthew 5:10-11

Reader, beware! Discipleship, following Jesus, can be costly. Following Jesus has never been easy. He never promised health, wealth, popularity, or prosperity to his followers. If you choose to live these Beatitudes, you may find yourself persecuted, insulted, and slandered. It is not easy to live these teachings. I would suggest it is humanly impossible. We need God's help. We also need some kind of community or small group support for encouragement. Discipleship is too difficult to do alone. We need companions, teachers, and cheerleaders for encouragement. We need to nurture an inner spiritual maturity as we choose daily to live the Jesus way.

It is especially important to remember that "discipleship is joy." [50] People throughout the ages have joyously endured persecution, insults, and slander to follow Christ. He is the greatest spiritual leader world history has known. You will find in your Gospel readings that Jesus never asked people to endure what he had not experienced. This includes persecution.

Take the time to reread the previous Beatitudes. With these special words Jesus teaches us about humility, grief, gentleness, righteousness, mercy, purity of heart, and peacemaking. Will you follow these teachings? Yes, there may be hardship experienced along the way, but showers of blessings await you. Whatever your lot may be, these Beatitudes will bless you with spiritual abundance and joy.

Blessed are the persecuted, insulted, and slandered. Blessed are the pure, humble, comforted, gentle, merciful, and those who love peace.

God, give me understanding and willingness to live these Beatitudes with joy. Amen.

---

[50] Bonhoeffer, Dietrich. *The Cost of Discipleship*, p. 41.

† April 26 †
Rejoice and be glad
Matthew 5:12

Jesus taught many things about heavenly rewards. Our suffering is never wasted. God sees and cares. God will honor our pain in the hereafter. I do not pretend to understand it, but heavenly reward is a promise from the Teacher. We are not blessed for doing evil. We are blessed and rewarded by God when we suffer for doing the Beatitudes. God is compassionate and concerned. We will be given what we need in our hour of need. We stand in a great spiritual tradition of others that have gone before us and suffered for doing right.

The Bible includes many examples of persecuted prophets. Some are described in Hebrews 11. Over the centuries, some were tortured, mocked, flogged, chained, and jailed. Others were stoned to death, sawn in two, and suffered death through other violent and malicious deeds. We are told the world was not worthy of them.

Divine justice is not easy to understand. Following Jesus (discipleship) through living the Beatitudes can bring us joy through suffering. Rejoice and be glad. Another New Testament writer puts it this way, "Be always joyful, pray continually, give thanks whatever happens" (1 Thessalonians 5:16-18).

God, I do not pretend to fully understand your ways. Help me to understand both the joy and the suffering in my life. Help me rejoice and be glad. Amen.

† April 27 †
Rediscover your passion and purpose for living
Matthew 5:14a

A few years ago, I joined a lighthouse society and served as a lighthouse keeper with other volunteers, walking the rugged Washington coastline and spending many hours enjoying walks on the beach. One of the lighthouses is five miles offshore and determined hikers have a rigorous journey along the world's longest natural sand spit. For some, it is their Holy Grail. Hikers come from near and far, journeying towards its distinctive guiding light. One woman hiker said to me, "I came here because I wanted to rediscover my passion and purpose in living."

Those who sail these mighty waters have nicknamed this area, "Cape Shipwreck." In the old days before there was a Coast Guard, when ships went down, the lighthouse keepers went out in small boats in dangerous waters to save lives often at great personal risk.

Every lighthouse has a distinctive signature light, to help navigators at sea determine if they are heading towards dangerous waters. This particular lighthouse light flashes every five seconds, day and night. While serving as a lighthouse keeper, I noticed the flashing light became more visible and brilliant as each night grew darker. When foul weather blankets the area, a foghorn blasts every two minutes, an audible sound warning those at sea of immediate danger.

The lighthouse is a universal symbol of hope and faith. We are called to be both keepers and senders of the light. We must always remember that there are many pilgrims locally and globally searching for sustaining, meaningful, life-giving, healing, and loving God-light. Many a sailor lost at sea has been brought home into safe harbor through the glimmer of a faint light in the distance.

Share your God-light generously. By doing so, you will rediscover your passion and purpose in living.

O Holy Light, shine brightly in our darkness and guide our way with wisdom. O Light Divine, teach us how to journey in Your light. Amen.

† April 28 †

Religious legalism or the teachings of Jesus?

Matthew 5:19

Moses offered many rules, regulations, and restrictions that were unique to his time in world history, and his specific religion. Not all of his teachings are applicable for everyone today. Christians believe Jesus is the fulfillment of all the Old Testament Law as taught by Moses. In Jesus, we are offered spiritual freedom from the law. Through him, we are invited into lives of grace and truth. God's truth is found through the teachings of Jesus Christ.

Many modern people are unacquainted with the teachings and stories in the Hebrew (or Old) Testament. The Hebrew Testament is worthy of great respect as sacred literature. The majority of Biblical scholars believe Moses authored the first five books in the Bible thousands of years ago. Jewish people refer to these as *Torah*, the Law. Moses brings us an ancient, patriarchal, religious understanding based on what he understood to be divine law. There are some very broad universal principles such as the Ten Commandments (Exodus 20:1-17), which are empowering and life giving even today.

Jesus was a spiritual revolutionary from the very beginning of his ministry. His radical teachings about God did not endear him to the ecclesiastical leaders of his day who revered their cherished religious laws, traditions, and commandments. Rather than burden people with impossible legalistic religious traditions and rules and regulations, Jesus encouraged people to live the spirit of the Beatitudes in his Sermon on the Mount.

The Sermon on the Mount provides timeless guidance for seekers yearning for spiritual greatness and freedom from religious legalism even today. Your life will never be the same if you practice what Jesus teaches in these empowering words for life.

Give us the courage to identify areas of religious legalism in our own lives, God. Give us the courage and wisdom to change as we strive to live the commands of Jesus – one day at a time. Amen.

† April 29 †

Murder, anger, insults, contempt

Matthew 5:22-24

What does Jesus have to teach us about murder, anger, insults, contempt, accusations, and legal action? Quite a bit, if you are interested. In just a few sentences (verses 21-26), we are given a summary of his teaching on reconciliation with our figurative and literal brothers and sisters. He gives us some fresh insight about anger.

Anger is as dangerous as murder. It is spiritually impossible to offer gifts to God with anger and bitterness in our hearts. The best gift we can give God is our peaceful reconciliation with each other. This is easier said than done, but well worth the effort and persistence. It may take years. We may be refused or ignored, mocked or slandered, but reconciliation is necessary for our spiritual wholeness. We need to make genuine efforts, even perhaps swallowing our pride. We may even need counseling, therapy, a spiritual director, or to talk with a trusted friend or pastor for help. Nothing is easy about reconciling deep hurts.

After my mother died, my brother did not speak to me for more than twelve years. Years later, during a family crisis, we spoke on the telephone and are now reconciled. We both regret many misperceptions we carried in our hearts over the past. We will never be able to get those years back and relive them. Our relationship deeply affected my spiritual life. It still does. He is my brother.

If we are to know peace, we need to seek reconciliation with those we have hurt, or who have hurt us. If we are to live and die in peace, we need to do the same. We need reconciliation for our spiritual healing. Blessed are the peacemakers, for they shall be the children of God (Matthew 5:9).

God, help us be reconciled with our brothers and sisters in the world. Bless our peacemaking, we pray. Amen.

† April 30 †

Lusty eyes and straying hearts

Matthew 5:28

I find myself reflecting that it is easy to become obsessed with the details of sexually explicit acts. It makes news. Sex is powerful. But more importantly, how do we integrate our sexuality with our spirituality in a way that honors our body and spirit, and our God?

According to Jesus, I am guilty of adultery. I have eyes that look at the world around me. I live in a twenty-first century American culture that is sexually sophisticated and lust saturated. I also live in a world full of lonely people, hungry to be loved and to love fully in return. John Milton is said to have written, "Loneliness was the first thing that God's eye named not good." Over the years, as a chaplain and minister, I have had many people come to see me as they agonized through extramarital relationships. People of all sexual orientations are deeply affected by adultery. Adultery is a spiritual concern.

Adultery was actually a popular global topic of discussion as we closed the twentieth century with the infamous Starr Report. This Internet document gave the world instant information on the alleged sexual practices between President Bill Clinton and Monica Lewinsky. An entire generation of small children began asking parents many questions about adultery and oral sex.

Jesus has a number of difficult teachings. This is one of them. If we harbor lusty eyes, we have straying hearts. Jesus cuts to the heart of the matter. Our inner sexual thoughts and practices affect our life with God.

Read the other verses (Matthew 5:27-30) around this difficult teaching. Jesus continues his teaching by saying that if some part of your body causes you to sin, cut it off and throw it away. Please realize this is a figurative and not a literal saying. We are not called to self-mutilate our body parts or blind ourselves. We can cut out enticements that could lead us into adultery. On the Internet, pornography proliferates and comes to our e-mail boxes. Links can lead us into steamy cyber alleys of spiritual danger. In both virtual reality and in our daily lives with others, we are called to be pure of heart. It is the Jesus way.

God, help us in our life today with this hard saying of Jesus. Help us to learn from it. Amen.

† May 1 †
Divorce and remarriage
Matthew 5: 31-32

Divorce is deeply wounding to people of all sexual orientations. Perhaps we can find grace, hope, and mercy through this teaching of Jesus. We can learn from our mistakes and life experiences. We can heal through counseling and time. Be gentle with yourself because a loveless or abusive marriage is always tragic.

What is the relevance of this teaching by Jesus? After all, first century marriages had very little to do with love. Women were considered property and the men had all the legal advantages. In ancient Jewish relationships, only the men could decide to get a divorce. During Jesus' time both prevailing viewpoints of divorce were based on Moses' prior teachings. Moses assumed divorce was part of life (Deuteronomy 22:13-21; 24:1-4). His patriarchal view assumed the woman is always at fault. It is well for us to note that "God hates divorce" (Malachi 2:16), but divorce has been happening for thousands of years.

F. F. Bruce makes an important point in his book *The Hard Sayings of Jesus*. Old Testament divorce was to a man's advantage. Women were not allowed any choice in the matter. They could be divorced if their husband found someone more attractive or who was a better cook.

Jesus taught about divorce (Matthew 5:31-32; 19:3-9; Luke 16:18; Mark 10:2-12), and did not endorse the traditional anti-women viewpoints of his day.

Even today many people of faith struggle to understand what Jesus really meant. Unfortunate people trapped in loveless marriages have agonized over literal and simplistic interpretations of these divorce statements. Others have remarried without a second thought. Then there are individuals who opt for the celibate life after a bitter divorce. Yet another point of view argues that these divorce teachings are only applicable to heterosexual couples who are allowed legal marriages.

Whatever your situation and circumstances, let mutual respect, healing, and God's grace be evident in your intimate relationships. Work hard at nurturing your relationship and strive to honor your commitment vows. Many relationships are worth salvaging if both people in the relationship are willing to try and to work things out.

But sometimes even with the best of intentions and effort, divorce is unavoidable and the relationship is clearly over. Strive to be amicable whenever possible. Seek counseling before remarriage and learn what went wrong in former relationships. Then humbly ask for God's blessing on your new life. Commit yourself to your new life partner daily above all others. Pray for your new relationship and ask for God's help one day at a time. Remember, to love and be loved are life's richest blessings.

God, many of us have been divorced and remarried. Or perhaps the love has gone out of our holy unions or marriages. Give us grace and mercy as we reflect on this hard saying of Jesus. Amen.

† May 2 †

Keeping your word

Matthew 5:33-37

Jesus' words in today's verse are intended to help listeners avoid perjury, according to F. F. Bruce. [51] Bearing false witness and breaking our vows are significant legal and spiritual concerns. Scripture lessons in Exodus 20:7, Leviticus 19:12, Numbers 30:2, and Deuteronomy 23:21 offer further guidance. In short, followers of Jesus should be women and men of their word.

While writing this reflection I watched a wonderful movie *It Could Happen to You.* This entertaining 1994 movie is about a New York City cop, a waitress, and a lottery ticket. To the cop's embarrassment, as he paid his bill, he lacked money for a tip. All he had left was a lottery ticket. Not expecting to win anything, the police officer promised to share his lottery winnings with the waitress in lieu of a tip. To everyone's surprise and delight, the officer held the winning ticket for millions of dollars.

Being a man of his word, he honored his promise and endured much criticism for doing so. But his word was his pledge and he was determined to do the right thing. He had made a promise. Being a person of integrity, he kept his word. What would you have done in his situation?

---

[51] Bruce, F. F. *The Hard Sayings of Jesus*, pp. 66-67.

So for today, let your "yes" be "yes" and "no" be "no" before making hasty promises. Consider the cost of your words. Think twice before offering vows, oaths, promises, and good intentions. As a follower of Jesus, keep your word.

God, help us honor our words, promises, vows, and oaths. Amen.

†   May 3   †

An eye for an eye

Matthew 5:38-42

Once again Jesus is prescribing a course of action that simply does not come naturally to us. Jesus' teaching is a standard for Christians of all sexual orientations. Jesus' is the most demanding lifestyle we can imagine. It is more difficult than living up to the standards of Moses. At least according to Moses, one could seek an eye for an eye, and a tooth for a tooth as compensation (Exodus 21:24).

F. F. Bruce wisely notes this limited excessive retaliation and bloodshed in primitive Jewish culture. Gandhi understood this is not limited to ancient Jewish culture. He once said if everyone lived by an eye for an eye mentality, the world would soon be full of blind people.

But Jesus takes us one step farther. And this is a hard saying. We are not to seek vengeance. We are not to retaliate. We are not to harbor a spirit of resentment. We are to be willing to go the extra mile and be inconvenienced. We are to have the mind of Christ. This is extremely countercultural and humanly difficult, if not impossible. God will give us strength.

Is this teaching relevant for our twenty-first century lives? Is it just for our personal behavior? Are we to use this principle for entire nations and communities? Is there a single "Christian" answer? How are we to live our lives with this teaching of Jesus Christ? So many questions and so few clear answers.

God, you need to help us with this teaching. It is very difficult to follow. Amen.

†   **May 4**   †

Love your enemies

Matthew 5:43-48

I heard a remarkable story about a military chaplain serving with the United States Marine Corps during the first Persian Gulf War in 1991. They had many prisoners of war (POWs) in the desert camps. The days were blazing hot. Cans of fluid were precious and wise soldiers carefully rationed them throughout the day. This particular chaplain was thirsty and tempted to drink his water early in the day. Instead he determined to save it for later. He would drink it before going to sleep. This thought consoled him as he went about his duties in the terrible heat of the day. His thirst grew hourly.

Many of the American and Allied soldiers treated the Iraqi POWs harshly. War is war. Kill or be killed. And the prisoners were also thirsty. Fluid priorities went to the American soldiers as they guarded their prisoners. As the chaplain made his rounds, he noticed one Iraqi prisoner almost dead with thirst. His own thirst was powerful. It would have been so easy to look the other way. But he did not. His soldiers discouraged him, reminding him that he should take care of himself so he could take care of them. There was not enough water to go around, but the chaplain slowly knelt and held his can of water to the dying enemy soldier's lips.

Love your enemies. "If your enemy is hungry, feed him; if he is thirsty, give him something to drink…do not be overcome by evil, but overcome evil with good" (Romans 12:20-21).

God, help us love our enemies. Help us pray for those who persecute us with the love of Christ. Amen.

† May 5 †

Righteous acts

Matthew 6:1-4

Jesus explains clearly that to give, to pray, and to fast are "acts of righteousness" (Matthew 6:2-4, 5-15, 16-18). Another translation interprets "acts of righteousness" to mean to practice your piety. Reading a variety of translations is helpful for additional insights.

Jesus is simply telling us not to brag about our charitable almsgiving or our acts of kindness and mercy. I sometimes forget there will be a heavenly reward waiting with my name on it. And my humanness deeply appreciates being publicly acknowledged for good that I have done. We all need moments of affirmation in our lives, but when we do brag and strut about our piety we lose our heavenly reward.

It is very easy to become a religious hypocrite. Rather than quietly do good from the heart, it is extremely tempting to do good in order to receive public recognition. We may not even know we are doing this. Our dear heavenly Parent knows what we are doing even when others do not. And so, we are to wait patiently for that day of heavenly reward. Every act of kindness, every charitable act, every time we quietly give of our abundance, God sees and remembers. We do not need to sound our own trumpet.

Oh God, help us not be religious hypocrites! And if we are, help us change into gracious, humble, quiet doers of good and charitable acts. Amen.

† May 6 †

Non-hypocritical prayer

Matthew 6:5

As an ordained minister, public prayer is one of my occupational hazards. I publicly pray in a number of local churches, ecumenical and interfaith events. Jesus' message is for all who pray, not just professionals. It is easy to pray flowery speeches to impress and please our listeners with poetic prose that is disguised as prayers. It is easy to be more concerned with content and delivery than to honor prayers of the heart. It is easy to be in love with the sound of our own voice. I have been guilty of all of these failings.

How do we publicly pray? Carefully. Humbly. Thoughtfully. Prayerfully. Wisely. Respectfully. My wise father insisted on brevity! Public prayer is both an art and a sacred responsibility.

At times I write down my prayers in advance and at other times they pour out of me straight from my heart. I have studied public prayers from different religious traditions. There are times and places to pour out one's heart before God at great length. There are also public prayer times when this is inappropriate and we must be aware of the occasion and others' time. Flowery speeches disguised as prayers can actually hinder the prayers of other listeners.

God, teach me how to pray sincerely. Help me pray non-hypocritical prayers. Amen.

✝ May 7 ✝

Personal prayer closets
Matthew 6:6-7

Everyone needs some kind of a personal prayer closet. This does not mean we are to literally go into our closets to pray, but we do need quiet and somewhat secluded places where we can be alone with God privately. We need these prayer sanctuaries. We can weep, shout, rage, laugh, or pray with feelings too deep for words in our special prayer place. These are places just for God, places where we can be ourselves and not hide anything, places where we meet God, places where we can be ourselves and not hide or hold back anything. These prayer places help us hear God's whisper in our hearts. Prayer closets can be our gardens, cars, garages, attics, basements, quiet park benches, in the forests or mountains, or along the beach. In these secret prayer places, God-seekers often find relief, renewal, and divine resources.

We can relax as beloved children and be safe with God in our prayer closets. Celebrate these prayer places by enjoying your connection to God. You will be empowered for life. Expect God to hear you. Even better, wait for God to answer.

Oh God, thank you for hearing our prayers. Help us find quiet places for prayer. Amen.

† May 8 †

The Great Prayer
Matthew 6:9

The Lord's Prayer, often called the Great Prayer, has energized and encouraged people of faith throughout the centuries. If you have ever struggled with prayer, this prayer taught by Jesus can guide chaotic, scattered thoughts and feelings. By praying this great prayer, we change the world and ourselves, while experiencing a divine connection different from any other.

Over the next couple of days, we will examine each part of this prayer. The first section of the prayer names God, and compares the role of God to that of a parent. But as a woman, I struggle to find feminine, inclusive, loving, and intimate names for the Divine. I wish with all my heart that Jesus had used a feminine name for God in this great prayer. Yet I realize through this profound prayer, he was ahead of his time while also being a product of his time in world history.

By praying a tender, intimate, male parental name for God, Jesus was remarkably bold. By using such a personal holy name in prayer, Jesus invited seekers into a Divine relationship never before experienced. But Jesus was also pragmatic and understood the limited understanding of the listeners in his patriarchal culture. He lived during a primitive time when women were considered property and valued for their breeding abilities, not spiritual leadership. By using a masculine parental name for God, he offered a culturally relevant bridge that encouraged a stepping stone to the Sacred. Had he used a feminine Divine name, the people he was striving to reach would have refused to listen to him. It would have been too outrageous for them to contemplate.

But in today's world, we can use any variety of sacred names in our prayers. These names are not limited to male parental images and as a result, seekers from many backgrounds experience breakthroughs to the Holy. Through our life experiences, training, and memories we will discover our own cherished holy names for the Sacred as we pray.

"My God, You are a Spirit, neither male or female. You have been my Father for so many years, today I ask to know you as Mother. You are too vast to fit into only one compartment. How foolish of us to confine you to one image. It feels uncomfortable to call you Mother. They have spoken of you as Father for centuries. Yet I have always wondered how there could be a father without a mother. How is it that the feminine face of God has been obscured for so long? They tell me now that there is a God who looks like me. It's hard to take it all in." [52] *Amen.*

† **May 9** †

Fourteen words to change the world
Matthew 6:10

Today's verse is one of those incredible smaller prayers within the Great Prayer, also known as the Lord's Prayer. Be very careful as you pray these fourteen sacred words today. The Great Prayer consists of six beloved major petitions. Today's section of the prayer is for spiritual revolutionaries who want to change the world. This prayer request is only for those willing to become involved as change agents of God's grace and mercy.

People who have the courage to pray these audacious words are petitioning God to transform the world. It is a remarkable prayer full of holy boldness. This is not for the indecisive and weak of heart. Those brave enough to pray it are asking the Almighty, maker of heaven and earth, to usher in heaven on earth. We are asking for God's will to be done. We are partnering with God to heal our sin sick and broken world.

---

[52] Vardey, Lucinda. Editor. *The Flowering of the Soul: A Book of Prayers by Women*, pp. 45-46.

The kingdom of God is radical. God's reign brings in the marginalized, outcast, and rejected. In the dominion of all that is sacred, the afflicted are comforted and justice will prevail. The rich and the powerful will be last and the last will be first.

Our human nature hesitates to truly comprehend the coming reign of God. It is costly and might turn our known world upside down. Yet the kingdom of God is near and dear to the heart of Christ. To fully understand, thoughtful people would be wise to read the ninety-nine accounts throughout all the Gospels where Jesus preaches and teaches about God's kingdom. To do so can change your life and perspective forever.

Are you willing to let these fourteen sacred words linger in your heart today? This is a prayer of spiritual greatness. Will you ask for God's will to be done on earth as it is in heaven? Will you accept your call to respond as God leads you through continued prayer and action?

Your kingdom come, God. Your will be done. Begin in my life on earth. Help me be a change agent of your grace and mercy. Amen.

† May 10 †

Practical prayers
Matthew 6:11

Jesus is concerned about hunger, both spiritual and physical. "Not mine, but ours – everybody's. Our responsibility to the starving world is implicit in [the Lord's Prayer]. As long as any part of the body is hungry, the entire body knows starvation," [53] writes Madeleine L'Engle. She suggests we simply do what we can, offering our small loaves and fishes and leaving the rest to God. We are to offer what we have with compassion. In praying this request, we are praying for those who hunger in all parts of the world, for the hungry in our neighborhoods, and for nourishment for ourselves.

We live in a desperately hungry world. According to the United Nations World Hunger Programme, hunger afflicts one of every seven people on earth. The UN's vision is for a hunger-free world. They believe

---

[53] L'Engle, Madeleine. *Glimpses of Grace*, p. 62.

there is enough food in the world today for every man, woman, and child. But tragically, there are 24,000 deaths from starvation daily. More than 800 million go to bed hungry every night. More than 50 million suffer from acute hunger. A child dies every eight seconds from malnutrition-related complications. There are many fine charitable groups dedicated to relieving world hunger, but the World Hunger Programme feeds most of the world's refugees and internally displaced peoples (www.thehungersite.com).

As followers of Christ, we must be concerned with local, national, and international hunger. A significant number of homeless and troubled youth live in my town. Members of a community outreach organization bring them free food throughout the week. The community food bank is always looking for donations. Local businesses periodically have food drives. And I know plenty of struggling students with limited budgets who would deeply appreciate a home cooked meal. I also know of youth groups and Sunday school groups who give up meals to help raise money for the hungry. There are abundant opportunities to share food with hungry people.

But there are also many other creative ways to help those who hunger and raise awareness for the starving. I was completely unaware of the desperate circumstances of Zimbabwe until a dedicated Christian physician living in that country contacted me by e-mail. Starvation was their main problem and her country was facing one of the worst food deficits the world has yet to experience. Knowing that I had written other devotional material, she asked if I would prayerfully write "some encouraging words about God's love for Zimbabwe and her people." She would then distribute these meditations via e-mail, nationally to Christians in Zimbabwe and to her colleagues throughout Africa.

With some trepidation, I agreed to her request and suggested the meditations be titled, "To Zimbabwe with Love." (These meditations may be found at http://soulfoodministry.org/docs/English/ZimLoveIntro.htm).

I cannot cure world hunger, but I can be more mindful of those around me who hunger daily and offer my small gifts. I can pray more compassionately for those who lack food for today.

God, give us today our daily bread. Amen.

† May 11 †

Forgiveness

Matthew 6:12

Quite frankly, I do not always want to forgive. I want to hold on to my anger, hurt, and sense of injustice. Yet Jesus taught we need daily forgiveness in our relationships with God and others (Matthew 18:35, Mark 11:25). We are to forgive from our hearts those who have wronged us. We are not to be vengeful, bitter, unforgiving, or harbor resentment.

Forgiveness is a critical issue and greatly affects our mental and emotional health. A friend of mine recently completed her training as a social worker. Her internship had been at a mental health center. While it was fascinating to discuss the psychological and philosophical theories about the cause and affect of mental health disorders, a spiritual dimension seemed to be missing.

One day I asked her if she or her colleagues had ever considered doing a spiritual assessment with their clients. She had never considered the possibility and was intrigued. She listened closely as I spoke of my experiences while working as a hospital chaplain with clients struggling with alcohol and drug abuse issues.

Many of those clients had never forgiven themselves for ruining their lives and the lives of people who had once loved and trusted them. As a result, some had harbored soul deep feelings of bitterness and re-sentment for years. Their unforgiving attitudes festered into a spiritual poison, which sabotaged their success in defeating their drug and alcohol addictions.

Forgiveness is a critical spiritual concern. Sooner or later, an un-forgiving attitude will affect our well being. This can severely damage our mental, emotional, and physical health. Important personal relationships will eventually be poisoned and lost.

Ask God for help with today's reflection. Forgiveness is never easy but the peace of mind that results is priceless.

God, forgive my sins and forgive those who have sinned against me. Amen.

✝   **May 12**   ✝

Temptation prayers

Matthew 6:13

Sometimes the Bible is difficult to understand. It seems full of contradictions. Why would God tempt anyone? F. F. Bruce notes that this request is very similar to the Jewish service of morning and evening prayer, "Do not bring us into the power of temptation." It is important to remember that "God cannot be tempted with evil and tempts no one" (James 1:13 NIV). Yet James writes that we are blessed when we endure temptation and the testing of our faith produces steadfastness (James 1:2, 12).

The apostle Paul encourages us with the reminder that, "No testing has overtaken you that is not common to everyone. God is faithful and will not let you be tested beyond your strength. But with the testing God will also provide the way out so that you may be able to endure it" (1 Corinthians 10:13, *The New Testament and Psalms: An Inclusive Version*).

A fifth-century Eastern Liturgy of St. James, recites this after the Lord's Prayer:

> Yes, O Lord our God, lead us not into temptation which
> we are not able to bear, but with the temptation grant also
> the way out, so that we may be able to remain steadfast;
> and deliver us from evil.

I have often jokingly said, "And lead me not into temptation, for I can get there by myself, thank you very much!" Be aware today of what entices you into evil. If possible, avoid it.

God, lead us not into temptation and deliver us from the evil one. Amen.

† May 13 †

Reality prayers

Matthew 6:14-15

The word "trespasses" refers directly to ethical transgressions. It is translated from a different Greek word used for debts.

Forgiveness remains central in Jesus' teachings. If we want God to forgive our ethical and moral failings, then we must forgive the imperfections of others. This is our reality in God. Forgiveness begets forgiveness.

There have been times in my own life when I have wanted to cling to my hurt feelings and grudges. That does not help my life in God. An unforgiving spirit leads to stress, remorse, anger, bitterness, and a desire for revenge.

The bottom line is this – if we want God to forgive us, we must forgive others.

God, help us forgive the ethical and moral failings of others. Amen.

† May 14 †

Fasting prayers

Matthew 6:16-18

Fasting is an important spiritual discipline. By going without food for selected periods of time (fasting), we identify with those who hunger and our prayers are more intentional. By emptying ourselves physically, we can experience a deeper awareness of God. Fasting is something Jesus assumes we will do throughout our lifetimes on our path toward spiritual empowerment.

Jesus has an important insight for us. When we do decide to fast, do it quietly. Be well groomed and clean. Fast privately without calling attention to yourself. In ancient Judaism, people would put ashes on their heads and wear sackcloth while fasting as a visible symbol. Putting oil on the head and washing the face were reserved for joyous occasions. God, who is invisible and unseen, sees everything we do in secret. God will honor our private fasting prayers.

God, teach us how to fast and pray. Amen.

† May 15 †
Orientation to God
Matthew 6:19-21

I will always remember coming home and seeing the broken window. While at school during my early seminary days, thieves broke into my home. I immediately went to neighbors where we called the police. The thieves had first tried the window and had eventually gotten in the house by destroying the basement door with a power saw. I felt violated. All my belongings were scattered throughout the house. Cherished family heirlooms were either destroyed or missing. They would be irreplaceable. My grandparents had brought them to America as they left their birth countries to begin a new life. I was heartbroken, but grateful that the thieves had overlooked a few items.

Is this what Jesus means? Or was he referring to excessive greed and acquisition of wealth at the expense of our souls? What are riches to God? Is it bad to have material things? Quite honestly, as a non-salaried minister, I would be grateful for some of that treasure on earth. So what does this mean?

Could it be that we all yearn for God? Could it be that materialism would never satisfy the hole in our hearts? There will always be thieves and those eager to take what is ours. But no one can take God away from us. God will sustain, empower, protect, shelter, and care for us when everything we value is stripped away, destroyed, or stolen. That is treasure on earth and in heaven.

God, fill our hearts with the wealth of your loving Presence in our lives. May we all have treasure in heaven. Amen.

†   May 16   †

Healthy eyes

Matthew 6:22-23

The meaning of life is to see. How we see is profound. And the blind can teach us a great deal about spiritual sight. Every so often I travel into a nearby city for medical care. Sometimes I see a blind man and his seeing-eye dog. I marvel at how he sees through that dog and with his God-given senses. Within seconds he "sees" people who speak to him through their words and actions. His dog is an extension of himself as they weave through traffic, navigate buses, and commute to and from work. We have become friends. When he recognizes my voice, his face lights up and he smiles with pleasure. He *sees* me more clearly than if he had perfect vision. His spiritual eyes are healthier than the spiritual eyes of many sighted people.

The two greatest truths about God that I know are simple. God is light. God is love. Light is healing and cleansing. Where do we need the loving light of God in our spirits today? A popular saying is that we can either be the light, or reflect it.

God, give us healthy spiritual eyes. Fill us with your light and love. Help us be and reflect divine light in our world. Amen.

†   May 17   †

Whom do you serve?

Matthew 6:24, Luke 16:13

Jesus taught a great deal about money. Our attitudes towards money can actually prevent us from serving God. Wealth can even become an idol for us, that is, the object of our worship.

F. F. Bruce suggests these verses are to teach us how to use our material property more worthily, rather than hoard it for only ourselves. And he cites the parable of the rich man in Luke 12:16-21. This man had so much accumulated wealth that he had no need for worry regarding his future. In the parable, he went to bed with this comforting thought and never woke up. He died and had to leave his property behind. His wealth had been his ultimate concern and it did not help him in his hour of greatest need.

"As for me and my house, we will serve the LORD" (Joshua 24:15). This includes how we spend our money. Money is a spiritual concern. Money by itself is not evil. We need it for daily sustenance and to help others who are less fortunate than ourselves. But the love of money can replace our love for God. God is to be first in our hearts.

God, teach us about money and serving you. Amen.

† May 18 †

Trusting God

Matthew 6:25-27

Trust God to provide for your needs. God will take care of you. Look at the birds, as Jesus suggests. God feeds them, yet we are more valuable than they are. And will worry add even a minute to our lives? Of course not. But I am sometimes a slow learner. I fear that perhaps God will forget or overlook my needs. Fear is the belief that all will not work out.

Recently my housemate and I put a bird feeder in our yard. It took a few days for the birds to find it, but now we have a yard full of happy birds. The birds bring us great pleasure and I delight in watching them. I marvel at their beauty and variety. Their presence reminds me daily that God will feed them. These birds are valuable to God. And I am worth far more than our happy birds. They do not seem to worry and they live one day at a time. The birds remind me to "keep looking up," as my Grandmother would say. God will provide. God always does.

God, this life is a constant classroom and I am a slow learner. Teach me again and again. Help me trust you, celebrate my worth, and worry less often. Amen.

† May 19 †

Priority prayers
Matthew 6:28-32

I need to relearn certain spiritual truths again and again. God surely has exquisite patience with me. It is often very difficult for me to trust God's gracious care and divine timing. It is much easier to try and trust in my own ability to provide. My distrustful attitude has often hindered my spiritual life. Has this ever happened to you?

One of my favorite places is Dayspring Retreat Center in Germantown, Maryland. [54] The quiet grounds are full of beautiful trees. A reflective pond enhances the solitude. A dear friend describes the silent retreats held there very well, "A falling acorn is an explosion of sound."

In the sleeping quarters, every room has a Bible verse on the door from the Sermon on the Mount. During one retreat, my assigned room had today's passage on it. All during the retreat these simple words formed my prayers again and again. I clearly remember marveling at the tall grasses in the field and the birds of the air. I remember praying these verses with gratitude.

How has God cared for you in the past? Perhaps we all need a reminder today. God continues to care for us day after day. God never forgets us. God cares deeply for our needs and will never fail or abandon us. Thank God!

God, you know all our needs. Thank you for the flowers of the field. Thank you for your goodness and care. Amen.

---

[54] Visit Dayspring's Web site at http://www.serve.com/dayspringretreat/.

✝   May 20   ✝

Daily perspective

Matthew 6:33-34

My beloved Grandmother would often sing, "One day at a time, dear Lord, one day at a time." Today's scripture was one of her favorite Bible verses. Stay with today. Live in the moment and serve God one day at a time. Do the best you can with what you have and trust God to provide for your needs. Grandma understood that for she worked hard to provide for her family while praying for her daily bread. Even in the North American Great Depression, there was always some food to share with others who hungered.

Many people do not know what it means to live and work for the "kingdom of God and God's righteousness." Jesus is giving us a wonderful roadmap of how to live. These teachings are timeless, multicultural, multigenerational, and vitally needed for our world today.

God, thank you for this reminder to stay with today's concerns. Help us live one day at a time through the power of your words. Amen.

✝   May 21   ✝

Judging others

Matthew 7:1-2

Only the Bible has appeared in more editions and in more languages than the devotional treasure *The Imitation of Christ* attributed to the German ecclesiastic Thomas á Kempis. His fifteenth century wisdom remains relevant and timely. á Kempis offers this mature spiritual insight, "Study to be patient in bearing the defects of others, and their infirmities, be they what they may; for thou hast many things, which others must bear withal. If thou canst not make thyself what thou wouldst be, how canst thou expect to have another so exactly to thy mind? We would fain see others perfect, and yet our own faults we amend not. We would have others strictly corrected, and we will not be corrected ourselves. . . . We wish others to be kept within the rules, and we ourselves will not bear to be checked ever so little. And so it is clear how seldom we weigh our neighbor in the same balance with ourselves . . . God hath thus ordered . . . that we may learn to bear one another's burdens; for no one is without a fault, no one but hath a burden; no one is sufficient for himself, no one is wise enough for himself: but we have to support one another, comfort one another, help, instruct and admonish one another." [55]

God, teach us this timeless wisdom. Forgive our judgmental attitudes. Amen.

†   May 22   †

Judging ourselves

Matthew 7:3-5

We constantly judge others. Yet none of us are perfect and we are often blind to our own faults. I have frequently been guilty of this. It is not easy to receive loving criticism. Nor is it easy to follow the Alcoholic Anonymous admonition to perform fearless personal moral inventories and make amends whenever possible to those we have hurt in our lives. A famous ancient dictum is "Know thyself." There is great value in self-knowledge.

One spiritual discipline frequently overlooked is known as the "Prayer of *Examen*." It is a word unfamiliar to many. *Examen* comes from the Latin and refers to the tongue, or weight indicator on a balance scale. This conveys an image of a highly accurate assessment of the situation. Richard Foster describes the prayer as having two aspects. The first is an "*examen* of consciousness." In this, we discover how God has been present to us throughout the day and how we have responded to God's loving, holy presence. The second part is personally uncovering areas where we need inner cleansing, purifying, and healing. "The Prayer of *Examen* produces within us the priceless grace of self-knowledge," he writes in *Prayer: Finding the Heart's True Home.* [56] We give God both our strengths and our weaknesses.

---

[55] á Kempis, Thomas. *The Imitation of Christ*, p. 28.

[56] Foster, Richard J. *Prayer: Finding the Heart's True Home*, p. 27-28.

People of faith have welcomed this spiritual practice over the centuries. It is the "scrutiny of Love." [57] We invite God to search the depths of our hearts. The Psalmist wrote, "Search me, O God, and know my heart; test me and know my thoughts. See if there is any wicked way in me, and lead me in the way everlasting" (Psalm 139:23-24, NRSV).

For today, take some time for introspection. Where have we judged others while neglecting our own inner reflection? Where have we been blind to our own faults?

God, search us and know our hearts. Test us and know our thoughts. Show us where we have wicked ways and help us walk with you in your way. Help us see the planks in our own eyes. Amen.

† May 23 †

Pigs and pearls
Matthew 7:6

F. F. Bruce suggests that the dogs will turn and bite the hand that feeds them and the pigs will trample the pearls. "Objects of value, special privileges, participation in sacred things should not be offered to those who are incapable of appreciating them," Bruce writes in the *Hard Sayings of Jesus*. [58] And pearls are objects of beauty and value. There are some people who will not feel grateful to anyone who gives them spiritual food and moments of priceless beauty.

Bruce shares an important thought. This is the only Gospel that recorded this saying of Jesus. It comes immediately after a discussion on judgment. We need to carefully discern like Jesus when to share God's good news. Jesus knew when it was useless to dialogue with Herod Antipas when Herod questioned him at great length (Luke 23:9). Some do not have ears ready to hear. Their hearts may be hardened.

---

[57] Foster, Richard J. *Prayer: Finding the Heart's True Home*, p. 29.
[58] Bruce, F. F. *The Hard Sayings of Jesus*, p. 86.

God, help us understand the context of this saying. Teach us the wisdom of Jesus to know when to speak and when to be silent. Amen.

✝ May 24 ✝
Ask, seek, and knock
Matthew 7:7-8

Sometimes we have not because we ask not. At other times, we are fearful to ask because we just might get what we ask for! Yet God is extremely approachable. God can handle our most honest and tentative prayers. We are invited to ask, seek, and knock. Our answers will be in God's timing and way. But God will answer our prayers one way or another. We might even get more than we asked for. Expect to be surprised by God. Prayer is learned by praying. Ask. Seek. Knock. Persist. Wait. Expect answers.

God, hear the prayers of our hearts. Amen.

✝ May 25 ✝
Good gifts from God
Matthew 7:9-11

Over the past fifteen years I have listened to many people share their fears about prayer. For some, God is a vengeful, angry, demanding, critical, and miserly God. Often we inherit our understandings of God through families, friends, society, and our religious leaders. How we perceive God affects our prayers. That is, if we pray. Why pray to a miserly, dysfunctional God? Why bother to seek a relationship with that kind of Higher Power?

We have just been encouraged by Jesus to ask, seek, and knock on heaven's door. Now Jesus is giving us a wonderful picture of God. God is a loving, caring, responsible, generous divine Parent who cherishes us. All

God's children may approach this Tender One with confidence, including people of faith among all sexual orientations. This loving heavenly Parent will never ridicule, reject, or denigrate us. This loving God is healthy, functional, and generous.

While writing this particular reflection in 2000, the people in the state of California in the United States tragically voted against recognizing same-sex marriages as being valid and equal to heterosexual relationships. For many weeks anti-gay people of faith have aggressively lobbied against this basic civil rights measure. As a result many of God's cherished gay and lesbian children feel despised by God and the people of God. Many of the children who have been told they were despised believe God hates or condemns them for simply being who they are. Their prayers are hindered. Their spiritual lives are damaged through the traditional anti-gay rhetoric of many churches. Many lack loving, trusting, intimate relationships with the God who created them gay and lesbian, in the divine image. Many people have been taught they can never be God's beloved children, that somehow they are flawed or not good enough.

It is my prayer and hope that today's reflection will be a blessing for every reader. God is loving and caring. God delights in people of all sexual orientations and blesses loving families of choice. So take a chance on God. Ask God for what you need. Trust God. Ask. Seek. Knock. Persist in your prayers. And God will bless you beyond your innermost dreams and secret hopes. God loves you.

God, thank you for loving all your children. Thank you for loving me. Amen.

† May 26 †

The Golden Rule

Matthew 7:12

Today's scripture is known as the Golden Rule. Treat others the way we would wish to be treated. As a Jewish rabbi and teacher, Jesus was well acquainted with scriptural Jewish Law and the Prophets. I am deeply grateful for this summary of the Old Testament, which are often called the Jewish or Hebrew Scriptures.

The Bible is a very large collection of writings that literally span thousands of years. Some writings are extremely difficult to understand. Some ancient laws seem culturally irrelevant and the context is not always clear. Spiritual revelation is progressive. Our ongoing challenge is to determine what is culturally relevant and universal for our contemporary society.

For instance, some of the Levitical laws which prohibited eating certain foods, wearing certain fabrics, having tattoos, and numerous other restrictions are not appropriate for all of us today. The early writers were patriarchal and many practiced polygamy. Women had little voice and were often treated as property. As a twenty-first century North American woman in a monogamous relationship, those ancient practices have no relevance for me. Those teachings are not universal.

But I am suggesting the Golden Rule is timeless. It is worth passing on to the next generation. It can change the world. Most importantly, it can change us. Yes, this is easier said than done. But the Golden Rule is worth a lifetime of practice. We reap what we sow. So treat others with respect, dignity, charity, grace, and a bit of humor. When in doubt, err on the side of kindness and mercy. Treat others better than how they treat you. And ask God for frequent help along the journey.

God, how have I been treating others? Help me live this Golden Rule. Let this be engraved in all our hearts. Amen.

† May 27 †

Narrow and wide gates

Matthew 7:13-14

As a minister, I am involved with international seekers who use the Internet as a spirituality resource. More than a million Web sites are devoted to faith, God, spirituality, and religious concerns. People are finding God through the Internet. Lives are being transformed. With a click of a mouse, cyber-seekers lurk and surf, leaping from virtual Jerusalem to cyber Vatican, many e-mailing intensely personal prayer requests to Internet prayer chapels.

I met with someone who had found God years ago in this way. The Internet was just beginning to explode in popularity and was quickly being integrated into society and daily life. This particular woman used the Internet to find spiritual friendships and information. Eventually she discovered a particular Web site that had a cyber-monk. Cyber-monk faithfully responded to her numerous e-mails and patiently answered her many questions. Over time, the woman decided to make a spiritual pilgrimage to the retreat center where this monk served. Gradually she made the decision to make a profession of faith and be baptized in the name of Jesus Christ. While being respectful of all religious faiths, she came into her own personal relationship with Jesus as her guide and companion for life.

I believe we are all pilgrims in search of our sacred path. Our human nature searches for the divine mystery. We seek our sacred center for personal renewal. We need to touch holy places and be touched by the journey. Sometimes the journey may be to a distant place on the other side of our planet, or it can be as near as our back yards or even through cyber-space.

Where have you journeyed in your search for the holy? Have you found your way? Can you describe your sacred path? Who is your spiritual guide?

Consider Christ as your companion. Walk with him and you can trust the path. His guidance will bring powerful resources of faith, hope, and love for your journey.

O Sacred Guide, bless my steps and prayers throughout this day. Be my companion, I pray. Amen.

† May 28 †
In sheep's clothing
Matthew 7:15-16

Not all who claim to be prophets, priests, ministers, chaplains, doers of good are who they appear to be. This is certainly true on the Internet. It can be very confusing to determine who is authentic and who is false. Not all Web pages offer truth. Imposters and predatory people will ask for money, credit card numbers, and other personal information to take advantage of trusting, gullible, and vulnerable people. There is a dark side in life and on-line encounters are not immune to it.

Watch out for phonies and fakes, Jesus reminds us. Take time to thoroughly investigate and research references from self-proclaimed spiritual leaders. Be careful. Not everyone is what he or she initially appears to be. Caution, discretion, and prudence may save us a great deal of remorse and heartache. Check professional and personal references before risking your soul to strangers.

Jesus never took advantage of vulnerable people. He always told the truth. He never cheated, schemed, or presented false claims. He had integrity and honesty as his lifestyle. He did not build an earthly power structure, but devoted himself to God's rule on earth.

God, give us wisdom and insight to recognize authentic spiritual leaders, mentors, and friends. Protect us from danger hidden in sheep's clothing. Amen.

†   May 29   †

What are my motives?

Matthew 7:21-23

Ask three very important questions while reading the Bible. What is the passage saying? What does it mean? And specifically, what does this mean to me in my personal life and situation? Valuable insights can also be gained through reading different Bible translations.

Jesus' warning reinforces what he is teaching us about false prophets and other spiritual impostors. God truly looks within our hearts and knows our motives. What is our motive in following Jesus? Are we using him to promote our own power agenda and to manipulate people for prestige?

Eugene Peterson translates these verses in a contemporary interpretation, "Knowing the correct password – saying 'Master, Master,' for instance – isn't going to get you anywhere with me. What is required is serious obedience – doing what my Father wills. I can see it now – at the

Final Judgment thousands strutting up to me and saying, 'Master, we preached the Message, we bashed the demons, our God-sponsored projects had everyone talking.' And do you know what I am going to say? 'You missed the boat. All you did was use me to make yourselves important. You don't impress me one bit. You're out of here.'" [59]

God, help us identify our true motives for following Jesus. Help us take heed of this stern warning. Amen.

† May 30 †

Wise and foolish builders
Matthew 7:24-25

My father was a master carpenter. While in my teens, he and my mother built the home of their dreams. I will always remember his painstaking attention to detail as he laid the foundation, installed plumbing and wiring. Most of his friends were plumbers, electricians, carpenters, and laborers. They helped him build the house. Many were the nights that my father would quietly redo much of the work. He would only be satisfied with the best work and sturdiest house. Houses are just not made like that anymore in our prefab construction world. My father's house could withstand most of what Mother Nature could offer. The foundation was rock-solid.

The words of Jesus offer us a rock-solid spiritual foundation for our lives. We will be wise to put them into practice. Whatever life brings us, we will have the inner resources to withstand adversity, temptation, despair, grief, persecution, injustice, and evil. Jesus is our rock.

Some Bibles will have the words of Jesus in red print. If you have never read them before, it can be a transforming experience. You will be given wisdom, insight, faith, courage, peace, and joy. As we say in North America, "Try it, you'll like it."

---

[59] Peterson, Eugene. *The Message: The New Testament in Contemporary Language*, p. 22.

God, let the words of Jesus Christ be the foundation of our lives. Amen.

† **May 31** †

This amazing teacher

Matthew 7:28-29

While teachers of the law quoted other rabbis to support their own teaching, Jesus simply spoke with divine authority. The crowds were astonished at his teachings. Jesus is simply the greatest spirituality teacher the world will ever know. His words are worth pondering and offer wisdom for our lives. Jesus can teach us something new, fresh, and relevant through daily gospel readings. His words bring us peace, joy, and courage. He walked his talk. His words will stand the test of time throughout eternity.

We have now finished our meditations on his famous Sermon of the Mount (Matthew chapters 5-7). Read them again and again. Memorize words of inspiration. When in doubt over important decisions or how to resolve conflict, pray, spend money, reduce stress, combat worry – Jesus' words in red can change your life and perspective. Jesus' words will bring you help and comfort in your times of need. You will be spiritually empowered.

Jesus, amaze us with your wonderful words of life. Amen.

† June 1 †

Spiritual diseases

Matthew 8:1-4

Jesus is extremely willing to help us become clean, to heal us from spiritual disease. He is the compassionate healer who is available to all who suffer spiritual, physical, psychological, mental, and emotional illnesses. There is no need to be embarrassed or fear being shunned by this compassionate teacher.

Today's verses hold meaning for all people who seek spiritual health. Our healthy and unhealthy bodies and feelings can either help or hinder our prayers. It is helpful, even empowering, to remember that Jesus is extremely approachable by those perceived as outcasts and unclean in their society. He continually brings people back into community and out of isolation.

God, where do I feel unclean? Where am I out of community? With the help of Jesus Christ, bring me into wholeness and fellowship. Amen.

† June 2 †

Great faith

Matthew 8:10

This is a story of a great faith that astonished even Jesus. This story is about faith, love, courage, and hope by a desperate person deeply concerned for the life of his servant-boy, someone who was obviously very dear to him. Have you ever wondered what great faith could look like? Rather than be destroyed by fear and doubt, a centurion, a Roman soldier with great authority who Jesus talks to in today's verse, steps out in bold, public faith in Christ, the Healer.

Many of us are often fearful as we strive to be faithful, but the centurion's courageous example shows us how we can likewise take a chance with God through the Healer, Jesus Christ, expecting divine compassion and concern for our loving relationships. Perhaps it is time to quietly converse with Christ through prayer. Tell Jesus what ails your body, mind, and spirit. Ask for healing help. Be willing to actively pursue your recovery program. Let your journey begin today. How do we get this astonishing great faith? Begin by reading today's remarkable story in Matthew 8:5-13.

There is a popular saying about faith, "When you have gone as far as all the light you know, and you are about to step into the darkness of the unknown. . . . Faith is knowing that one of two things will happen . . . you will step onto firm ground, or you will learn how to fly."

God, bless us with the kind of faith this centurion had! Amen.

† June 3 †

Many are healed
Matthew 8:14-17

Before becoming an ordained minister, I worked for sixteen years as a registered nurse in many emergency rooms and outpatient clinics full of waiting, sick people and their families. Often children would be crying. Some times some were unable to get a bathroom in time and were sitting in soiled clothing. Others struggled with schizophrenia and other psychiatric disorders. Feverish people would often be wet with perspiration and their skin would feel hot to the touch. Often they were exhausted and dehydrated by their raging fevers. I remember the smells and sights of sick, lame, abandoned, hopeless, and discouraged people. Many could only hope for a moment of relief. Cures were humanly impossible for those in advanced stages of terminal illness.

I bring all these memories with me as I read these four verses and marvel at the images in my mind. Jesus understands illness. He took up our infirmities and carried our diseases. He is amazing. He understands our human sufferings.

Perhaps our response to him should be similar to Peter's mother-in-law. In her gratitude, she began to humbly serve Jesus in the only way she knew how. She began to linger in his presence while delighting in his voice, touch, and companionship. She is a timeless model of servant leadership for us today.

God, help us serve Jesus Christ with gratitude like that expressed by Peter's mother-in-law. Amen.

† June 4 †

The cost of following Jesus
Matthew 8:18-22

This passage has been dear to my heart for many years. While studying for my masters in divinity, I cared for my mother as she struggled with advanced cancer. She died shortly before I graduated. It literally broke my heart to leave my grieving family to serve as a military chaplain on active duty so soon after her funeral. Years later as I struggled with ministerial loneliness while serving in a remote overseas area, I remember reading these verses again with fresh power and a new awareness of Jesus' own loneliness. Now, a decade later, I again pause and reflect on the personal cost of following Jesus in my life. Even after finishing a doctor of ministry program, I still need to sit with these verses as if for the first time and hear them with fresh new power and awareness. These verses contain a lifetime of spiritual lessons for all readers who desire to follow Jesus.

Not all are called to leave everything to follow the Teacher. Sometimes we are called to stay home and be a local witness of God's truth in our lives. We may also be called to leave familiar surroundings and friends to serve overseas or relocate elsewhere. Following Jesus is not easy locally or globally.

Jesus continues to call people to live remarkable lives of faithful obedience to his teachings. Following Christ involves listening and learning, alertness and practice. When we follow him, we can expect great moments of joy. Anticipate an adventure with God.

Jesus, I will follow you all the days of my life. Show me how to begin today. Amen.

† June 5 †

Storms are calmed

Matthew 8:24-25

I have been in furious storms on some of the world's mighty oceans. As life-threatening waves sweep over the boat, sometimes all you can do is hang on for dear life while desperately praying for calm seas. Sometimes I have gotten caught in vicious summer squalls while sailing small boats. One night, a fellow shipmate fell overboard and I feared he had drowned. I heard his voice from the dark waters and threw a lifeline. He was able to climb back into the boat as the waves churned in fury and we were flung from side to side in the boat. When the squall passed by, we became becalmed. There was not even a whisper of wind. We could hear and feel the stillness. In the quiet we could hear fish jump. The stars came out. The sea looked like dark velvet. Bruised and battered, we managed to sail home. After we docked the boat, I knelt down and kissed the ground in profound gratitude for our safety.

In today's story, the terrified disciples were seasoned sailors and professional fisherman. They too, feared for their lives while Jesus was sleeping. In their terror, they shouted a profound prayer, "Lord, save us! We are going to drown!"

Jesus woke up and chastised them for their little faith. He asked why they were so fearful. Then he stood up on the wildly rocking boat and rebuked the waves and the wind. It became completely calm. The terrified disciples were amazed and asked a question we need to answer today. "What kind of man is Jesus?" Even nature obeys him! I have always wondered if they knelt down and kissed the ground in gratitude after landing their boat.

Who is Jesus? Who is he to you? Is there something in your life that feels out of control? Have you ever wondered if Jesus could help you?

Feel free to ask him for help. Ask for calm seas, rest from the bruises of life, and safe harbor for your souls. He is our wonderful Navigator through life's troubled waters. He is our divine lifeline.

Lord, save us! Protect us from spiritual drowning! Help us get into safe harbor. Amen.

† June 6 †

Healing

Matthew 8:28, 34

Tormented people experience Jesus the Healer in this powerful story found in its entirety in Matthew 8:28-34 and in Mark 5:1-17. Both gospel writers were deeply impressed with this event. Matthew mentions two demon-possessed men. Mark only mentions one. But the numbers are irrelevant. It is a profound story of mental anguish, inner violence, insanity, and loneliness. Life is forever changed but at significant economic cost for the local community. The Healer sends the tormenting evil spirits into the large herd of feeding pigs. The entire herd then rushes into the water. They drown. The pig herders rush into town and tell their news. And the entire town goes out to meet Jesus and see the situation for themselves. They beg Jesus to leave their region.

Perhaps we need healing ourselves but fear the cost of following Jesus. Or perhaps we have ample resources and wish to keep them for ourselves, rather than alleviate the sufferings of others.

I am amazed at the value of a human life. Jesus was willing to travel out of his way to meet those who needed healing. He was approachable to those who suffered deep inner torment and inner violence. He is just as approachable today.

God, where are we in this story? And what are we to do with Jesus in our lives? Amen.

† June 7 †

Spiritual paralysis

Matthew 9:1, 2

I suspect the man's paralysis is a spiritual metaphor for all of us. Everyone has missed the mark (sinned) somewhere in life. Probably we have felt frozen with guilt and remorse, anger and frustration, regret and other feelings. Perhaps we have become spiritually paralyzed through sins of omission and those sins intentionally committed. All of us have sinned. Only Jesus is the sinless one. Only God is perfect.

Another powerful story of Jesus the Healer, recorded in Matthew 9:1-8, Mark 2:3-12, and Luke 5:18-26, is a story about spiritual paralysis, faith, sin, forgiveness, and hope. This liberating tale can transform our perspectives and our lives.

In today's story, these remarkable friends earnestly believed Jesus would heal their companion. They awkwardly carried him to the Healer. When Jesus saw their faith, he said to the paralytic, "Be encouraged, child, your sins are forgiven." The religious leaders of the day were outraged. Only God could forgive sins. According to Orthodox Jewish law, Jesus was blaspheming. This offense was worthy of death.

We see yet another new picture of Jesus. Nature obeys him, but he can also read our human thoughts and hearts. He reads the minds of the critical teachers of the law. He confronts them with spiritual questions. Then he proves his authority to forgive sins through healing the paralytic and tells him to get up, pick up his mat, and go home. The paralytic springs to his feet, a new man in Christ! And the crowds marvel in awe. They praised God who had given such astonishing authority to Jesus.

Where are we in this story? Are we the paralyzed, the faith-filled friends, the astonished crowd, or the disciples? Or are we so deeply religious that we cannot see the power of Christ with fresh eyes? Where have we missed the mark in our lives and experienced spiritual paralysis?

God, show us where we are spiritually paralyzed and heal us. Amen.

†   **June 8**   †

Gifts from God

Matthew 9:9

Matthew's birth obviously had been a source of deep parental joy and celebration because his name literally means "God's gift." Yet little Matthew grew up to be an adult who broke his parents hearts. Their beloved son grew to be an outcast among his own people as a result of his lifestyle of bad decisions and moral failings.

Jesus was God's gift to Matthew. Jesus searched for Matthew with a startling invitation to become part of his beloved community of faithful disciples. From Matthew's spontaneous response, we learn there is a place at God's table for everyone. Each reader is invited to respond to Jesus with the enthusiasm, joy, and gratitude of Matthew. This is our gift to God.

Still another divine gift awaits us. On the evening of Matthew's dramatic calling into discipleship, he hosted a lavish dinner party with Jesus as his honored guest. Many of Matthew's friends and colleagues attended along with the Pharisees. The Pharisees classified Matthew and his tax collector associates as despicable sinners. These sanctimonious religious authorities were scandalized by the fact that Jesus ate with such relish in the presence of such people. Jesus' gift to us is his response to his critics, "It is not the healthy who need a doctor, but the sick. But go and learn what this means, 'I desire mercy, not sacrifice.' For I have not come to call the righteous, but sinners" (Matthew 9:12). This gift challenges us to reexamine our attitudes towards people we believe are unforgivable sinners and outcasts.

God has many gifts for us through the example of Matthew. Perhaps the greatest gift is the call of divine mercy and forgiveness to all people, including lesbians, gays, bisexuals, and transgendered people excluded by legalistic, judgmental, and abusive religion. The Bible contains many unspoken yet intriguing life stories. Priceless gifts are waiting to be found by every thoughtful searcher willing to sift and ponder the meaning of these stories.

Merciful and compassionate God, we thank you for so many spiritual gifts today. Teach us more of divine mercy and forgiveness. Help us get up and follow Jesus with the courage, joy, and gratitude of Matthew. Bring us into new life with Christ. Protect us from the judgmental attitudes of the Pharisees. Amen.

† June 9 †

An old saying with new truth
Matthew 9:14-17

Jesus often answered questions with a question or two of his own. This valuable teaching technique empowered his listeners to think more clearly and stimulated growth and understanding. The disciples of John the Baptist asked probing questions as they sought to understand the theological differences between the Baptist and Jesus. They had correctly identified John as one of the greatest spiritual leaders known in Jewish history. But John consistently pointed them to Jesus as being far greater. The baffled disciples were inquisitive and persistent. What can a wedding, new cloth, and old wineskins teach us about God?

The disciples realized John the Baptist was an important prophet, but he was not the Messiah. Jesus was the Messiah they were waiting for. It was Jesus who was God's very special messenger that cherished prophets had yearned for throughout the ages. Jesus was the joyous bridegroom in the story.

But being the master teacher that he was, Jesus understood these seekers needed more help as they struggled to understand the immensity of what he was saying. He used two old sayings to bring his students into new truth. His words are brilliant in their simplicity. Just as new and unshrunken cloth cannot be used to repair an old garment, so Jesus cannot be manipulated into old garments of understanding. We need new spiritual rebirth in God to understand the joy of Christ in our lives. And new wine cannot be put into old wineskins. To be preserved, new wine needs new wineskins. In the same way, our new lives in Christ need new lifestyles and attitudes.

The questioning disciples left with more than they expected. They had found Jesus approachable. He had been hospitable and generous in his answers. They had been treated with great respect in their search for deeper truth in God.

Jesus is a source of joy for those who seek God. Ask the Bridegroom for new garments and the new wine of spiritual understanding through today's teaching. Pray until something happens. Persist and be patient. Ask God to surprise you with joy.

Joyous Bridegroom, surprise us with the new wine of spiritual understanding and new life in God. Clothe us anew with the joy of our salvation. Amen.

†   **June 10**   †

Desperation and hope

Matthew 9:18-21

Who has not felt desperate or struggled with despair at some time in life? There are moments when all hope is lost and God seems silent. How can we find comfort and strength through this story?

There are some things worse than our own deaths. I remember my beloved grandmother often said the greatest fear of any parent was outliving their children. She knew from heartbreaking experience the bitter grief and desperation of seeing her children die as adults through incurable diseases marked by great suffering. Some sufferers believe another fate worse than death can be living with debilitating, progressive, and painful chronic diseases without hope for a cure. They feel as if they are dying by inches.

Today's Gospel offers a timeless snapshot of desperation and hope. The first was a desperate parent whose little girl had unexpectedly died. The second was a chronically ill woman who had suffered for many years without a cure. Desperate people do desperate things in times of need. Both had run out of options and in desperation reached out to Jesus, hopeful for a miracle.

Although the bereaved father and chronically ill woman came from different walks of life, Jesus gave each his full attention and compassion. The frantic father had interrupted Jesus in the midst of his teachings, and Jesus listened carefully to his pleas. He graciously agreed to immediately accompany the father to his home where the little girl lay dead. When the desperate woman pushed her way through the crowd to touch the hem of his cloak, Jesus stopped again. He refused to go any further until he met the person who had touched him. This story has a happy ending. The woman experienced healing and the little girl was raised from the dead.

Whatever our life situation might be, Christ walks with us. When we cry out for help in times of need, he stops and compassionately listens to our pleas. As we reach out to touch the hem of his cloak, his healing power continues to flow. So "turn your eyes on Jesus. Look full in His wonderful face, and things of earth will grow strangely dim, in the light of His glory and grace" [60] and you will be moved from desperation to hope.

Oh God, thank you for understanding our experiences of human despera-tion. Help us find hope through Jesus Christ in our times of need. Amen.

† **June 11** †

Blind faith

Matthew 9:27-30a

This wonderful story teaches us about blind faith. Jesus has just performed a dramatic miracle of bringing a little girl back from the dead. As he leaves this rejoicing family, two sightless men persistently, insis-tently follow him, calling out, "Have mercy on us, Son of David!" (Mat-thew 9:27 NIV). They refused to be silenced and followed Jesus indoors. They were then blessed with a personal conversation with the Healer. Je-sus asked, "Do you believe that I am able to do this?" (Matthew 9:28 NIV). Their instant and enthusiastic response was "yes!" They knew Je-sus was God's Sent One, the Messiah ancient prophets spoke of over the centuries. That is why they called him the popular Jewish title for the coming Messiah, "Son of David!" Matthew records the use of this title numerous times (Matthew 12:23; 20:30; 21:9; 22:41-45).

Jesus honors their unwavering faith, touches their eyes and said, "According to your faith will it be done to you" (Matthew 9:29 NIV). Their sight was restored! Then Jesus does a strange thing. He sternly warns them to keep their healing a secret. But in their joy they went throughout their region and spread the news about him everywhere.

---

[60] From the hymn, "Fix your eyes upon Jesus," words and music by Helen H. Lemmel, 1922, first published in *Glad Song*, by the British National Sunday School Union. http://cyberhymnal.org/htm/t/u/turnyour.htm.

What is blind faith? Is this something we should strive for? How did the sightless ones "see" Jesus? What do they offer us in spiritual instruction? Quite simply, their hearing was acute and compensated for their lack of sight. They heard and intuitively felt the power and goodness of the Healer. They knew how to "holy listen," while wholly listening with their other senses. They were also well acquainted with Holy Scripture and the prophets, and clearly understood that Jesus was God's special messenger for planet earth. They refused to leave until they received their miracle. They had heard about the little girl being raised from the dead. This was a once in a lifetime opportunity and they insisted, persisted, and refused to leave until they literally saw Jesus. And they were additionally blessed with his healing touch.

Their bold faith came as a result of hearing the Word of God, Jesus Christ, the Messiah, God's Sent One. Through reading the Gospels, we too, can experience their "blind faith" and gain spiritual sight.

God, give us this admirable and courageous faith in Jesus. Amen.

† June 12 †

Even the mute speak
Matthew 9:32-34

I once brought a portable indoor labyrinth to an ecumenical retreat entitled, "Finding our voice." Women attended from throughout the USA. It was a powerful experience. The women represented all ages, a variety of cultures, and spiritual diversity in Christ. One woman even "came out" as a Christian lesbian to her small group as she reclaimed her voice over the weekend.

What was striking to me, was that all struggled to be heard with dignity and respect in their personal and professional lives. As women, many were expected to be seen and not heard. It was exciting to hear women find their voices, strengths, and gifts with each session and small group experience. There was strength in numbers and gathered community.

Henry David Thoreau said, in "Where I Lived and What I Lived For,"[61] that many people "lead lives of quiet desperation." Powerful authorities sometimes maintain the status quo and exclude certain minority voices. Even the Christian church has muted the voices of selected people over the centuries. This is slowly changing as growing numbers of people are finding their voice in Christ.

The Pharisees claimed Jesus was the evil one, Satan, the devil, who healed the mute man. Often in our contemporary culture, religious authorities from many traditions have insisted those claiming their voice were in the thrall of the evil one. Jesus was being accused of being evil incarnate as he compassionately gave this man his voice. He has healed the sick, raised the dead, given sight to the blind, voice to the mute, and now he is being accused of being the "prince of demons." We are not told what words the formerly mute man spoke, but I have always wondered if he thanked Jesus for his miraculous healing.

Where do we need to find our voice in Christ? How can we help those muted by society and legalistic religion? How do we reclaim their voice and dignity?

God, if we have been silenced or have silenced others through bias, prejudice, or harmful religion, help us and them regain our voice from Christ. Amen.

† June 13 †

A critical shortage of workers
Matthew 9:35-37

Believe it or not, Jesus is asking for our compassionate prayers. We are to pray for workers willing to share God's loving message with others. The apostle Paul makes a similar profound observation in 1 Corinthians 1:26-31. God is looking for people who are often considered inconsequential by the standards of our societies. God often chooses the foolish, the weak, the lowly, and the despised to bring the liberating and inclusive

---

[61] "Where I Lived and What I Lived For," is chapter 2 in *Walden, or Life in the Woods*, by Henry David Thoreau, 1854.

good news from Jesus Christ into our world. God delights in using ordinary people in extraordinary ways. The bottom line is that we be humble and available to God's call in our lives. And we are to pray for many workers.

I preached this message of outreach and mission at an evangelical church many years ago as their guest preacher. After the worship service, an angry and indignant woman rushed up to me with her husband reluctantly following behind her. "How dare you," she wagged her finger in my face. "How dare you preach this to us? Just who do you think you are? You are nothing, nobody." Her embarrassed husband later apologized to me for her rude behavior, puzzled at his wife's tirade against me. Later I would discover she had been under a counselor's care. Even so, her words gave me pause for reflection. Yes, she was correct. I fall into the category specified by the apostle Paul. By the world's standards, I am weak, lowly, sometimes despised, and actually quite ordinary. But I am willing to be used by God in extraordinary ways. Are you?

The harvest is great. The need is enormous. Who will go? Who will share Jesus with others? Crowds of searching people seek spiritual truth. How will they hear if we do not speak? Faith comes by hearing. We are called to be messengers of God's peace through Jesus Christ. We are to tell our stories of faith and pray for others to share their faith stories.

For several years I worshipped in a large Christian church of primarily gay and lesbian members known as the Metropolitan Community Church of Washington, D.C. (MCC-DC). In the sanctuary was a rainbow chair, which was always left empty. The chair was a silent reminder that many people around the world had not yet heard of God's compassionate loving message through Jesus Christ. People are searching in every town, village, and city. They have not yet met Jesus Christ, the Good Shepherd of our souls.

How dare we be silent? How dare we keep the good news of God to ourselves and not share with others who hunger for spiritual food and drink? How dare we turn our backs and silence our voices? We are often our own people's best missionaries, for we hear the cry of their hearts. How dare we not pray for them to experience God's peace, through Christ?

Just who does Jesus think he is, asking us to pray for others?

God, open our eyes to see your searching people. Help us compassionately share Jesus, the Good Shepherd, with others. Amen.

† June 14 †

Called by name
Matthew 10:1-4

There is great power and significance in naming. Scripture recognizes how important names are. Names affirm people as significant. We are more than a social security number, zip code, credit card number. Names are personal, insightful, prophetic, and revealing. Our names are often carefully chosen before birth by eager parents. These names frequently reflect their hopes and dreams for us.

Some dear friends are expecting their first child. They have struggled mightily to find the perfect name. Because of ultrasound technology, they know their baby's gender in advance and have chosen to name him Matthew, meaning "God's gift."

People have often asked why I initially wrote Internet reflections under the pen name "Surprised by Joy" over the years. God blessed me with the pen name "Surprised by Joy" in 1997. It had been an extended time of crisis, major transition, deep grief, loss, and upheaval for me. When asked to write anonymous reflections for a church under a pen name, I struggled to find a name that accurately described my spiritual pilgrimage from darkness into light. I signed that first reflection, "Surprised by Joy." As the years passed by, I missed being known by my real name.

All this to say, I am deeply moved by these simple verses where Jesus names his inner circle of disciples. He speaks their names and knows them intimately. Even the future betrayer is named.

Jesus knows our names. He knows us better than we know ourselves. I rejoice in being known personally by God. The Psalmist puts it this way, "O LORD, you have searched me and you know me" (Psalm 139:1 NIV). God knows us by name. Amazing.

God, thank you for knowing our names. Amen.

✝ June 15 ✝

A difficult teaching
Matthew 10:5-10

Sometimes Jesus is not easy to understand. If these specific instructions were to be literally interpreted for today, I would be excluded. You see, I am not a Jew. I am a "Gentile." I work in towns and cities where "Samaritans," that is, people with mixed-blood through intermarriages, live. Quite honestly, I do not know many of the "lost sheep of Israel" that Jesus mentions. I do not have the power to heal the sick, raise the dead, cleanse lepers, and drive out demons. It also seems irresponsible, dangerous, and foolhardy to travel without money or supplies as a twenty-first century woman living in an increasingly violent society.

Jesus sometimes seems to contradict himself. He went to the Samaritans early in his ministry career (John 4). He "went to the other side" where the Gentiles lived (Matthew 8). He even taught about personal responsibility and fiscal stewardship (Matthew 25). At the very end of Matthew's Gospel, he commands his disciples to teach everything he taught them locally and globally to all the nations.

What does this passage mean today? The Bible tells us Jesus is the same yesterday, today, and tomorrow (Hebrews 13:8), but does that apply to all his teachings?

Perhaps I need this reminder that I have freely received God's generosity. I am to pass that spiritual generosity on to others. And yes, a worker is worth his or her keep. And those groups who ask for such services need to honor the time, effort, and labor involved by the workers through hospitality and honorariums.

God, help me linger with today's teaching and learn what Jesus truly means. Amen.

† June 16 †

Sheep, wolves, snakes, and doves
Matthew 10:11-16

Not everyone is interested in hearing Jesus' message of God's peace. We are called to share this good news with prudence, discernment, wisdom, and discretion. Evaluate your surroundings. Carefully assess who is friend or foe. Be wise and innocent both at the same time. Realize some will refuse to hear and may act with violence against you. If refused a hearing, shake the dust off your feet and go on to other places. Do not stay where you are not welcome. Those who refuse to hear the gospel message of God's peace will someday face a judgment far more severe than Sodom and Gomorrah (Genesis 19).

Sometimes those we love and trust will not welcome us. That happened to me after a decade of ordained ministry when planning to visit some old seminary friends. Over the years, I had changed denominations from a conservative evangelical denomination to a more inclusive and affirming Protestant group that welcomes people of all sexual orientations, the Metropolitan Community Churches (MCC). I had reached out with open arms and a loving heart to my dear friends. Their words of rejection and refusal of hospitality cut me deep to the heart. I could not visit their home as formerly planned. They referred me to a motel room. They had researched my denomination and disagreed with its statement of faith and judged me as being "incompatible with Christian teachings." I was no longer a welcomed guest and friend. That was the day that these biblical verses became intensely personal for me.

So be wise. Listen to the Spirit before speaking. Sharing God's grace and mercy can be hazardous work. Live and serve Jesus as very wise sheep surrounded by wolves.

God, help us serve you with wisdom, prudence, and holy boldness. Amen.

† June 17 †

Be on your guard
Matthew 10:17-20

Often we forget the Church was built on the blood and suffering of martyrs. Being a Christian may be hazardous to your health, prosperity, and popularity. Some countries continue to actively persecute Christians for their faith even today. And all too tragically, throughout history zealous Christians have been equally guilty, persecuting and oppressing others who failed to subscribe to their cherished religious beliefs. Many horrific religious wars have been committed in the name of God. Believe or die. Believe my way or be tortured, imprisoned, exiled, or even executed. This was never the intention of Jesus as he taught his disciples that suffering for his teachings is sometimes a part of discipleship.

The inner circle of disciples had no idea of what their future held as they eagerly followed Jesus. Most of the twelve disciples eventually experienced martyrdom. The beloved disciple, John, was exiled to the island of Patmos (a Roman penal colony) for his activities as a Christian missionary.

Hatred, violence, slander, and injustice can even be experienced within the church. Ireland has been racked with violence between Catholics and Protestants for years. Gay and lesbian Christians are often excluded or excommunicated from churches in many countries. "Ethnic cleansing" in the name of religious holy wars continues around the world.

Whatever our situation, if we find ourselves accused and standing before the courts, beaten and bruised for our faith in Christ, the Spirit of God will speak through us. We will not be left alone. We will be given the words to speak through the power of God. So be very brave. Be comforted. We will not be abandoned in our hour of need.

God, bless your martyred people. Help us to pray for them and to be brave in our faith. Amen.

† **June 18** †

Stand firm

Matthew 10:21-23

Sometimes I forget that some people deeply hate those who follow Jesus. Hatred is deeply divisive among families, friends, colleagues, and sometimes even our neighbors. It is difficult to be neutral about Jesus.

And when heterosexual Christians harbor prejudices against gay, lesbian, bisexual, and transgendered (GLBT) Christians, bitter debates divide and cause much harm throughout the Church when such hatred is expressed towards fellow believers solely based on sexual orientation. This I believe, deeply grieves our Savior, harms our common witness, and does enormous harm locally, nationally, and internationally. Some of the most dedicated, loving, prophetic, and courageous Christians I know are found among GLBT communities worldwide. They do much good and our world would be a poorer place without their inspiring witness. Slanderous words, malicious intent, and odious behaviors against people because of their sexual orientation is displeasing to our God and sorrows the Holy Spirit.

If you are being persecuted for whatever reason, take heart and remember those famous verses from the Sermon on the Mount, "When you are reviled and persecuted and lied about because you are my followers – wonderful! Be happy about it! Be very glad! For a tremendous reward awaits you up in heaven. And remember, the ancient prophets were persecuted too" (Matthew 5:11-12 TLB).

Cling to your belovedness in God through difficult times. "Beloved" with every breath you take. God will get you through the difficult, discouraging, frightening, and despairing times. The Holy Spirit will comfort, enfold, guide, and empower you one breath at a time when one day at a time feels overwhelming. Never, never, never give up. God is with you always, even to the ends of the earth. And let your sexual orientation be God's gift to you and a blessing to the world.

God, help us learn love, tolerance, respect, and inclusion for people of all sexual orientations. Help us experience joy and comfort through the words of Jesus when we are in the midst of trials and persecution. Amen.

† June 19 †

Be like Jesus

Matthew 10:24-25

Over the past thirty years of my life, I have sat through and also taught many local church membership classes. Usually the classes are devoted to teaching potential members about that particular denomination. Often the membership classes attempt to recruit volunteers to assist in chores and other needed tasks and ministries of the church. It is also popular to have the students complete spiritual gift inventories as part of their membership classes and encourage each one to sign up for a ministry as they enter the life of that particular church. Sometimes we are so intent on jobs, chores, and needful things to do, that we neglect the teachings of Jesus, the early church creeds and basic spiritual rebirth, baptism, and discipleship training. Many new members have never read a gospel and have no understanding of who Jesus is and what he taught!

The early church understood it was costly to follow Jesus. They often insisted on a thorough teaching of the Christian faith for prospective members, for publicly identifying with Christ could possibly bring them martyrdom.

What if we insisted prospective church members read all "the words in red" found in the gospels of Matthew, Mark, Luke, and John before joining a local church? What if we discussed the costs of publicly identifying with Christ in our communities? What if our churches more closely identified with Jesus? What would happen if each of us did these things in our personal lives?

God, help us remember we are students and servants of Jesus. Amen.

† June 20 †

Fear not

Matthew 10:26-31

Sometime ago I was preparing a sermon on fear. One commentary mentioned the Bible specifically teaches us to "fear not" in more than 300 scripture references. I find that greatly encouraging. I have experienced violence at both knifepoint and gunpoint and have felt paralyzing fear. Yet Jesus is telling us to "fear not." Do not be afraid of evil perpetrators of violence. Rather, revere and fear God who can destroy body and soul. I have to confess that this is easier said than done.

Look at the birds. Once again we are reminded that not one will fall to the ground without our heavenly Parent's will and consent. Even the hairs on our head are numbered. So do not fear. We are worth more than many little birds. We are deeply valued by God. Be strong and of good courage. Fear not. God is with us. We will not be left alone in our hour of need.

God, help us not be afraid. Thank you for valuing us so highly. Amen.

† June 21 †

A spiritual revolution

Matthew 10:32-36

Jesus emphatically refuses to sugarcoat his gospel message with easy promises of peace, prosperity, and popularity. Throughout history, some have experienced mockery, criticism, and even hostility in their efforts to live out his radical wisdom. Blessed are the peacemakers (Matthew 5:9), but realistically there are occasions when our attempts might be met with varying degrees of scorn, conflict, and in extreme cases, virulent verbal abuse and life-threatening physical violence. If this is your experience, take courage and trust God to give you strength for the day.

One of the most powerful and influential books I have ever read is *Behold the Beauty of the LORD*, written by the late Henri Nouwen. He writes about four beloved Russian Orthodox icons. One of the icons is a partially damaged face of Christ that war, violence, destruction, hatred, and despair could not remove from the world. The famous 15th Century icon is known as "Christ, the Peacemaker."

Christians and non-Christians alike quickly discover this holy face brings a spiritual revolution into every receptive heart. Also known as "The Savior," this dramatic image is located in the State Tretyakov Gallery in Moscow, Russia.

Sometimes Jesus is difficult to understand. He is the Prince of Peace (Isaiah 9:6). His name is elevated above all others (Philippians 2:9). He is the Sent One from God (Luke 2:14) who brings true peace on earth. His divine peace is inexplicably and mysteriously not of this world (John 14:27). This inner peace with God is freely and abundantly available to all seekers through personal faith in Jesus Christ.

Jesus also calls us into spiritual warfare. We are part of a spiritual revolution in a world that aggressively tries to remove His face in many places through violence and injustice. We are to joyfully identify with Christ in word and deed, even when his message it met with opposition. Truly, God's thoughts are not our thoughts and God's ways are not our ways (Isaiah 55:8). Take comfort – Christ is always with you.

God, help us publicly identify with Christ the Peacemaker. Amen.

† June 22 †

Take up your cross
Matthew 10:37-39

A dear friend carved a simple wooden statue for me years ago. It is a statue of a person standing tall with both arms upraised to heaven. I often use it for personal reflection and when leading retreats. The carving reminds me to surrender my pride, ego, personal issues, mistaken priorities, and hidden agendas at the door. Often I find myself using the wooden statue for my prayer. I will light a candle, stand on a prayer rug, and lift my arms in surrender while confessing personal human failings and other issues.

I struggle with the cost of taking my cross and loving Jesus more than family and friends. I struggle with spiritual values and the cost of remaining faithful to my ministry call. It is human nature to do so. So I invite you to linger with me through these verses and surrender whatever keeps you from taking your cross and following Jesus in your life.

For our prayer today, stand with arms upraised in silence. Let God guide your quiet time. Ask for a new outlook on everything.

Oh God, give us your divine perspective today as we linger in prayer. Help us take up our cross and follow where Jesus leads. We ask for more love for Christ. Amen.

† June 23 †
Even a cup of cold water
Matthew 10:40-42

One of my dearest friends never married. She loves little children. Neighborhood children adore her. Their parents trust her completely. Children call her the "Popsicle Lady." Her freezer is full of them. All the children know a simple knock on her door anytime of the day or evening will get them a smile and tasty, cool treat. They are always welcome and treated as valued, precious, special friends. My friend never complains as she cleans their sticky fingerprints off her furniture. She reminds me of Jesus, even though she usually gives the children frozen popsicles instead of cups of cold water.

Someday I imagine her getting a wonderful, heavenly reward for her special kindness to children. There are none too dirty or sticky. She delights in holding the little ones. Truly, her reward will be great.

God, teach us how to be kind and welcoming to people. Amen.

†   June 24   †

Doubt, faith, and encouragement
Matthew 11:1-6

We see today an honest picture of doubt by a real spiritual giant. John the Baptist was a great prophet and messenger of Jesus Christ. He was a man of great faith. Because of his prophetic messages, he was imprisoned. We find him languishing in prison. Even the strongest can experience doubt through isolation and loneliness. John has a very human response to his situation. He sends his loyal followers to find Jesus and ask a question that demonstrates his vulnerability and inner doubt. Is Jesus God's Sent One? Or should they wait for someone else?

Jesus offers a sensitive and encouraging reply to their earnest questions. Rather than chastise John's doubt, he sends them back with a blessing for the imprisoned prophet. John is given freedom to doubt and ask very honest questions through his painful ordeal. We have much to learn from this story.

God, give us the honesty of John the Baptist. Bless our doubts, increase our faith, and encourage us when we are languishing in isolation. Amen.

†   June 25   †

Greater than John the Baptist!
Matthew 11:11

After John's disciples are gone, Jesus begins teaching (Matthew 11:7-19). There is much to ponder. John the Baptist is God's honored prophet sent to announce the Messiah's coming. He was God's very special messenger and worthy of great honor, not imprisonment. Then Jesus said something astonishing. Even the least in heaven is greater than John the Baptist.

Sometimes we doubt our value to Christ. He loved and respected John the Baptist. John was a spiritual giant and great prophet. He has a very special place in heaven. Yet we too, have enormous value to God.

God, thank you for valuing us. Help us have the faith of John the Baptist. Amen.

✝ June 26 ✝

Confidence before God
Matthew 11:20-24

Jesus had performed numerous miracles. Today we find him strongly denouncing specific cities where many had not repented after seeing his miracles or hearing his message. Some cities are Jewish and others are Gentile. Then Jesus speaks of Sodom on the Day of Judgment and addresses his unrepentant listeners with a strongly worded admonition. For those unfamiliar with the Sodom and Gomorrah story (Genesis 19), it represents God's holy judgment towards rebellious humanity. It is worth noting that "woe" can also be translated as "doom."

We are the people of Korazin, Bethsaida, Capernaum, Tyre, Sidon, and Sodom. Just change the names of these cities to our local regions: Moscow, London, New York City, Jerusalem, Rome, Tokyo, Sydney, and others.

Through reading Matthew's Gospel, we have also heard the Jesus message of repentance and many miracles. Do we believe in the Miracle Worker? If so, we can have confidence before God.

Our timeless human condition calls us to inner repentance from sin, while turning towards God for restoration and renewal. Jesus is our bridge to God. We are called to life-sustaining belief in this Miraculous One. All of us have missed the mark in life. All of us need periodic moments of repentance and inner transformation. Through personal faith in Jesus, we can face the Day of Judgment without fear. Jesus can help us experience confidence before God.

God, hear our prayers. Help our unbelief. Amen.

✝ June 27 ✝

The wisdom of little children

Matthew 11:25-27

Truly God's ways are not ours. The little children will always lead us. Our adult wisdom and education can actually hinder our spiritual journey. We forget God is extremely approachable as a loving, heavenly Parent. We are invited to be God's children. Childlike faith will transform us. This is God's good pleasure. Jesus actually praises God for hiding spiritual treasure from wise and learned adults. The Son reveals God to the childlike in heart. Blessed are the children, for they shall see God.

Perhaps we need to reclaim our inner child for spiritual wholeness and healing. Or perhaps our inner child has been injured and/or betrayed by our earthly parents. Whatever our experience, God will never turn us away. God will never abuse or abandon us. God will never reject, ridicule, belittle, or demean us. God's loving arms are open to us. Perhaps we need a hug from the Dear One who invites us into childlike faith and trust. Consider using these simple body movements as part of your prayer: Gently lift your open arms to heaven. Slowly embrace yourself as a beloved child of God. Imagine God tenderly hugging you with love, joy, and delight.

Dear One, thank you for accepting and cherishing me as your beloved child. Help me love you in return with renewed trust and gratitude. Amen.

✝ June 28 ✝

For the weary and burdened

Matthew 11:28-30

Have you ever been exhausted? Burdened with many worries and anxieties? Stressed with inner turmoil and conflict? When was the last time you really rested and just breathed with God? When was the last time your soul felt full of rest?

Come to this soul teacher. Jesus' lessons are instantly available and free to every student. His yoke is easy and burden is light. This Teacher is gentle and humble in heart. He is available to all and offers profound rest for our souls. We can lay our burdens on him. He cares for us. Jesus is fully trustworthy. His very presence offers us spiritual hospitality and generosity. He offers us inner sanctuary.

Rest is good for our souls. Never underestimate the power of a nap. I have lived and worked with people who sometimes had to work more than twenty-four hours at a time. Some would be too exhausted to eat at the end of their shift. All they wanted to do was sleep. Sleep can produce miraculous restoration of perspective, strength, humor, courage, and endurance. Rest is a precious gift from God. For those who are sick and in pain, sleep can mean blessed relief from suffering. Rest rejuvenates. Exhaustion debilitates.

Rest brings us into wholeness and healing. Sometimes we just need to rest with God. Jesus invites us to rest in his presence through these gracious words of comfort and help.

Yes, God, I need this soul rest today. Amen.

✝   June 29   ✝

Lord of the Sabbath
Matthew 12:8

The disciples of Jesus were hungry. We find them traveling on the Jewish Sabbath. Then they broke religious laws by eating grain in the fields. The Pharisees (Jewish religious leaders) confront Jesus on the spot, "Look! Your disciples are doing what is unlawful on the Sabbath" (Matthew 12:2 NIV).

Jesus gives them a lesson from history and reinterprets their ancient story of beloved David. Many years ago, David was fleeing for his life. He and his companions illegally ate consecrated bread. Jesus hammers home his point and clearly lets it be known that "one greater than the temple is here." And then he quotes Hebrew scriptures (Hosea 6:6; Micah 6:6-8 NIV) to reinforce his teachings, "*I desire mercy, not sacrifice.*"

Jesus then makes a significant revolutionary statement about himself, "For the Son of Man is Lord of the Sabbath." The expression, "Son of Man," was Jesus' most common title for himself. It is found 81 times in the Gospels and was only used by Jesus. But what does it mean for twenty-first century readers unfamiliar with the Jewish theological understanding of this audacious and astonishing title? Why were some listeners outraged and religiously offended, and others overjoyed and eager to learn more?

For starters, the Son of Man is a mysterious heavenly figure found in the Old Testament book of Daniel (7:13-14), entrusted with divine authority, glory, and sovereign power from God for use during the final judgment of the world. This title is every bit as powerful as the theological title, "Christ," meaning Messiah, or God's anointed one. Jesus also used "Son of Man" as an expression of his humanity. He experienced hunger and thirst, discouragement and exhilaration, joy and sorrow, temptations and frustrations. This is why Jesus can fully identify with our human condition with sovereign power and compassion, helping us during our times of need.

Who is Jesus? He is obviously more than a healer and teacher. Claiming to be the "Son of Man" and "Lord of the Sabbath," he has the authority to overturn Sabbath laws. What will happen next? How does this affect our personal lives? Where are you in this story? Are you outraged and deeply offended by this teaching or eager to learn more?

God, I ask that you bless my understanding about Jesus and his self-proclaimed titles, "Son of Man" and "Lord of the Sabbath." Give me a renewed appreciation of Jesus and his teachings. Transform my life with this knowledge, I pray. Amen.

† June 30 †

Accused!

Matthew 12:9-14

Did Jesus walk into a trap? A man with a shriveled hand was in the synagogue. The rabbis prohibited healing on the Sabbath, unless it was feared that the victim would die before the next day. The Pharisees were looking for a reason to accuse Jesus. Jesus compassionately chose to heal the man with a shriveled hand on the Sabbath in the synagogue. The rest is history. The Pharisees begin plotting how they might kill Jesus.

What has Jesus done to deserve death? He has healed many, fed the multitudes and even raised a little girl from the dead. He has traveled to many cities, towns, and villages preaching and teaching. He has called people to repent from their sins and turn to God. People were astonished at his power and authority. Crowds pushed to get close and hear his wonderful words of life. Jesus brought a fresh message from God about faith, love, and hope. The religious authorities could not tolerate his teachings. He disrupted the status quo. Jesus claimed divine power and authority. He was "Lord of the Sabbath." The Pharisees decided he had to be destroyed.

So what about you? What do you think? Who is Jesus? Should he be put to death? Depending on your answer, then how does Jesus affect your life and spiritual journey?

God, perhaps our souls are shriveled with misunderstandings about Jesus. Show us where we are in this story. Amen.

† July 1 †

God's hope for the world

Matthew 12:15-21

Today's readings include the words of the prophet named Isaiah, who had spoken about Jesus centuries earlier. Jesus is God's beloved servant and chosen messenger. God is enormously pleased with Jesus. Jesus has a mission of bringing justice to the nations. He is God's hope for the world. Nations will hope in his name. Jesus came for all people, from every culture, nation, ethnic background, sexual orientation, and religious tradition.

After the miraculous healing in the synagogue of a man with a shriveled hand, the Pharisees met and began plotting to destroy Jesus. Their response is in sharp contrast to the compassion of Christ.

As Jesus left for a safer area, the eager crowds followed him. Even while in danger, Jesus stopped and cured all of them. As he healed people, he ordered them to keep quiet about his whereabouts. Jesus was no fool. He wisely chose to leave harm's way, in order to minister for another day. It was not his time to die.

There is something to be learned from his example. Sometimes confrontation is immediately needed. At other times, we would be wise to assess the risks and possible dangers of the situation at hand. Wisdom, prudence, and common sense may lead us to hope, and to perhaps wait for justice, one more complete than is possible for people to deliver.

Consider an experiment with God. Ask for new ears to hear the words of hope and justice that Jesus offers us. Ask for new eyes to see the wonder of Christ and for a compassionate heart for those who suffer. Expect the Spirit of God to bless you.

God, help us pray with new awareness of Jesus in our lives. Amen.

† July 2 †

Jesus and Beelzebul
Matthew 12:22-28

The crowds continued to be amazed by Jesus. They wondered if he was the one of whom the prophet Isaiah spoke. Jesus mystified and intrigued them. Who was he? The crowds wondered out loud if he could possibly be the Messiah, the "Son of David." But the Pharisees disagreed and conspired for his death. They accused Jesus of being the evil ruler of demons before the marveling crowds. Jesus knew their thoughts and spoke with tremendous insight. A kingdom divided against itself cannot survive. Evil cannot cast out evil. Only the Spirit of the living God can cast out evil. If Jesus is casting out demons by God-power, then God is in our midst.

I have always wondered what the newly healed formerly blind and mute man believed about Jesus. Surely his first spoken words were of deep gratitude. He probably would have been horrified to realize religious authorities were planning to destroy his compassionate healer. His miracle was obviously from God.

Could God be in our midst today? Do we need new eyes and new ears to experience the Spirit of God in our lives? Where are we in the story? Perhaps we identify with the blind and mute individual. Perhaps we identify with the Pharisees and resist God's voice when it extends beyond our religious understandings. The Pharisees were spiritually blind and obtuse when it came to Jesus, the compassionate Healer.

God, give us new eyes and ears of faith to experience Jesus Christ. Amen.

† July 3 †

Speaking against the Holy Spirit
Matthew 12:29-32

Ask many questions while reading sacred words. Our answers may be revealing and transforming. When I read these verses, I find myself wondering if I am with Jesus or against him. Am I serving him or serving myself? What is this unpardonable sin against the Holy Spirit? Do I have it in my own life? Could I be in spiritual danger? Other gospel writers mention this confusing sin (Mark 3:28-29; Luke 12:10), but what does it mean for my time in world history? Jesus spoke in the first century. Are these words still culturally relevant? I believe they are timeless. The challenge is to interpret them with cultural relevance for each generation.

Have we ever spoken against the Holy Spirit of God? F. F. Bruce notes that literature abounds with stories about people who commit "the unpardonable sin." He suggests we read these passages with care. Matthew's Gospel seems to imply that unforgivable sin is to deliberately shut one's eyes to the light and to call good evil. But quite honestly, many Biblical scholars are in disagreement about what this actually means. If they are in disagreement, what hope do we have for understanding the message?

Living without full understanding can actually create a healthy tension for growing moments of introspection and reflection. A helpful spiritual practice is when in doubt, stay with the passages or parts that are clearly understood. Revelation is progressive and some answers may not be fully understood this side of eternity.

With this said, it is clear that we are to identify with Jesus while living on this earth. If our spiritual anchors are set deep in the foundation of Christ, clear answers will come in God's time and ways. We are all works of grace in progress. Be patient! God is not finished with us yet. I am confident that all who chose to identify with Jesus have nothing to worry about with this passage.

God, I do not have all the answers I would like to have with these verses. But I clearly understand I am for Jesus. Help me live in such a way that this is clear. Forgive the sin in my life and help me not blaspheme against your Spirit. Amen.

† July 4 †

Our words and deeds
Matthew 12:33-37

I marvel at the bluntness of Jesus. He calls his religious critics vipers or evil snakes directly to their face. Perhaps this is why so many are not neutral about him. I respect his directness. It is such a contrast to his enemies who met secretly while scheming against him. But there is more to this admonition addressed to the religious authorities of his day. There is something for us across the centuries.

Our mouths speak from the abundance of our hearts. Good begets good. Evil begets evil. Our words are powerful. They can heal or harm. Even the most careless words can have long lasting effects. Once spoken, they cannot be taken back. And even when words are overheard by accident, they transform lives.

A future day of judgment comes for all of us. Every careless word will be revisited. Our words will come back to us. They will haunt some and edify others. Be careful of what you speak. Silence can be golden. Let your words be seasoned with wisdom, prudence, love, and truth. Rash words cause deep regret.

From time to time, people come to me for spiritual direction. The temptation to speak personal words of advice is sometimes overwhelming. My sincere words could actually hinder someone's spiritual journey towards healing. Sometimes it is better for me to speak less and listen more closely.

But it is also important to have our words reflected back at us. They mirror our hearts and speak volumes of our spiritual condition. Words of slander, malice, and abusive language reflect and reveal our true heart condition.

The rich words of Christ can help transform the spoken and unspoken words in our hearts. Let Christ's words fill the inner chapel of your hearts.

God, help us choose our words carefully today and think twice before we speak. Amen.

† July 5 †

Greater than Solomon!
Matthew 12:38-45

Who among us has not asked God for signs and answers to our prayers and spiritual quests for meaning? The answer Jesus gave two thousand years ago continues to be relevant today. He refers us to the Hebrew scriptures in the stories of Jonah, Solomon, and the Queen of the Sheba.

Jonah is a profound story of one man's rebellion and ethnic prejudice in the face of God's compassion and willingness to forgive an evil people (from Nineveh). Children are often told the story of how Jonah was swallowed up by a great fish. He was held captive in the belly of the fish for three days and nights. Even when he was released from the fish to do what God commanded him to do, he was a reluctant prophet who detested the people to whom he was sent. The people of Nineveh listened to Jonah's message, repented of their sins, and found life. Jesus used this story to indirectly refer to his future death and burial for three days in the tomb. This would be his sign to the religious leaders; he would rise from the dead after three days in the grave.

The Queen of Sheba was a wise queen who traveled a great distance to learn even more wisdom from King Solomon (1 Kings 10:1-13; 2 Chronicles 9:1-12). She was willing to go to the ends of the earth to find truth and life-sustaining knowledge to bring back to her people.

The Pharisees had asked for a miraculous sign. Jesus offered them, and offers us, the Easter miracle. Death is conquered through the empty tomb.

Oh God, these old stories bring us exciting new perspectives. Help us learn from the mistakes and prejudices of Jonah. Encourage our pursuit of wisdom and excellence through the Queen of Sheba's example. Empower us with the wisdom of Solomon. All three point us to Christ. Through Jesus Christ, teach us resurrection hope. Amen.

† July 6 †
God's family
Matthew 12:46-50

Have you ever been curious about what Jesus' mother and brothers wanted to say? Were they worried for his safety? Did they want to warn him to be careful? Perhaps they wished to give him an encouraging word of affirmation and encouragement. I have always wondered if his mother wanted to remind Jesus to take time to eat and rest. We will never know.

We do know that Jesus has just taught us a new understanding of God's family values. God's family is generously expanded for all wanting to follow God's will. There is room at God's table for each of us. We are included in the beauty of all our human diversity. So live as a child of God. Live in close relationship with other family members. Get to know each other. Welcome to the family of God!

God, what does it mean to be in your family? Show us how to live in your will. Amen.

† July 7 †
The parable of the sower
Matthew 13:1-9

Sometimes we forget Jesus was a famed teacher. Such great crowds gathered around him in this event, that he had to get into a small boat in order to be heard by the eager people. He taught many things in parables. Parables are stories with a message. Through the use of parables, he taught those who could not read and who did not have access to books. These timeless parables are worth reclaiming in our lives. They help us listen and learn new truths and insights about God.

We are often too busy to listen. Listening is a lost art. I invite your holy and wholly listening to this parable over the next few days. Consider centering breath prayers with the word "listen." Listen for God's whisper in each part of this parable. Listen to Jesus and think about what he might be teaching as he tells us about the seeds in the four different kinds of ground. What kind of spiritual soil is in our hearts as we listen to Jesus today?

The parable of the sower reveals the heart of the Gospel. Can you find it? Meister Johann Eckhart (1260-1328), a Christian mystic, once wrote, "The seed of God is in us. Given an intelligent and hard-working farmer, it will thrive and grow up to God, whose seed it is, and, accordingly, its fruit will be God-nature."

God, help us to listen to your complete message and to learn the lesson that you teach. Amen.

† July 8 †

Spiritual dullness

Matthew 13:10-15

Spiritual dullness has always been among us. If we would truly hear with our ears and look with our eyes, and understand with our hearts and turn from the errors of our ways, God would heal us beyond our wildest dreams.

Many of us struggle with honest introspection. We often hear and see ourselves selectively. As a result, our hearts dull to God's full truth and revelation. Our ears become spiritually hard of hearing and, yes, we become spiritually blind to God.

I would personally prefer to think of myself as spiritually clever and astute. Yet in lingering quiet moments of prayer and meditation, silence is truly the greatest revelation. Silence can speak louder than words and reveal the inner cracks and blemishes of a soul grown dull and jaded. My spiritual direction colleagues and friends all realize we have great gifts of self-deception. We need spiritual friends for accountability and encouragement. We need those who care enough to question if we are becoming dull of heart.

I have found in my own life that I need to intentionally seek out those friends and colleagues, individually and in community. Those who love me may mention I seem to be working all the time. One friend would call and encourage me to take an afternoon off, or to take a walk. These are refreshing moments. When deep fatigue or chronic tiredness pervades, it is helpful for me to take a nap, review my eating and exercise habits. A little bit of self-care can work wonders, and healthy perspective can return. All these simple things affect my daily inner life. Spiritual alertness and awareness can be improved dramatically.

Are there identifiable factors that dull you to the power of God's healing words from taking root in the soil of your hearts? If so, pray from your heart and be encouraged. God wishes to bring us into alertness and restore our spiritual joy.

God, help us be alert and open to you. Help us listen and give us understanding. Amen.

† July 9 †

Blessed are your eyes

Matthew 13:16-17

God's deepest blessing is ours when we hear, see, and respond with spiritual alertness and willingness. Many faithful saints across the centuries have longed to see and hear what we have been given through the Bible. We have the teachings of Jesus to help us along our path of spiritual empowerment. These wonderful words of life are our blessing from God.

Do you want to be blessed with spiritual sight and hearing? Do you want to understand and live what the ancients longed for but did not have? Are you ready for your blessing? Then begin lingering in the Gospels as a resource for inner strength and joy. Woodrow Wilson is credited with saying, "I am sorry for those who do not read the Bible every day. I wonder why they deprive themselves of the strength and pleasure."

Perhaps fatigue, stress-filled events, or illness limits or detracts from your reading abilities. Consider lingering in the Gospels or the Psalms. Perhaps a word, a phrase, or a verse will bless you with strength for your day. Focus on getting through one day at a time, even when the day feels overwhelming. And you will be blessed with what many people of faith yearned to see and hear through your Bible reading.

God, bless us with spiritual strength, clarity, and responsiveness! Amen.

†   July 10   †

Listen again

Matthew 13:18-22

When our hearts and ears are open and receptive to understanding, we will someday harvest spiritual results in God's way and God's timing. But first we need to be honest with God about the rocks, weeds, and thorns in the soil in our hearts.

Where are we in this parable? What is the soil of our hearts? Do we need God to replant spiritual seed in our souls? Have we lost our understanding? Have we fallen away in trouble or persecution? Have the cares of this world and the lure of wealth choked our spiritual lives? Every life has a story. What is our story? Perhaps our hearts need replanting with the illuminating and inspiring life giving words.

I learned to better listen to the word of God in my life when I began to walk the labyrinth, a very old spiritual tradition. Several months ago, I made a labyrinth in our yard. They are amazingly easy to make when you know the basic pattern. [62] With a stick or broom handle, it is a simple matter to draw the path in the earth. After the path was drawn, finding sticks, stones, and seashells to line the path was even easier. When in the labyrinth, the single path leads the walker into the center. It is a wonderful meditation tool. St. Augustine is quoted as saying, *Solvitur ambulando*, ("It is solved by walking").

This seems to be so in my own life. I have been noticing that during the summer, weeds seem to sprout overnight in the labyrinth. The weeds seem to proliferate in the good soil and I need to periodically get out in the dirt! Pulling weeds on my hands and knees is good for the labyrinth and good for my soul. The weed roots often extend for great lengths under the topsoil.

So it is with our own souls. We need to carefully and lovingly weed and cultivate the soil of our hearts. So get in some spiritual dirt today. Consider getting on your hands and knees. Dirt is full of surprises.

---

[62] Please visit the Labyrinth Society Web site at www.labyrinthsociety.org.

You may be surprised by God and surprised by joy as you linger thoughtfully with this parable. Listen to it again and again, and let God be your Gardener.

God, sow your good seed in our hearts. Plow the soil of our souls. Help us listen again and understand. Amen.

† July 11 †

Hear and understand

Matthew 13:23

For twenty years I have lived mostly in apartment buildings. I have had little opportunity to dig in the dirt and grow anything other than flowers and cacti on the balcony – until the year when I moved into a house with a yard. I was surprised at the amount of effort required in basic yard work. During summer months, the lawn needs watering, mowing, and weeding on a weekly basis. The soil in our yard is not good and requires fertilizer and other additives throughout the year. Previous renters had constantly struggled with the lawn and flower garden.

The lawn and garden are teaching me about the "good soil" to which this parable refers. Even with the best heart soil, our hearts still need regular care and attention just like the soil of our fields, lawns, and gardens. We need to become spiritual gardeners. Everyone has spiritual weeds to be pulled. We all need pruning to promote new, healthy, and abundant growth in God. If we neglect the garden in our hearts, our life with God will suffer. Now some growth takes time, labor, commitment, and patience if we want to bear good fruit. There are no short cuts in the garden.

Certainly my inexperience is obvious to neighbors. Both yard and garden constantly improve as I learn the rhythms of growth and bloom, fertilization and care. Various stores in town offer free gardening classes, and many books and Internet resources offer practical wisdom. Best of all, when I ask for help neighbors are more than happy to loan tools and share advice based on years of experience. One neighbor in particular has a green thumb. His love for the earth and growing things is beautiful. He always has a moment to walk over, look at a plant, and make a helpful suggestion to improve the garden. I call him Saint Harold.

The bottom line is this: if we wish to have a fruitful and bountiful spiritual harvest in our lives, we need to cultivate the soil of our hearts with prayer, sacred words, spiritual readings, and affirming community, and to be in step with the rhythms of life. Very few people do all these things well by themselves. Most of us need mentoring in the spiritual life by the more seasoned, experienced gardeners of the spirit. This is an important aspect of Christian discipleship. Disciples mentor young babes in the faith and help each other grow up in Christian maturity and service and yes, accountability.

In my home, we have a tile that has the saying, "Plant a garden and magic will grow." Yes, magic will grow! But magic grows best with loving, thoughtful, committed, frequent care.

God, bless our hearing and understanding with this parable. Amen.

† July 12 †

Weeds

Matthew 13:24-30

The parable reminds us that God is in control and knows the tactics of the evil enemy very well indeed. God is an eternal strategist, patiently giving people an opportunity to respond to the Gospel and turn from evil before the day of reckoning, a spiritual harvesting. People of faith understand there will someday be a judgment day. Followers of Christ need not fear.

Imagine it is your job to harvest this field of weeds and grain. Even with the sage advice of the householder we realize the kingdom of heaven is touched by enemies armed with the intent to harm, destroy, and sabotage the work of God in the world. Like the householder, we are in a struggle of good versus evil. Evil may begin in subtle ways, extending its tentacles of influence before we notice. Those who work for God are sometimes at a loss for knowing how to respond to the malicious deeds of sin and destruction, but this particular householder did not forget to have faith or about how to care for his crop.

What does this story mean in our lives today? How are we living the kingdom of heaven on earth? Are we identifying evil and drawing on wise, God-focused advice to extinguish it? Are we making the world a better place by how we live? Write your thoughts and prayers in a journal. Ask God for insight and new direction.

The next six parables specifically illuminate spiritual truths about the kingdom of heaven, a new direction for all the faithful – straight or gay, Christian or not. The parables bring us into the heartbeat and soul of the message of Jesus and help us understand God's strategy and God's love. Each of the parables begins with this simple phrase, "The kingdom of heaven is like. . . ." If you have ever wondered what heaven was like or what heaven on earth could look like, read on through the next reflections. These six parables are simple enough for a child, yet profound enough to offer adults a lifetime of insights.

God, open our hearts to respond to you. Bring us into a fuller understanding of how we should be living your kingdom of heaven on earth today. Bless us as we work for good and fight evil in our world. Amen.

†   July 13   †

The truth of the mustard seed
Matthew 13:31-32

I had the most amazing prayer experience today while walking the labyrinth in my yard. For those unfamiliar with labyrinths, they are a cherished form of walking meditation, consisting of a single curving, twisting path often based on a sacred geometry, and can be made from all kinds of materials. For thousands of years people from many different cultures have enjoyed the practice of walking labyrinths. Labyrinths differ from mazes. Mazes require choices and problem solving. The maze walker might not find the center. The labyrinth only has one path, which always brings you to the center, a place to linger, meditate, reflect, and pray.

I love walking them in the early morning. Often I will pause every few steps and just enjoy looking and listening to the glorious sights and sounds of birds singing, chirping, and flitting about as they happily perch among the tree branches. Woodpeckers, wrens, thrushes, sparrows, robins, and crows daily fill the air with their songs. Today I thought of this parable of the mustard seed and how the birds of the air come and sit in the branches of a mustard tree.

The mustard seed was the smallest known seed used by first century Palestinian farmers and gardeners. When conditions were favorable, the plant could grow ten feet in height. The smallest seed becomes the largest plant. The kingdom of God is like a mustard seed. People from every nation, tribe, culture, ethnic identity, language, economic background, political persuasion and sexual orientation can find a joyous welcome into God's realm through this glorious parable and their local birds.

God, help us pray with the birds today to better understand and experience our beloved welcome into the kingdom of heaven. Amen.

For more labyrinth information, several excellent web sites are www.labyrinthsociety.org, www.geomancy.org, www.labyrinthproject.com, a worldwide web labyrinth locator is at www.gracecom.org, and www.relax4life.com (which is very LGBT friendly).

---

† July 14 †

Heavenly yeast

Matthew 13:33-35

My father was the bread baker in the house while I was growing up. He would always make bread during the winter when the weather would slow the pace of his construction work. We would come home from school to find fresh, hot bread waiting for us. That was always a wonderful treat! He would mix the yeast into the dough and knead it thoroughly with his strong, capable hands before baking it.

But the yeast needs to be good. I remember the disappointment of making bread with old yeast. It did not rise or taste good, and eventually it was thrown out for the birds.

The kingdom of heaven is like yeast as it mixes and mixes with the dough. What a wonderful image of God kneading the universe and our lives with heavenly yeast of faith, hope, and love. God is the master bread maker of heaven. God's spirit is the yeast of our lives, permeating every fiber and cell of our being. We are in good hands with the Almighty. Trust God to knead your soul thoroughly!

God, let your Spirit permeate our lives as yeast permeates dough. Amen.

† July 15 †

Weeds explained

Matthew 13:36-43

The gospel has always comforted the afflicted and afflicted the comfortable. The parable is about choices and consequences. Some readers will be highly offended. Others will be challenged. Few of us will be indifferent or neutral. You might disagree with my understanding. Consider writing your responses to this parable and the explanation in your journal as part of your prayer today.

Jesus is the one sowing the good seed of God in the world. The good seeds are the people who follow Jesus. The weeds are people from the evil one. And that enemy has a name. The devil. In other places in the Bible, the devil is called the father of lies, an imposter, the tempter, and accuser.

Someday the world as we know it will come to an end. Angels will harvest all the good seed sown in the world. The weeds will be pulled up and burned. All that causes sin and does evil will be thrown into the fiery furnace where weeping and gnashing of teeth will be heard forever. Good will triumph eternally over evil in the kingdom of our heavenly Parent. Hear the word of Christ. Listen.

Who does Jesus think he is to say such things? Perhaps the more important question is, who do we think he is to say such things? Our answers to these questions might teach us something about our lives. Where are we in the parable? What are we going to do about it?

God, what do I believe about Jesus? Where am I in this parable? Amen.

† July 16 †

Hidden treasure
Matthew 13:44

The kingdom of heaven is hidden treasure worth everything we have. It is worth all our money, our relationships, our material things, and personal hopes, dreams, and ambition. It is for those who seek God. God delights in being found and loved. Some time ago, an e-mail came to me with a saying that I believe summarizes what Jesus is teaching us with this parable, "To seek God is the greatest of all adventures; to find God is the greatest of all achievements; to fall in love with God is the greatest of all romances."

God is wonderful to be with. God is easily found. All we have to do is open the eyes of our heart. Let God surprise you with joy today. Seek, find, and fall in love with God. This is worth everything! Your life will be changed forever.

God, bless us with the joy of knowing you personally. Amen.

† July 17 †

Fine pearls
Matthew 13:45-46

I have a bumper sticker on my car that invites people to commit random acts of kindness and senseless acts of beauty. I have often thought that the saying should be changed to commit many acts of kindness and constant acts of beauty.

The world is full of many beautiful things. Sunrises and sunsets are freely available on a daily basis for those with the eyes to see. I once had a blind roommate who taught me about this. She lost her sight as a child, but never forgot her colors. She was not afraid to ask her sighted friends to describe the skies and everything they saw.

The pearl merchant brings us a different perspective. He was an expert in his field who appreciated priceless treasure. The kingdom of heaven is like a pearl merchant who finds one pearl of enormous value. It is worth all his earthly possessions.

A personal relationship with God is the most valuable relationship we can have in this world. But God cannot be bought. The good news of God is freely available to the poorest person in the world. Rich or poor, God is lovely to be with. A life with God is worth everything. It is like finding one pearl of great value.

God, thank you for being beautiful in a world that can sometimes be ugly. Amen.

† July 18 †

Fishing nets

Matthew 13:47-50

Readers may easily skim over selected parts of the teachings of Jesus when the teachings make us uncomfortable. Anything with judgment, consequences, weeping, and the end of time as we know it should cause us to pause and ask some questions. What does this mean? Where am I in this story? What is Jesus saying? Does this mean anything in my life? Is there something I need to change?

Once again we learn that the kingdom of heaven is huge, like the largest fishing net the world will ever know. Every kind of fish will be caught and eventually be sorted. Good fish will be kept, but the bad fish will be thrown away at the end of time. A day of judgment will come. Evil will be thrown into the fire where there will be weeping and gnashing of teeth.

Where are we in this parable? Diogenes (412-323 BC), a Greek philosopher, once said, "We have two ears and only one tongue in order that we hear more and speak less." Certainly we can argue this parable's meaning. Today, let us just hear it.

God, let me just sit with this parable today and hear it with new understanding. Amen.

† July 19 †

New and old treasures

Matthew 13:51-52

One commentary suggests these verses specifically referred to the Jewish teachers of the law during the time of Jesus. The teachers had been trained in the ancient Hebrew scriptures. With the kingdom of heaven teachings of Jesus, they had now been given new treasure. Perhaps that is correct. Yet I think there is also something for us in the twenty-first century. This is a teaching for all who chose to follow Jesus.

"To acquire knowledge, one must study." The Gospels are worth our time and effort to study. They bring us spiritual treasure. So I offer this insight. Accept it if you can. As we read about the kingdom of heaven through the Gospels, we are blessed with new spiritual wealth. Each of us can informally teach others in different areas of our lives. As we live, work, converse, share ideas and insights, these wonderful words of life in the Gospels can bring relevance to our world.

Listed in the Guinness Book of World Records Hall of Fame under "Highest IQ," popular columnist of *Parade Magazine* and noted host of the weekly "Ask Marilyn" segment for CBS television evening news in New York, Marilyn Vos Savant offers this profound insight for us, "[T]o acquire wisdom, one must observe." [63] If you desire wisdom, observe the life of Christ in addition to studying his words. Jesus walked his talk. He led by example. Jesus never asked his followers to do what he himself was unwilling to do.

Knowledge and wisdom can be ours. All of us are offered spiritual treasures through reading the Gospels.

God, fill our storehouses with your treasures. Help us generously share our spiritual wealth with others. Amen.

---

[63] Found on http://quotationspage.com/subjects/wisdom/ quoting from http://askmarilyn.com.

† July 20 †

Rejection

Matthew 13:53-58

Yes, it is very hard to return to our hometowns and experience rejection by those we know and love. Yes, Jesus was the local person who achieved fame through his teachings and miracles. The townspeople were very human in their angry rejection of him. Jesus upset their religion. He taught with an authority that infuriated religious leaders of his day. Not only did he heal physical infirmities, but he also preached about sin, repentance, and God's judgment. Jesus continually called people to follow his leadership. Anger was their honest response to Jesus. But what really caused their anger?

I believe it was their unbelief. To the townspeople, Jesus was just the kid next door. His family was of humble means. Rumors had circulated about the legitimacy of his birth for years. His brothers and sisters were ordinary common folk. The townspeople's astonishment at the wisdom and miracles that Jesus offered quickly turned to fury. They took personal offense at him. Jesus was "amazed at their lack of faith" (Mark 6:1-6 NIV) and as a result, performed only a few great miracles.

Where are we in the story? Is unbelief blocking God's transforming work in our lives? I wonder if unbelief is limiting God's mighty power and work in my own life. What about you?

God, hear our prayers. Amen.

† July 21 †

Revenge

Matthew 14:8

John the Baptist had been languishing in jail for some time. We last saw him as he struggled with doubt and despair while in isolation (reflections for June 24 and June 25, Matthew 11:1-14). John was initially imprisoned for speaking candidly. Powerful people did not want to hear his sincerity. They imprisoned him. And now he dies for his truth telling.

The tragic story is found in the first twelve verses of Matthew 14. Herod Antipas is a powerful man in government. He is having a birthday party. The daughter of his current wife dances sensually for the guests. Herod was so impressed that he promised to give Salome whatever she asked. The girl immediately asked her mother, Herodias, for guidance. Salome could have requested and received enormous wealth and power. But her mother's immediate response was clearly tainted by hate and revenge. The Baptist had dared to publicly disapprove of her sordid second marriage when she left her former husband for his brother, Herod Antipas. Marriage to one's brother's wife while the brother was still living was clearly forbidden by Mosaic Law (Leviticus 18:16). In Herodias' mind, this was a heaven sent opportunity to permanently silence any public religious condemnation regarding her marriage that had been generated by this troublesome prophet. Prompted by her mother, the obedient daughter publicly asks Herod for John's head on a platter.

Herod is deeply distressed, but he caves in to this gruesome request. Soldiers march to the prison and behead John. His head was brought in on a plate and given to the girl who then gives it to her mother. John's grieving followers bury his headless body and then go and tell Jesus.

Truth is not always popular, safe, or easy to tell.

God, why did you allow this to happen to faithful John? Why do bad things happen to good people? Where are you in the midst of evil? Amen.

✝   **July 22**   ✝

Grief

Matthew 14:13

Jesus went to a private and solitary place to grieve the death of beloved John the Baptist. John had baptized Jesus at the beginning of his earthly ministry, referred his disciples to Jesus, and courageously called people to repentance. John clearly understood he was not worthy to untie even the thongs on Jesus' sandals. John was a great prophet. He was also a friend, cousin, and colleague. Jesus would miss him. We see a picture of good grief. Jesus withdrew to a private place to grieve before the crowds would surround him with their neediness and demands on his time.

Jesus reveals his vulnerability in his mourning and offers us a healthy example of self-care. He did not pretend everything was fine. He sought some privacy. We need moments of privacy and solitude with our deep feelings. Sometimes we all need to get away for a time and sit with our emotions.

The crowds, eager to see and hear Jesus, learn of his whereabouts and travel on foot from many towns to find him. How will Jesus respond to them in his raw grief?

Help us find private places to pray for a few minutes today, God. Amen.

† July 23 †

Compassion and abundance
Matthew 14:14-21

It was quite a large crowd. They pushed and shoved to get closer to Jesus. They probably did not realize Jesus was deep in grief. The sick clamored for his touch. Even in his sorrow, Jesus compassionately healed them all. It must have been a long and arduous day. Evening approached and the practical disciples remind Jesus they were in a remote place. The crowds needed to go away and find food. And we see yet another example of the compassion of God in action. Jesus refuses to send them away hungry. He challenges his inner circle of disciples to feed them. All they had were a couple of fish and some loaves of bread.

The miracle of loaves and fishes never ceases to amaze me. The people sat down as directed. Jesus took the bits of food and gave thanks to God. The astonished disciples distributed the food. All who ate were satisfied. Basketfuls of broken pieces of food were left over. Thousands had been fed. Critics will say the massive crowd unselfishly shared their food among themselves, inspired by the giving of Jesus and the disciples. But I personally believe God is fully capable of multiplying our smallest gifts into abundance. And this generous God delights in healing broken, fragmented, hurting humanity.

Jesus has been called many things in Matthew's Gospel. He is teacher, healer, miracle worker, prophet, friend, son, spiritual leader, and much more. John's Gospel gives us another name for this amazing one. Jesus is the bread of life. All who hunger and thirst for God will be satisfied in his company.

God, satisfy the hunger in our souls with the words of Jesus Christ in the Gospels. Amen.

† **July 24** †

Take courage

Matthew 14:22-27

I have been at sea in rough and stormy weather. I have stood watches throughout the night. Who would not be terrified to see someone walking on the water? Exhaustion combined with fear is easily experienced by all of us. These paralyzing feelings leave us vulnerable to terror, doubt, and disbelief.

I have also heard many sermons on these verses criticizing the terrified disciples. After all, they had been with Jesus for a long time. They had lingered with his remarkable words, enjoyed his friendship, marveled at his miracles, and had participated in miraculous ministries. You would think nothing would surprise them about Jesus at this point in their lives.

We see Jesus in his humanity and divinity. Jesus now needs time alone. After sending the crowd home, Jesus sends the disciples away so he could go up on the mountain and pray by himself. He needed to be alone with his feelings and to pray without interruption. The disciples obeyed him and began sailing their boat to the other side of the lake. It was difficult sailing against the wind and the waves, but they were making progress. Late in the night, they see Jesus walking on the water towards them and they are terrified.

Jesus says, "Take courage. It is I. Do not be afraid." The Bible encourages us not to be afraid in more than three hundred places. We are to release our fear and trust Jesus, God's water walker.

God, help us take courage and not fear in the strong, protective presence of Jesus Christ. Amen.

† July 25 †
Seeing is believing
Matthew 14:28-33

I love this story and greatly admire Peter for his impulsiveness. I probably would have remained in the wildly rocking boat being battered and bruised. But Peter gives us a lesson in courage and faith. As long as he fixed his eyes on Jesus, he walked on the water without fear. But when he saw the wind and the waves, he began to fear and sink. He cried out, "Lord, save me!" Rather than let him flounder in the water, Jesus immediately rescues him and asks why did he doubt. They climb into the boat and the wind becomes still.

Have you ever cried out to Jesus in panic and need? Will you consider worshiping Jesus as God's Son? We all need to be saved. Jesus will immediately reach out to us. And even nature obeys him. Our highest calling is to worship God through Jesus Christ.

God, we join the disciples in worship. Amen.

† July 26 †
Who is Jesus?
Matthew 14:34-36

People brought their sick friends and family members to Jesus. They stopped their daily routines and rushed to him. Many desperate ones begged just to touch the edge of his cloak for healing. All who touched him were healed. Once again we see the fame of the Miracle Healer.

A cherished practice of scripture reading is to imagine ourselves in the Gospel stories. Be present in the crowd. Perhaps you are sick and needing a touch from Jesus. Or perhaps someone you love is gravely ill. If only you could bring your loved one close enough to touch the Healer! Write down your thoughts and feelings describing the scene. Imagine Jesus saying something healing to you. What is it like being with the Healer? Let this be part of your prayer.

God, let us touch Jesus and be healed in our spirits today. Amen.

† **July 27** †

Traditions

Matthew 15:1-9

This story *should* make us uncomfortable. We all have cherished traditions that have stood the test of time, but some traditions can in fact be called sacred cows. When something is done more for comfort and out of habit than renewing a fresh connection with the spirit, that is known as a sacred cow. All of our cherished traditions certainly are well intentioned, but sometimes they can actually keep us from obeying the Spirit of God.

This is the situation we find as we read of these Pharisees and teachers of the law. They deeply loved God and earnestly desired to obey every jot and tittle of their religious law. In their religious zealousness, they lost touch with basic human kindness and responsibility towards even their parents. They honored their tradition more than God and became hypocrites through their religious practices.

The prophet Isaiah prophesied about both them and us. It is easy to honor God with our mouths, but our hearts are distant from God. We worship in vain and our teachings are human rules, not God's rules.

Cherished human traditions can both help and hinder our spiritual lives. When they hinder us, we limit others and ourselves from experiencing God's mighty power.

Do we find ourselves in this story? Where? Let us sit with God and let these words linger in our hearts. Perhaps we need to let some cherished traditions and preconceived biases go. Perhaps we need a new look at God and how our religion affects our spirituality. "Sacred cows make the tastiest hamburgers," as the popular saying goes. Perhaps we need a fresh taste of God today.

God, let our hearts be very close to you as we reexamine our religious traditions and our roles in them. Amen.

✝ July 28 ✝
Listen and understand
Matthew 15:10-11

Jesus' own disciples did not understand, so Jesus had to explain the lesson more fully. What makes us unclean are the thoughts of our hearts. Jesus reminds us that from our hearts come "evil thoughts, sexual immorality, theft, murder, adultery, greed, malice, deceit, lewdness, envy, slander, arrogance, and folly" (Mark 7:21-22). People have not changed over the centuries.

My mother frequently said during my childhood that if people could read others' thoughts we would all certainly be in trouble. We may look saintly on the outside, but our thoughts might be quite unsaintly on the inside. It is possible to fool others, but God knows our hearts.

So here is our challenge. Ancient Jewish religious law was concerned with sins of the outward acts. Jesus is concerned with our impure hearts. Even our thoughts are spiritual concerns. We all need spiritual cardiac care through the words of Christ and the Spirit of God. Mahatma Gandhi said, "It is for us to make the effort. The result will always be in God's hands" (1931 press release after the Round Table Conference). If we make the effort to clean our inner thoughts and heart, God will empower our efforts and bless our intent.

Perhaps our prayers should follow the example of the Psalmist who prayed, "Have mercy on me, O God, according to your unfailing love; according to your great compassion blot out my transgressions. Wash away all my iniquity and cleanse me from my sin . . . you teach me wisdom in the inmost place. Cleanse me . . . wash me. . . . Hide your face from sins and blot out all my iniquity. Create in me a pure heart, O God, and renew a steadfast spirit within me" (Psalm 51:1-10 NIV).

God, examine and know our innermost thoughts. Let us know if any impure thing is affecting our inner hearts. Wash and cleanse us of our inner faults. Bless us with a renewed spirit and inner joy. Amen.

†   July 29   †

Difficult to be neutral

Matthew 15:12-14

The disciples were deeply concerned that the Pharisees, powerful religious leaders, were personally offended at Jesus. The Pharisees zealously obeyed God's laws. They were deeply religious people who dedicated their lives to their faith. Who did Jesus think he was to say the things that he did? It is difficult to be neutral about Jesus and his teachings. His teachings continue to console the suffering and trouble the complacent and indifferent.

Jesus also challenges the comfort zone of the disciples. He tells them to leave their spiritually blind religious guides before they both fall into a pit. The religious ones had become blind towards God. The blind were leading the blind. Do not allow yourself to follow spiritually blind leaders, but follow Jesus Christ, the Light of the World.

It is very hard to leave cherished religious leaders who cannot see Jesus for who he is. Even conservative and zealous Christian leaders can become blind in this way. We forget Jesus came for all people. This includes the outcasts, marginalized, rejected, and forgotten people that formal religion is sometimes reluctant and disinclined to include and embrace. It is very easy to become spiritually blind to this simple truth.

Much of my ministry is offering what I call "damage control" among sexual minorities who have followed religious leaders and traditions that falsely labeled them as unclean, abominations, and perversions. Because of their former leaders' well-intended but damaging teachings, many now live lives with deep spiritual injuries. The most important truth in the Bible is that God is deeply in love with us. Some are actually amazed to realize that their sexual orientation is actually a blessing and gift from God. We are God's dearly beloved people. Jesus Christ invites each of us to live with peace and wholeness as we are, as God's beloved people.

Open your eyes. See yourselves and others in the divine image, blessed by God for who you are. Do not follow blind leaders who will lead you into a pit of pain, despair, self-rejection, self-hatred, and a lack of belovedness.

Instead, follow Jesus. Be loved. Be blessed with all the blessings of Ruth and Naomi. Share your blessedness with others. Live with spiritual sight and gratitude.

God, give us your eyesight to see truth in Jesus. Help us live as your beloved people. Amen.

† July 30 †

So dull

Matthew 15:15-16

I love Peter. I love his faith, courage, impulsiveness, and even his dullness. I can relate to him in many ways. He is so very human. As a teacher, I recognize his request for yet another explanation. Sometimes we ask repetitive questions even though we know the answers. The deeper knowledge and truth becomes a mixed blessing. If we truly learn a new lesson, then we might be required to change our ways. Change is something many people often fear, fight, resist, avoid, and delay. Peter speaks for all seekers who cautiously explore a fuller understanding of deeper commitment and the ensuing consequences of following and serving Jesus.

Knowledge can empower. Knowledge can also threaten our security. Fuller understanding might cause change and totally disrupt our comfort zone. We may need to leave the comfort and security of our birth and cultural religions in order to follow Jesus with more alertness. It is easier to remain spiritually dull with the status quo.

In my kitchen is a dull knife. It is practically useless. I need to sharpen it so it can be useful. At the moment, it only takes up space and can barely slice through soft butter. It is dull from my neglect and probably from overuse. Our spiritual lives can also become dull through unconscious neglect and fatigue resulting from overuse. We can also become dull through exhaustion, stress, and abusive religious practices that can stifle God's creative spirit in us.

Jesus wants us to be sharp, that is, alert and attentive to his teachings. We are to be intentionally open to God. And guess what? We might be surprised with God. Our lives could be transformed. We could find ourselves being used by God for great things. Are you ready?

Show us where we are spiritually dull, God. Help us become alert and sharp-witted in our understanding of your words. Sharpen us. Amen.

† July 31 †

From our hearts

Matthew 15:17-20

Jesus is concerned with our inner thoughts and desires. Buddha has said, "The mind is everything; what you think, you become." And so it is. Our innermost heart reflects who we really are.

Jesus was referring to the religious customs of his time. They had ceremonial washings that had been handed down from their elders ever since Moses. Jesus allowed his disciples to eat without washing their hands. Religious authorities were shocked and dismayed at the perceived religious uncleanness of the disciples. The concern of the elders was skin deep. To them, perception was everything.

Jesus brings us to the real heart of the matter. What is in our heart? This is what counts before God. What are we thinking? What are we saying about others? Have we even thought about adultery, sexual immorality, theft, lying, or slander? Then we need to confess these thoughts, desires, and actions to God as they occur. I find in my own life, it is better to flee temptation than to tempt fate. Truly the spirit is willing but often the flesh is weak.

Let Jesus clean your hearts, and let Jesus help you change your behavior. When tempted to do things which make us unclean, consider reading, memorizing, or meditating on the words of Jesus in the gospels of Matthew, Mark, Luke, and John. Be accountable in your life to another person or small group. Sometimes we need to find new friends to affirm our choices in life.

For practical health reasons, it is good to wash hands before eating. But hand washing does not clean our hearts before God. Confession of personal sin is one way to begin to clean our hearts. Confession is good for our souls. Confession helps us become right with God. Confession has its own challenges, but sometimes getting started is the hardest part. We need moments where we confess personal sin in prayer, so we can make confessions of great faith in life.

I am sorry, God. Forgive me for those specific thoughts that are negative, destructive, denigrating, ridiculing, and displeasing to you. With the help of Jesus, give me a new heart. Help me live a better life that is pleasing to you in word, thought, and deed. Amen.

†   August 1   †

When God seems silent
Matthew 15:21-28

What do we do when God seems silent? Do we stop praying and give up hope? Or do we turn every stone and knock on every door until we receive an answer? All these questions find answers in this story of a desperate mother.

Biography magazine has a simple motto, "Every life has a story." And this woman has a profound story about faith, hope, and love. She was not Jewish yet somehow learned about the Healer, who miraculously was in her country and vicinity. Her precious daughter was suffering terribly and nothing could help her. She would move heaven and earth to have a hearing with Jesus.

She searched for him and when she found him, began shouting for mercy. She immediately called him by the distinguished Jewish title, "Son of David," showing some degree of recognition of Jesus as the Messiah who would heal the people. She urgently called his name again and again. And God seemed silent. Jesus refused to answer her. She was loud and bothersome to the male disciples, who urged Jesus to send her away. Her noisy cries for mercy and healing for her daughter bothered their rest. It was not their daughters who were suffering.

The ensuing conversation initially appears harsh and insensitive as Jesus reminds the woman and his disciples that he was sent only to the "lost sheep of Israel." But the woman refuses to take no for an answer. She drops to her knees and begs for mercy. Jesus replies that it is not right to take food from children to give to their dogs.

There are times when popular English translations fail to convey subtle theological nuances conveyed through the original Biblical languages and author's intent. Jesus was not being harsh. I suspect he had a smile on his lips and a kind twinkle in his eyes as he used the word the Gospel Greek rendered as the diminutive word, *kynaria*, meaning little house dogs, pet dogs, and even puppies. In no way was Jesus being insulting or comparing the petitioning woman to the despised and troublesome wild dogs roaming the countryside.

I wonder if the courageous woman smiled with relief as she persisted with her supplication for mercy in response to the Healer's humor and kindness. "Yes, Lord, but even the *kynaria* eat the crumbs that fall from their masters' table." She refused to leave until Jesus offered her a crumb of healing and mercy. Jesus complimented and blessed this determined woman. "Woman, you have great faith! Your request is granted." And her daughter was instantly healed.

How do we pray when God seems silent? This determined woman teaches us how to pray with persistent faith and courage. She experienced divine compassion, healing, and even a moment of humor with Christ. Her story can be ours. We can approach Jesus for mercy. We can move heaven and earth with our prevailing prayers. And when you see little house dogs and puppies, let them be a blessed reminder to pray during moments of need.

God, have mercy on us and hear our prayers. Amen.

✝   August 2   ✝

Praise as our response
Matthew 15:29-31

Praise should be part of our response to God's mercy and intervention in our lives. God's gifts are often overlooked. Our humanness cries out with our neediness. We frequently forget to thank and praise God for our healing and the daily miracles of life. Praise is something we need to learn again and again. Praise is good for our souls and is a healthy part of gratitude.

Once again crowds of hurting, sick, despairing people came to Jesus with their sick, lame, maimed, blind, and suffering friends and family members. They placed them at Jesus' feet and he cured them. The amazed crowd praised God for the astonishing miracles they so dramatically saw, heard, and experienced.

We may not have such dramatic experiences, but praising God is good for us. God delights in our praise. Our highest calling is found through praising and blessing God. This is why we are created. Worship is our highest calling.

What is praise? Awe, adoration, love, and reverence come to mind. Sometimes we need to learn the language of praise that the Psalms teach us. Psalms 145 through 150 can help us.

✝   Praise the Lord with singing.

✝   Remember God's remarkable deeds.

✝   Lift up God's name in honor and love.

✝   Praise God through music.

✝   Praise God through nature.

✝   Sing new songs to God while in community and while alone.

✝   Praise God in the sanctuary.

✝   Be glad in God with dancing.

✝   Praise the Lord.

✝   Alleluia. Amen.

God, we praise your holy name. Amen.

†   August 3   †

Give us a sign

Matthew 16:1-4

The Pharisees and Sadducees, two powerful religious groups within the Jewish tradition, struggle to discern the possibility of a miracle in the presence of Jesus. These two groups' stubborn adherence to the rules of their faith unfortunately leads to their unbelief. Despite having witnessed many of the miracles Jesus performed and listened carefully to his teachings, they refused to believe Jesus was both from God and *was* God. They demanded even more signs from heaven.

The error of these two groups was their refusal even to consider a glimmer of new truth from God when it came through Jesus Christ. In their not-so-humble opinion, Jesus was a mere mortal just as they were. Their sin was in their persistent unbelief and refusal to be open to in-creased revelation and truth from God by having faith in this remarkable messenger. Jesus was a great threat to the cherished beliefs of many Pharisees and Sadducees. Jesus threatened the foundation of their religious faith by suggesting that such a close connection between God and humans was possibly manifested in him. Jesus insisted his critics needed to believe in his message without spectacular and miraculous signs on demand. Seeing does not always lead to belief, and that was the case among the majority of the Pharisees and Sadducees.

Believing helps us see the world through the eyes of faith. The New Testament urges people to have faith, keep the faith, and pursue faith while asking for more faith in God through Jesus Christ. Faith is a mystery, and it is the only way to salvation. Faith is available to "whosoever," "all," and "everyone." It is more than being concerned with heavenly signs or facts versus feelings. Faith is also more than a one-time statement of intellectual or emotional belief. Faith is a continuous, ongoing, intimate, deeply personal, and loving relationship with the living Christ.

The stubborn Sadducees and Pharisees refused to believe in Jesus Christ. Will we too insist on signs from heaven or will we believe in the life-giving message of Jesus?

God, open our hearts to the truth of Jesus' message. Let us be open to new possibilities while we yearn for heavenly signs to help us believe. Let us journey by faith, not by sight. We pray these things in the name of Jesus Christ. Amen.

† August 4 †

Spiritual yeast

Matthew 16:5-12

After the confrontation with the Pharisees and Sadducees, Jesus and his disciples get into their boat and sail across the lake. The disciples forget to bring some of the leftover food from the earlier miraculous feeding of the four thousand. Using yeast as a spiritual metaphor, Jesus warns them to beware of the evil teachings of their respected, revered, and recognized religious instructors and leaders of Jewish law who were hostile to him.

The confused disciples think Jesus is upset because they forgot to bring food with them. Jesus chides them for their little faith. They still do not understand and fail to remember recent miracles. They see and believe in the excitement and drama of the moment, then promptly forget what they saw and experienced. Patiently Jesus repeats his admonition against their religious leaders. Finally the spiritually dull disciples understand Jesus is warning them to beware of the formal teachings of the Pharisees and Sadducees.

We too can find a place in this story. Perhaps we have religious leaders who might be popular and respected, but their God is small. Their understanding of Jesus is limited. We need to beware of their teachings and act responsibly on what we know to be true. Going against the flow of popular opinion has never been easy. Test everything by the words of Christ. Be a humble learner and ask for wisdom to discern the difference between good and evil when listening to religious teachings. It is a sad fact of life, but corruption and compromise with wickedness influences a number of religious leaders found in every faith tradition among every generation.

God, help us become familiar with the spiritual yeast that represents a fresh awareness of you through the teachings of Jesus Christ. Protect us from being influenced by the yeast of corrupt religion. Amen.

† August 5 †
What about you?
Matthew 16:13-20

Jesus and his inner circle of disciples have been together for several years at this point. They lived, traveled, worked, learned, and socialized together. Jesus has carefully trained them. It is time for the Teacher to ask his students a very important question. Who do people say that he is? They reply with the names of several famous prophets from their religious heritage. Then comes a personal question by the One they love and trust. "But what about you? Who do you say I am?"

Perhaps this is a good place for us to pause and sit with the disciples as they remember all they have experienced with this remarkable

Teacher, Friend, and Healer. We have also experienced some of the miracles, lingered with famous teachings, and struggled with parables about the kingdom of heaven.

Impulsive Peter blurts out his conviction that Jesus is God's Messiah. Jesus blesses Peter for his rock-like, sturdy faith and promises to use him to build the foundation of the ecumenical Christian church. The gates of Hades will not prevail against this amazing institution dedicated to bringing the reign of God on earth. Even the very keys of heaven are given to Peter, who is so clearly destined for spiritual greatness, anointed with awesome authority by Christ.

But this spiritual power is not limited to the apostle Peter. Every believer in Christ, gay or straight, has a vital role to play in the building and furthering of the mission of Christ through participating in the life of the Church. The Greek word for church is *ecclesia*, meaning the called out people.

The traditional face of Christianity is slowly but surely changing as growing numbers of gay, lesbians, bisexual, and transgendered people are participating in churches as a called out people, confronting many churches and societies of institutionalized homophobia around the world. The spirit of Christ is every bit as evident in their lives as in that of the apostle Peter.

What say you? Who is Jesus? Are you participating in the life of the *ecclesia*? If not, why not? Your answer may change your life forever.

God, bless us with the faith of Peter. Help us live into our full potential as people called out into the world through the Church, sharing our hope in Christ through words and deeds. Amen.

† **August 6** †

Stumbling blocks

Matthew 16:21-23

What has happened? In the preceding verses, Peter has made a great statement of faith, and Jesus promises to build his church with Peter. Now, just minutes later, Jesus confuses Peter and the other disciples. To their dismay, he begins teaching them that he must suffer and be killed by their religious leaders. Impulsively Peter takes Jesus aside and rebukes him for saying such negative and frightening things.

Jesus instantly turns to Peter and tells him to back off. He calls Peter a "stumbling block" and "Satan." He chastises Peter for having in mind the things of people instead of the things of God. How confusing this must have been for poor Peter. Elevated by profound spiritual insight one moment and severely rebuked by Jesus with the next breath.

Are we experiencing a spiritual stumbling block like Peter? What is keeping us from having God's point of view and perspective? What is Jesus saying to us through this story?

God, how are we like Peter? What are the spiritual stumbling blocks in our lives? Amen.

† August 7 †

Take up your cross and deny yourselves
Matthew 16:24-28

On one of the walls of my writing study hangs an inexpensive copy of a very old Byzantine or Slavic icon called "Christ, *Pantocrator*." I am not talking about computer icons, but a sacred art form providing visual focal points for reflection and meditation on Christian revelation and aspects of discipleship. These cherished religious images are the result of the prayers of many icon painters, providing a powerful prayer form that has continued to evolve over nearly 2,000 years. They help people pray with their eyes and hearts, without any need of rationalization or even verbalization. You simply gaze at them in silence and stillness. I often light a candle by mine when writing meditations, trusting the Spirit of God to work deep within my soul. Many of these beautiful icon images are available online, providing powerful prayer experiences using modern technology.

The Greek word, *Pantocrator*, translates as "Ruler of All." This popular icon has been often used in the high, main domes of churches for centuries, acknowledging Christ as Ruler of the universe, Creator and Savior. Christ typically is painted facing directly frontally, holding the Gospel, Book of Judgment, or an Orb representing the world in his left hand, with his right hand raised in blessing. He is often painted with riveting eyes staring straight at the viewer, although sometimes his eyes are averted.

My particular copy has an unusual feature, which a woman noticed when I facilitated an indoor Lenten labyrinth walk, for which I placed icons throughout the room for meditation purposes.

She came up to me and asked if the eyes of Christ were different. Yes. The artist painted one eye open and kind. The other eye is keen and piercing.

The Christ sees deep within our souls and all hidden inner thoughts. Words and actions are revealed for what they truly are. Sometimes we forget that someday Jesus Christ will repay everyone for what has been done when he returns in power and glory to judge the world of its sin.

But through the brush of this particular artist, the kindly eye of Christ, *Pantocrator* reveals an invitation for every viewer to experience God's amazing grace. This brings to my mind the ever-present reminder that Jesus has always been a great friend of sinners such as myself. We are all sinners saved by grace. Christ is indeed a great Savior.

God, help us appreciate the powerful image Christ, Pantocrator *brings through the powerful words of today's gospel passage. Thank you for the amazing grace that gives us confidence now and when Christ returns. Amen.*

†   August 8   †

Beloved

Matthew 17:5

Jesus is preparing for his pending death on the cross. He needs to go up to the mountain and talk with God and gather spiritual strength, wisdom, and encouragement. He brings along Peter, James, and his brother John. Before their stunned eyes, Jesus becomes transfigured, that is, becomes shining, radiant, and dazzling. The three astonished men probably think they are hallucinating, for they see Moses and Elijah talking with Jesus. Peter babbles something ridiculous to Jesus and suddenly the men are shrouded in a brilliantly bright cloud where they hear a heavenly voice, "This is my Son, the Beloved; with him I am well pleased; listen to him!"

The transfiguration of Jesus is recorded in three Gospels (Matthew 17:1-13, Mark 9:2-8, and Luke 9:28-36). If you have time, read all three accounts. It is a wonderful and marvelous story offering us many insights to ponder.

The disciples are overcome by fear and fall to the ground. Jesus comes and touches them, encouraging them to get up and to not be afraid. When they rise up, all they see is Jesus. Moses and Elijah are gone. As they return to the valley, Jesus orders the three men to keep silent about this moment until after he suffers, dies, and is later raised from the dead. How confused they must have been.

The story of Jesus' transfiguration is still difficult to understand even now. What I do understand is that Jesus is God's Beloved Son. I am to listen to him. And so are you.

God, help us listen to your Beloved Child. Amen.

✝   **August 9**   ✝

Mustard seed faith

Matthew 17:14-21

I have known people who have actually lost their faith in God through these verses. They too, have knelt in prayer while asking Jesus for mercy and healing. They have diligently prepared themselves to receive a miracle. They have worked to have the faith of a mustard seed. They think, if they believe enough, God will heal them, for nothing is impossible for the faith-filled. Then upon awakening in the morning, they are still sick and unhealed. They become bitter at God and disillusioned with the promises of Christ.

So what is this all about? What did it mean at the time of this miracle and what does this story mean for us today? How do we understand and apply something of value to our daily lives?

We often overlook what has just happened. James, John, and Peter just had a mountaintop experience with Jesus. Jesus had specifically chosen these three over the others. We do not know why only three were chosen and the others left behind with the impatient crowd.

The disciples who were left behind were doing the best they could while Jesus was gone. They tried to share what Jesus had given them to the crowd. The desperate father wanted his child healed. Perhaps he did not have faith that the disciples could heal without Jesus being present. Perhaps the disgruntled disciples who had been left behind did not have faith either. The crowd wanted Jesus, not the disciples. Jesus was the famed and trusted miracle worker from God.

After Jesus heals the child with a word, the disciples approach Jesus privately and demand answers for their lack of power. And Jesus tells them the truth. Their faith was too small. Their faith was smaller than even a mustard seed, the smallest known seed. Without Jesus, they could do nothing. With deeper faith, they could move mountains.

I believe in miracles. Yet I do not have a gift for healing epileptic children. Is my faith too little? Sometimes it is. I forget God is big and generous. I forget the other miracles in daily life. I forget that there is no such thing as a little prayer. I forget about previously answered prayers for healing that are too numerous to count.

But God cannot be manipulated. God's timing may not be ours. And sometimes we do not have the eyes of faith to see the true spiritual healing we are given.

God, give us this mustard seed faith. Amen.

† August 10 †

Grief and dismay
Matthew 17:22-23

As difficult as these verses are to read and contemplate, from time to time we must reflect on the life, suffering, passion, death, and resurrection of Jesus Christ. Today's verses should give us pause as we pursue our daily routines. So often these verses are glossed over and read superficially. A closer reading reveals this is a dramatic story about deep grief and consternation when the disciples hear their beloved Jesus speak of his impending doom. The distraught disciples could not comprehend the bitter reality that lay ahead for their cherished friend and spiritual leader. Their overwhelming sense of anguish blinded them to the glorious possibility of resurrection.

All who choose to follow this remarkable Jesus need to realize there can be no Easter joy without the horror and tragedy of the cross. There can be no resurrection without Gethsemane. Every generation of believers must learn these lessons afresh. We also need to share the disciples' horror as Jesus speaks of his betrayal and death so calmly. We must ask the same questions as these grief-stricken disciples. Why would anyone in their right mind want to kill this remarkable healer, teacher, rabbi, and miracle worker who spoke such astonishing insights about God? With the disciples, I am grieved in my spirit. I wish Jesus did not have to suffer and die. I wish the cross were not necessary. I dread his awful betrayal, torture, and death.

But we must not linger in the horror. We must hear the hope offered by Jesus that his disciples were unable to hear. Death will not be the end. Evil will ultimately be defeated. Because Jesus suffered, he understands our human condition. He understands betrayal, torture, injustice, cruelty, and death. As a result, divine love conquers hate. Good wins over evil. Death loses its fearful grip on our hearts for the grave is not able to hold Jesus. We can be joyful in suffering and courageous in the face of evil. So take comfort and keep looking up. Fix your eyes on Jesus. Through him God will provide us with strength for the day and hope for tomorrow.

God, deepen our understanding of why Jesus had to go to the cross and experience betrayal, torture, injustice, cruelty, and death. Bless us with resurrection hope through our thoughts and prayers today. Amen.

†   August 11   †

Paying religious taxes
Matthew 17:24-27

Even Jesus paid taxes! This temple tax was an annual tax on adult Jewish males to support temple sacrifices. While I am not a Jewish male, I too, belong to a religious institution that expects a percentage on any financial gifts and offerings that come through my ordained denominational ministry. Perhaps I need to sit with this teaching and its meaning in my own life today. Jesus not only paid his religious tax in full, but he generously paid twice the amount that was required.

One commentary suggests, "True children of God do not need to contribute to the support of God's house." But as I know in my own ministry, it costs money to turn on the lights and pay the bills. The money has to come from somewhere and if God's people fail to give generously even the best ministries are forced to shut down and permanently close their doors. When the economy struggles, even the most faithful people of God consider reducing their financial contributions to their local churches, favorite ministries, and other worthy causes. Yet that is exactly when the needs are usually the greatest.

Fortunately the gospel is always free and independent of the economy. I thank God for such a priceless gift in my own life, and strive to model the generosity of Christ as best I can.

Our gospel story today is a reminder to give generously without calculating what's in it for us. While we are not obligated to give, when we do dig deep in our pockets, many others are blessed and the world becomes a better place. Talk is cheap by itself. Sometimes living our faith requires we pull out the checkbook and write a larger than usual contribution. When in doubt, err on the side of generosity and trust God to bless you in the process.

God, bless me with the generosity exhibited by Jesus. Amen.

† August 12 †

Who is the greatest?

Matthew 18:1-9

One of my good friends is a fiercely competitive bowler. She is one of the best and is frequently called "THE bowler." Many fear bowling against her because she is very, very good. She is the greatest woman bowler in her state. But this is not the kind of greatness Jesus is teaching about.

At this point in the story the disciples have been with Jesus for three years. They wanted to know who was the greatest among their inner group. Jesus brings in a young child for a lesson in spiritual greatness. According to the kingdom of heaven, spiritual greatness is found in those with childlike humility and trust in Christ. And woe to any who place stumbling blocks before these little ones. Woe to any who cause them to lose their faith in Jesus.

Jesus is not calling people to disfigure or mutilate themselves literally in their self-examination. Jesus does call us to moments of introspection and reflection. We are all God's children. Are we placing stumbling blocks and discouraging certain people from faith in Jesus?

I will always remember the story of a young gay Christian. He grew up in a legalistic church, listening to his pastor preach about how much Jesus hated homosexuals. This young man believed his pastor through his teenage years as he struggled to become heterosexual so Jesus would love him. One day, as a young adult, he asked a priest friend just where in the Gospels did Jesus preach such condemnation.

Nowhere, exclaimed the priest. For the young man, it was a profound moment of revelation and hope. He soon found a Christian church consisting of many gay and lesbian parishioners. He now sings in the choir and brings his dates and friends to this welcoming church. He was one of the lucky ones fortunate to overcome his spiritual stumbling blocks. The homophobic church of his childhood had caused him years of tears and inner torment, attempting to change what could not be changed. His childhood pastor had actually lied from his pulpit, inflicting great harm to this young man and the entire congregation.

God, are we helping or hindering people from trusting in Jesus? Amen.

†   **August 13**   †

Angels watching over us

Matthew 18:10-14

"Where can I find God?" This question has been echoed throughout history. It is fundamental for our well being. We may have different names for our Deity of choice, but we are spiritual people and need loving, holy Presence in our lives. Jesus is teaching people not to hinder others from experiencing God. Woe to those who do!

Have you ever been despised? I have. Throughout my life, various groups and individuals have despised me because of my sexual orientation, skin color, gender, and spiritual convictions. Intolerance and hate is taught and caught.

Yet Jesus is teaching us that respect is a holy word. We should not despise those different from us. Our bias and prejudice actually prevent people from experiencing God's loving care and empowerment.

Do you believe in angels? Jesus obviously does. Scripture tells us guardian angels exist (Psalms 34:7, Psalms 91:11, Hebrews 1:14). God's angels are watching over us even now. And we are not to despise those over whom the angels watch.

Jesus is the good shepherd ever on the search to find people, bringing them into loving spiritual community. God is delighted and the angels rejoice when one person is found and returned to God.

We are missionaries with good news to share with those wandering in search of a spiritual home. Jesus has come for the despised, the rejected, the ridiculed, the marginalized, and the outcast. Angels are watching over all of us.

So where are we in this message? Is there someone we despise? Are we hindering them from experiencing God's loving kindness through our personal bias? Whom are we hindering from experiencing the Gospel? Or are we wandering in search of a spiritual home? Do we seek God?

Take courage. God is as near as our breathing, closer than our hands and feet. Let God embrace you today and seek affirming spiritual community through Jesus Christ. God is in the search and rescue business. Come home to God.

God, thank you for the angels watching over us. Bless each reader with a sense of your loving Presence through a personal relationship through Jesus Christ. Amen.

†   **August 14**   †

Direct and loving confrontation

Matthew 18:15-17

Benjamin Franklin wrote, "Those things that hurt, instruct." Sometimes the truth hurts. Tough love might lead us to privately speak with another and honestly share how we have been injured by another's words and actions. In our relationships with others diplomacy and respect often win us a hearing to share our truth. But there are times when diplomacy is not always helpful. Sometimes we must be more direct and to the point. Loving confrontation is needed.

I appreciate this teaching of Jesus. He is refreshingly honest and uncomplicated. It is much easier to gossip and criticize people behind their backs. It takes courage to approach a person who has sinned against us and tell it like it is from our perspective. While this teaching is often the foundation of church discipline, it also offers us rich insights about individual conflict resolution.

Always approach the other person privately and try to resolve the issue at the source of contention. Remember that respect is a holy word and that diplomacy might open a more frank and honest conversation. Have the courage to humbly confront and the grace to listen. But be very careful. We are not always right in our judgments, fervent opinions, and beliefs.

Just the other day I saw two friends have the courage to live this teaching in their interpersonal conflict. One woman had been extremely upset and deeply offended by an embarrassing comment made by a trusted and valued friend. The friend had unintentionally but publicly hurt her feelings with a thoughtless comment. The offended woman made the effort to privately approach her friend and share how the comment embarrassed and angered her. Her friend was mortified and apologized profusely. Their friendship was actually strengthened through honest, direct, and caring conversation. They were able to reach a peaceable resolution and deeper understanding.

There are no guarantees that all conflict and hurt can be resolved at this personal level. Honesty can be a risky business. Wisdom encourages us to try to resolve issues privately whenever possible.

God, is there anyone I need to approach privately in loving honesty? Give me the courage to act on this teaching of Jesus. Amen.

†   August 15   †

Two or three

Matthew 18:18-20

There is no such thing as a little prayer. There is a saying that one plus God is a majority. Imagine the power of two or three people praying together for God's will to be done, in the name of Jesus Christ.

As a former U.S. Navy chaplain, I lived on an ammunition ship for two years. A small group of Christians gathered for worship services and prayer throughout our six-month overseas deployment to the turbulent Middle East. International tensions were strained at that time in the Persian Gulf. Some of my sailors talked eagerly about showing force and bombing their perceived enemy.

I would often privately and quietly go the bomb storage area. In solitude and privacy, I would place my hands on the various bombs and pray for peace. During the worship services, sometimes with only two or three others present, we would pray for peace through the name of Jesus Christ.

Never underestimate the power of prayer in the Name that is above all other names. We are actually told that someday at the name of Jesus, every knee shall bow and every mouth confess him as Lord (Philippians 2:10-11).

If you have never prayed in the name of Jesus Christ, consider such an experiment with God. Intentionally close your prayers in the name of Jesus for the next thirty days and see how you are changed. And consider finding a small prayer group or prayer partner for ongoing prayer. Your prayers can change the world in the name of Jesus Christ.

God, teach us to pray in the name of Jesus Christ. Amen.

†   August 16   †

Forgiveness seventy-seven times
Matthew 18:21-22

I believe it was Winston Churchill who said, "We shape our dwellings, and afterwards our dwellings shape us." If we are unforgiving in our spirits, our dwellings will be shaped by bitterness, resentment, hatred, and intolerance. We become spiritually damaged when we refuse to forgive. Forgiveness begets forgiveness.

The other evening I was watching a World War II documentary about American prisoners of war (POWs). The POWs suffered horrible atrocities at the hands of their Japanese captors. Their suffering defies description. Many shared their memories of beloved comrades who died of torture, malnutrition, and disease. Some wept. One veteran said, "I can forgive them but I can never forget what they did."

That same day I happened to read a newspaper article from a Japanese-American citizen who was unjustly imprisoned simply for his ethnic heritage during that war. His comments were strikingly similar. His family also suffered terribly at the hands of their fellow American captors.

Several years ago I read the autobiography of Corrie ten Boom. This remarkable woman and her family were also POWs. Her captors were German. Their "crimes" were those of Christian compassion. They protected Jewish refugees from Hitler's holocaust until they were discovered and put in a brutal concentration camp. Her beloved sister and father died cruel deaths at the hands of the Nazis.

Years after the war, to her dismay while speaking at a church group, a former Nazi prison guard approached. His hand reached out to her in friendship and she instantly remembered his cruelty toward her and especially to her sister. The former tormentor personally asked her forgiveness.

For years, this man had been deeply troubled in his spirit for his crimes against humanity and yearned for forgiveness. When he saw Corrie ten Boom, he eagerly rushed to meet her. It was only with the help of God that she could forgive him, but it was a struggle. Corrie ten Boom remembered her sister's suffering as if it had happened only yesterday.

Jesus is teaching us through a parable about forgiveness and the kingdom of heaven in the following verses. The parable concludes with his comment, "This is how my heavenly Father will treat each of you unless you forgive your brother [or sister] from your heart" (Matthew 18:35 NIV). Jesus never asks us to do what he was unwilling or unable to do.

At the Washington National Cathedral, in a tiny prayer area, a large cross of nails hangs on a wall in front of a prayer kneeler. The words "Father, forgive" are engraved on the plaque. These two words sear into my soul. It is good to learn from ancient wisdom and "be quick to listen, slow to speak, and slow to become angry" (James 1:19 NIV). We must learn to forgive as Jesus did.

God, help us forgive! Amen.

†   August 17   †

Divorce

Matthew 19:3

The agony of divorce is not new. One day I listened to a friend agonize about her marriage. She finally said, "I guess I'm looking for someone to give me permission to divorce my husband." I know many friends and colleagues who have divorced their life partners. Divorce is a painful life event and spiritual concern.

His teaching about divorce is one of the hard sayings of Jesus. He taught about divorce in Matthew 5:31-32, Matthew 19:3-6, Luke 16:18, and Mark 10:2-12. His male disciples were quite dismayed with his teachings, for he treated women with enormous respect. In ancient times, divorce was always to a man's advantage. Women were not allowed any choice in the matter. While Malachi 2:16 tells us "God hates divorce," even Moses acknowledged it as a reality of life (Deuteronomy 22:13-21 and 24:1-4).

So yes, it is lawful for men and women to divorce their life partners. And it is deeply wounding for spousal relationships of all sexual orientations. But we can learn from our mistakes and experiences. We can heal through time and counseling. A loveless marriage is always tragic; it may take years or a lifetime to recover from one.

I lived in a family where one set of grandparents had a loveless marriage. Theirs was an arranged marriage in Russia during the 1930s. When my grandfather immigrated to North America, it took thirteen years before my grandmother reluctantly joined him. As I search my memory, I can recall no loving words or expressed affection between the two of them. They argued and fought about everything: money, children, and religion. It was a miserable marriage. My father frequently said that while he personally does not believe in divorce, it would have been "better for them if they had." Just one of the tragic outcomes of my paternal grandparents' loveless marriage was that my father had to learn to be a loving husband and father without positive role models.

God, be in our relationships. Heal and reconcile us whenever possible. Give us courage to divorce and resources for healing from loveless unions. Amen.

† August 18 †

Jesus and little children
Matthew 19:13-15

Madeleine L'Engle is one of my favorite writers. She has this to say about a child's understanding of Jesus, "A teacher of small children told us of a child who said to her, 'Jesus is God's show and tell.' How simple and how wonderful! Jesus is God's show and tell. That's the best theology of incarnation I've ever heard. If we do not understand Jesus as a little child, we will not be able to enter the kingdom of heaven. That child's insight works more powerfully for me than dogma."[64]

Let the little children teach us. Recently I was at the home of the single mother of an eight-year-old. We were talking about the preaching

---

[64] L'Engle, Madeleine. *Glimpses of Grace*, p. 111.

invitation a local Unitarian church had graciously offered me. I had used the expression "pulpit supply" in our conversation. Later the child exclaimed, "I want to see your puppet supply!" We had a good laugh at my expense! But I marvel at the child's insight. Am I a mindless, entertaining, and harmless puppet in the pulpit dancing to the tune of popular public opinion on contemporary and controversial issues? Or am I a gracious representative of God's presence? Do I speak and write thoughtfully, prayerfully, and prophetically after thorough study and preparation? Let the little children teach us and do not hinder them!

Jesus loved children. The harried disciples attempted to protect Jesus from the young ones, but he always took time for them. All were precious in his sight. Jesus offers us an example as God's show and tell. He was never too busy to hold and bless a child. Let the little children teach us. May we treat all children with the love of Christ.

God, help us see Jesus with childlike trust. Help us see children with the eyes of Jesus. Amen.

✝ August 19 ✝
What must I do?
Matthew 19:16

A wealthy person wants to know from Jesus what he has to do to get eternal life. The Teacher answered his question with a question, and the two have a profound conversation. It does not matter if we are rich or poor, old or young, male or female, lesbian or gay or heterosexual. It is a question we all have. What do we have to do to get eternal life? How can we live forever?

Jesus and the wealthy man engage in respectful conversation. You have to obey the commandments, replied Jesus. Which ones, asks the Jewish seeker. Jesus cites only six of the Ten Commandments. Oh, the Jewish man exclaimed in relief. I have done all those. What do I lack?

We are told that the rich man's face became very sad when he heard the Teacher's answer. Jesus bluntly told him to give all his possessions to the poor. He would then have treasure in heaven. This nameless, wealthy man then received a personal invitation by Jesus to come and follow him. The young man had great wealth and left saddened. All his money could not buy, barter, or bribe God into giving him eternal life.

Does this story mean we each must give away all our possessions before following Jesus in discipleship? Of course not! But perhaps there are possessions, wealth, or relationships that we worship and honor more than God in our lives. What might they be? Are they hindering our life with Jesus? What must we do for eternal life? Salvation is free. Discipleship is a lifetime of following Jesus. This includes how we use our money.

Richard Foster wrote, "Our study of money leads us to one inescapable conclusion: we who follow Jesus Christ are called to a vow of simplicity. This vow is not for the dedicated few but for all. It is not an option to take or leave depending on our personal preference. All who name Christ as Lord and Savior are obliged to follow what he says, and Jesus' call to discipleship in money can best be summed up in the single word simplicity. Simplicity seeks to do justice to our Lord's many-faced teachings about money – light and dark, giving and receiving, trust, contentment, and faith. Simplicity means unity of heart and singleness of purpose. We have only one desire; to obey Christ in all things . . . we have only one use for money: to advance his kingdom upon the earth." [65]

God, where are we in this story today? What does this mean in our lives? Are we willing to follow Jesus? Teach us how to use our money for you. Help us give with generous hearts. Amen.

†   **August 20**   †

Who can be saved?

Matthew 19:25-26

The disciples listened with great interest as Jesus continued his teaching after the wealthy man sorrowfully left. The affluent young man had everything money could buy, except eternal life with God. That could not be bought for all the silver or gold in the world. The prosperous seeker was spiritually impoverished, blinded by material possessions and his

---

[65] Richard J. Foster. *The Challenge of the Disciplined Life: Christian Reflections on Money, Sex, and Power,* p. 71.

laudable external good deeds performed to the letter of his religious laws. He failed to realize his true state of inner poverty and need for complete dependence upon God's amazing grace for salvation. These faithful disciples were not rich people. They worked hard and lived simply. The disciples were "greatly astonished" to learn that wealth and possessions and commendable charitable deeds and religiously oriented actions can actually hinder our life with God. Money and possessions and praiseworthy activities cannot save us. In amazement the disciples ask Jesus what we all ask, "Who then can be saved?"

And Jesus replied, "Humanly speaking, no one. But with God, everything is possible" (Matthew 19:26 TLB). Only God can save us. Our very best efforts are futile attempts to buy, barter, earn, or bribe our way into heaven. We are saved by faith. It is a free gift from God. Will you humbly ask for your gift of eternal life? And then come, follow Jesus, and experience an adventure with God that will transform your life!

God, give us this eternal life. And bless us as we follow Jesus. Amen.

† August 21 †
What is in it for me?
Matthew 19:27-30

I deeply appreciate the blunt honesty of the impulsive Peter. He has eagerly been following the conversation between Jesus and the rich young man. Like the other disciples, he has been amazed at Jesus' teachings on wealth and the realm of God. He was shocked that the wealthy man was challenged to give up his possessions before following Jesus. So he blurts out a question that I imagine was on the minds of all the others. "We have left everything to follow you! What then will there be for us?" Meaning, I suspect, what is in it for me?

There is nothing wrong in that question. He and the others gave up their jobs and financial resources to follow this remarkable teacher, Jesus. I can identify with his question because I also am not salaried as I serve the Gospel in a full time ministry. If there is a prosperity gospel, I have not seen it!

We find Jesus patiently explaining their future reward to the entire group of the original disciples. Someday friends, he said, when I am on my glorious throne, you will also sit on thrones with power, honor, and glory. I will honor your faithful service. That is as good as it gets.

The Teacher continued with timeless words for today. Everyone who has served the Gospel sacrificially in obedience to the call of Christ will someday be abundantly rewarded in the hereafter. The last will be first, and the first will be last.

Delayed gratification is never easy. We are to serve faithfully in the here and now. We may never see the rewards of our sacrificial service to the Gospel in this life. But someday we will hear a "well done, good and faithful servant" from the One who has called us by name. And that is as good as it gets. It is more than enough.

God, help us be faithful servants of Christ. Help us serve with loving and willing hearts. Amen.

† **August 22** †

God's generosity

Matthew 20:1-16

We will find ourselves in today's parable. Perhaps we are among the laborers who toiled in backbreaking work throughout the relentless heat of the very long day. If so, we are probably those who grumbled and bitterly resented those who experienced the generosity of the landowner. Others might find themselves rejoicing for those unsuspecting day laborers who found such surprising good fortune. They had arrived late, worked the fewest hours, and expected a much smaller salary than they received. As they gazed incredulously at the money in their hands, they realized they had been paid for a full day's wage. These day workers were jubilant. All received an honest day's wage regardless of hours actually worked. The workers varied in their response to the landowner's generosity with every conceivable emotion ranging from dismay and consternation, to gratitude and delight, to jealousy and anger depending on how long they had toiled.

But how does this parable affect us in the twenty-first century? This story often comes as a surprise for many who either believe they must earn their salvation, or who have been living under the fear that God is miserly. It can also be uncomfortable for faithful people who have sacrificially and devotedly toiled for God in obscurity, hardship, and through the tedium of long-term committed service. By reading this parable, countless generations of seekers, skeptics, doubters, and spiritual pilgrims from all walks of life have found God to be generous beyond their wildest imaginings.

God's ways certainly are not ours. Someday the least and the last will be first in the realm of God. Because God is generous to saint and sinner alike, we can be greatly encouraged. It is never too late to approach God for mercy and enter the realm of God. Divine generosity is abundantly lavished on the least deserving, eleventh hour, repentant reprobates and prodigals without measure or miserliness. This is a great gift if we will freely receive it. So enjoy the generosity of God today. Always remember God's heart is bigger than ours. God is charitable and kind, characterized by open-handedness and large heartedness for saints and sinners.

God, thank you for being so generous to saints and sinners alike. We bless you for your mercy and kindness. May we always remember this parable when we feel bitterness and resentment, dismay and consternation when those we feel are less deserving approach you for mercy and entry into your realm. Amen.

† August 23 †

The ultimate reality of the Gospel
Matthew 20:17-19

From the very beginning of his ministry, Jesus was a man with a mission from God. He knew why he was born and what was required of him. The looming cross was to be a critical and essential part of the gospel message. Without the cross, we could not have Easter and resurrection hope. But the disciples did not understand this at all. To them, Jesus was a wonderful prophet, teacher, healer, miracle worker, and friend sent from God. He was wonderful to be with and they loved him. They had left everything to serve him. The disciples did not want Jesus to suffer and die.

Matthew's Gospel describes Jesus preparing the disciples again for the inevitable harsh reality awaiting them. He was going to be betrayed and denied justice. Jesus was going to be tortured before dying a shameful and agonizing death. Then he was going to conquer both death and sin through resurrection power, that is, by being raised to life!

Our sins and the sins of the world led him to the cross. On the cross, Jesus paid the full price and penalty for all our sins of omission and commission. None of us are perfect. Only Jesus Christ is the sinless one. He is the great friend of sinners. "All of us have sinned and fallen short of the glory of God" (Romans 3:23 NIV). There is no greater love than when Christ willingly went to the cross for us. This is the ultimate reality of the Gospel message.

Jesus was innocent. He did not commit crimes; he had no sin in his life. Madeleine L'Engle calls Jesus "a great universe-disturber, so upsetting to the establishment of his day that they put him on a cross, hoping to finish him off. Those of us who try to follow his Way have a choice, either to go with him as universe-disturbers, or to play it safe. Playing it safe ultimately leads to personal diminishment and death." [66]

L'Engle tells us more about what it means to be a disturber, "If we disturb the universe, no matter how lovingly, we're likely to get hurt. Nobody ever promised that universe-disturbers would have an easy time of it. Universe-disturbers make waves, rock boats, upset establishments. Gandhi upset the great British Empire. Despite his non-violence, he was unable to stop the shedding of blood. . . . Anwar Sadat tried to work for peace . . . knowing that he might die for what he was doing, and he did." [67] Jesus calls us to join him in being universe-disturbers.

Evil constantly attempts to conquer Love. The good news and ultimate reality of the Gospel is that God conquers evil with the divine Light and Love of Jesus Christ revealed on the cross.

God, bless us as we reverently contemplate the ultimate reality of the Gospel message. Help us understand what it means to be a universe-disturber as we strive to follow Jesus. Amen.

---

[66] L'Engle, Madeleine. *Glimpses of Grace*, p. 108.
[67] Ibid.

†   August 24   †

Selective hearing

Matthew 20:20-26

People have a tendency to hear what they want to hear. It is very easy to do. We all do this. Today's story is a perfect example of selective hearing. Jesus has just told the twelve original disciples that he must be betrayed, arrested, tortured, and crucified. In these verses we see two of the disciples and their mother privately approaching Jesus. Together they kneel before Jesus and the brothers' mother asks Jesus for a favor. Give my sons power, prestige, promotion, and privilege over the other disciples, she asks. James and John had obviously remembered Jesus' earlier answer to the impulsive Peter about their eventual heavenly reward with selective hearing. With their own interests at stake, they overlooked the conversation about the pending cross. They had selective hearing and heard only what they wanted to hear.

Amazingly, Jesus did not scold them. They obviously did not understand what they were asking. Jesus asked the brothers a question that he might still ask today of all who wish to follow him, "Can you drink the cup I am going to drink?"

Oh yes, James and John eagerly assure Jesus. They had no understanding of what was ahead for Jesus. They would soon receive the answer to their prayers. St. Teresa of Avila wisely said, "More tears are shed over answered prayers than unanswered ones." [68]

Henri Nouwen makes the observation that before we drink the cup of Christ, we must hold it. He uses the cup as a metaphor to articulate the basics of spiritual life. The cup is a powerful image in human experience. It is a cup of sorrow, joy, blessing, and salvation. We must hold it, lift it, and drink it. "This question – one that Jesus asked his friends James and John – has the power to crack open the hardened heart and lay bare the tendons of the spiritual life." [69] This question can radically change our lives.

Yes, Jesus said to James and John. Yes, he says to us today. "You will indeed drink from my cup" (Matthew 20:23 NIV). But only God can grant power and promotion.

---

[68] Quoted in Rueben P. Job and Norma Shawchuk. *A Guide to Prayer for Ministers and Other Servants*, p. 168.

[69] Nouwen, Henri J. M. *Can You Drink the Cup?*, p. 20.

The other disciples are enraged when they learn of James and John's attempt to get power and status. Jesus calls them all together and gives a lesson on spiritual greatness. To be spiritually great, we must be servants and slaves. We need to be like Christ. He came not to be served, but to serve. He came to give his life as a ransom for the sins of many. This is the message of the Gospel.

Will you drink of Jesus' cup?

God, help us know what it means to drink from Christ's cup. Amen.

† August 25 †

Jesus stopped
Matthew 20:29-34

As usual, a large crowd was excitedly thronging around Jesus as he and his disciples departed from yet another city. We will never know if the two blind men sitting on the roadside were waiting for him. It might have been just a routine day for them as they begged passing travelers for alms.

But when they heard through the noisy commotion, that the re-markable Healer, Jesus, was passing in front of them, they knew their lives could change forever. In a flash of a second, they realized this was a once in a lifetime opportunity. They seized it with gusto and shouted again and again, at the top of their lungs, for Jesus to have mercy on them. They re-fused to be hushed by the annoyed crowd. They had nothing to lose and everything to gain. They could not and would not be silenced.

Jesus heard their cries for mercy and stopped. He halted in his tracks and came to a complete standstill. Through the din of the crowd, he heard their voices of blind faith. Their persistent shouts touched his com-passionate heart. Even though many others were competing for his atten-tion, Jesus focused on the blind men with tunnel vision, boring into the innermost depths of their souls as he inquired what they wanted from him.

The blind men eagerly blurted out their desperate request for sight. They wanted to see and Jesus immediately granted their desire. It was a miracle and the astonished crowd cheered and praised God. The newly sighted men joyously joined the exuberant and celebrating crowd. They followed Jesus, close on his heels. They could not take their eyes off of their gracious Benefactor, memorizing every detail and gazing deeply into his wonderful face.

These two men help us see Jesus with the eyes of faith. Even before Jesus stopped in his tracks, these desperate ones had seen Jesus more clearly than the sighted crowd. How could this be? Through their other God-given senses, they had learned to listen and hear with great alertness and attentiveness. As a result, their physical disability had taught them spiritual wisdom and discernment. Their faith in the Healer was not a foolish, reckless, or stupid faith. Even before Jesus stopped, they were utterly convinced Jesus would help them.

There may be times when we feel blinded by doubt, despair, sorrow, disillusionment, hate, confusion, and exhaustion. Perhaps we need a new vision of God and these blind men can lead us into a clearer view of God's compassion and mercy through the Healer. These two men help us gaze deeply at Jesus. As Jesus stopped and listened so compassionately to them, he will likewise halt and listen to our cries for help. We can be comforted and strengthened through this knowledge.

God, we want to see Jesus with new eyes. Bless us with the clarity of vision these blind men had. Give us, we ask, eyes full of faith. Amen.

† August 26 †

Hosanna!

Matthew 21:1-11

Jesus was at a crossroads. Some might call this fate or destiny. Others would say he is at a divine appointment. At the crossroads, he consciously made the choice to courageously go forward to his death on the cross. The disciples and cheering crowds had no idea of what was to come. This was why Jesus was born. He knew and accepted his divine fate. In doing so, Jesus forever changed the world.

Everything he did was with intention and obedience to prophecy. The donkey symbolized humility, peace, and Davidic royalty (Zechariah 9:9). The very large crowds spread their cloaks as an act of royal homage

(2 Kings 8:28). "Hosanna" means both prayer and praise. Jesus was being recognized as a king, a leader, and a prophet from God. For a moment he enjoyed the accolades of adoring crowds. The soon to be fickle crowds enthusiastically cheered Jesus. The entire city was stirred. Many asked, "Who is this?" Perhaps you have the same question, Who is this Jesus?

Usually we read this passage (commonly called "the Triumphal Entry") for Palm Sunday. But the drama of the gospel is appropriate anytime of the year. Other Gospel accounts of this dramatic event are located in Mark 11:1-10, Luke 19:29-38, and John 12:12-15. If today were Palm Sunday, we would begin what the Christian Church calls "Holy Week" with special Maundy Thursday and Good Friday worship services. This is the week when people of faith around the world remember the cross, death, burial, and resurrection of Jesus. Easter celebrates the empty tomb.

We need to remember King Jesus, Son of David, the Messiah, is the Christ. He not only rode into Jerusalem on a donkey, but even today Jesus wishes to ride into our hearts and live with us forever.

The crowds cried, "Hosanna!" They blessed Jesus publicly as he rode by. We would do well if we followed their example. So the questions beg asking. Who is this Jesus? Who is he to you? Have you praised and blessed him with the adoring crowds? Or are you still wondering who he really is?

Lord Jesus Christ, Son of David, Child of God, Hosanna! Blessed are you! Amen.

† **August 27** †

Let the little ones lead us

Matthew 21:12-17

The children were shouting and dancing. Children led the praise chants. "Hosanna to the Son of David!" The blind and the lame eagerly came to him in the holy place. Jesus healed them all. Those in need were blessed beyond words. The religious authorities were indignant at the healing, the upset businesses, the noisy children, and Jesus. How dare he upset the status quo? How dare he let people infer he was King and Divine? How dare he act with such divine authority?

Jesus answered their irate questions with a quotation from Hebrew scripture, "From the lips of infants and children, you have ordained praise" (Psalm 8:2)! The little ones intuitively knew Jesus was someone very special and wonderful.

God's house is to be a house of prayer for all people. Jesus was not known for his diplomacy, but for his holy boldness. When he saw the temple full of shops, moneychangers, and profiteers he overturned their tables and benches. This act did not endear him to the local businesses that were taking financial advantage of the worshippers, but Jesus publicly called them a "den of robbers."

Jesus prudently left the area to stay overnight in a safer place several miles away from Jerusalem. He knew he had made many dangerous enemies in the temple with his actions and words.

Where are we in this story? Where are we in God's house of prayer? Are we among the lame, the blind, and the children? Perhaps we are protecting the status quo of our religions. Are our businesses robbing people? Are we interfering with God's house of prayer?

O God, thank you for children. Let the little ones lead us in praise today. We wish to see Jesus with childlike delight. Amen.

† August 28 †

Judgment and a prayer lesson
Matthew 21:18-22

What in heaven's name does this unfruitful fig tree and prayer lesson mean for us? Matthew describes the tree as withering immediately. The fig tree event takes a bit longer in Mark 11:12-14, 20-25. Some biblical scholars suggest this is an example of God's immediate judgment. [70]

Bearing fruit is a spiritual metaphor common in scripture that I struggle with as an urban woman. I have no agricultural expertise and provide great entertainment to my neighbors as I am learning to differentiate between the weeds and flowers in my yard. But I do understand what

---

[70] Barker, Kenneth, General Editor. *The New International Version Study Bible*, p. 1472.

it means to be barren in spirit and life. Someday my own life will also come into divine judgment.

All of us will someday be asked if our lives were fruitful or barren in goodness, generosity, hospitality, kindness, love, mercy, and justice. Perhaps it is time to cultivate and nurture a new spirit as we follow Christ.

What about this teaching on prayer? Jesus says it is "the truth." If we have faith without doubt, we can do even more than he did with the fig tree. He concludes this teaching with this empowering comment, "If you believe, you will receive whatever you ask for in prayer" (Matthew 21:22 NIV).

Now I have asked for many things in life through prayer. I do not remember receiving answers to every request. Yet I have often been more prayerless than prayerful. My prayer life is imperfect at best, and I am an ordained minister with more than forty years in the Christian life. Perhaps my prayers have been as barren as this fig tree. The fruit of our prayers can change the world, help many people, and transform our personal lives. So why do we hesitate to pray and believe nothing is impossible for God?

God, I personally lack the faith to pray strongly enough to move mountains. Oh, help my unbelief! Teach me to pray in such ways that my life and the lives of many others will be productive, loving, and blessed. Amen.

✝   **August 29**   ✝

By what authority?

Matthew 21:23

The chief priests and religious elders want to know where Jesus had received his theological authority. He was a mere upstart, an itinerant and unschooled street preacher in their opinion. They, on the other hand, were trained scholars and had dedicated their lives to maintaining the strict standards of the religious purity of their faith. So these critics were throwing down the gauntlet. How dare Jesus teach with such authority and upset their cherished religious traditions? Who did he think he was to challenge their powerful influence on the people?

Jesus was well aware of the chief priests and religious elders' hostility. As the story continues, he astutely answers his enemies with a theological question based on the prior teachings of John the Baptist. The frustrated priests and elders have a heated discussion among themselves. Now matter how they answer, Jesus has cleverly put them in an uncomfortable spot where public opinion would flow in his favor. Finally the thwarted leaders avoid any more public debate and admit ignorance to the question Jesus had posed to them about John the Baptist.

These questioning priests and elders offer a valuable insight for us as they question the authority of Christ. There have been times in my own spiritual journey when I have questioned and doubted him. I clearly remember part of my journey involved a time when I overtly rejected any of his teachings, turned my back on Jesus, and fled away from anything even remotely Christian. I personally needed time to look at other worldviews and spiritual traditions while experiencing life as a young adult. My journey to faith involved years of skepticism before I got on my knees in prayer one day, and admitted I needed whatever Jesus Christ had for my life. I knew once I did, the divine authority of his words would change my life forever.

What about you and your spiritual journey? How have you struggled with faith in God and the teachings of Jesus Christ? What and who is the spiritual authority in your life? Does this divine influence empower and energize you? If not, perhaps it is time to reexamine your personal beliefs and spiritual practices.

God, we are all on a spiritual journey searching for meaning and purpose. Bless our memories and reflections today as we consider the authority of Jesus. We live in a confusing world where many conflicting deities of choice abound. Help us this day to determine whose we are and who we are. Amen.

† August 30 †

The prostitutes
Matthew 21:28-32

The religious leaders who had been debating with Jesus were probably very unhappy with this conversation! While the truth hurts, it also instructs. Our cherished religions can sometimes prevent or limit us from experiencing and sharing God's incredible spiritual generosity and hospitality.

"God has no religion," said Mahatma Gandhi. Jesus did not seem to promote any particular religion. He did however, preach and teach the radical lifestyle and spiritual revolution of the inclusive kingdom of God. The religious leaders of his day overwhelmingly rejected his teachings. Jesus was pushing their boundaries. His God was too big for them to fathom in their rigid religion.

This was also the message of John the Baptist, get ready for this amazing realm of God to come, repent and turn from your sins, believe and be baptized, follow Jesus Christ, realize you are not worthy to even untie his shoes, become a follower (disciple) of Jesus.

The despised, marginalized, outcasts, and common people heard Jesus gladly. Jesus confronted the "religious right" of his day with this amazing truth. Sometimes the rowdy, irreverent, rambunctious, and rejected sinners are more spiritually receptive than the rigidly religious to God's grace and mercy. Many such people become eager disciples of Jesus and are grateful for being included and welcomed into the realm of God. God's family is inclusive and welcoming.

Is this the kind of heaven you want to enter? Imagine being in heaven full of such companions for eternity. Imagine being in the realm of God where people of all sexual orientations love and care for each other. Imagine living in heaven with former prostitutes as your neighbors. Imagine God's delight to see us all living harmoniously together as the body of Christ.

Imagine both irreverent and reverent people becoming devoted followers of Jesus Christ.

God, I too, want to experience your grace and mercy along with the prostitutes and tax collectors as a devoted follower of Jesus Christ. Amen.

✝   **August 31**   ✝

Listen

Matthew 21:33-40

Robert Farrar Capon shares this insight about how Jesus used parables in his book *The Parables of the Kingdom.*[71] Parables are hard to understand yet one of the oldest teaching techniques in the world. They make a point by comparing one thing to another. Jesus often spoke in parables without interpreting them for the crowds. Either the disciples or other listeners would then ask questions for clarification. Jesus would often teach the meanings of the parables to his disciples privately. Sometimes the parables are confusing and seem full of paradox and contradictions. Sometimes we assume their meaning and really do not understand them at all. So listen with fresh ears and an open heart.

Listen to the answers of his listeners. The owner of the vineyard will severely punish the violent tenants and bring them to an end. The vineyard owner will then rent his vineyard to new tenants who will give the owner his share of the crop at harvest time.

What does this really mean? Jesus clarifies this disturbing parable about the realm of God. "Therefore I tell you that the kingdom of God will be taken away from you and given to a people who will produce its fruit" (Matthew 21:43). When the chief priests and the Pharisees heard this comment, they knew he was talking about them. We are told that they looked for a way to arrest him but were afraid of the popular public support of Jesus the prophet.

God, help us listen closely to this parable and find our place in it. Amen.

---

[71] Capon, Robert Farrar. *The Parables of the Kingdom*, page 1.

246

† September 1 †

A wedding parable
Matthew 22:1-14

We are individually responsible for our response to Jesus Christ, the Son of God. God is our gracious host, offering us an invitation to eternal life with Christ. What will we do with that invitation? The parable teaches us there will be consequences in refusing this divine offer.

This parable, also found in Luke 14:15-24, makes me squirm. In my dozen years as an ordained minister, I have only preached it once as a required assignment in a class. It is an uncomfortable parable about heaven and hell. According to Jesus, not everyone is going to heaven. This should make us pause and reflect. Where are we in this story?

Do you believe in heaven and hell? It was C. S. Lewis who said, "The safest road to hell is the gradual one – the gentle slope, soft underfoot, without sudden turnings, without milestones, without signposts." Today's parable is a definite signpost in our reading. It is an important teaching of Jesus that most of us quite frankly prefer to overlook.

Greek philosopher Epicurus (341-270 BC) is credited with saying, "It is never too early or too late to care for the well-being of the soul." Will you accept this invitation for eternal life in God through Jesus Christ, the Son? Our souls need what Jesus so generously offers us.

God, we thank you for this generous invitation to sit at your banquet table with Christ Jesus, your Son, in the kingdom of heaven. Help us live as your faithful servants and be assured of our salvation this day and forever. Amen.

† September 2 †

Trickery, Caesar, and taxes
Matthew 22:15-22

Political and religious enemies have always made strange bedfellows. Normally the Herodians and Pharisees did not get along. Their political beliefs differed sharply. But they shared a common desire to eliminate Jesus and so joined forces in a clever trap. First they flattered Jesus. Then they asked him a highly charged, politically dangerous question about Caesar and paying taxes. Their country was under Roman rule. If Jesus responded by defying Caesar and his oppressive taxation, this would place Jesus in very dangerous situation. He could be arrested and severely punished as a revolutionary.

Being no fool, Jesus instantly saw through their trickery. He knew their motives and felt their deadly hatred. He called their bluff and let them know he understood their attempt to trap him. What began as a potentially deadly trap instantly became one of his most famous sayings. "Give to Caesar what is Caesar's, and to God what is God's."

People of faith have long struggled to understand what it means to be a good citizen even when living under the rule of repressive, harsh, and evil governments. While honoring God in our lives how can we advocate justice and mercy, fight hunger, work for world peace, and make the world a better place to live? Even when we try to put politics aside, what does this teaching mean in our private, religious, social, professional, and recreational lives? How do we do this as we struggle to pay our bills and put food on the table?

I personally know of no easy answers to these questions. A popular question, which asks what Jesus would do in various situations, sometimes feels simplistic. But I know of no better way to begin.

Our story today concludes with Jesus' enemies baffled and astonished by his answer. They leave while shaking their heads in dismay and anger. But their conflict with him will only intensify. They are determined to rid their world of this upstart theologian.

God, teach us to give Caesar what is Caesar's. Bless us with the mind of Christ so we may know how give you what is yours. Amen.

† September 3 †

Heaven and marriage
Matthew 22:23-33

The Sadducees challenge Jesus by telling a hypothetical story of a bereaved woman who survived seven husbands. They wanted to know if there was a resurrection of the dead, like Jesus taught, whose wife would the woman be who had been passed on to so many brothers? As odd as their custom might seem to us, they did not have a social security system to assist widows and provide bereavement benefits. When husbands died, widows were handed down to the next surviving brother of the deceased in marriage. The brother was mandated by the law of Moses to marry his brother's widow and procreate children if the widow was childless. The purpose of this law was to continue the family line and protect the vulnerable widow in a patriarchal society. If the widows were not protected in this way, they would either starve or be forced to survive through prostitution. As the children grew, they would be able to care for their aged mother.

However, Jesus understood the Sadducees had a hidden agenda in their questioning. This was a test. With a few words, Jesus thoughtfully reinterpreted Levitical law (Deuteronomy 25:5-6) and offered a revolutionary new understanding of life after death. Traditional marriage was for this world only.

Marriage and traditional family values are often in public debate these days as growing numbers of same-sex couples around the world seek public recognition and legal protections equivalent to those of heterosexual couples. But back in the time of Jesus, there was no such public dialogue about what makes a family. Whatever our sexual orientation and however we define marriage, we would do well to remember that in the next world, the institution of marriage will not exist as we know it. According to Jesus, we will be like angels in heaven. There is life after death.

The ancient crowd was astonished by his answer. Even today, this is impossible to fully understand. But what I understand is this – there is hope of a resurrection for all of us. It is a living hope through a living God. The grave is not the end but the beginning of something beyond our human comprehension. Someday we will find ourselves singing with the angels. So as death approaches, have no fear. We will dwell in the presence of God forever and it will be glorious.

God, this teaching of Jesus is difficult to understand. Bless our comprehension and comfort those who live in hope of resurrection. Amen.

†   September 4   †

The greatest commandment
Matthew 22:34-40

Love is the greatest commandment in biblical law. With just four concise sentences, Jesus sums up the entire Old Testament (Hebrew Scriptures) for us. Love God with every fiber, breath, and cell of our being. Then love our neighbors as ourselves. Love ourselves as we love our neighbors. A teaching for all cultures, this Great Commandment, speaks to every generation, every nation, and every sexual orientation.

We all fall short and miss the mark in loving God, our neighbor, and ourselves. Today many mainline Christian denominations often practice intolerance and discrimination, causing great pain and suffering for sexual minorities. Christian churches that do not recognize same-sex love are not practicing the Golden Rule as taught by Jesus. Some Christian ministries explain their prejudice against same-sex love by saying they "hate the sin and love the sinner," but often they reject, refuse, and prohibit sexual minority people's basic human courtesies and human rights. Sometimes these Christian ministries go further than withholding blessings, they distort this basic teaching of Christ to justify fund-raising for themselves and political candidates that continue these policies of oppression of LGBT people, policies that often contribute to a lack of job security and health insurance for LGBT people, as well as acts of physical violence against them. Tragically, these non-welcoming Christian churches can cause profound spiritual injuries to many seekers who have been demonized and denigrated by these houses of worship.

I am often considered "too controversial" to lead centering and contemplative prayer groups at those non-affirming churches. Does this surprise you? When will we learn to live and practice our highest calling? When will we finally obey Jesus and live this commandment to love?

More love, O God, to You, our neighbors, and ourselves. Amen.

† September 5 †

A theological dilemma

Matthew 22:41-46

Jesus' listeners face a dilemma. If Jesus proclaims himself to be the Messiah everything would change. People would need to choose sides in a spiritual-political-religious revolution that would turn their world upside down.

Nonetheless, "[t]he large crowd listened to [Jesus] with delight" (Mark 12:37 NIV) as he asked these challenging questions (see also Luke 20:41-44 for another version of this teaching). Jesus tells the crowds and Pharisees that the Messiah was more than a descendant of David. The Messiah is David's Lord and superior, radical theology for the listening crowd.

Suddenly the mood of the crowd shifted to apprehension and fear. The throng sensed the embarrassed Pharisees' cold hatred towards Jesus. Any more questions would be far too dangerous for askers and listeners alike. Jesus was clearly on thin ice as he spoke with such authority and presence. People shifted uneasily on their feet, some coughing and clearing their throats in the thick and uncomfortable silence. The Pharisees were not interested in engaging in good natured, jocular debate. They were dead serious in their growing resolve to permanently silence Jesus.

Many times I find myself wondering what relevance particular biblical passages have. It can be difficult in the best of times to understand and appreciate some of these ancient stories. As one who grew up in a distinctly Protestant home, I can only try and imagine with my limited ability just how outraged and determined these devout Pharisees were in their growing resolve to destroy Jesus. The furious Pharisees intimidated the great crowd with fear. Speakers and listeners alike realized any more being said could lead to a point of no turning back. There are times when silence is golden and this was one of them.

What are we to do with this story? Perhaps all we can do is linger with the tension in the crowd and think of what really was at stake. If Jesus is who he claims to be, then we too, face the crowd's dilemma. We must then accept or reject his astonishing spiritual-political-religious revolution that continues even to this day. Our decision is intensely personal and will affect how we live, love, work, play, rest, and serve God and humanity.

God, what do we believe about this person named Jesus? Help us live our beliefs about him today. Amen.

†   September 6   †

Religious hypocrisy and sickness

Matthew 23:1-12

An old calendar of mine has this saying, "Make your life your sermon." I must admit a feeling of caution as we approach this chapter in Matthew, commonly known as the "Seven Woes." Human nature, being what it is, encourages a rapid and shallow reading of uncomfortable scriptures. Oh, we may say, this does not apply to me. Yet all of us harbor the potential of being a religious hypocrite. It is so easy to do.

Who has not wanted others to do what we say and not what we do. Yet spiritual leadership calls for brutally honest moments of self-examination. We might find ourselves in these verses. So together, let us do something daily that helps us grow spiritually. Let us slowly digest the twenty-third chapter of Matthew over the course of a week as contemplative readers. Allow yourself to reflect on it in moments of silent stillness. Let the silence change, calm, and illuminate your understanding of these verses. Let this be time for inner change.

Who has not failed to practice what they preached? Who has not put burdens on others that we ourselves had no intention of assuming? Who has not done something during our lives for public acclaim, recognition, and fame? Who has not loved being in places of honor and the best seats? Who does not love being called by their full and official titles of respect and recognition?

Jesus calls us to look honestly within ourselves. Those among us who have exalted themselves at the expense of others will be humbled. Discipleship according to Jesus is humble living with the heart of a servant. God will exalt the humble in divine timing.

God, give us the inward courage for personal and fearless self-examination. Help us have the mind and heart of Christ. Give us the courage to change the things we can. Amen.

† September 7 †

Actors and masks
Matthew 23:13-14

All of us have the potential to be a "Pharisee." John A. Sanford offers us brilliant insight in his book *The Kingdom Within: The Inner Meanings of Jesus' Sayings.* "One reason that the requirements of the kingdom are both difficult and light is the necessity to shed the Pharisaic outer mask. The mask is the person we pretend to be – the false outer personality that we turn to the world, but that is contradicted from within. The mask is that which conceals our real thoughts and feelings, and which we come to use so habitually as a way to hide from others and ourselves that we become unaware that we have assumed it. . . . If we would belong to the kingdom, this false outer front must go. . . . This shedding of the mask is the primary point of Jesus' teachings against Pharisaism. Jesus is opposed to the Pharisees primarily because the Pharisees wear masks – they conceal themselves – and so mislead people because they themselves are false . . . the word hypocrite means an 'actor,' and actors in Jesus' time literally wore masks that depicted the roles they were playing." [72]

"Conscience is the voice of the soul," taught Jean-Jacques Rousseau. We would be wise to pray for a healthy conscience as we linger in this chapter with these brutally honest warnings from Jesus. You see, these are not simply addressed to the teachers of the law and Pharisees of Jesus' day. These lessons are timeless and appropriate for all people.

Perhaps this is why we are cautioned to not be so eager to teach. James, believed to be a brother of Jesus reminds us, "We who teach will be judged with greater strictness. For all of us make many mistakes" (James 3:1-2 NIV).

Have we somehow, somewhere, at sometime, prevented someone from experiencing the liberating and dignifying gospel of Jesus Christ? Have we let personal bias block a seeker of God by placing well intentioned but burdensome requirements on seekers?

God, give me the courage to confront myself honestly and without self-deception in these verses. What is Jesus saying to me? Give me courage to change the things that I can. Amen.

---

[72] Sanford, John A. *The Kingdom Within: The Inner Meaning of Jesus' Sayings*, p. 70

† September 8 †
Warning!
Matthew 23:15

Jesus denounces the scribes and Pharisees, saying, "Woe to you, scribes and Pharisees, hypocrites! For you cross sea and land to make a single convert, and you make the new convert twice as much a child of hell as yourselves" (Matthew 23:15, NRSV). Have I done this during my Christian life and ministry, God? If so, where? Help me learn from my mistakes. A daily spirituality calendar reminder says to "Keep your mind hospitable to new ideas." Have I created and trained zealots? Have I mentored spiritual babes in the faith to be proud, arrogant, and self-serving in the gospel? Am I a religious hypocrite?

I sometimes find international wisdom proverbs posted on the Internet helpful in such moments of self-examination. A sensible Ilocano saying (a popular dialect spoken by millions in the Philippines on the northern island of Luzon) is, "If you are going a long way, go slowly." Help me, God, go slowly in reflection, evaluation, and spiritual reassessment in how I live and share my Christian faith.

Forgive me, gracious God, where I have erred in well-intentioned efforts in the Christian discipleship and spiritual formation of myself and in others. Open my eyes and the door of my heart to respond to Jesus today. Amen.

† September 9 †
Be very careful
Matthew 23:16-22

I believe it was Ralph Waldo Emerson (1803-1882) who said, "Be very careful what you set your heart upon, for you will surely have it." Set your heart upon loving and serving God. Honor your oaths, vows, and promises to God. Today's verses remind us to be very careful indeed. Are we serving as blind spiritual guides? Does money blind us? Or have we blinded others by our own idolization of money? Have we valued anything more than our vows, oaths, and promises to God? Have we compromised our spiritual integrity for personal greed?

Life is a spiritual marathon. A photograph of a blind man running a marathon with a sighted partner, which I saw in a running magazine with an advertisement for the Marine Corps Marathon, deeply influenced me many years ago. The blind man wore a large sign pinned to his chest that said, "BLIND." I marveled at his courage and faith in his running partner to run 26.2 grueling miles. He trusted his partner's clear vision as well as his faithful and protective presence. The blind man could not have run the race with a sightless guide in that jostling crowd of thousands of fellow marathoners. He needed a sighted guide to finish the race.

In much the same way, we benefit by having clear sighted and reliable spiritual guides who offer us their experience and wisdom. Be selective and seek guides known for their integrity and trustworthiness. However, even the best spiritual mentors can disappoint. But Jesus Christ will never let you down or abandon you when the going gets tough. Whatever your circumstances, follow his guidance and you will find sure footing along with growing spiritual clarity and perception. You might be astonished at how God might bring seekers and believers into your life, seeking your experiences in the spiritual life, drawn to you because Christ is your guide in life.

God, give us eyes to see this warning. Give us spiritual insight to respond to it. Help us heed the words of Christ today and be wise spiritual guides. Amen.

† September 10 †

Blind guides

Matthew 23:23-24

Jesus did not endear himself to the religious leaders of his day listening to these comments. His brutally honest words continue to instruct people from all walks of life and every religious tradition. Every human being has great potential to be a hypocrite. Our external, public behavior can look marvelous. We can be applauded for our personal piety as we meticulously tithe our resources to the penny, promoting religious activities through our various churches, synagogues, temples, and multifaith and ecumenical institutions. We can excel in obeying the letter of the law while neglecting mercy, justice, and faithfulness.

When we err in these ways, Jesus bluntly reminds us that we have become blind guides and hypocrites. We can be so diligent and devoted to honoring the minutia of our laws that we become overzealous in our judgments and condemning of those who do not meet our strict standards of behavior.

It is good to remember that we are all sinners saved by grace. Yes, it is important and spiritually pleasing to God when we tithe of our resources. But God is not pleased when we neglect the most important matters of justice, compassion, and faithfulness. The Gospel is quite practical. If we chose to follow the Christ, God expects us to bring a little heaven on earth to others less fortunate than ourselves.

How then should we live? By doing justice, offering mercy, and walking humbly with God. When in doubt, err on the side of justice with mercy and mercy with justice, while seeking divine wisdom every step of the way. Be accountable to others who have the courage to confront us when we become legalistic and inconsistent. When we find ourselves straining out gnats, ask God for forgiveness and humbly learn from those mistakes.

God, protect me from harsh legalism, from any lack in justice or mercy in secular, religious, and spiritual settings. Help me walk humbly with you as I strive to be faithful in word, thought, and deed to the teachings of Jesus. Give me courage to confront my own inner blindness. Amen.

†   September 11   †

Inner attitudes and cleansing

Matthew 23:25-26

Jesus says, "Woe to you, scribes and Pharisees, hypocrites! For you clean the outside of the cup and of the plate, but inside they are full of greed and self-indulgence. You blind Pharisee! First clean the inside of the cup, so that the outside also may become clean" (Matthew 23:25-26, NRSV). These stinging words are as relevant today as when Jesus uttered them. Religious people have often been quick to point the finger and condemn others, while neglecting to first look in the mirror. Our human nature is often blind to our own faults and eager to pass the blame on to others. September 11, 2001 is a powerful example of such religious condemnation, bigotry, and hypocrisy.

That morning four hijacked planes had been used in a carefully planned, well-coordinated attack. Two had deliberately crashed and destroyed the twin 110-story towers of the World Trade Center building in New York City. Minutes later another crashed into the Pentagon in Washington, DC, causing the White House to be evacuated while the fourth plane crashed outside Pittsburgh. Scenes of hell could not be any worse than these horrific moments as thousands of innocent people died in fiery infernos.

Wise spiritual leaders from around the world quickly urged the dazed public to refrain from retributive hate crimes. Within hours, people from many faiths came together and began many extraordinary interfaith vigils mingling Jewish, Christian and Muslim prayers for peace and healing. Our prayers connected us in our common human condition of mourning.

Tragically, before the dust of the rubble settled, prominent television evangelists, powerful voices of the religious right, pointed their fingers in judgment and accused liberal civil liberties groups, feminists, homosexuals, and abortion rights supporters for being partially responsible for the terrorist attacks. These self-righteous contemporary Pharisees proclaimed these were the people who made God angry at America. They vilified many innocent citizens. Ignorant, bigoted, and fearful people responded with savage violence against fellow Americans in their eagerness to retaliate because of the hateful religious rhetoric. The hate-filled extremist terrorist rhetoric of the 9/11 highjackers had met its match.

According to Jesus, all human beings have great potential to be self-indulgent religious hypocrites, pointing fingers in judgment towards others while neglecting to take care of the inherent potential for evil in their own souls. This seems to be an especially dangerous occupational hazard for religious professionals. We would be wise to remember we are all sinners in need of grace. None of us are perfect or without sin except God. Together, we should weep with God as we meditate on the words from Jesus and grieve the events of September 11, 2001.

God, help us look in the mirror and see ourselves through your holy eyes. As we remember September 11, 2001, we ask you heal the broken hearted and pray for our world. Amen.

† **September 12** †

Take off the mask

Matthew 23:27-28

Our morality needs to be more than skin deep. Jesus knows our inner make-up. We can try to pass ourselves off as someone we are not, but God is not fooled. God knows our hearts (Luke 16:15).

John A. Sanford reminds us that the Pharisees were perceived as the perfect examples of what God wanted people to be like. [73] They were the respectable, virtuous people in society. Now Jesus compares them to tombs of corruption and cups of filth. They hated him for stripping away their façade. Jesus had preached this earlier in his Sermon on the Mount, "If your virtue goes no deeper than that of the scribes and Pharisees, you will never get into the kingdom of heaven" (Matthew 5:20).

How are our hearts before God today? Do we need some serious spiritual heart surgery? Our greatest delusion, Sanford tells us, "is thinking that we can avoid the unconscious and solve the moral problems of life by creating a righteous exterior, or by an ethic of outer obedience to laws. But this is of no avail, for God sees into the human heart; ruthlessly his eye penetrates into the deepest recess of the soul." [74]

With God, nothing can be kept in darkness. God sees all that is done in secret and understands our motives better than we understand ourselves.

God, examine and know us. Read our thoughts. Change our hearts. May our virtue be deeper than that of the scribes and Pharisees. Amen.

---

[73] Sanford, John A. *The Kingdom Within: The Inner Meaning of Jesus' Sayings*, p. 73.
[74] Ibid.

† September 13 †

Sins of our ancestors

Matthew 23:29-32

The sins of our ancestors come back to us. Sooner or later we reap what we sow. Every family closet has skeletons that need to be examined and purged. The good news of the gospel is that we do not have to be stuck in the past. With the help of God, we can learn from our family and spiritual histories, gain insight and strength, and be spiritually empowered for present and future living.

Our ancestors can teach us many lessons. Just the other day, some missionaries from another faith denomination came to my door. They graciously offered free genealogy services at their own expense "with absolutely no obligation." Their card said, "Families are forever." If we do not learn from the lessons of history, we are bound to repeat those mistakes again and again. The "sins of our forebears" are worth learning from. We can save ourselves from repeating their mistakes such as abusive and spiritually destructive behaviors and attitudes.

Who has not been spiritually blind at some point in our lives? Who has not failed to honor the prophets among us? They might be religious figures or social activists, family or teachers, friends or preachers, famous or unknown. Prophets come in many forms.

God, help us learn from the sins of our ancestors and all who preceded us in our faith. Help us recognize and respect the prophets in our midst. Amen.

† September 14 †

Snakes in the grass

Matthew 23:33-39

Several nights ago, the television news was filled with rattlesnake warnings. Long grass and warm weather combined to make perfect conditions for the snakes to thrive and multiply. The news broadcasters cautioned people to watch where they walk and be careful where they put their hands as they climbed over fallen logs along the park trails. Look, listen, and pause before you step out on the path before you, encouraged the U.S.A. Park Service. There are "snakes in the grass!"

There are religious rattlesnakes among us, says Jesus. Watch, look, and listen for them. Be careful!

How dare Jesus call them "snakes and vipers!" The religious leaders were infuriated. Those receiving this judgment from Jesus hated him. They would later kill, crucify, flog, chase out of town, and stone the people Jesus would send to them in the future. Their hearts were hardened. They were spiritually blind to God's truth through Jesus.

We see God's heartbeat through Jesus. In another gospel passage, he weeps as he cries out, "O Jerusalem, Jerusalem" (Luke 13:34-35). How Christ longs to gather us under his protecting arms, as a mother hen protects her wee chicks. People sent from God are still killed, tortured, persecuted, and exiled around the world. The blood of martyrs since the beginning has built the Church. The Christian Church remains a persecuted church in many countries around the world.

Sometimes God's truth comes to us through the most unlikely messengers of grace and mercy. The face of the Christian church has changed forever with the growing prophetic global voices of gay, lesbian, bisexual, and transgendered Christians. Yet even the Church persecutes its own, for many hearts are hardened to these Christian brothers and sisters. Could we call these persecutors religious rattlesnakes?

Prophets, wise men and women, and teachers come in the name of Christ representing all sexual orientations. Be open to their voices. God is big and not limited to our finite understandings. You who have ears to hear, listen! Watch out for religious rattlesnakes in the grass!

God, help us listen to this stern teaching of Christ. Amen.

† September 15 †

Signs of the end times
Matthew 24:3-8

Many devout Christians sincerely believed the end of the world was coming as we greeted the twenty-first century. I received numerous e-mails explaining their understanding of why Jesus was returning specifically in the year 2000. Profiteers made a fortune from selling elaborate year Y2K (year 2000) supplies to the gullible and fearful. Some people even sold their homes, moved to rural areas, armed themselves against possible thieves, and prepared for the worse. They thoroughly prepared for violence and other natural and human disasters based on their fallible understanding of Holy Scripture.

Other Christians insisted the end of the world could not take place until the gospel had been preached to the whole world. Devout people have believed the end was in sight as they experienced famine, earthquakes, and other natural disasters throughout world history. Wars and rumors of wars always bring this speculation. As one United Church of Christ (UCC) minister put it, "Christian disunity isn't news. Christian disunity is as old as the New Testament."

The Bible tells us that someday there will be a great and terrible day of God's holy, righteous judgment. Jesus came to prepare us for that day so we can stand before God with confidence as beloved children. Many Christians differ in their interpretation of when and how and if this will actually happen. The original disciples approached Jesus privately for a fuller explanation. Today's scripture is a very difficult and controversial teaching to understand.

Someday this world will come to an end. Jesus Christ is coming again. The signs of the end times will be very chaotic and confusing. Many will claim to be Christ. Do not be deceived. The world will experience suffering beyond description. Be brave. Christians of all sexual orientations will be persecuted, put to death, and hated because of Christ. Be faithful unto death. Many believers will waver in their faith and lose their love for God through their suffering. We must stand firm through our last breath. When the entire world has heard the liberating gospel message of Jesus, in God's timing, the end will come and a new heaven and earth will be ushered in.

My beloved grandmother would often say, "Keep looking up. Jesus is coming. Maybe even today."

God, help us live one day at a time as faithful and courageous Christians. Amen.

†   September 16   †

Hard times

Matthew 24:15-25

Famous scholars disagree about the meaning of some Bible passages. Depending on which commentaries and study notes you refer to, you will find a number of wide ranging interpretations on these verses.

There are some areas of agreement. Most of the resources I consulted agreed that Jesus was referring to prophetic passages in Daniel 9:27; 11:31; 12:11. [75] Many people believe Jesus was speaking of a double reference to the catastrophic event when the Roman army would destroy the Jerusalem temple in A.D. 70 and to the Antichrist. [76] One commentary suggests the Sabbath reference was clearly a Jewish perspective by the Gospel author Matthew. [77] The author of Matthew was Jewish. It would have been against the Jewish law to travel on the Sabbath. Another scholar states that this horrible disaster that affected Israel was limited in scope and had a definite end. History continued. The events were "catastrophic but not apocalyptic." [78] They were not the end of world history.

This passage remains very difficult to interpret and understand. What I clearly understand is this: Jesus has told us ahead of time that there will be many false Christs and prophets. I do not have to be deceived. The Gospels are our standard of measurement for when the going gets tough.

Rather than be fearful of the end times, get to know Jesus through reading the Gospels of Matthew, Mark, Luke, and John. Get to know him personally and be spiritually empowered for whatever life brings your way. Jesus' words and wisdom are timeless for your era of world history

---

[75] Bruce, F. F., General Editor. *The International Bible Commentary with the New International Version*, page 1902.

[76] Hendriksen, William. *New Testament Commentary: The Gospel of Matthew*, pp. 860-861.

[77] Guthrie, D., and J. A. Motyer, Editors. *The New Bible Commentary*, p. 845.

[78] *Ibid.*

and global culture. We can be secure in the words of Christ and know truth when deceit surrounds us. So take courage and rest in Christ.

God, sometimes the Bible is difficult to understand. We live in a world where fearful and distressing events occur locally and globally. Give us insight and discernment as we strive to know Jesus, sometimes in the midst of chaos and confusion. Amen.

†   **September 17**   †

Global mourning

Matthew 24:29-35

World history as we know it will come to an end someday, according to Jesus' teaching. Theologians debate and disagree vigorously on details, timing, and various theologies of divine judgment and reward. Generally speaking though, since the earliest days of the Church the majority of Christians have expected Jesus to return to earth in heavenly glory and power.

Those first generations of excited and expectant believers fervently and impatiently awaited for Jesus to return after he arose from the grave. Some people were so convinced of the immediate return of their beloved Jesus that they were reluctant to work and waste time on activities that would keep them focused on earthly concerns. Their bags were packed for heaven.

During the first century, spiritual leaders such as the apostle Paul became concerned about the fiscal irresponsibility of these heavenly dreamers. Although their faith was commendable, it was becoming obvious that Jesus was taking his time in returning. Bills needed paying, crops had to be harvested. Paul wrote letters to circulate among various churches urging believers to live in eager expectation while diligently working to bring heaven on earth as they served their employers, paid their earthly bills, and honored their personal, family, and business responsibilities.

As generations lived and died, it became obvious to the church at large that Christ would return in God's time. The church gradually developed a liturgical calendar to assist the faithful in remembering the teachings of Jesus. [79] As time went on, the church developed seasons of worship and remembrance through selected scripture readings and particular prayers and songs. Advent, Christmas, Epiphany, Lent, Easter, and Pentecost offer reminders of the entire Jesus story from his first Advent, coming as a baby in a manger, to his second Advent, when he will return as Savior of the world. Although today's scripture reading is sometimes reserved for Advent, it is helpful to look at these difficult passages throughout the year so we do not become complacent in our faith.

Christ's return will generate two major responses. Those who believe in him will rejoice, while the unbelieving world will mourn. Heaven and earth will pass away. In the great Mystery of God, there will be a new heaven and new earth. The things of this current world will pass away and be no more. Christians of all sexual orientations are urged to work and wait, pray and live in expectation of this day.

These Bible verses in Matthew's gospel remind me of a great woman of faith, my beloved grandmother, Inga Gunderson, who used to croon a prayer whenever life circumstances were overwhelming, summarizing her belief that this world would someday come to an end, but Jesus would eventually make things better upon his return. She would often pray, "One day at a time, dear Lord, one day at a time. Jesus is coming again. Perhaps even today." While that prayer might bring a skeptical smile to many lips, my grandmother had wisely conceptualized and summarized this very difficult teaching of Jesus in her memorable prayer. She understood Jesus could come any hour of the day or night. God alone knows the hour.

So live, work, play, pray, worship, and conduct your life with alertness and expectation of Jesus' return. When that day occurs, the faithful will celebrate and the faithless will mourn. Here lies the tension of the Gospel. If Jesus were to return today, would you celebrate or mourn? The choice is yours.

Oh God, help me live as your beloved follower one day at a time. Remind me to keep looking up in eager hope and expectation of the second return of Christ. Amen.

---

[79] Chi Rho Press publishes an annual *Liturgical Calendar and Lectionary*, based on the *Revised Common Lectionary*. Find the latest edition at http://www.ChiRhoPress.com.

† **September 18** †

When?

Matthew 24:36-44

Life is full of many different kinds of surprises. Some are good and others are dreadful. I love a good surprise birthday party or receiving an unexpected present from someone I love. The surprise Jesus is describing is not something anyone would wish for. His words urge us to live with the alert expectation of Christ's eventual return, for we do not know the hour or day this will occur.

It is easy to drift back into complacency after having experienced a dramatic wake up call or life changing event. Resolutions to live more alertly are easy to make in the initial horror of catastrophic events. We sometimes vow to live better lives that will be pleasing to God with the best of intentions. As the memories of our earlier spiritual awakenings fade, old habits and the monotony of daily routines lure many of us into casual and careless attitudes of living. That is exactly what Jesus is addressing in today's verses. We will be living our routine lives when Jesus' unexpected second return will occur. Jesus will crash into our awareness when we least expect him. Life will never again be the same.

I find it very difficult to remain spiritually alert and ready for this moment by myself. My mind and body become tired. I have heard these admonitions to remain alert for decades. Mentally, spiritually, physically, and emotionally I find it humanly impossible to live in a constant ready and waiting mode. This is why we need to find and identify with spiritual community for encouragement and empowerment. To be renewed and invigorated in our faith, we need to participate in a worshipping community.

Through our participation with the church and community of faith, Jesus crashes into our lives when we least expect or invite him. He continues to surprise us with his remarkable presence through some of the most unlikely messengers of grace. We do not have to wait for the Second Advent to experience his power and mercy.

It may be a little more difficult to find a church that welcomes seekers of all sexual orientations due to religious homophobia. Be patient in your search and ask God for help along your journey. Be encouraged. The number of open and affirming, more light, welcoming, and reconciling churches is growing every day. If there are none in your immediate community, go online and at the very least, connect with affirming virtual

Web sites and cyber-churches. Throughout your journey, keep the faith and keep looking up. Remember, Jesus is coming, perhaps even today through friend and stranger.

God, bless me as I look for worshipping communities that can help me grow stronger in my faith. Help me live with renewed spiritual readiness and alertness daily, I pray. Amen.

† September 19 †

How shall we live?

Matthew 24:45-51

We have a charge to live faithful and wise lives as disciples (followers) of Christ. God has work for us to do. Some disciples might be famous and globally influential, but probably most of us are called to faithful lives serving in relative obscurity. It is easy to become lulled into complacency and careless stewardship of our precious lives. We might think Jesus would never return during our lifetime, but we never know when that day will be.

The gospel message comforts the afflicted and afflicts the comfortable. I am very comfortable in my faith. These words disturb my comfort zone. I get stuck. I am a creature of habit. Perhaps I am not alone in these thoughts. Can you identify with me?

These stern words from Christ call for an honest reassessment of "call" and "ministry." Each follower of Christ has meaningful service to contribute during our lifetime to promote the kingdom of heaven on earth. As long as we breathe on earth, we have something to contribute.

God, energize my life with new awareness and love for serving you and your kingdom. Help me be a faithful and wise servant of the gospel. Help us all. Amen.

† September 20 †

The parable of the ten virgins

Matthew 25:1-13

Are we wise, alert, and prepared? Or are we foolish and unprepared? Today we need honest self-discernment to understand this lesson about the kingdom of heaven.

It is a disturbing parable for the latecomers who miss the wedding feast and find the door closed in their faces. The doorkeeper has these chilling words for the foolish virgins, "I tell you the truth, I do not know you." F. F. Bruce notes in *The Hard Sayings of Jesus* that the ten virgins did not appear to have been bridesmaids or even specially invited guests. He suggests they were local village girls who decided to form a torchlight procession and escort the bridegroom and his party to the house where the wedding feast was to be held. They knew if they did, there would be a place at the feast for them, where they could share the good cheer. Even today centuries later, there are parts of the world where a wedding feast is a public occasion for the neighborhood. All who come will find a welcome and something to eat and drink.

There was no time announced for the event. Some of the waiting women were wise and brought extra oil for their lamps. Others were foolish and unprepared. Those who had prepared did not share their oil supply with the foolish ones. Those refused entry to the wedding banquet returned to their homes in the dark, tired and disappointed.

All the oil was good while it lasted, but not everyone prepared enough for tomorrow's needs. We cannot always rely on yesterday's experiences of grace. We must be prepared and watchful every day. Times of testing come without warning. Will we be prepared and wise? Or will we be foolish? So it will be when Christ returns for the second time. We do not know the day or the hour.

God, Jesus had a reason for teaching this parable. Bless my understanding and help me live more alertly today. Amen.

†   **September 21**   †

The parable of the talents

Matthew 25:14-30

The kingdom of heaven is like a master leaving on a long trip and entrusting servants with varying amounts of talents depending on their ability. Some people are very faithful and productive with what they are given. Other people are miserly in spirit with their gifts for the kingdom of heaven. There are rewards and consequences to how we use what God gives us.

In the early 1990s I served as a U.S. Navy Chaplain on an ammunition ship. I was the first woman chaplain to serve on that vessel. Some of the senior male officers were very angry to have a chaplain onboard and a female at that. I often faced overt and covert sexual harassment and internal sabotage of my assigned duties in the Command Religious Program. It was my responsibility to deploy with the troops, be confidential counselor, be an advisor, provide interfaith pastoral presence, lead Protestant worship services, and provide nightly public prayers for the entire ship while at sea. Those were difficult and exhausting years. The ongoing verbal abuse and disrespect by those senior officers caused me to pause and consider quitting. I was not afraid of hard work. I was however, getting emotionally and spiritually fatigued and sometimes felt very isolated.

This particular parable was a great source of comfort to me during that time. I actually penciled my dated initials by the statement, "Well done, good and faithful servant! You have been faithful in a few things." God had entrusted me with this ship and I gave my best efforts to be faithful. I was often tempted to quit and give up. I strove to serve even the difficult people with the loving spirit of God. It was a great comfort to remember God saw and empowered me one day at a time. Someday there would be heavenly reward for my faithful service. That is as good as it gets.

Many people find it difficult to believe that our lives are indeed accountable to God. Someday everything we do, say, think, and intend will be assessed before God. Our highest praise will be hearing God say, "Well done, good and faithful servant!"

Here is a glimpse of grace for the day. God is eager to use ordinary people in extraordinary ways for the kingdom of heaven. In *Glimpses of Grace*, Madeleine L'Engle writes, "And then there is time in which to be, simply to be, that time in which God quietly tells us who we are and

268

who [God] wants us to be. It is then that God can take our emptiness and fill it up with what [God] wants, and drain away the business with which we inevitably get involved in the daily-ness of human living." [80]

How is God quietly speaking to you in this parable? Who does God want you to be? How does God want you to use your talents?

Come, Holy Spirit, come. Fill me with your power and might. Show me where I am in this parable. Help me to use my talents to live a faithful life for God. Amen.

✝   September 22   ✝

The parable of sheep and goats
Matthew 25:31-46

In *Picturing God*, Ann Belford Ulanov writes, "Picturing God must precede any speaking about God, for our pictures accompany all our words and they continue long after we fall silent before God. Images – the language of the psyche – are the coin of life; they touch our emotions as well as our thoughts; they reach down into our bodies as well as toward our ideas. They arrive unbidden, startling, after our many years of effort to craft them." [81]

This is the final parable Christ taught before his betrayal, arrest, and death by crucifixion. It is a picture of God that gives us images that touch our innermost souls and hidden hearts. This touches our thoughts and daily lives.

Where are we in this parable? Are we among the sheep or the goats? Have we lived compassionate lives as disciples of Christ? Have we reached out to the sick, hungry, imprisoned, and needy? Or have we been indifferent to them? Truly, the gospel is a blessed burden. It offers divine encouragement and hope for those in need, and mandates a sacred

---

[80] L'Engle, Madeleine. *Glimpses of Grace*, p. 118

[81] Found in Job, Rueben P., and Norman Shawchuck, editors. *A Guide to Prayer for all God's People*, p. 132-133

responsibility for those with the resources and means to ease the pervasive suffering of so many near and far.

One of Jesus' brothers is believed to have authored the New Testament letter (epistle) titled, *James*. James clearly understood his big brother's teachings! James writes about faith and deeds, "What good is it, my brothers and sisters, if you say you have faith but do not have works? Can such faith save you? If a brother or sister is naked and lacks daily food, and one of you says to them, 'Go in peace; keep warm and eat your fill,' and yet you do not supply their bodily needs, what is the good of that? So faith by itself, if it has no works, is dead" (James 2: 14-17 NRSV).

The beloved disciple John also understood this teaching and later wrote these words of encouragement, "This is how we know what love is: Jesus Christ laid down his life for us. And we ought to lay down our lives for our brothers [and sisters]. If anyone has material possessions and sees his brother [or sister] in need but has no pity, how can the love of God be in them? Dear children, let us not love with words or tongue but with actions and in truth" (1 John 3:16-18 NIV).

Mother Teresa has had great influence on my spiritual journey. I deeply admire her life and faith. When asked if she ever felt overwhelmed by such dire poverty among those she served in India, her response was no. Her life was like a drop of water in the ocean. If her drop were not offered, it would be deeply missed. When encountering human misery in the streets, she encouraged people "not to wait for your leaders, do something!" [82] Perhaps we should all follow her advice and do something when we encounter human need as followers of Jesus.

The gospel is profoundly simple. Those who have ears to hear, listen!

God, speak clearly to us through today's parable and teach us how to live. Amen.

---

[82] Muggeridge, Malcolm. *Something Beautiful for God*, p. 29

†   September 23   †

A sly plan to kill Jesus
Matthew 26:1-5

Over the years of his public ministry, Jesus had made a number of deadly enemies within the leadership of his own birth religion. His opponents had had enough of his message, and with stealth and malice they gathered to make an evil plan to entrap and arrest him. Their intent was deadly. His enemies would not rest until he was dead and buried. Jesus was clearly in harm's way.

But the public loved and respected Jesus. He had healed, blessed, preached, and taught life-nourishing insights about God and a new way of spiritual living with real life applications. His miracles had convinced huge crowds that Jesus had a very special relationship with God. Whatever premeditated murderous plan was being hatched, it had to be done carefully or the religious leaders in power would have a riot on their hands. If that happened, the occupying Roman authorities would quickly become involved. So the religious leaders carefully and perhaps even prayerfully searched quietly for an effective way to eliminate Jesus. He had to be terminated in such a way that the public would be on the religious officials' side.

History has a tendency to repeat itself if we fail to learn from the past. Consciously or unconsciously, those in positions of religious leadership and influence often have the best of intentions as they passionately defend and protect their long standing, cherished religious interpretations of sacred texts and their traditional ways of life from perceived real or potential apostasy and heresy. I have seen deeply devout people capable of verbal and physical violence when it comes to defending their most cherished belief systems. We can become so involved in protecting and defending our faith that we might fail to recognize new and progressive revelations from God.

Yes, we do have a holy responsibility to hold those in ecclesiastical power to a standard of accountability locally and globally. It is spiritually healthy to examine contemporary issues and respectfully question and challenge certain stances held in our religious hierarchies. It is all too possible for religious institutions to become so bureaucratic and politically motivated, that they fail to discern fresh new movements of the Holy Spirit in our midst. We must always remember that people in positions of religious authority killed Jesus.

Ultimately we are responsible for how we individually respond to or stifle the spirit of Christ within others and ourselves. Jesus comes to us disguised in many forms. He might come to us in gay apparel or as a homeless person. Jesus is often revealed through those people who are often neglected, despised, overlooked, and ignored. We must remember God is bigger and more compassionate than we can ever imagine. Prayerfully consider how our words, actions, and attitudes kill or give life to the spirit of Christ in others.

God, give us courage for moments of honest and fearless self-examination today as we consider our cherished ways of believing and thinking about you and others. Bless us with a deeper understanding of the message of Jesus Christ. We also pray for those in religious leadership around the world. Help us hold them accountable to the life-giving, dignifying spirit of Jesus. Amen.

† September 24 †

Anonymous greatness

Matthew 26:6-13

This anonymous woman demonstrates great spiritual leadership and insight. While the male disciples were dismayed and avoiding the topic of the crucifixion, this brave woman took it upon herself to lovingly anoint Jesus. She anointed him with the best perfume money could buy to prepare him for his burial. She understood and accepted what Jesus had told them time and time again. He must die. If so, she would spare no expense to tenderly offer this beautiful service of love to Jesus. She could do no less than give her best in his moments of need. She affirmed his mission and accepted her own calling to humbly demonstrate anonymous spiritual leadership with her profound insight and actions.

This woman received instant and indignant criticism. The male disciples vociferously called her loving act wasteful. They piously insisted the lovely perfume should have been sold and the money given to the poor. Jesus told them to stop bothering the woman. The poor will always be with us. Her gift was beautiful and honored him. She indeed prepared his body for burial. Wherever the gospel is preached throughout the world, what she has done "will also be told in memory of her."

Spiritual greatness is often anonymous. Spiritual greatness is lived humbly and in loving adoration of God. Spiritual greatness is often not the popular or easy thing to do. Spiritual greatness comes at great personal cost without expecting a reward. Spiritual greatness can generate criticism from our own people.

Do you want to be spiritually great? Then be like this anonymous woman. Study the life of Jesus and follow his teachings in the spirit of love and sacrificial service. Be willing to anonymously serve in obscurity.

God, help me listen to this story and teach me about spiritual greatness. Amen.

† September 25 †
Sold for a price
Matthew 26:14-16

Cynics will insist everyone has a price and loyalty can be bought. For Judas Iscariot, thirty silver coins represented approximately four months' wages. Why would he betray Jesus? After three years of being with this remarkable teacher, healer, and miracle worker, what prompted him to sell out to the religious authorities? Was it greed? Or is there more to this story? Did the anonymous woman who so lovingly anointed Jesus influence his decision? The other gospel accounts do not tell us the motives of Judas Iscariot (Mark 14:10, 11; Luke 22:3-6). They do tell us that the hostile religious leaders were "delighted" with his decision to betray Jesus into their hands (Mark 14: 11 NIV).

Luke and John specifically mention that "Satan entered Judas." This expression is found twice, first in Luke 22:3 and later during the description of the Last Supper in John 13:27. One commentary notes that Judas never had a high motive of service or commitment to Jesus. [83] Judas had even stolen money that had been given to support Jesus and the other disciples in ministry (John 12:6). From the very beginning of his experi-

---

[83] Hendriksen, William. *New Testament Commentary: The Gospel of Matthew*, pp. 902-903

ence with Jesus, he compromised his ethics and integrity for personal gain and ambition.

Judas Iscariot began watching for an opportunity to betray his master, friend, mentor, and rabbi. Judas was receptive to evil influence in his life, and Satan is a great opportunist and strategist.

Judas Iscariot had the soul of a traitor. He was a hypocrite and a sneak. His story continues to enlighten people, for the Christian church has always had some disciples who merely pretend to serve Christ out of loving devotion. Jesus is useful to them as they seek to further their careers, special agendas, and personal fortunes. But nothing is more demoralizing than being betrayed by someone you love. It is frighteningly easy to become like Judas Iscariot. Hypocrisy can take many forms and the spiritual profile of Judas serves as warning.

Do our lives model the life of Judas Iscariot? Do we share his lack of commitment and self-serving motive to serve Jesus? Have we ever compromised and taken what is not ours? Do we live with integrity? What are our ethics? Have we, like Judas Iscariot, intimately known Jesus, been involved in ministry, and been in spiritual leadership? What is our price to compromise the Gospel of Jesus Christ?

God, help us humbly learn from the mistakes of Judas Iscariot. Amen.

✝   September 26   ✝

Take and eat

Matthew 26:20-30

All the gospels bring us to this remarkable final Passover meal Christ ate with his disciples the night before his crucifixion. Christian churches have called this meal a variety of names, "Holy Communion," "the Eucharist," and "the Last Supper." It is a sacrament that has been reclaimed by every generation of believers.

All the disciples were deeply saddened at Jesus' words. They could not understand who the betrayer would be. Jesus had known from the very beginning of his ministry when he handpicked the twelve disciples. At this holy symbolic meal, Jesus gave Judas Iscariot permission to leave the table in order to betray him (John 13:30). Even at the table, Judas had a chance to change his mind and dedicate himself to Jesus. Instead, Judas allowed evil to lead him into unholy actions.

Christian Protestant and Catholic churches often differ on how to remember Christ through this meal. Some insist formal church membership and denominational identity are required to partake of communion. There are churches who offer this meal daily and others only on a monthly, quarterly, or even annual basis. Certain denominations prohibit "practicing" gay and lesbian Christians from this table. Others insist women must take this meal with their heads covered and believe only men are allowed to serve the bread and wine. I have known youth pastors who have served this meal with soda pop and potato chips in an attempt to be "culturally relevant." Regrettably, bitter disagreements can exist among Christians when it comes to sharing this holy meal. Religion can be terribly divisive.

The table of God, however, is bigger than our differences. Everyone is invited. Jesus simply said, "Take and eat." Seekers, skeptics, doubters, betrayers, loyal disciples of all sexual orientations are invited to this meal.

Whenever possible, experience this sacrament in the community of believers. But through the centuries, many have shared this sacred meal in the privacy of their homes and at retreat centers. Begin by preparing your heart in advance to receive divine grace and blessing, allowing some scheduled time for silent listening to God before reading your selected scriptures. You can include other readings for contemplation – perhaps even today's reflection! Give yourself some quiet time for personal meditation and prayer. Write down your thoughts in a journal. Then take a bit of bread or crackers and some juice or wine. Ask God to consecrate these simple elements as you remember what Christ has so lovingly done for you. Give thanks to God. Meditate in silence and sit at the table with Jesus. Enjoy the sweet communion and friendship he offers you. It is that simple.

Bless us as we partake of this holy meal, God. Help us see Jesus as we sit at the table. Amen.

† September 27 †

The best of intentions
Matthew 26:31-35

Perhaps it was the drama at the Passover dinner table and the solemn mood of the gathered group of disciples. Impulsive Peter blurts out his loyalty and love for Jesus. Even if all others desert you, Jesus, I never will! And Jesus assures Peter that he will indeed deny knowing and following his beloved Teacher not once, but three times before the rooster crows.

I have heard a number of sermons over the years about this event. Peter has been thoroughly criticized for his inadequate faith and courage. But let us pause for a moment of honest self-reflection. What would we have done if we had been in Peter's sandals? I would like to think I would never disown Jesus, as the emotional Peter will soon do, but we would be wise to never say never. Our words and promises can return to haunt us. The best of intentions fail under pressure, fear, isolation, loneliness, and the threat of violence and personal harm.

Peter had every intention of remaining loyal to Jesus as he fervently spoke from the depths of his heart. The other disciples quickly chimed in with assurances of their support and loyalty, heartened by Peter's bold words. Yet all too soon, these disciples would run for their lives and abandon Jesus to the mercy of his enemies.

The followers of Jesus are only human. Along with Peter and the other disciples, we too, might find ourselves experiencing the great temptation to play it safe and deny our spiritual loyalties in the face of ridicule or rejection. There are places in the world where those who identify with Christ might even encounter physical danger, persecution, and even death. When we are afraid or at risk because of our personal beliefs, our survival instinct may be stronger than our earlier words of faithful allegiance.

Life is full of many good intentions. We let others know we intend to stop smoking, excessive drinking, drug use, or overeating. We intend to exercise more and take better care of ourselves. We offer our assistance and loyalty to people and causes important to us, but when the going gets tough or inconvenient, perhaps we fail to show up or neglect to provide promised support of all kinds. We mean to be helpful but sometimes overlook the cost of our promises. Talk has always been cheap. Commitment is costly and requires endurance, resolve, and periodic rededication throughout our entire lives.

Where is the hope in Peter's story? I find great hope in the realization that Jesus understands our human fallibility and the deepest motives of our hearts. No matter how often we fail, with the help of God, we can try, and try again. So never give up trying to live for Jesus. When we are faithless, he is always faithful. Learn from past failures and confess them to God. Peter offers us a great role model. Although he would soon deny Jesus, he was able to rededicate his life to the risen Christ and became a great leader in the early Christian church. Never underestimate God's ability to transform our failures into divine success stories.

God, we have all failed in our good intentions somewhere or at some point in our lives. Perhaps we have deeply hurt others as a result. Show us today if there are areas in our lives where we have denied our loyalty and allegiance to Jesus and his teachings publicly or privately. Give us the courage to recommit ourselves to him and start anew. Amen.

† September 28 †

Gethsemane

Matthew 26:36-46

Jesus enters deeper and deeper into the dark night of his soul as he and the remaining disciples arrive at Gethsemane, a place many scholars believe to have been a secluded spot, containing some olive trees and perhaps even an oil press. It was a quiet place to rest, teach, pray, and even sleep. I personally find it remarkable that even Jesus needed human companionship and encouragement in his most vulnerable hours of deep anguish and fear. So he brought three of his closest companions among the inner circle of disciples, Peter, James, and John to be with him as he prayed. He begged them to keep watch with him. The three disciples tried their best, but kept falling asleep in their exhaustion. In urgent need, Jesus woke them as he desperately prayed for divine intervention and rescue from his fate. When their beloved Teacher needed them, the disciples failed him completely.

It is significant that even in deepest soul agony, Jesus spoke to Peter and chided him for his sleepiness. Even in Gethsemane, Jesus offers us timeless words of wisdom for our own lives today. "Watch and pray so that you will not fall into temptation. The spirit is willing, but the body is weak" (Matthew 26:41 NIV).

Through his prayer, Jesus begged God three times as he sought help in his dire time of need. He recoiled in horror of what lay ahead, fervently begging God for another way. He asked that the cup of suffering not be part of his fate. Through his brutally honest prayer, Jesus was able to face his future ordeal with strength and courage. He prayed until the betrayer and the large crowd armed with swords and clubs arrived in Gethsemane. Strengthened through prayer, Jesus rose up and went to greet them.

So what does this mean for us? Through the inspiring example of Christ in Gethsemane, we are given freedom to beg God for help and mercy in our direst hours of need. We need prayer partners and encouragement from friends and through meaningful community. We need to watch and pray, as Peter was encouraged to do, for our spirit is willing but our bodies are weak. We are all deeply tempted to take the easy and safe way out.

All of us will face crisis points and personal times of anguish and indecision in our lives. Our lives may feel chaotic and scattered. We may feel fragmented and broken with doubt and fear. Through his brief but poignant words spoken in Gethsemane, Jesus provides us with a powerful example of prevailing, persistent prayer when life is overwhelming and when we are near death.

God, thank you for the humanness of Jesus. Help me watch and pray with him during the difficult times in life. Not my will, dear God, but yours be done in my life. Amen.

† September 29 †

Betrayed, arrested, and deserted

Matthew 26:47-56

Even in those confused and emotional moments preceding this kiss of death, Judas Iscariot had opportunity to change his mind about betraying his dear friend, mentor, rabbi, and teacher. Judas kept his word to the obviously hostile religious leaders who wished Jesus dead. We see this profound moment of Jesus' betrayal by a friend. Jesus did not publicly chastise Judas. Neither did he make any attempt to escape his fate. Jesus even gave Judas permission to betray him.

Rough men in the crowd seized this gentle teacher-healer and arrested him. The frightened disciples cowered in confusion except impulsive Peter. In his fear and confusion, Peter resorted to violence. A head wound was inflicted to a servant of the high priest responsible for this travesty of justice. As the servant cried out in pain, Jesus called for nonviolence and spoke prophetic words fulfilling scripture. The gospel of Luke reveals that even in his moments of arrest, Jesus stopped and healed the injured man.

The eleven terrified disciples then deserted Jesus and ran for their lives. Only a few hours earlier Peter had sworn he would die with Jesus and never disown him.

Where are we in this story? Who are we? How do we apply these verses to our lives today? Could we ever find ourselves in the sandals of Judas, the betrayer? Have we ever denied our faith or someone we loved? Have we betrayed friends while smiling to their faces? Do we use violence towards others? These verses are worth quiet moments of reflection and prayer.

Betrayed with a kiss. Seized. Arrested. Deserted. Jesus has experienced the worst human behavior possible through the betrayal by a dear friend.

God, bless me with divine insight as I linger with Jesus today. Amen.

† September 30 †

Fear and courage

Matthew 26:57-58

Jesus was being roughly pushed into the assembly of all the religious authorities who waited to condemn him. We are given a picture of combined fear and courage through Peter's example. Yes, it is true that he had earlier deserted Jesus. Quite frankly he fled for his life. Do you blame him? What would you have done in his place?

Peter conquers his fear enough to discretely follow the arresting mob at a distance. He enters into the very courtyard of the high priest so eager to put Jesus to death. Peter stays until the outcome is decided. He courageously swallows his fear enough to sit down with the guards. His own personal safety is at risk, but his deep love for Jesus gives him enough courage to literally sit with the enemy.

Have you felt terror and helplessness in your own life? Sometimes all we can do to is quietly wait in situations beyond our control. Love is what gives us courage to return to our loved ones. Love is what gives us the bravery to remain near them even when it is personally dangerous and unpopular. Love is the greatest motivator on earth. Peter loved Jesus and is to be applauded for his fearful courage.

Where, dear God, am I in this story? Increase my love and courage for Jesus. Amen.

† October 1 †

Christ suffered in silence
Matthew 26:59-68

Jesus chose to be silent while many came forward and lied about him. Finally two came forward and intentionally distorted his words. Their testimony gave the high priest what he so ardently sought. A blasphemy charge would put Jesus to death according to their religious traditions and laws. I find it utterly incomprehensible that these religious leaders were so hateful and intent on destroying Jesus. Yet world history reveals horrific brutality and terrible suffering has been inflicted on millions through centuries of well-intentioned and zealous (un)holy wars, inquisitions, and religious crusades.

Jesus remained silent throughout this travesty of justice. Chaos erupted as the chief priest and the assembly of spiritual leaders unanimously issued their verdict of blasphemy. They began to physically attack and brutalize the Silent One. They spit in his face, slapped him, and beat him with their fists. The horrible ordeal was just beginning.

Years later, Peter would recall the prophetic ancient words spoken centuries earlier as he wrote these encouraging words to suffering fellow believers about his beloved Jesus, "To this you were called, because Christ suffered for you, leaving you an example, that you should follow in his steps. 'He committed no sin, and no deceit was found in his mouth' [Isaiah 53:9 NIV]. When they hurled their insults at him, he did not retaliate; when he suffered, he made no threats. Instead, he entrusted himself to God who judges justly. He himself bore our sins in his body on the tree, so that we might die to sins and live for righteousness; by his wounds you have been healed. For you were like sheep going astray, but now you have returned to the Shepherd and Overseer of your souls" (1 Peter 2:21-25 NIV).

Our souls need this Shepherd. His courage and dignity in the face of hatred and violence can be ours. Let us follow in his steps, and likewise entrust our souls to God who is just.

God, bless me with the spiritual empowerment that comes from Christ alone. Amen.

†   October 2   †

It is safe to cry with God
Matthew 26:69-75

Peter's tears remind us that fear can sometimes overpower loving courage. Peter had done his best to stay near Jesus while the other disciples had fled for their lives. His public outing by the servant girl proved to be terrifying. Peter was faced with a dangerous and potentially deadly dilemma. If he identified as one of Jesus' disciples, he could possibly share the same fate as his beloved master. Instinctively Peter denied his best friend again and again without thinking.

In several panic stricken moments, Peter betrayed Jesus more powerfully than Judas Iscariot. Judas had the soul of a traitor and had carefully premeditated his actions for some time. Peter had the soul of loyal friend who loved Jesus passionately, but when the chips were down and his life was as stake, Peter impulsively betrayed Jesus by denying their relationship. He lied to save his own skin. Can we really blame him for his cowardice? What would we have done in his situation?

The rooster crowed as Jesus had earlier predicted. Overcome with remorse, Peter fled outside the courtyard and wept bitter heartrending tears. His grief only intensified as he remembered the loving look Jesus gave him as Peter cursed and repeatedly insisted he did not know Jesus. Jesus had looked him right in the eye and gazed into the depths of his soul. Peter then ran for his life, berating himself with a self-hatred and loathing we can only imagine. He would carry the memories of his bitter betrayal of Jesus to his grave.

As Peter wept bitter tears of shame, grief, and regret he unwittingly found it was safe to cry with God. I suspect he was unaware of God's tender presence in his defining moment of human failure. God was with him throughout the horror of the moment, and would help him live through the terrible events that lay ahead. After the resurrection, Peter's tears would eventually lead him to a life transforming and soul refining repentance, bringing him an empowering resolve to serve the risen Christ and build his church. He would become a great preacher and influential pastor to many churches before dying a martyr's death for his loyalty to the new Christian faith.

So often in life we minimize our pain and try to stifle and hide our tears. Tears are something many of us are ashamed of as a sign of weakness and inadequacy. We even apologize when crying in our deepest agony. But God created tears for a purpose. They cleanse our souls and hearts, bringing healing and strength. The next time tears well up in our eyes, let them become an agent of God's grace. Have a good cry and you too, will find it is safe to cry with God. There are times when even a tear rolling quietly down our cheeks is a silent prayer.

God, today Peter's tears have become mine. With Peter, may I find you safe to cry with and find comfort and courage in my times of need. Amen.

† October 3 †

Reach out to God

Matthew 27:1-5

Suicide is dangerous. Do not do it. We are most vulnerable when in despair. Judas Iscariot took his life during lonely moments of shame, self-hatred, grief, and profound emotional remorse. He died as a fallen disciple of Christ. We may never fully realize his true motives for betraying Jesus. We can never understand the agony of his final thoughts. Judas took those to his grave, but we can learn from his death.

The day Judas died was a tragedy for everyone. He lost hope in God's mercy. After spending three amazing years with Jesus in intensive spiritual formation, within a few hours, he completely self-destructed. Jesus was to die because of Judas' words and actions. The victorious religious leaders did not care for Judas at all. To them, he was just a pawn in their plot. Judas was no longer useful to them.

But Jesus, even while experiencing his profound moments of betrayal, had called Judas, "Friend." He will forgive with his final breaths his taunting tormentors as he dies on the cross. I believe Jesus forgave his friend Judas, even as he was being betrayed. If only Judas had waited a little longer. Perhaps he could have become a great example of divine forgiveness such as the great early Christian missionary Paul. Perhaps he too could have been used by God to write profound letters to the Christian churches.

Many people struggle with suicide ideation. No matter what we have done, I believe God will forgive a truly repentant heart. If you are struggling with thoughts and feelings about suicide, reach out to a friend.

Reach out to God. God is as close as your breathing, nearer than your hands and feet.

Years ago a woman shared with me her remarkable story. One night in despair she took a loaded weapon, locked the door, and placed the gun in her mouth. She heard within her a still, small voice that said, "Don't do it." She removed the gun and called a friend. The next day, she contacted a therapist. She began living one day at a time. One day at a time with the power of God has helped her live a blessed life. You can too.

The Founder of the Franciscan orders, St. Francis of Assisi (1181-1226) gives us this prayer:

Lord, make us instruments of thy peace; where there is hatred, let us sow love; where there is injury, pardon; where there is discord, vision. Where there is doubt, faith; where there is despair, hope. Where there is darkness, light. Where there is sadness, joy. O divine master, grant that I may not so much seek to be consoled as to console; to be understood as to understand; to be loved as to love; for it is in giving that we receive, it is in pardoning that we are pardoned, and it is in dying that we are born to eternal life. Amen.

† October 4 †

The potter's field
Matthew 27:6-10

The same religious leaders who had Jesus condemned to death on a blasphemy charge now had two new problems. Both the corpse of Judas Iscariot and his betrayal money raised questions. What were they to do with the blood money returned to them by Judas Iscariot? While he was alive, Judas had been a useful pawn in betraying Jesus. Dead at his own hands, what were they now to do with the body?

In the agony of remorse, Judas tragically hung himself. According to religious laws, the money was tainted and could not be used for the temple or synagogue. There was no way it could be legally laundered for religious spending. Not only was Judas' money difficult to use, but he had to be buried according to the law. In their religion, those who committed suicide were not allowed to rest in peace among their honored dead. Judas could not even be buried among his own people.

Although scripture does not tell us exactly where Judas was buried, I have often wondered if his body was laid to rest in the potter's field under the tree where he hung himself. The authorities could then solve two problems at once by buying the field where the desperate Judas took his life with the tainted money and still honor their burial practices. The field could then be used as burial site for foreigners, for it was against their religion to bury non-Jewish corpses among Orthodox Jews, a custom still practiced today.

I also wonder if any family and friends came to his grave to weep and mourn, or if any priest cared enough to offer prayers and words of solace at his gravesite. Was Judas shunned in death by the remaining disciples? We will never know.

I am convinced of one thing. I am confident God had mercy on his tortured soul. Judas' evil betrayal of Jesus had unwittingly fulfilled divine prophecy. Without the death of Christ, there could be no resurrection hope!

God, through this final meditation on Judas Iscariot, help me continue to learn from his life and death. Open my eyes to corrupt religious and secular practices that result in blood money in our contemporary society. Help me whenever possible to be an agent of change and reform. May I also comfort those grieving over loved ones who have committed suicide with compassion, not judgment. Amen.

✝ October 5 ✝

In Pilate's sandals

Matthew 27:11-14

Let us use our imaginations for a moment and put ourselves in Pilate's sandals. As the appointed Roman governor in the area, he was politically astute and aware that these religious leaders hated the occupying Roman rule. It was obvious to Pilate their religious hatred of Jesus far exceeded their dislike for the harsh non-Jewish government Pilate represented. The chief priest and elders lacked the legal and political power to put Jesus to death. As much as they hated the occupying Roman government, these religious authorities needed the assent of the governor to get the death penalty for Jesus. They would be satisfied with nothing less. The enemies of Jesus were politically sensitive and knew Caesar would never tolerate a self-identified Jewish king.

Pilate was a cunning politically adept ruler who now found himself in a dilemma, holding the power of life or death over Jesus. Pilate was no fool. He knew the charges against Jesus were hate inspired. He began to interrogate Jesus. Amazingly, Jesus remained silent as his religious enemies hurled their bitter accusations.

Pilate was now in an impossible situation. If Jesus would not verbally defend himself, Pilate would have to make a very difficult verdict. He had to weigh the words of the chief priest and elders over the silence of Jesus. If he let Jesus go free, these powerful and pesky Jewish leaders could make his governing rule difficult at best. However, if Pilate condemned Jesus without adequate proof, it was possible that an innocent man would die. Pilate had the power to stop a corrupt religious leadership from committing a horrific hate crime. But he knew his political survival depended on how well he could govern these fanatical leaders. Would he choose justice or political compromise?

Perhaps we can learn some important lessons about religious hate crimes and political compromise through today's Bible story. Throughout the ages, intolerant people of many faith traditions have caused the deaths of others who threatened their beliefs about God, morality, and justice. Religious wars, inquisitions, crusades, and pogroms result when intolerance, bigotry, prejudice, and discrimination are unchecked and unchallenged by weak political leaders and corrupt governments.

It can be hard to believe, but even in today's world, overzealous religious leaders have the potential to kill and destroy through political maneuverings as they protect and promote their agendas and special interests.

God, open my eyes to see where contemporary religious corruption and weak politicians allow injustice and death to innocent people. Empower my understanding of religious-based hate crimes and help us stop legalized hate. Amen.

† October 6 †

Weak leadership

Matthew 27:15-18

As a politician, Pilate was squirming with discomfort. He was at best a weak leader and too fearful to serve justice. He caved in to the pressure of the rabidly hostile Jewish religious leaders determined to see Jesus dead and buried. Rather than assert his legal authority as governor, Pilate decided to not make a decision and let a gathering crowd get him off the hook. According to the Jewish religious custom with this feast day, the gathered crowds annually choose the release of a prisoner. Pilate offered the crowd a decision to release Jesus Christ or Barabbas, a notorious prisoner.

Perhaps Pilate rationalized his inept leadership decision. Who in their right mind would chose Barabbas over Jesus Christ? Jesus was a popular healer and teacher. Barabbas was not the kind of person anyone would want in their own neighborhood. For Pilate, it was a politically wise solution. If he placed Jesus at the mercy of the crowd, he felt confident enough that the crowd would overwhelmingly chose to liberate Jesus. Pilate would then be rid of the unpleasant, envy-driven chief priest and elders.

Pilate reminds me of many contemporary leaders in positions of political power and authority. Rather than serve justice, these weak leaders opt either not to make a decision or make politically motivated decisions to maintain their prestigious positions. This is not limited to secular politics. I suspect all of us know people who have compromised their integrity and ethics to keep their jobs. Perhaps there have been times when we have had to make similar choices and buckled under the pressure. Perhaps we too have failed to exert our leadership potential and chosen not to make a decision and passively let public opinion chose for us.

What lessons can we learn from today's story? Could there be contemporary parallels in our own society? Have there been situations in our past or present where we have succumbed to public pressure and neglected to do the right thing?

Oh God, Pilate's weak leadership in the face of raw religious hatred and jealousy is unnerving. Show me where similar weak leadership exists in our own political arenas. Help me vote for officials who will not give way to intolerant religious voices. *Open our eyes to our own weaknesses, and give us courage to stand up for justice even in the face of hostile opposition. Amen.*

† **October 7** †

Holy dreams

Matthew 27:19

The Bible is full of holy dreamers. They have sometimes changed the course of world history. God can and does speak to people through holy dreams even today. Dreams are sometimes difficult to interpret and may even wake us up as nightmares. Such was the case with the wife of Pilate. Somehow, God gave her a dream so troubling that she sent her husband an emergency message as he wavered indecisively, waiting for the fickle crowd to choose between Barabbas and Jesus.

We do not know many things about Pilate's wife. We do not know her name or background or any details about her marriage to Pilate. Perhaps Pilate habitually came home from the office and discussed his business affairs with her, seeking her opinion on controversial issues. She may have been a trusted sounding board to him. It could even be that she had followed with keen interest the ministry of Jesus from afar.

We do know that she had a terrible nightmare about Jesus and her husband. Without hesitation, she reached out to her husband with all the influence and power she had at her disposal. She begged her spouse for the life of Jesus. She knew he was innocent and in great danger, for her husband was a weak and ineffectual leader. Her courage in speaking out in the face of hate and public opinion is commendable. She could not let an innocent man be given the death penalty. Even if it came at the cost of her marriage, she would not be silenced.

I am sure her husband hesitated on the judgment seat. Perhaps he dismissed her message or was annoyed with her interference. On the other hand, he may have regretted his earlier decision to let the crowd make a life and death decision about Jesus. But how could he take control of this situation that was so rapidly getting out of hand?

Pilate's wife offers us a profile in courage and spiritual discernment. Through her example, honor your dreams. Do not brush them aside. Be open and attentive to what God might be saying to you. It is helpful to write down our dreams so we do not forget them. Talk about them to trusted friends, pastors, chaplains, spiritual directors, counselors, and therapists. Who knows, God might speak to you too through a powerful dream.

God, help me be sensitive to holy dreams. If you chose to speak to me through dreams, bless me with insight and understanding, as well as the courage to act on what I recognize as your divine leading. Amen.

† October 8 †

Easily persuaded

Matthew 27:20-22

Despite the urgent message received from his wife, Pilate hesitated too long. The influential chief priests and elders easily persuaded the crowd to choose the life of Barabbas, a convicted felon, over the life of Jesus. The hostile authorities smelled blood and seized their opportunity without hesitation. They would never again have Jesus so vulnerable and within their malicious reach.

Humans sometimes have a herd mentality and are easily persuaded. Every crowd has a personality that can be influenced and swayed by skilled and determined ringleaders. These ringleaders were leading citizens and leaders in the religious community. It is hard, if not impossible, to stop the momentum when the masses collect and begin to shout. The most law-abiding citizens can get swept up with the rioting crowds. Violence erupts and can quickly escalate out of control.

Pilate was faced with a potential riot on his hands, and he lost his courage in the face of the frenzied shouts to crucify Jesus. He was dumbfounded by the intensity of the entire situation. Whatever resolve Pilate had to rectify this grievous situation was lost in the chaos of the tragic and regrettable situation. Barabbas was a hardened criminal. Jesus had done nothing wrong, but he was clearly a victim of religious hate. A riot was brewing and Pilate had to make a decision within seconds or lose complete control of the crowd and situation. Crucifixion is a horrible way to die, and it was usually reserved for the worst offenders. What would he do?

Again pause and learn from the crowd and Pilate through our holy musings. Can you imagine being as easily swayed by corrupt religious leaders and their rhetoric of hate? Has there ever been a contemporary situation where an innocent person was condemned through public opinion, swayed by influential leaders with a special interest agenda? Where are you in this riled crowd? What would you do if you were Pilate?

God, give me courage and strength to learn the hard lessons in today's scripture reading. As this holy story continues, transform me with understanding and insight as I ponder this horrific situation. Amen.

✝ October 9 ✝

Not my responsibility
Matthew 27:23-26

An ancient Persian proverb tells us if fate throws a knife at you, you can catch it either by the blade or the handle. Pilate dodges the knife by refusing to accept the responsibility of his office. Rather than quell the disturbance and maintain Roman justice, he takes the easy way out. Pilate washes his hands of this sordid event and tells the rioting crowd that Jesus is "your responsibility." The crazed crowd shouts back, "Let his blood be on us and our children." Barabbas disappears into the crowd as a free man. Pilate had Jesus flogged. Roman floggings were so brutal that sometimes the victim died before crucifixion. Jesus survived and went on to be crucified.

I cringe from the horror of this event and my own self-knowledge. There have been times in my own life where I have dodged or avoided responsibility. By stepping back and letting others take over, I have acted like Pilate. By silent assent or passive behavior, evil can triumph. Power and authority always carry responsibility.

God, where have I acted as Pilate? Please forgive me. Amen.

† October 10 †

Crown of thorns

Matthew 27: 27-31

Institutionalized cruelty comes in many different forms. Consider the situation of Jesus Christ. We often fail to appreciate the physical and emotional anguish Jesus experienced during his pre-crucifixion ordeal. For hours on end, brutal soldiers tortured him. First they shamed him by stripping off his clothes. Then they mocked him by dressing him with a scarlet robe fit for a king. Then they began to deliberately torture him, beginning from his head and working their way down the entire length of his body by flogging him with stone tipped whips. The soldiers made a cruel crown of thorns and jammed it on his head. Blood streamed into his eyes. They teased him, spit on him, and hit him repeatedly on the head with blinding blows from their fists and clubs.

When they wearied of their sport, the soldiers stripped Jesus again before dressing him in his own clothing. His back, bloodied and raw with every nerve ending in agony, stained his clothing with his own blood and sweat. Exhausted by pain, faint with thirst, fatigued from his sleepless night, swollen and bruised, Jesus was barely recognizable even to those who loved him. Only then did the soldiers lead him away to be crucified, forcing Jesus to carry his own cross with his last ounce of remaining strength.

Perhaps these soldiers had been desensitized by the nature of their terrible work assignment. By torturing and mocking their condemned prisoners, it may have been easier for the soldiers to carry out their grisly task. The torture dehumanized their captives. As the hours went by, I imagine the soldiers were swept up by a mob mentality. Some may have even enjoyed the bloodletting. People can be cruel. Even those who are normally kind and gentle can surprise us with their brutality when with a group of peers. Wearing a uniform can help the violence feel more anonymous. Perhaps this is why so many invading and occupying armies have raped and pillaged throughout history.

No matter what we believe about the historical Jesus, the brutality of his death sentence cannot be minimized. A man innocent of a crime was condemned to the most shameful and painful death Imperial Roman society could devise. As the soldiers led Jesus away to be crucified, his religious enemies rejoiced while his friends and family wept in dismay and horror.

What is your response to Jesus in this situation as you use your imagination, hearing the sickening thud of clubs striking his head, while listening to the soldiers curse and berate him? Take a few minutes and journal your thoughts and prayers. In your own life experience, have you ever experienced such dehumanizing mockery and shame? If so, take comfort. Jesus understands and can help you find strength for the day and your situation. Because he suffered, he understands pain, ridicule, shame, torture, injustice, brutality, and evil.

God, as I contemplate Jesus wearing his crown of thorns, help me find healing in my own experiences of shame, mockery, and physical abuse. Give me courage to compassionately intervene and stop cruel behavior to others when I see it. Amen.

† October 11 †

A divine interruption
Matthew 27:32

As the soldiers herded Jesus and two other condemned prisoners to the dreaded place of crucifixion, curious onlookers gathered along the road. They were forced to halt and wait for the grim death march to pass them by. Some gawked while others shook their heads in pity or wailed their grief. Many onlookers knew Jesus was a good man unjustly condemned to die. The horrible news swept through the crowd like wildfire. It was Jesus, the kind miracle worker, going to his death.

Jesus was greatly weakened by his ordeal. He had been beaten and cursed. His entire body was bruised and swollen. While carrying his cross, Jesus tripped and fell. The soldiers were faced with a pragmatic problem. It would do them no good to beat their victim anymore. Jesus was already near death. Their solution was simple, for it was customary for Roman soldiers to stop travelers and force them to help carry supplies along their marches. The public had no choice but to submit without protest, for the occupying Roman soldiers would not hesitate to beat reluctant citizens into service.

The soldier in charge scanned the crowd of onlookers and without hesitation picked sturdy Simon from Cyrene (modern day Libya) for the job. Simon probably felt he was in the wrong place at the wrong time when the bloodied stranger collapsed before him in agony and exhaustion. As Simon shouldered the heavy wooden cross beam on his own broad back, he provided Jesus with precious moments of physical relief. Simon's body became an altar. His great strength became a sacrament of grace.

I wonder what Simon was thinking as the noisy crowd followed them to Calvary. He may have initially felt annoyed, but as the death march continued, there was such peace and dignity in Jesus, that perhaps Simon was drawn to pray for this unfortunate stranger. Simon had no idea that he was in a divine appointment. Of all the people in the world, for reasons known only to God, Simon of Cyrene was chosen over all others to carry the cross of Jesus Christ to Calvary. His life would be forever changed. Over the centuries, some Christian traditions have honored Simon by including him in the fifth station of the cross.

Have you ever been in a divine interruption? Often it is only in hindsight when we realize something or someone greater than ourselves had been present in a situation. These are the moments when we too become a sacrament of grace to friends and foes alike, or perhaps to a complete stranger, sometimes in moments of injustice or during times of great human need and suffering. God often uses ordinary people like us for extraordinary moments of grace and mercy.

God, I ask to carry the cross of Jesus. Use me in divine interruptions throughout my lifetime. Help me provide others with precious moments of relief from their human suffering. May my life be transformed as I serve the crucified Christ. Amen.

✝   **October 12**   ✝

Death watch

Matthew 27:33-36

Over the past twenty years, I have sat with many families as loved ones were dying. These heart wrenching hours are often exhausting. Usually the loved ones are heavily medicated so they may die with dignity and comfort. Family members and friends sometimes request prayer, scripture, and appropriate religious rituals such as last rites or anointing by various clergy of their faith traditions. Usually the atmosphere is subdued. In all my years of ministry, I have never experienced anything like this situation. I find myself recoiling in horror and grief at what is happening to Jesus.

According to ancient custom, the women in Jerusalem usually furnished gall, a pain-killing narcotic, to prisoners who were crucified. Jesus refused this act of mercy. He chose instead to remain fully conscious until his death. Then the soldiers crucified him. The Gospels tell us Jesus was stripped before being cruelly nailed to the cross. For those unfamiliar with crucifixion, it was a slow, painful execution by binding or nailing a victim to a cross, stake, or tree. It was used by the Romans especially for those convicted of violent crime, slave revolt, army desertion, or rebellion against the state. The soldiers then gambled to divide Jesus' clothing, unwittingly fulfilling prophecy (Psalm 22:18). The soldiers began their deathwatch over Jesus. It was a dirty job they had been assigned, but was all in a day's work.

I have recently made arrangements to have the soil in my front lawn aerated. Holes are literally punched into the ground. This allows water and other nutrients to penetrate the surface to help the lawn grow. Our hearts also need periodic spiritual aeration. The words of scripture can then soak more deeply into our souls, penetrating and transforming our awareness of God's loving presence in our lives. Read these verses aloud. Read them slowly. Read them quietly again and again. Quietly sit in silence and imagine being near Jesus during his death. What would you say to him?

Many years ago, while conducting a Good Friday service on a U.S. Navy ship, a young sailor listened attentively to this story. At the conclusion of the service, he approached me. "Chaplain," he said, "I need what Jesus did for me on the cross. I want to be a Christian." We all need what Jesus did for us on the cross. Jesus took upon himself all the sins of the world so that we might believe and have eternal life through his saving work on the cross. Would you like to be a Christian? It is as simple as breathing.

Lord Jesus Christ, I too, need what you did for me on the cross. Come into my heart, I pray. Amen.

† October 13 †

It is never too late for God's mercy
Matthew 27:37-44

It is never too late to accept God's mercy and forgiveness. Even on our deathbed, we can reconcile with God through Jesus Christ. There is grace and mercy at the foot of the cross as long as we have breath in our bodies.

This powerful scene brings us to Jesus, nailed to the cross with the written charge against him, "THIS IS JESUS, THE KING OF THE JEWS." On each side hangs a crucified criminal. People are rudely hurling crude insults at King Jesus. They mock him. "Hey you, Jesus, come down from the cross if you're God!" The religious leaders join the mob in public ridicule. I find it amazing that even the crucified robbers jeered insults at Jesus as they writhed in pain.

A careful reading of the other Gospels reveals it is never too late to receive God's mercy in our deepest moments of need. One of the jeering robbers becomes strangely drawn to Jesus as they are dying together. The two robbers have a profound conversation with Jesus. "Aren't you the Christ? Save yourself and us!" cried the one. But the other criminal rebuked him and said, "Don't you fear God, since you are under the same sentence? We are punished justly, for we are getting what our deeds deserve. But this man has done nothing wrong. . . . Jesus, remember me when you come into your kingdom" (Luke 23:39-42 NIV). Jesus answered him, "I tell you the truth, today you will be with me in paradise."

It is never too late to receive God's mercy and forgiveness for our sins while we have breath in our bodies. There is no crime, no sin so terrible, that Christ cannot forgive when we approach the cross in repentance. This includes Christ's executors, accusers, betrayers, and tormentors. We can go from hell on earth to paradise. Jesus Christ is the way, the truth, and the door to the kingdom of God.

Jesus, remember me too. Thank you that it is never too late to receive divine mercy and forgiveness. I want to be with you in paradise for eternity. I need you. I need you for living and dying. I need what you did for me on the cross. I need your resurrection hope. Amen.

†   **October 14**   †

Honest to God

Matthew 27:45-46

Hour after agonizing hour went by. A strange and eerie darkness fell over the land. As Christ experienced the full pain of the curse of sin, darkness pervaded the earth. When the earth was at its darkest hour, Jesus cried out in despair, "My God, my God, why have you forsaken me?" (quoting Psalm 22:1 NIV)

Who among us has not experienced the darkness of despair, loneliness, betrayal, torment, ridicule, rejection, verbal and/or physical abuse, and suffering? The darkest despair of all is feeling forsaken and separated from God. Jesus, even Jesus, cried out in despair.

I have listened to many suffering people cry out similar heartfelt words. Sometimes people of faith discourage this kind of spiritual honesty. "It's not nice to question God," these well-meaning comforters will say. "You need to have more faith," they remind us. Even Jesus felt forsaken in his darkest moments before death. We too, can cry out and feel safe with our questions and doubts.

My mother eventually lost her battle with cancer after years of chemotherapy and radiation. When she was on hourly morphine, she still struggled to breathe without pain. I would often hold her and rock her gently back and forth as she cried in pain. "Why is God doing this to me?" she often asked. I never knew what to say. I only know God cried with us and provided strength for the moment, sometimes one breath at a time. I had the privilege of being with her when she died and will never forget her last words. "God is calling my name," she struggled to say, "and I'm not afraid." Throughout her illness, she had been honest to God with her diagnosis and prognosis. God honored her spiritual honesty and provided her with the courage and faith she needed at the hour of her death.

Jesus was honest to God on the cross. His words give us courage to share our doubts, questions, and fears with God. God can help us in our darkest hours when we feel abandoned, forsaken, and forgotten. Be honest to God. Your circumstances might not change, but you will be spiritually empowered.

God, give us the spiritual honesty of Jesus as we struggle with darkness in our lives. Give us spiritual empowerment for one breath at a time. Amen.

†   October 15   †

The Jesus way to die
Matthew 27:47-50

The moment of death is sacred. We both fear and respect it. I have been at many hospital and hospice bedsides as people breathed their last breath. I have seen the light in their eyes dim and become extinguished. It is a holy moment when we are reminded of our own mortality.

We each have a time to be born and a time to die. Dying is part of life. Despite the poet Dylan Thomas' adjuration, "Do not go gentle into that good night, / Old age should burn and rave at close of day; / Rage, rage against the dying of the light" [84] sometimes death is actually a blessing after great physical suffering from lingering or debilitating illnesses.

North American culture does not often let people either die or mourn gracefully. Many people completely avoid the topic and will not even use the word "death." People say the departed ones "passed on." Another phrase I have often heard is, "God took them home." Others quietly will say, "They've gone to be with the Lord." Society continues to frantically search for the fountain of youth, but death will eventually happen to all of us.

There is a Jesus way to die that offers us courage, hope, and dignity. It is the way of faith and it is available to all of us. We see this enormous faith through the final prayer of Christ as he breathed his last. "It is finished" (John 19:30) and "Father (translated from the Greek word, *Pater*), into your hands I commit my spirit" (Luke 23:46 NIV). Then he died. Jesus knew his time was up. His lifework was finished. For Jesus, God was his beloved, tender, compassionate heavenly *Pater*. Christ's prayer life helped him live with greatness and die with dignity and courage in his deepest moments of need. He confidently placed himself into the loving hands of his dear heavenly Parent whom he loved and served. God ushered him into eternity.

Even in death, Jesus reminds us that God is as near as our breathing, closer than our hands and feet. Whatever our cherished sacred names

---

[84] From *The Poems of Dylan Thomas*, published by New Directions. Copyright © 1952, 1953 Dylan Thomas. Copyright © 1937, 1945, 1955, 1962, 1966, 1967 the Trustees for the Copyrights of Dylan Thomas. Copyright © 1938, 1939, 1943, 1946, 1971 New Directions Publishing Corp.

for God may be, we can be assured our Divine Companion and Guide will usher us into eternity when it is time. There is no need to be afraid of death. Commit yourself to God and remember that God is faithful. We will never be forsaken or abandoned in our final breaths. We are in divine loving hands as we are ushered into Paradise.

Hold me close to your heart, God. Be nearer than my breathing and closer than my hands and feet even in death. Amen.

†   October 16   †

The earth shook
Matthew 27:51-53

The earth shook while many other strange and frightening things began to happen the moment Christ died. The curtain of the Jewish temple in Jerusalem was torn from top to bottom. Rocks shattered. Certain graves actually released their dead, and many corpses of known holy people were raised to life. They came out of their tombs. How terrifying this all must have been. The sun had disappeared and all was dark. Where was God in this dark moment in world history? I imagine many people huddled in fear and wonder.

We are told that the raised dead actually appeared to many in Jerusalem after Christ was resurrected. Even in the moment of Christ's death, death was conquered. The power of the grave was shattered forever as faithful and holy people were miraculously raised from the dead, testifying to God's great grace and power. There were many empty tombs the moment Christ died.

What does this mean for us? We can personally claim the Christian hope that we too can experience resurrection through Jesus Christ, God's crucified and beloved Child. Jesus himself experienced death for us and understands our human frailties and fears. We can take courage at the moment of our death and experience spiritual comfort when loved ones die. Death has been conquered forever.

Someday the dead in Christ will be raised again (1 Thessalonians 4:13-18). Oh death, where is your victory? Where is your sting? (See 1 Corinthians 15:54-56.) Christ has conquered the grave even in death.

Death cannot hold him. Death is not the end. We have hope beyond the grave (1 Corinthians 15).

Beloved Christ, you have tasted death for me and offer all of us resurrection hope. Help us encourage each other with these words. Amen.

†   October 17   †

Fear and faith

Matthew 27:54

This single verse offers us great insight for today's reflection on fear and faith. The military personnel responsible for carrying out the order to execute Jesus were absolutely terrified at all these earthshaking events. They had watched Jesus die. They had heard his gracious words of forgiveness as he prayed for those who nailed him to the cross. They had listened to Jesus struggle for breath as the public hurled verbal abuse and insults at him.

As the earth shook and other strange, unexplainable, and miraculous events occurred, the soldiers unanimously exclaimed, "Surely he was the Son of God!" (NIV). Their statement of faith is timeless and can be ours. Their eyewitness account can be part of our spiritual journey and understanding of this remarkable Jesus Christ.

Their fearful experience can actually encourage our faith today. We can affirm their statement of faith but without the fear. "Perfect love casts out fear" (1 John 4:18 NRSV). Our call is to love God with every fiber of our being, along with our neighbors and ourselves. We can pray fearlessly and with confidence as God's beloved people. Seekers of all sexual orientations are invited to approach God without fear.

Years ago, a friend e-mailed me this saying from St. Augustine, which has offered me great spiritual insight and which I offer to you, "To fall in love with God is the greatest of all romances; to seek [God], the greatest adventure; to find [God], the greatest human achievement."

Jesus Christ, you are God's Beloved! Help me experience the greatest of all romances. Amen.

† October 18 †

Mothers

Matthew 27:55-56

An ancient Hebrew proverb tells us, "God could not be everywhere, therefore he made mothers." Today's verses offer us profound insights through the combined knowledge, wisdom, love, and courage of these mothers at the cross. Many women grieved at the cross, observing from a distance.

They had faithfully followed Jesus and cared for his needs and those of the disciples. Many had used their own personal resources to provide for this remarkable spiritual leader. Even in the midst of danger, they courageously stood by the cross and watched their beloved friend, teacher, healer, and rabbi die an agonizing and shameful death. Who were these remarkable female spiritual leaders of such great courage, love, loyalty, and wisdom?

Mary Magdalene had experienced profound spiritual healing and community with Jesus (Luke 8:1-3). We really do not know who Mary the mother of James and Joses is, but the biblical text soon tells us she watched with Mary Magdalene as the tomb in which Jesus was buried was sealed (Matthew 27:61; Mark 15:47). Many women had joyously followed and served Jesus in humble, practical ways throughout his ministry. He had always treated them with the utmost of respect and as valued people of great worth and equality. He was thousands of years ahead of any human rights movement.

We have seen the mother of Zebedee's sons earlier (Matthew 20:20-28). She and her sons had approached Jesus privately. They made a request for power, prestige, privilege, and promotion that outraged the other loyal disciples when they learned of it. They had made their requests known to Jesus from their knees in postures of humble supplication. At that time, Jesus asked them all if they could drink of the cup he was to drink. They eagerly said they could. I wonder if this mother was remembering that conversation with Jesus as she watched him die. I wonder what her thoughts and prayers were at the cross.

Let us observe this scene for a few moments. Jesus is dead on the cross. Many women watched and grieved from a distance. The earth has been shaking and the sky is dark. The soldiers are terrified. The religious leaders are satisfied their enemy, Jesus, is finally dead.

Where are we in this picture? What are our thoughts and prayers? What spiritual direction are we given through these verses?

Oh God, bless us with the love, courage, loyalty, and wisdom of these women who watched from a distance. Amen.

† October 19 †

Burial of Jesus

Matthew 27:57-61

What would happen to the body of Jesus? A rich man from Arimathea named Joseph had become a follower of Christ in secret because he feared the Jewish leaders (John 19:33-34, 38). In an act of quiet heroism, he publicly approached the governor who had condemned Jesus to death. Pilate was a weak leader who had been swayed by public opinion and the hostile Jewish religious leaders. Joseph was willing to risk imprisonment or worse. He asked for the body of Jesus. Pilate ordered the corpse to be given to him.

In a combined act of loving devotion mingled with fear and courage, Joseph took the body. He wrapped it in a clean linen cloth and placed it in his own new tomb. I have always wondered if Joseph had to remove those terrible nails from the hands and feet of his beloved Jesus. Joseph then rolled a large stone in front of the tomb entrance and left. Two loyal women still refused to leave. They sat by the tomb and observed everything. Beloved Jesus was dead and buried.

As a former U.S. Navy Chaplain, I have performed many burials at sea. Burials are the final act of caring for our own. Our loved ones deserve dignified burials and we need to grieve. I find myself awed at the courage of Joseph of Arimathea and humbled at the steadfast devotion of Mary Magdalene and the other Mary. These must have been their darkest hours.

These three people offer us lessons in discipleship. We are called to publicly identify with the crucified Christ even when our hearts are breaking and our world seems chaotic and shattered with grief. It has never been safe or easy to follow Christ. Yet we are to faithfully follow him in life and in death. It might be dangerous for us. Following Jesus may bring us against the flow of public opinion and popular leadership. These three disciples clearly understood the cost of following Jesus. Rich and poor, their unified motive was love for Christ. They deeply loved their crucified friend and refused to abandon him even in death.

God, bless me with this spirit of love for Christ. Amen.

† October 20 †
The guarded tomb
Matthew 27:62-66

I wonder what Pilate was actually thinking. Did he regret his previous weakness when he allowed these hostile religious leaders to influence his decision? These fanatic leaders were determined to eliminate Jesus in death as well as in life. Was Pilate weary of these religious leaders who refused to be pacified? Perhaps it was just easier to cave in to their demands yet again and secure the tomb as they wished with an armed guard. This probably seemed a small thing after such a horrific act of condemning an innocent man to death. Pilate now had to live with the consequences of his actions.

What is truth? Pilate's earlier musings are ours. Who is the deceiver and who the deceived? What deceives us today under the guise of religious purity and zealotry?

The insistent religious leaders went and made the tomb as secure as they knew how. They sealed the tomb and posted an armed Roman guard. They did their best to hold Jesus in the grave.

Where am I in today's story, God? Has religious zealotry blinded me to the spirit of Christ? Or have I been Pilate, condoning religious violence because it was too difficult to stand for justice? Amen.

†   October 21   †

Go and tell!
Matthew 28:1-7

The first evangelists were women who had courageously served Jesus Christ while he was alive. These brave souls had refused to leave him as he painfully died on the cross and risked their lives in their public identification with him. These loyal women had even followed the body of Jesus to the borrowed tomb where he was so hastily buried before their Sabbath. They were reluctant to leave him even in death.

At dawn on the third day, these faithful women had hurried to the gravesite with what they believed would be their final act of love and devotion. Their plan was to anoint the body with burial spices. Who would roll away the enormous stone that blocked the entrance to the borrowed tomb? Even with their combined strength, the huge boulder would be far to heavy for them to budge. The two determined Marys stepped out in the faith they had; trusting God would help them in their great need for physical assistance. Although it seemed highly unlikely, perhaps the Roman guards at the gravesite might take pity on them and lend their brute strength, if only for a moment.

The women never expected to find the heavily armed guards unconscious. What the guards had seen was too fearful to bear for even the bravest and strongest professional soldiers among them. As the women tentatively approached the chaotic scene, littered with rubble from the earthquake and limp soldiers on the ground like rag dolls, they saw a dazzling angel. His clothes were more brilliant than snow. As the women gasped in shock and amazement, the angel spoke reassuring words to them; they could scarcely believe their eyes and ears. The tomb was empty. Jesus was not there. The angel joyously proclaimed Christ was risen. Death was conquered. The trembling and terrified women were ordered to go and tell the inner circle of disciples that Jesus was alive and planned to meet them in Galilee.

As one reads the other Gospel accounts of this universe-shattering event, while details may vary, the message is basically the same. Jesus was alive. Death could not hold him in the borrowed tomb. The world would never again be the same.

Perhaps we should all tremble in holy awe and fear as we grapple with the enormous significance of this event and what it means for us. Today's story offers many lessons. Through the risen Christ, we have all received a divine message of hope that must be shared with others. Share that hope through word and deed.

Death no longer has victory over our lives. There is life beyond the grave. From the very beginning of the resurrection, God broke traditional gender barriers and cultural role stereotypes by using women to share spiritual truth through egalitarian leadership roles with men. Do not be afraid, for God is willing and eager to use you too. It matters not if you are gay or straight, male or female, partnered or single, young or old. Go and tell!

God, thank you for this message of hope and resurrection. Open our eyes to new life in Christ. Help us as we share our faith in Jesus Christ to others in word and deed. Amen.

† October 22 †

Women apostles!
Matthew 28:8-10

Have you ever been afraid and joyful at the same time? As these women rushed to tell the disciples, guess who met them? Jesus himself! Can you imagine what the women were feeling? As Jesus greeted them, they came and fell on their knees, holding his feet while worshipping him. Jesus blessed them and said, "Do not be afraid." They were both fearful and joyful. Who would not be after seeing someone raised from the dead?

Women were the first to see the risen Christ. Now they were to go and tell the male disciples to meet with Jesus in Galilee. They were entrusted with the first commands uttered by the risen Christ. Jesus was using women as apostolic messengers. Jesus was breaking traditional patterns of male spiritual leadership.

Even today, certain Christian churches do not allow women to preach, publicly read scripture aloud during the church service, or serve communion. Some leaders insist women cannot teach little boys older than the age of six. Women are to be seen but not heard in some traditions, sometimes even in those that say otherwise.

In my own childhood, it never crossed my mind that women could be pastors, preachers, seminary professors, and spiritual directors. My role models taught that women's work was limited to the church nursery and kitchen, and they were always given permission to dust and clean the sanctuary.

Imagine my astonishment while in an evangelical seminary, I received a call to ministry. One day, when in deep prayer, I offered myself to God in any capacity, to any country, for any people. While praying, the telephone rang and it was a Navy chaplain recruiter. He was looking for ordained clergywomen. Would I be interested? Yes, but I felt both fearful and joyful.

In my joy, I could hardly wait to meet with my pastor and share this amazing answer to prayer! My beloved church actually disowned me when I eagerly shared this wonderful moment. My male pastor said, "Yes, you are called. But you must leave. You see, God doesn't call our women to this kind of work. You have to go to another denomination. You cannot stay with us." What would his response have been if I had been male?

Thus began several years of spiritual turmoil while searching for a church home that would allow me to follow God's gracious calling. Through it all, I learned God is big. God is bigger than the fallible people in the church. I found there are Christian denominations that ordain women and place them in positions of leadership. There are Christian denominations that have fought against slavery and for human rights. There are even Christian denominations that offer affirmation, blessing, marriage rites, and ordination for gay and lesbian people.

My ministry has changed throughout the years, but God has not. Jesus Christ remains the same yesterday, today, and tomorrow. The risen Christ uses people among all walks of life in extraordinary ways. Who am I to limit God's calling in another person's life?

God, bless us with joyous worship as we contemplate the risen Christ in our lives. Thank you for calling us by name. Amen.

✝ October 23 ✝

Religious deception and bribery
Matthew 28:11-15

What is the price of truth? We are not told how much money the soldiers received, but it was a large sum. To the poorly paid soldiers, it probably represented a small fortune. The soldiers agreed to accept the money and lie about what actually happened at the tomb where Jesus had been buried. Certain religious authorities were now desperate in their attempts to silence the resurrection event. All conspired and agreed to perpetuate an intentional lie. All agreed to circulate the story among the Jewish people. Lies beget lies.

What was the truth? Jesus had risen from the dead. Death had been conquered. God was moving in mysterious and powerful ways that disturbed religiously powerful men. They tried to cover the truth with money and deception. They tried to lie to the world.

Over the years, I have worked with religious leaders representing many different faith traditions. Most are devout, sincere, God fearing, honest, and holy leaders. Yet our religious institutions are fallible. Sometimes the truth is subconsciously or deliberately silenced and hidden in order to maintain the status quo and please the financial donors. Such was my experience while studying evangelism during my Doctor of Ministry program. For an elective, I chose to attend one of the famous Billy Graham schools of evangelism. During that week of intense study, I was in conversation with a Graham employee about the possibility of teaching an inclusive gospel, which would welcome people of all sexual orientations. He totally discouraged any further conversation with the comment, "Our funders barely support our inclusion of women at this school of evangelism. We'd lose them in a minute if we supported your proposed workshop!"

While religion can deepen our faith experiences, it can also corrupt us. God is bigger than all our combined religions. Religion can sometimes fail us in our search for truth. Well-intentioned people have used religion to inflict deep suffering on people who believe differently. They have demonized certain groups such as gays and lesbians, crusaded against those whom they call infidels and pagans, and burned books that offered different outlooks on life.

Yet it must also be said that religious organizations have done much good as they have fed the hungry, cared for the destitute, provided for the orphan, and worked for improving conditions for the impoverished.

Religious corruption is not new. It is good to question our religious authorities and our own motives thoroughly. Leaders and believers representing all world religions are vulnerable. Bribery, deception, and lies can affect all our cherished religious institutions and leaders.

Perhaps it is enough to simply sit with the tension of these verses and consider where we are in the story. Perhaps we too, have been tempted to lie, deceive, bribe, and cover the truth somewhere in our lives. This is a wonderful opportunity for personal reflection and confession of sin. We need these moments of soul care. Each of us has an enormous capacity for self-deception.

God, as I linger quietly in your loving presence, speak to me about truth and deception, honesty and bribery. Amen.

✝ October 24 ✝

Doubt

Matthew 28:16-17

What did the eleven disciples discuss on their way to this astonishing reunion? I would have many strong doubts about seeing someone alive who had been dead and buried. As much as the eleven men valued the two women's testimony, surely they felt many conflicting emotions as they journeyed to the mountain. When the eleven men saw Jesus, they immediately worshipped him. But some doubted. Perhaps they thought they were hallucinating. Or perhaps they thought this reunion was too good to be true. Their worship offers us rich insights for today. If I were there, I too, would want to touch Jesus. I would probably pinch myself to make sure I was awake and not dreaming.

The great metaphysical poet, John Donne, writes, "To come to a doubt, and to a debatement of any religious duty, is the voice of God in our conscience: Would you know the truth? Doubt, and then you will inquire." [85]

Madeleine L'Engle reminds us through her lovely daily thoughts and reflections in *Glimpses of Grace*, that "doubt is a doorway to truth. And if our religion is true, it will stand up to our questionings." [86] She shares a story about belief and doubt as she held an after-school seminar for high school students. One student asked her, "Do you really and truly believe in God with no doubts at all?"

Her response was, "I really and truly believe in God with all kinds of doubts." She bases her life on her belief and accepts the presence of doubt with her gift of reason while letting her inclination to God guide her life.

Seekers, doubters, and skeptics! Wherever we are in our spiritual journey and understanding of this risen Christ, we can worship honestly about our doubts. God will honor our doubts and questions. Doubts help us reconnect with our souls. Continue your spiritual pilgrimage one day at a time. Honor your doubts. An anonymous writer tells us, "When in doubt, write." Journal your doubts and you will marvel at your faith journey. Let doubt be your doorway to truth. Perhaps this is why the Gospels of Matthew, Mark, Luke, and John were initially written. Doubtful disciples shared what they knew about this amazing Jesus and their experiences can help us in our journey towards understanding.

God, honor our doubts as well as our beliefs about this amazing Jesus who rose from the dead. Amen.

✝   **October 25**   ✝

Ultimate authority

Matthew 28:18

In the aftermath of the September 11, 2001 terrorist attacks, many prayers were said in many faiths and in many languages during that time of global grief. As someone who is committed to respectful interfaith dia-

---

[85] Quoted in Madeleine L'Engle. *Glimpses of Grace*, p. 28.
[86] Ibid.

logue and ministry, I began speaking about this tragedy as a distinctly Christian minister. I realized all our voices were needed to offer solace and comfort to a grieving and shocked nation and world where thousands of different world religions struggle to coexist peacefully.

In the difficult days immediately following September 11, my personal faith in Jesus Christ was what sustained and encouraged me. As the rubble from the World Trade Center buildings and Pentagon gradually settled, I found myself frequently on line gazing into the eyes of a beloved Russian icon painted in Svenigorod, Russia, by the famous fifteenth century artist Andrei Rublev. It was the compassionate face of Christ, the Peacemaker.

To gaze into this beautiful face is to see the face of God, a face that war, injustice, hatred, betrayal, and violence cannot remove from our world. To look into the compassionate eyes of this icon is to experience the kindness and unlimited goodness and love of God. It is a face full of love and strength, courage and comfort. It is a holy face that reminds us of God's deep compassion for a suffering humanity. It is a sacred face worthy of contemplation for Christians, Muslims, Jews, and Buddhists.

In a religiously pluralistic world full of competing voices calling for your allegiance, what faith sustains you in times of chaos and pain? What divine authority do you answer to and call on for help? Consider trusting Jesus Christ as your ultimate authority, and you will find direction, strength, solace, courage, and hope in your times of need.

God, bless us with renewed faith and trust in Jesus Christ. Teach us how to live under Christ's divine authority, leadership, and guidance in our daily lives. Amen.

† October 26 †

Make disciples
Matthew 28:19a

Everyone who chooses to follow and serve Jesus Christ has a great commission. We are to make other disciples. According to Jesus, this is not a suggestion or an idea to do whenever it is convenient. When one looks at the original Greek texts in the New Testament, it quickly becomes evident that Jesus is actually issuing an order to everyone and anyone who decides to follow him.

Discipleship is our holy calling. Not only are we to live as contemporary, culturally relevant disciples, but Jesus expects us to nurture, reproduce, and develop others in discipleship as well. Even more amazing, Jesus expects and mandates every generation of believers to reach out to others locally and globally with his message of faith, hope, and love. Each generation has the responsibility and the charge to tell the story of Jesus from his birth to the resurrection while sharing the love of God through compassionate acts of service to others in the world around us.

The many Christian denominations and various spiritual traditions understand discipleship in many different ways. We must ask, how can we know the way to make disciples? The most basic understanding of discipleship comes from Jesus himself.

A former seminary professor of mine often said 80% of what we need to know about discipleship is found in the Gospels. Begin reading and rereading all the Gospels. We can learn more about being a disciple by studying scripture with the help of devotional readings, by worshiping in a local church community, and by participating in small fellowship groups. By saying prayers daily we can learn to be in step with the Holy Spirit's leading. Seek communities of faith that welcome and accept seekers of all sexual orientations. Invest in yourself by learning more about your faith through different classes and study guides.

We benefit by the wisdom and experience of mentors in school and business. In the same way, we increase in personal insight and understanding when more mature believers mentor us. Search for those who walk the talk and ask to spend time with them, while asking many questions. Be available and generous with your time, willing to mentor and befriend others in their spiritual journeys.

Making disciples is the calling of every Christian of every sexual orientation as we share our truth in Jesus Christ. Discipleship is about people reaching people with their experiences through Jesus Christ as Savior, Sovereign, and Friend. We are to be witnesses in word and deed of God's great love in our lives. We all have the potential to be good news messengers in a world full of bad news as long as we have breath in our bodies. Jesus expects his followers to make a difference in the lives of others locally, nationally, and even globally. Discipleship is a lifetime process, offering moments of great joy even in times of difficulties, suffering, and sorrow.

Follow Jesus with all your heart. Pray every day and throughout your day. Attempt great things for God. Expect great things from God. Seek the fellowship of other believers while reaching out to others. Your life and the lives of others will be transformed.

God, let me live as a follower of Jesus Christ today. Help me graciously and generously learn to share my faith. Bring me into discipleship friendships. Give us courage to both mentor and be mentored by others. Amen.

† October 27 †

Baptism

Matthew 28:19b

Ever since Christ instituted this sacrament of grace, people have often remembered the day of their baptism as a source of spiritual comfort and encouragement when life is difficult. Baptism is a holy sacrament mandated by Jesus Christ himself for every believer. It is an outward and visible sign to the world, indicating our public identification as a disciple of Christ. Baptism helps us focus on the life, death, and resurrection of our Savior. Different churches and denominations vary in their interpretation of baptism, but all agree that Jesus expects this of us as a willing act of obedience. Baptism is part of Christian discipleship and signifies the beginning of our new life in Christ. It is also a rite of initiation into the Christian church.

In today's verse, Jesus gives us the Trinitarian statement for baptismal use. Some churches and believers prefer the original language of Father, Son, and Holy Spirit. As language continues to evolve, more inclusive and contemporary formulas are sometimes preferred. One such inclusive Trinitarian formulation is "Creator, Christ, and Holy Spirit." All, I believe, are worthy of our deepest respect, for baptism is an intensively personal decision.

Realize that baptism does not make us Christian; rather, it symbolizes our public confession of faith and personal commitment to Jesus Christ as our personal Lord and Savior. It symbolizes that we are buried with Christ by baptism into death, and as Christ was raised from the dead, we too, are raised to walk in newness of life.

Jesus himself was baptized at the beginning of his earthly ministry and thus gave us an example to follow. He never asks us to do anything he himself was unwilling to do. It is significant that as part of his immediate post resurrection ministry, he insisted disciples be baptized. This is for every generation of believers.

If you have never been baptized before, consider it. The blessings are endless. Depending on where you worship and hold church membership, you might be sprinkled with water or fully immersed in a church tank in a sanctuary, or find yourself getting dunked in a nearby river, swimming pool, or even hot tub, as friends and family and church members watch and sing.

Some churches require a series of preparatory classes. These sessions vary in length, intensity, and time, providing a valuable framework of spiritual formation for those considering baptism. Other communities of faith invite people to come forward for immediate baptism, as a public commitment of first time Christian faith, in response to the worship service and sermon. Certain denominations and faith traditions baptize children and infants, while others will only baptize adults.

I regret to say, gay, lesbian, bisexual, and transgendered Christians sometimes experience frustration as they search for churches who will baptize them. However, be encouraged in your journey. The number of churches that will baptize you is growing. The Internet also can be a great blessing in identifying those welcoming churches in your area. If you have been refused baptism because of your sexual orientation, continue to trust God in your spiritual journey. Jesus understands your situation and walks with you.

Thank you, God, for Christian baptism and all that it signifies. Continue to open the doors of growing numbers of welcoming churches, which will be willing to baptize believers of all sexual orientations. Amen.

† October 28 †

Wonderful words of life
Matthew 28:20a

The Gospels of Matthew, Mark, Luke, and John offer us wonderful words of life. They offer us hope, courage, joy, peace, and strength for the day. By reading them, we learn how to better love God, our neighbors, and ourselves. As we slowly read the stories, we learn many things from Jesus. We are blessed with his spiritual hospitality and generosity. Jesus also fully expects us to share the goodness of God with others, and we are expected to pass it on. God's good news is to be shared and not hoarded! We are blessed with this charge to teach others what Jesus commanded.

We all teach others whether we realize it or not. We teach by example. How we live deeply influences our children, friends, and neighbors. Our attitudes and actions impact even the stranger on the street. Our lives are actually our sermons. Sometimes our actions are so loud that people cannot hear our words.

While some of us teach in formal classrooms and small group settings, most of us probably teach others informally. Perhaps someone asks for personal advice or a recipe. Or maybe there is a young mother seeking mentoring by an older woman. Work friends and colleagues might come to us for suggestions regarding money, health issues, or an ethical situation. We are all teachers in some capacity. Some of us teach best without words, but by serving others. Because none of us are clones, we will teach in many creative and diverse ways.

Our challenge is to teach the gospel humbly, graciously, thoughtfully, whenever people are interested. We are to live and share the teachings of Jesus and offer them in culturally relevant ways to each generation. This is our calling. In doing so, we help make Jesus audible and visible in the lives of others.

People need to learn the story of Jesus in safe places as they explore the concept of discipleship. Spiritual rebirth is free indeed, but discipleship is costly. Discipleship is a seven day a week, twenty-four hour a day calling. There is nothing easy about following Jesus and people should know this before they are invited to "make a commitment." Obeying his teachings will bring us into countercultural living. By living his words, we will threaten the status quo of our religions, societies, political movements, and more. We will be called to feed the hungry, visit the sick and those in prison while sharing our wealth and resources with others in need.

Study his teachings closely before teaching others. The Gospels teach us that there is a welcome for everyone who is interested in Jesus. It takes time to carefully learn and relearn all that Jesus commanded and taught. Jesus carefully trained his inner circle of disciples for three intense years. Discipleship is a lifetime revelation. Disciples are to disciple new babes in the faith.

Consider rereading Matthew's Gospel as a primer in discipleship. Ask God for wisdom and insight as you strive to share the goodness of Christ with others.

Help me make the effort to become a gracious teacher in word and deed, God, as I learn and generously share these wonderful words of life with others. Truly, the results are in your hands. Amen.

† **October 29** †

God's Promise

Matthew 28:20b

I have begun jogging on a regular basis for health and fitness reasons. A local high school has an outdoor track that is available to the general public. I feel safe while running and walking laps. Sometimes the repetition of doing laps is boring, but it is off the road and away from heavy traffic. It is usually very quiet and I enjoy seeing and hearing the numerous birds in the area. In the distance I can see an inlet. On clear days I can even see one of the nearby mountain peaks.

It was deeply disturbing for me when I saw bloody feathers yesterday while walking laps. The poor bird! Those feathers told a grim story. Something had attacked it and the bird had put up quite a struggle. The trail of feathers extended into the woods. For the bird, death was violent and unexpected. It was nature's way. In the Koran we are told the facts of life, "There will nothing befall us but what God hath written down for us." This includes all God's creatures, great and small.

As we conclude our experience of reading Matthew's Gospel, it is important to remember that Jesus promises us strength for the day and hope for tomorrow. Whatever our situation and circumstances, we have this promise from the risen Christ. He is with us always. He will never leave or forsake us. He will always provide strength for the day. It is impossible to be separated from his loving, caring presence. He is closer than our breathing, nearer than our hands and feet. [87] Nothing can separate us from Jesus' loving presence. We can claim these words written by the apostle Paul, "For I am convinced that neither death nor life, neither angels nor demons, neither the present nor the future, nor any powers, neither height nor depth nor anything else in all creation, will be able to separate us from the love of God that is in Christ Jesus our Lord" (Romans 8:38-39 NIV).

Many years ago, my beloved Grandmother gave me a bookmark with a poem. The poem is titled "God's Promise" and the author is unknown. The bookmark is tattered and the words of the poem are faded,

> God hath not promised skies always blue,
> Flower-strewn pathways all our lives through;
> God hath not promised sun without rain,
> Day without sorrow, peace without pain.
> But God hath promised strength for the day,
> Rest for the labor, light for the way,
> Grace for the trials, help from above,
> Unfailing sympathy, undying love.

Thank you, God, that there is nothing able to separate me from your love that is in Christ Jesus. Thank you for your promises. Amen.

† October 30 †

Reading the entire Bible

Psalm 119:89-90

From April until now, the end of October, we have read through the Gospel of Matthew. Congratulations! Reading an entire book in the Bible is a marvelous accomplishment. These wonderful words of life up-

---

[87] Wuellner, Flora Slosson. *Prayer and Our Bodies*, p. 36.

lift, sustain, encourage, and provide us with moments of God-power. I love reading the Bible. No other book has so deeply influenced my life. The Bible is worth a lifetime of study. Perhaps this is why so many fondly call it "the Good Book."

If you have enjoyed reading the Gospel of Matthew, consider reading the other Gospels of Mark, Luke, and John. Each offers unique insights and lessons for living. Each shares the Jesus story in powerful ways. Mark offers a gold thread of discipleship. Luke is the beloved physician writing about Jesus as the Great Physician. John teaches us how to simply be with Jesus.

You may even find yourself wanting to read the entire Bible. There are many Bible reading plans. I used one for many years that a friend recommended. It involved reading ten chapters in the Bible on a daily basis. Many others have used it and have been transformed. It involves a bit of disciplined reading but is extremely rewarding.

The ten chapters divide into four daily sections: Old Testament, New Testament, Psalms and Proverbs. Daily read two chapters in the Old Testament, beginning with the first book in the Bible known as Genesis. When Genesis is completed, continue on to the next book in the Bible, Exodus.

While reading in the Old Testament, continue daily readings with two chapters in the New Testament, beginning with Matthew's Gospel, which we have just read. Throughout your reading discipline, include five daily Psalms with one chapter from the book of Proverbs. The Psalms are cherished prayers that have helped people pray throughout the centuries. We need the Psalms for the care of our soul. The Proverbs are a treasure of ethical insights for living.

What does this particular reading plan accomplish? By the end of a year, you will have read the entire Old Testament twice. You will have read the New Testament three times. You will have read the entire prayer book known as the Psalms on a monthly basis, including the marvelous ancient wisdom of Proverbs. If ten chapters seem too difficult, time consuming, or intimidating, do what you realistically can. Expect a daily blessing whether you read ten chapters a day or ten verses or even just ten words. The Bible will nourish your soul. God will honor your reading and efforts. These sacred words have been known to change lives.

God, help me to grow spiritually every day. Amen.

† October 31 †

Enjoying God

Psalm 90:1-2 and Psalm 121:1-2

Recently a friend and I went on a long anticipated hike that was two years in the making. The previous year had schedule conflicts and our mountain hike was cancelled. As months went by, we remembered our ambitious plan and rescheduled the hike. Inclement weather conditions canceled the hike yet again. This time we had actually driven near the vicinity of the trailhead. As a result, we were so inspired by the local beauty that we rearranged our schedules to try again several days later.

The third time around was a charm. The weather was glorious, but the road was poorly marked and we lost several precious hours searching for the trailhead. My friend had a cell phone and we used it twice to call the local ranger station and ask for directions. Each time, the ranger apologetically said, "I'm sorry, but I cannot help you." The maps for the area had not been updated.

We eventually found the trailhead and had a glorious hike. As the afternoon shadows grew longer, it was obvious that we were still several hours away from the summit. It would be impossible to complete the hike before darkness fell. So we lingered with the soaring hawks, ate lunch, and marveled at the panoramic view before reluctantly returning the way we came.

While on the rocky perch, I had pulled out my Gideon's *International Pocket New Testament with Psalms and Proverbs* and read today's lovely verses. I was tremendously impressed with the grandeur of the mountains, the silence, the beauty of the trail, and life in general. Surely God must have lingered and enjoyed the creation process. The good earth is full of beauty. It was wonderful to be in the high places with God!

During the long hike back, I found myself thinking about faith. There are times where the path seems lost. It can be hard to find the trailhead. The trail switchbacks can be discouraging when fatigue and blisters set in. Sometimes we go three steps forward and two steps backwards, unable to see the top or bottom of the trail. Hiking is a rich metaphor for life. God walks with us step by step. God has always been and always will be present with us. God will never forsake us, even if the trail seems to dead-end.

The spiritual life, like creation, is a process that is constantly evolving. God is patient with the process! Oswald Chambers once wrote, "Think of the enormous leisure of God! [God] is never in a hurry." [88] God is not in a hurry with our souls but invites us into moments of holy leisure. During those moments, we are not required to do anything, accomplish work, or complete chores. We are invited into moments where our highest calling is to enjoy God.

Yes, it would have been lovely to reach the summit, but the faith life is more than a single mountain top experience. The journey is sometimes more important than the destination. My publisher, Adam DeBaugh shared with me one of his favorite hymns after reading this meditation. It is by contemporary Christian hymn writer Ruth Duck and is called "Lead On, O Cloud of Yahweh." [89] The second verse is,

Lead on, O fiery pillar,
We follow yet with fears,
But we shall come rejoicing
Though joy be born of tears.
We are not lost, though wandering,
For by your light we come,
And we are still God's people,
The journey is our home.

"The journey is our home!" Remember to keep looking up. Lift up your eyes to the high places. God will help you step by step.

Dearest mountain-creating God, thank you for such a beautiful creation. Thank you for the high places. Thank you for being God. Help me enjoy being with you. Amen.

---

[88] Chambers, Oswald. *My Utmost for His Highest.* 1935, Dodd Mead & Co., renewed 1963 by the Oswald Chambers Publications Assn., Ltd., p. 95.

[89] Duck, Ruth. *Everflowing Streams: Songs for Worship.* 1981, The Pilgrim Press, New York, p. 77.

†   November 1 – All Saints Day   †

Anyone, everyone, whosoever, and all

John 3:16

After spending seven months in the Gospel of Matthew, it is now time to broaden our horizons. Today I want introduce you to John 3:16, quite possibly the most famous verse in the entire Bible, and the story of Nicodemus.

John 3:16 is also the most misunderstood verse in the entire Bible when well-intentioned people of faith put limitations and conditions on its message. I want you to know these twenty-seven words are for anyone, everyone, whosoever, and all who believe them. Let me emphasize God's great love for humankind, and the promise of eternal life through faith in Jesus Christ, is not limited to a particular sexual orientation, race, nationality, class, or gender. When Jesus offers God's promises to everyone, he means just that.

Whoever we may be, we all owe Nicodemus a debt of gratitude for his courage in approaching Jesus. Nicodemus was a prominent and well-respected Jewish leader, acutely aware that his career would be jeopardized if he were seen alone with Jesus. At great personal risk, he sought Jesus out for a private, late night interview. Jesus graciously agreed to meet with him and the two rabbis spoke long into the early morning hours. During their conversation, Jesus spoke these wonderful words of life now known as John 3:16 to Nicodemus, affirming God's great love for the world while explaining that eternal life is freely available for anyone who would believe in the message of Jesus.

In my study, I have some beautiful pencil sketches of Jesus by an unknown artist. In one of these simple drawings, Jesus is tenderly holding a wee newborn. In another, he is joyfully holding the hands of a very young child taking its first steps. The other sketches reveal Jesus laughing and playing, listening and gently holding children of various ages.

With Nicodemus, we need to birth our holy longings and live as children of God, trusting Jesus every step of the way. With Jesus, we can begin taking baby steps of faith towards spiritual adulthood and maturity. No matter what our age, when we believe in the message of Jesus, we will always find Jesus nearby, giving us guidance and strength for each day.

Yes, it is true. Jesus freely and unconditionally offers himself to anyone, everyone, whosoever, and all. Gay or straight, young or old, male or female, rich or poor, single or partnered, John 3:16 is for you.

God, thank you for offering eternal life to anyone, everyone, whosoever, and all who believe in Jesus Christ. Through the story of Nicodemus, help us experience your great love for us with a childlike faith. Amen.

† November 2 †

God and HIV/AIDS

Lamentations 3:21-22

As an Internet pastor, I receive astonishing e-mail. One that deeply touched my heart was from a seeker in Zimbabwe. Things were very bad in her country, she wrote. A deadly combination of drought, famine, poverty, and HIV/AIDS was expected to take the lives of millions of Zimbabweans unless outside world relief organizations quickly intervened with food and urgently needed medical resources. Would I please write a series of meditations that she could e-mail throughout Zimbabwe, to encourage Christians of all sexual orientations living in the midst of such terrible sufferings? Of course, was my response and thus began a series of reflections titled, "To Zimbabwe with Love."

I quickly learned Zimbabwe has one of the world's highest HIV/AIDS infection rates and wrote the following reflection. I invite you to think of your own birth country whenever you read, "Zimbabwe."

As Christians, we must constantly remind others and ourselves that HIV/AIDS remains a growing global epidemic. Although there is no cure for HIV/AIDS, there is spiritual strength for the journey. Through our lives and churches, we must reach out to those living with HIV/AIDS with God's generous and nonjudgmental love.

HIV is not "just a gay disease." AIDS is no respecter of sexual orientation, gender, culture, economic status, or religious preference. This disease affects and infects millions of people around the world. We must remind our young and old alike that HIV/AIDS is a reality in today's world. It is a local as well as global problem, for the majority of people do not know they are infected. Tragically, far too many live where life-saving medications are unavailable.

In twenty years, experts predict there will be more than 40 million orphans under the age of 15 in 23 countries. HIV/AIDS will claim the lives of both their parents. AIDS is quickly wiping out the gains made in life expectancy in many countries.

What can we do? Begin locally. Make a difference in HIV awareness right now. An old proverb reminds us an ounce of prevention is worth a pound of cure. The spread of HIV can be dramatically prevented through education. Learn how to prevent this disease. Pray for and support your doctors and educators who are training people in these lifesaving areas. Break the silence that so often surrounds AIDS. By doing so, you will save lives.

Do not shun those with the disease, rather, open your arms to them in love and concern. Comfort and encourage those struggling with HIV/AIDS with the compassion of Jesus Christ. When daily realities are overwhelming, remember God's enormous love for you and Zimbabwe never ceases. God is faithful and will not abandon you. God's mercies are new every morning; tenderly reaching out to Zimbabwe. Do the best you can with what you have, and live each day in the steadfast and unchanging love of God.

Faithful God, we pray for each person affected by HIV/AIDS around the world. We pray for a cure for this dread disease, and for equity and justice in the medical and drug distribution to those living with AIDS. May your unceasing, steadfast love for people living with HIV/AIDS be evident through our words and deeds of compassion. Amen.

† November 3 †

God-Power

Ephesians 3:14-21

The Bible has hundreds of great prayers. This is one of my favorites. The Letter to the Ephesians is wonderful to read. It was a letter written during the first century to the church in Ephesus (now in Turkey) by the apostle Paul. If you are interested in learning about your spiritual blessings in Christ, and experiencing more great prayers and empowering spiritual insights about faith, life, unity, new life in Christ, relationships, and experiencing "the whole armor of God," this Epistle is worth reading again and again. Ephesians introduces us to what can be abundant spiritual wealth that is available through prayer.

Today's prayer blesses us with what I call God-Power. God-Power begins with being rooted and grounded in love. God-Power is experienced through praying with a loving, intimate, and tender name for God. God-Power invites the Holy Spirit to strengthen our inner being, with Christ dwelling in our hearts through faith. We are called to pray greatly in order to live greatly. We are invited to comprehend the marvelous love of Christ in our lives. God wants us filled with divine fullness. God delights in powerfully working within us to accomplish great things through us.

Too often our prayers are puny and limited in understanding, but this scriptural prayer challenges us to pray to God for great things that are beyond our human imagining. Each one of us can experience spiritual greatness, and this prayer could be the first step.

Pray with God-Power!

We too, bow our knees before you, Holy One, in worship and awe. Help us comprehend your great love for us through Christ. Bless us with the power and fullness of the Holy Spirit. Teach us to pray. Amen.

† November 4 †

Praise the Lord and pass the ammunition!

Ephesians 6:10-13

As followers of Christ, we will experience spiritual warfare. We live in a world full of good and evil. Evil comes in many forms and disguises, and attempts to extinguish the light of God within us. Evil can be subtle and easy to miss. Evil can wear us down like a pebble in a shoe. We are in a struggle that is not against flesh and blood, but a struggle that is cosmic in nature. The struggle may come in the form of reasonable compromise or may be quite obvious, such as great movements of evil in world history.

How can we be strong in God? We can live in the strength of God's power and withstand evil by wearing the whole armor of God. Partial armor is not enough. Years of military experience reveal that the enemies will always look for a weak link in the line of defense. The enemy will study their opponent's weaknesses and when least expected, will attack and slaughter without mercy.

What is the whole armor of God? We put on our armor while standing firm in our faith. Wear your belt of truth. Put on the breastplate of righteousness. Wear shoes that will prepare you to proclaim the Gospel of peace. St. Francis reminds us to preach the Gospel at all times and if necessary, to use words. Hold on to your shield of faith. Wear the helmet of salvation and sword of the Spirit, which is the word of God. Pray in the power of the Holy Spirit at all times in every prayer. Pray alertly and frequently for other Christians in their struggles against the evil one. Our best ammunition against evil and doubt is prayer. Praise the Lord and pass the ammunition!

I used to have a bookmark that said something like this, "When we reach up, God is reaching down." When we clothe ourselves with the whole armor of God, we can be confident that God is standing alongside us. God is greater than all the combined forces of evil. One plus God is a majority. We need to pray for each other to succeed in our Christian lives. Through our prayers, we can help others put on their spiritual armor when they are battle fatigued and unprepared.

Many people say sexual minorities cannot be Christians, but the word of God invites seekers from all sexual orientations who are interested in Christ into the family of God. This is an important part of our armor. Without this understanding, we are vulnerable to the attacks of the evil one who delights in defeating us with lies and deceptions.

So praise the Lord and pass the ammunition! Wear the full armor of God. Remember, the Bible invites without discrimination *all*, *whosoever*, *anyone*, and *everyone* to a full and triumphant life in God.

God, thank you for your word, which so empowers us for spiritual warfare. Help us stand firm and stand tall in your armor. Amen.

† **November 5** †

Lessons from Mary

Luke 1:37

Have you ever experienced a visit from an angel? An unexpected angelic visit changed Mary's life forever. Her response to the message then changed world history. She and her older relative, Elizabeth, offer us rich insights on discipleship, spiritual leadership, and spiritual success.

The angel Gabriel gently informed Mary that God had a special mission for her. She was to be impregnated by the Holy Spirit with a child who would be called, "Son of God" (Luke 1:35 NRSV). To reassure this young and unmarried teenager, the angel then revealed that a distant relative by the name of Elizabeth was also pregnant. Elizabeth had long been barren. It was known that she was beyond the age of childbearing. But Gabriel reminded Mary, "nothing will be impossible with God." Mary's response to God was an unqualified "yes." "Here am I, the servant of the Lord; let it be with me according to your word" (Luke 1:38 NRSV), she said. Then the angel left.

Mary gives us lessons in discipleship. After the angel Gabriel's visit, she immediately sought out Elizabeth. Perhaps she realized she needed the older woman's mentoring. Perhaps Mary intuitively understood she needed a like-minded spiritual friend who would encourage her in this unusual and possibly life-threatening call from God. Young as she was, she understood that she needed human companionship to obey God's unusual and inconvenient call in her life. Elizabeth would be a great blessing to her. Mary would be a great blessing to Elizabeth. As modern disciples, we also need spiritual companions who will encourage us in our discipleship walk.

Mary also offers us a picture of spiritual greatness. She was wise beyond her years, obeying God's gracious leading in her life. She was God-sensitive. As she assented to this unusual call, she stepped out in quiet, unassuming spiritual leadership. She shows us how to live a new life in Christ from the moment of spiritual birth. She stepped out in the faith she had, knowing that God would provide, one day at a time. If God called, God would provide. She obeyed and was willing to trust God with her present and future. She did not know the entire story, but stepped out in faith with what she had. She knew God would be enough.

Finally, this unusual teenager teaches us about spiritual success. She heard God's quiet call privately, but she immediately sought out community and affirmation through her relative, Elizabeth. She needed to share her remarkable story with someone who would rejoice with her, encourage her through the obstacles, and spiritually bless her. She needed the older woman's strength, wisdom, experience in God and life, and friendship. Spiritual success is found in combination with solitude and community.

The spiritual walk needs accountability, obedience, encouragement and nurture. Disciples are made, not born. It takes time, effort, training, companions, learning, practice, and faith. Discipleship is a lifetime learning process. God will use us to mentor others in their spiritual lives.

For the next thirty-three years, Mary would study and learn from her remarkable child, God's Son, Jesus Christ. She offers us profound lessons in discipleship through her life experiences. Consider studying her life through the Gospels. She has much to teach us about obeying God's call.

Teach us, God, how to heed and obey your call. Help us find spiritual companions to encourage and nurture us in our faith. As we walk in discipleship, help us be as God-sensitive as young Mary. Bless us with spiritual success and greatness. Amen.

† November 6 †

Who, me?

John 20:21

Just as God sent Jesus to earth to walk among human beings, revealing divine grace and truth, so Jesus commissions everyone who believes in his message, to go forth and do likewise. Believe it or not, we are part of a divine plan.

Some of you might be incredulous, murmuring, "who, me?" Yes, God uses ordinary people in extraordinary ways. Through our faith in Jesus Christ, we are born into something much bigger than ourselves. Jesus himself sends us into the world to share the love of God, in word and deed, as long as we live, in our neighborhoods and workplaces, in local and even global communities.

Because none of us are clones, we will reflect the light of Christ through our lives to others in many different ways. Some of us are better at articulating our faith, while others have administrative gifts or a calling to help the sick and needy. Christ is eager to use our artistic and musical talents, along with our secular work areas of competence, to shine spiritual light in the world. Jesus can use us through interpersonal relationships, business networks, even our hobbies, to bring moments of divine hope and healing to a broken, hurting humanity. The ultimate divine plan is to bring God's enormous love through the message of Jesus to every human being, in every city, village, town, culture, and in every language.

You probably realize this is humanly impossible to do alone, although each individual with the help of God can accomplish enormous good. Gay or straight, we need the help of others to develop and serve to our fullest potential, as we obey our divine commission.

The divine plan revolves around the Church. We need the fellowship and encouragement of other believers, imperfect as we all are, to grow in our faith, while faithfully living out our individual and common callings for Jesus. We need to gather for moments of praise and prayer through worship services. These gatherings will energize and equip us, empowering our sense of mission and purpose. We are not in this great calling by ourselves. We are part of a great community of faith that stretches around the globe, which continues to be passed on from generation to generation. The Church represents human diversity, as we strive to serve God. Gay or straight, we bring a message of hope the world urgently needs to hear.

The majority of people have no church experience or memory. These folks have never read a Gospel and probably do not know what Christians celebrate on Easter. Although they may not be religious, they are often deeply spiritual, in search of the Sacred. Jesus is an unknown to them.

As God sent Jesus into the world, Jesus sends us with the divine message of faith, hope, and love. Not only does the risen Christ send us, but he equips us through the incredible power of the Holy Spirit. The God who calls, empowers, as we step out in faith and obedience.

God, we wish to serve you. Thank you for including us as part of your divine plan, bringing your message of faith, hope, and love, locally and globally through our words and deeds. Help us find churches accepting of human diversity, that can help equip and encourage us as we strive to spread the message of Jesus. Amen.

† November 7 †

No condemnation

Romans 8:1

Years ago I received a phone call on New Year's Day. A young man named David was dying. His lover was with him in the hospital. Their family story is all too familiar and tragic. Years earlier, when David came out as a gay teen to his father, he was forcibly thrown out of the house. David's father was a Protestant minister. As David struggled to survive on the streets, he became infected with HIV. Eventually a kind aunt in a distant city took him in and cared for him as her own son. Now David was dying. Would I come and pray with him before the inevitable?

Although David's father had refused to see his son for years, he had flown in to be at his son's bedside and was angrily waiting for me at the hospital. He rudely interrogated me on my ministerial credentials. He demanded to know what I planned to do with his son on his deathbed. It was a difficult situation. Eventually David's father grudgingly allowed me in the hospital room where his son was surrounded by loving friends and his life partner. We prayed. One by one, all of the loving friends said good-bye. We blessed David and thanked him for being such a wonderful friend. We assured him of God's gracious, gentle love and of the loving welcome awaiting him in heaven.

Then David's father ushered us out. He entered the room with an open Bible and began urging his son to repent of his homosexuality through reading a passage in Leviticus. When David died, his father insisted on preaching the funeral service. He publicly condemned his son's soul to hell and preached fire and damnation to his son's grieving gay and lesbian friends. David's father then left to return to his parish.

In the shocked silence that followed, people were unwilling to leave their dear, departed friend with such terrible words of rejection. Slowly, a deacon who was present opened her copy of the Episcopal Book of Common Prayer. She began to read loving words of faith, hope, and love appropriate for a Christian funeral. She blessed David's memory and soul to the loving God who created him gay. Together, they prayed in Jesus' name.

David lived and died as a Christian. The Bible tells us that there is no condemnation for those who are in Christ Jesus. People need to hear God welcomes everyone. God does not discriminate and has no preference over any sexual orientation.

God, thank you for our relationship with you through Jesus Christ. Amen.

†   **November 8**   †

The beautiful mind of Christ

Philippians 2:5-11

What is on your mind today? My beloved grandmother often remarked that if our true thoughts were ever known, most of us would probably be arrested. The mind may forever be a mystery to scientists and physicians, as they strive to understand the origins of human behaviors and find cures for mental illnesses. Certain thoughts can be harmful to others and ourselves, if we act on them.

As a minister, I often ask people what they are thinking. Whether we share our thoughts selectively or freely with others, I believe people of faith need to cultivate the mind of Christ, for as we think, we often become.

Today's Bible verses offer us insight into the mind of Christ, through the words of an early hymn of the Christian church. Because first century Christians lacked easy access to written materials about Christ, and many were illiterate, singing hymns helped them grow stronger in their faith, while passing on the truths of the Gospel to others. Countless generations of faithful believers have been strengthened through this particular hymn of praise, singing it in many different forms and chants, in their search to understand and experience the beautiful mind of Jesus. Perhaps you too, have sung some of these phrases, "every knee shall bow, every tongue confess, that Jesus Christ is Lord."

Now who among us can understand the mind of God? Our finite minds will never fully grasp the beautiful mind of Christ on this side of eternity. But today's Bible passage helps. Although Jesus has always co-existed with the Creator as an equal part of the Godhead, he willingly humbled himself to walk among us in human form. Christ voluntarily gave up his heavenly privilege, glory, and comfort, to share human hardships while confronting evil. He took upon himself the lowliest servant lifestyle imaginable, working as an impoverished carpenter, living in relative obscurity. He chose to work with his hands in rough, menial labor and eat peasant food. But there is more to his story. Jesus was ever mindful of God's plan for his life, knowing he was destined to die a shameful, horrific death on a cross for the sins of the entire world. Because of Jesus' willingness to suffer and die, God has forever exalted the name of Jesus Christ above all other names in the world. While other religions have much to teach us, it is only the name of Jesus that will someday bring us all to our knees in adoration, uniting our voices in praises to our Creator. Every knee shall bow, every tongue confess, that Jesus Christ is Lord.

My mind is nowhere near the mind of Christ. With you, I struggle with less than noble thoughts. As a sinful humanity, we have self-serving thoughts and ambitions, often at the expense of others. But here is the hope of the Gospel, as I understand it. Through prayer, familiarization with the scriptures, and cultivating a lifestyle of worship, we can experience in part, the beautiful mind of Christ. We can become less selfish and arrogant, while growing ever more loving and thoughtful of others. The mind of Christ transforms, redeems, and reconciles us with God. Truly, this is something to sing about.

Oh God, give us the beautiful mind of Christ and transform our ways of thinking and interacting with people. Empower us to think his thoughts in safety and in danger, in comfort and privation, in life and death. Amen.

† November 9 †
What was I thinking?
Isaiah 6:1-9

Sometimes God's call is so mysterious and subtle; it can be difficult and frustrating to discern. But other times are dramatic and unforgettable, such as the old, old story of the prophet Isaiah and his life changing call from God. Swept up in the holy emotion of an awe inspired, majestic moment in God's presence, Isaiah responded from the depths of his heart. Gay or straight, Isaiah has much to teach us, for as faithful people, we actively seek God's call in our own lives.

Perhaps you already know his story. While in a contemplative state of worship, Isaiah heard God ask, "Whom shall I send? And who will go for us?" Impulsively Isaiah blurted, "Here I am. Send me."

Usually most preachers and missionaries stop at this inspiring point in his story and offer an altar call. In many revivals and church services, this is where we respond by going forward to dedicate our lives to God, or raise a hand, indicating that we have heard God's call in our own life for a particular people, situation, or need.

We then go home on an emotional and spiritual high, full of holy fervor and good intentions. Reality shock usually begins the next morning, when we wake up with the thought, "What was I thinking?" If this has ever been your situation, relax. You are in very good company. Isaiah certainly would understand your feelings and second thoughts about answering a divinely inspired call.

Since the beginning of time, God has called human beings around the world to extraordinary acts of obedience, often going against the flow of public opinion and behavior. Within seconds of Isaiah's heartfelt response, God gave him a hefty dose of reality shock. Without sparing any punches, God bluntly told the idealistic Isaiah that he was being sent to a people who would not understand or respond to the divine message. God was sending Isaiah to a people who were spiritually obtuse and indifferent. They would not respond to the prophet's message until their cities were ruined, houses deserted, fields ruined and ravaged, and their entire land overtaken by an occupying country. Things would get very bad indeed, before getting better. I suspect Isaiah had the fleeting afterthought, "What was I thinking?"

If you have never read the entire book of Isaiah, consider doing so. While it is not always easy reading, it is important for our spiritual formation and understanding of human nature and divine calling. This prophet writes with courage, compassion, and honesty, speaking of divine judgment and repentance, comfort and salvation.

Most importantly, Isaiah teaches us how to remain faithful to God's call in our own lives, when we wake up the next morning, wondering, "What was I thinking?"

Holy, holy, holy God, bless us with the commitment of Isaiah as we respond to your call in our lives. Give us endurance, resolve, and even moments of humor, when we wake up the next morning, wondering, "What was I thinking?" With Isaiah, we yearn to live remarkably faithful and obedient lives. With Isaiah, we pray, "Here I am. Send me." Amen.

† **November 10** †

God chooses the weak, foolish, and despised

1 Corinthians 1:26-28

As a pastor, I hear remarkable stories about faith and quiet heroism by people living in obscurity. While quietly listening to an international guest, I learned today's verses had inspired her in a long term, dangerously overwhelming situation with no easy solutions in sight. "I find it hard to believe," she mused, "that God would use me in such important ways. I am a Christian, lesbian, and a racial minority in a country where there are no existing human rights. Yet God is using me to make a difference and save many lives."

God's ways are often not our own. God changes the world using people that societies often throw away or devalue and despise. Consider your call, the apostle Paul urges us in the scriptures. Not many of you are powerful, wise, or from socially prestigious families. God's way is to use the weak and the foolish in the world, those who are often detested by the wealthy and politically powerful and socially ambitious.

In the survival of the fittest, only the strong survive. But Paul had learned something of God's strategy the hard way, through hardships, suffering, and danger. When we are at our weakest, Christ's power is most evident in our lives. When we find ourselves up against humanly impossible odds, we learn our God is God of the impossible. God's grace is more than sufficient for us, for in the context of faith, divine power is perfected in human weakness. When we are at our lowest ebb and at the end of our wits and resources, God's strength abounds.

Take what the world may perceive as a physical, mental, spiritual, or emotional disability or limitation, and offer it to God as your unique and priceless gift. Let God use you as you are, for when we are weakest, Christ empowers.

A popular saying reminds us to make lemonade when life gives us lemons. Rather than whine and engage in self-pity, consider your own call. Ask God to use you in extraordinary ways and be a blessing to many. In weakness, hardships, insults, persecutions, difficulties, when we are weakest, through the power of God, we are at our strongest.

Thank you, God, for today's timely reminder to consider our own call. Use us in remarkable ways to make the world a better place. May the

power of Christ be evident through our human frailties, for your glory.
Amen.

✝ November 11 ✝

The grace of giving money

2 Corinthians 8:1-9

Today's Bible verses encourage the generosity of God's people to
give financially to those in dire need. The inspired author of this material
is the apostle Paul, writing to the first century Corinthian church in Greece.
Paul's timeless words of encouragement to complete the collection of
money for famine relief are appropriate today. World hunger should be a
Christian concern locally and globally, wherever people routinely go to
bed hungry, and children perish daily from starvation.

Christians must be generous in giving their money for hunger relief, teaches Paul, because of the example of grace of our Lord Jesus
Christ. Jesus was supremely generous and gave his all for humanity, so
we could experience the riches of God. We are to follow the generous example of Jesus and share our abundance with others in need.

Paul understood Jesus was very concerned with world hunger and
suffering people. But the Corinthian church was more concerned with
their own needs and was neglecting their earlier promise of famine relief to
the Jerusalem church in far away Israel. Perhaps we too, need this re-
fresher course in the grace of giving money today.

God loves a cheerful giver and is pleased when we share our resources generously with suffering humanity. Christians are to excel in
many graces – in speech, knowledge of God, sincerity, and love for the
saints. Christians are also expected by God to give willingly from their
abundance. When in doubt of how much to give, consider the supremely
generous act of Christ going to the cross, and be inspired to give without
any hidden agenda or expectations of payback, with or without interest or
profitable gain.

People of faith are often uncomfortable when the subject comes to
money. Paul expands his teachings through chapters 8 and 9 in this letter
to the Corinthians. We are to give freely from the heart and never reluc-

tantly or under compulsion. As we give generously to others in need, many will give thanks and honor God as a result.

The grace of giving financially is one very practical aspect of our confession of faith. Sometimes we have to put our money where our mouth is. Talk can be very cheap. It takes money to feed the starving, clothe the poor, shelter the homeless, help the orphan, and reach out with the compassion of Christ. A church that is not giving is not living up to its fullest God-given potential to make an impact in the world. When in doubt, give more and not less.

All Christians, gay and straight alike, rich and poor, are expected to open their wallets and pockets to assist others less fortunate. This is the heart of today's Bible verses.

Teach us, O God, to give generously to others in need locally and globally. Help us be very concerned with world hunger and act accordingly. May we always be inspired through the generous act of giving, demonstrated by our Lord Jesus Christ. Amen.

† **November 12** †

Priceless!

1 Peter 1:3-8

Our faith is priceless. Our yearning for God takes many expressions in the world. Yet I am distinctly Christian and my most nourishing forms of food for my soul come through the Gospels and other New Testament writings. I marvel at the wonderful words of Jesus. For me, he is the light of the world, the bread of life, the truth, and the best way to God. I have never seen him yet I love him. I have found my faith in Christ sweeter than honey, more precious than gold and silver. It is priceless!

Our spiritual yearnings can be satisfied with Christ's words. Chew, savor, enjoy, and linger with them through the banquet table of the Gospels. Reheat them, serve them in different ways. Meditate, reflect, imagine yourselves in the stories, and share them with your friends. There is something for everyone.

Yet through the study and exposure of other religions and cultures, we quickly learn how similar we are in our yearning for sacred faith.

Although I am distinctly Christian, I love participating in interfaith worship services and events. For years I have actively learned a great deal from the major world religions. They enhance my own spiritual expression and growth. When in the Orient, I respectfully visited many Shinto shrines and Buddhist temples. While in the Persian Gulf, I brought groups of sailors to several Moslem mosques. In other countries I have visited Hindu temples, Chinese roadside shrines, and many different Christian churches.

One year I was invited to participate in an interfaith Pride service. For the service, I helped develop a creative call to worship with a group who used Tibetan singing bowls. Those wonderful bowls helped us pray and worship as Protestants, Jews, Muslims, Buddhists, Wiccans, and Catholics of all sexual orientations in unity and peace.

Soul food comes in many different forms and shapes. I am deeply enriched by other faith traditions. They have much to offer me and help my inner growth. Likewise, they are enriched by my precious faith! We are on a spiritual journey together. We have different paths, but we all search for meaning and dignity in our lives. Respect is a holy word. We can live together in peace and unity. Cherish your faith. It will sustain you in times of need and bless others.

Oh God, people from all walks of life search for you. We yearn for precious faith that offers us a living hope. As we celebrate our Christian faith, help us always respect other traditions. Teach us how to live together in peace. Amen.

† **November 13** †

Knowing Christ is everything

Philippians 1:21; 3:7-13

I love reading the book of Philippians and helping others read it. It is full of God-power insights and can dramatically transform lives. It is only four chapters and worth reading, memorizing, and using for personal meditation. The author is believed to be the apostle Paul. He was originally an Orthodox Jewish rabbi who passionately hunted down the early Christians. He zealously had them imprisoned and delighted in their deaths. Then one day he had a dramatic conversion experience on the road to Damascus. His great change of heart forever altered his life. He became a tireless missionary for Jesus Christ to the astonishment of those he formerly persecuted and his rabbinical colleagues. He suffered greatly for his Christian faith. He wrote Philippians while in jail for sharing the gospel. Through this letter, we learn about the joy of Christian suffering for the Gospel.

Several years ago, a young lesbian activist had a spiritual conversion experience. She met Jesus Christ in a powerful, healing, and personally transforming way. She then began attending an affirming Bible study for gay men, lesbians, bisexuals, and transgendered seekers, doubters, and skeptics. Someone gave her a Bible. She began reading the Gospel for the first time. She then went on to a four week Bible study with a group of Christian lesbians. Together they read the lovely book of Ruth. By reading Ruth, all the women found a place in God's love story. The group was reluctant to stop meeting and decided another short book in the Bible would be a good experience. They chose Philippians for its brevity.

They were astonished at the spiritual riches of those four short chapters and eagerly read every word. Some were so deeply touched that they memorized favorite sentences. This way they could experience a portable chapel in their hearts. Several began a spiritual journal. Others began praying in the name of Jesus Christ for the first time.

The lesbian eagerly began sharing her spiritual experiences with other lesbian activists. They were confused that their beautiful, bright, and dedicated friend would identify as a Christian. Their experiences with many Christian churches had been abusive and damaging. One day a million Promise Keepers visited their city to pray as a large group of evangelical, heterosexual male Christians. The young woman eagerly went to meet them and joyfully shared her Christian faith with them. "There are many Christian churches for your gay and lesbian friends and children," she enthusiastically shared with them. Many of the Promise Keepers were astonished to learn of this growing, global voice of Christian faith among sexual minorities. The men were amazed at this remarkable lesbian. She was literally one in a million. Like the apostle Paul, she had learned that knowing Christ was everything. She wanted to experience resurrection power and share her faith.

Expect your life to be changed when you read these powerful pages.

Yes, God, we too wish to know Christ and the power of the living resurrection. Help us share our faith with the same courage of Paul and this anonymous Christian lesbian. Amen.

✝ November 14 ✝

Get back to the basics

Luke 15:1-2

The Christian life can become quite a complicated dance with our religious zeal, dogmas, rules, and denominational standards of conduct and worship. Most people simply need the basics that Jesus shares in the Gospels. He is the friend of sinners. While ancient Jewish religious authorities muttered and criticized him for spending time with sinners, there are contemporary parallels with these verses for Christians today.

We need to get back to the basics. We need to sit with sinners and learn to identify as one. We need to not be condescending friends and genuinely care for those the formal church views as outcast and less important. So let us sit with Jesus and review the basics through the next three reflections. Every word of scripture breathes God's love and compassion for human beings of all kinds. God is a missionary in search of the lost. God is the tender searcher who refuses to stop looking for us.

Dear God, I am a sinner. I wish to sit with Jesus and relearn the basics of your loving message. Amen.

✝ November 15 ✝

Lost and found

Luke 15:3-7

Though I am an urban woman and am not personally acquainted with sheep, I do understand the terror and vulnerability of being lost. While living in Washington D.C., I once saw an unforgettable example of such fear through the eyes of a small child. In a large crowd one night during a Christmas event in the city, a little boy who was about three or four years old became separated from his family. It quickly became obvious that he was terrified of being lost and equally terrified of strangers. When strangers attempted to befriend him, he would back away and try and hide in the crowds. Soon a policeman arrived on the scene and the little fellow visibly relaxed and placed his small hand in the officer's large one. Together, they began walking hand-in-hand in search for his parents and disappeared into the crowd.

Soon a frantic mother came in search of her lost child. She urgently and repeatedly called out his name and asked complete strangers if they had seen her little boy. "Yes," said one woman, "He went with a policeman," and she pointed in the general direction. Suddenly the police officer reappeared. The little boy saw his mother and stopped sobbing. He threw himself into her arms and she held him tightly in obvious relief. Even today, I have tears in my eyes with the memory of those two clinging to each other. The lost child was found. The worried crowd became joyful, for many had been concerned over the little child.

And so it is in heaven, as Jesus the Good Shepherd finds each of us in divine love. There is exuberant joy in heaven when we are found. The Shepherd's heart is full of compassion and will not be satisfied until we are found and brought back into loving, intimate community and personal relationship with God. Today's parable in Luke brings us the Gospel message of Jesus Christ in its most basic simplicity.

I have a cherished pencil sketch of Jesus in my study. He is lovingly holding a lamb in his arms. The lamb has a look of trust and contentment. The nail marks are clearly visible on the hands of the Good Shepherd. We are invited into those loving arms.

Searching Shepherd of our souls, thank you for finding us. From time to time, we have all strayed from your presence like a lost lamb. Now help us experience the joy of being found by God. Amen.

†   **November 16**   †

Repent and rejoice

Luke 15:8-10

This wonderful parable teaches us a fundamental Gospel lesson. Repent and rejoice. Confession is always good for our souls and in the process, we learn God has a big eraser. Through this parable, we learn God is eager to be found when we repent of sin, and has never left us even when we have misplaced or forgotten God. Throughout our search for divine love and fulfillment, God has always been with us, closer than our breathing, nearer than our hands and feet.

But sin separates us from God's loving yet holy presence. Unconfessed sin prevents us from rejoicing in God.

What is the solution to our unconfessed sin dilemma? As my beloved grandmother diligently searched high and low throughout the house and even in the garbage for her misplaced false teeth, I am reminded to search my own heart and memories periodically for unconfessed sin. This is something everyone can do and the spiritual reward is joy.

To experience deep joy in the spiritual life, get in the habit of daily asking God for forgiveness for remembered and even forgotten unconfessed sins. Divine forgiveness brings spiritual renewal and restoration, with an abiding joy that goes beyond temporary happiness.

So celebrate your clean slate with God. Each day is a new beginning when we repent and rejoice.

Dear God, teach us how to repent and rejoice. While confession of sin is good for the soul, as human beings, we tend to avoid such honest introspection. Give us the courage to honestly admit where we have erred, and the willingness to change our attitudes and ways when needed. Bless us with joy when we repent. We pray for these things in the empowering name of Jesus Christ. Amen.

338

† November 17 †
Hugged by God
Luke 15:11-20

The parable of the prodigal child is perhaps the best known in the entire Bible. As a master storyteller, Jesus leaves the interpretation open, so each listener can find a place somewhere in this timeless story. The parable is about people of all kinds coming home to God. The bottom line of this old, old story is that God loves us no matter who we are, where we have been, or what we have done. It is a tale of hope, love, and joy with a happy ending.

Through the parable, we experience the Gospel at its best, purest, and simplest form. God is generous to forgive and eager to reconcile with us. Although human beings may break our hearts and refuse reconciliation, restoration, and forgiveness, God will never refuse us. Even if people are unwillingly to accept us back into healing and healthy, joyous relationships, God is eager to embrace and restore us.

When we drift away from the Eternal by our own life choices, it is never too late to return back to God. Gay or straight, young or old, rich or poor, male or female, when we tentatively approach God we can expect to be greeted by God's welcoming arms. God is already knocking at the doors of our heart. This is very good news indeed.

Today's parable is more than a story about a wayward child, a loving parent, and an angry sibling frustrated with the parent's instant and generous forgiveness. It is a compelling story worth retelling in our own words about being hugged by God, while experiencing divine forgiveness with celebration. It is about repentance and reconciliation.

We are ever so grateful, God, for this wonderful parable inviting reconciliation, restoration, and forgiveness with you. Embrace us with your love. Help us live as a beloved child of God, snug and secure in your loving arms, for the rest of our lives. Amen.

† November 18 †

Precious names for God

Mark 14:36

From childhood through his time at Gethsemane where he prepared for the crucifixion, Jesus called God tender and loving names that were counter-cultural and unconventional in his religion. He called God *Abba*, (Aramaic for "Daddy") and *Pater* (Greek for Father). Jesus is recorded using precious names for God more than 200 times in the Gospels. Once would have been significant. God is our loving Divine Parent. Feel free to call God "Father/Mother," "Daddy/Mummy," "*Abba/Amma* (Dearest Mommy)."

Through the example of Jesus, we can also use intimate, tender, precious names for God. There is great power in names. They will bring us into transforming relationships with our dear heavenly Parent as beloved children.

In many families, parents have unfortunately been abusive and cruel towards their children. Some seekers among us might find using any parental name for God deeply painful. Consider reclaiming your spiritual power through other tender names in your prayers such as "Dearest," "Tender One," "Healer," "Loving One," or others.

We have just spent several days in God's heartbeat through the three back-to-back parables in Luke 15. The prodigal child parable is typical of Jesus' teachings about God. Our common call with the prodigal is to enter God's heartbeat of love. We are encouraged to be embraced by our loving, tender, caring, heavenly Parent-God.

When we pray with such powerful and tender names, we will be transformed and never be quite the same. Ask God for help in praying a tender name for the Holy One. God will honor your request.

In Christ's deepest hour of human need, he was able to call out for divine help to his "dearest Daddy." God yearns to hold us in loving arms when the world abandons us. God will never leave us when others betray, deny, abandon, or abuse us. Through using precious names for God, we can reclaim our spiritual heritage and birthright. We will be empowered for life and death.

Dearest, loving, tender Abba/Amma *God, bless us with precious names*
for you that will transform our relationships with you. Amen.

†   November 19   †

God knows us

Psalm 139:1

I have often reflected with amazement that God knows *ME*. God
knows you. God *KNOWS* everything about us. God knows when we sit or
stand. God knows what we are going to say even before we know. God
actually knows us better than we know ourselves. God hears our prayers
and cares deeply for us. God knows if we are closeted or out. God has
searched us before our birth and has known us before our conception and
birth.

Our caring God loves us and invites us into prayers with our feelings that at times may be too deep for words. We can be assured that God
cares. God sees. God stops, looks, and listens to our cries. It is wonderful
to be with God. We can never hide from our loving God. Planet earth is
too small. We can be comforted with the few words in today's meditation.
God knows and loves us deeply. The God who knows us is enough for all
our concerns. We can approach this knowing, loving God with all our cares. Truly this knowledge is too wonderful for words! We often forget
that we are a gift to God.

We also frequently forget or find difficult to believe that God
wants to be known by us. It is a wonderful two-way relationship that can
be personal and intimate. I know many people who believe in God but are
afraid. Perhaps they have experienced abusive religion or religious per-
sons who have told them they are unforgivable or abominable sinners.
Their fear factor is high. It is extremely difficult in my own life to deeply
love someone who has hurt me.

People, not God, are the abusers. God will never refuse, reject,
denigrate, or ridicule us. God wants to be known by us. Take courage and
leave past and damaging stereotypes of God. Take a risk with God and
begin spending some leisure time together. A Jewish prophet revealed the
heart of God for us through these words, "I don't want your sacrifices – I
want your love; I don't want your offerings – I want you to know me"
(Hosea 6:6 TLB).

Continue to search us, O God. Know us and help us know and love you. Lead us in love one day at a time. Amen.

†   **November 20**   †

Only God is perfect

Romans 3:23

Only God is perfect. Only Christ is without sin. Sin is an unfortunate but real aspect of our common human condition. The Bible tells us that Christ died for the sins of the world. This may come as a surprise for some well-intentioned Christian churches and pastors, but even churches and their spiritual leaders sin. Sin is a guarantee for spiritual indigestion. Sin offers no nourishing soul food.

Jesus actually came for the sins of all people, people from every imaginable sexual orientation. The cross is our common denominator. We are equally needy for spiritual cleaning and restoration from sin. We need to begin with a contrite heart. It is good to remember that Jesus is kind to people of all kinds. He never insisted on a change in sexual orientation. He did insist all change their sin orientation.

The Reverend Eugene Peterson writes this revealing insight in his beautiful book, *Answering God,* "Sin is not what is wrong with our minds, it is the catastrophic disorder in which we find ourselves at odds with God. This is the human condition." [90]

Homosexuality is not a sin. Neither is heterosexuality or bisexuality. All sexual orientations are a good gift from God. We need to remember God delights in human diversity and honors our differences and loving relationships. A popular saying in my youth was, "God doesn't make junk!" We are all precious to God. God does not prefer one sexual orientation to another. People might be biased or prejudicial, but God is not.

Sin is not precious. It is harmful. Many words describe sin in the Bible. The ancient Hebrew and Greek words have very specific and special meanings that we often do not appreciate in the 21st century. Words like trespasses, transgressions, iniquities, and debts reveal sin to be a real and complex part of human nature. We may try to avoid or deny sin as

---

[90] Peterson, Eugene. *Answering God,* p. 113.

part of our humanity, but it is a reality in our lives. Sin coexists alongside creation and confuses life. "All have sinned and fallen short of the glory of God" (Romans 3:32).

We can take moments in our lives and confess our failings to God in a spirit of humility. All of us have missed the mark somewhere in our lives today. Perhaps it was through a thought or an unkind word. Or in a moment of anger we refused to hug someone we loved or intentionally "forgot" to do something we had promised. Where have we missed the mark in life today? Where are we at odds with God?

The good news of the Gospel is that when we confess our sins, God forgives them (1 John 1:9). Confession is good for our souls and is the key to our spiritual renewal, rebirth, reawakening, and rededication to God.

God, forgive me. Forgive me where I have sinned in words, thoughts, and deeds today. Help me live a better and more loving life with you. Amen.

† **November 21** †

More than a religious concern

Psalm 51:1-12

Sin is more than a religious concern. [91] Sin is socio-religious and corporate. Every social crime, adultery, oppression, injustice, theft, cruelty, inhumanity, and neglect of the poor, with land, nations, and neighbors is sin (Exodus 20:12-17; Job 31; Isaiah 1:12-20; Amos 1:3-2:16).

Sin also has individual origin and responsibility. [92] The first book in the Bible traces sin to deliberate misuse of God-given freedoms from the beginning of human history, as we know it through Adam and Eve.

The Biblical Jewish prophets insisted on individual responsibility for inner cleansing, renewal, and reformation. They also called their na-

---

[91] Douglas, J. D., F. F. Bruce, J. I. Packer, N. Hillyer, D. Guthrie, A. R. Millard and D. J. Wiseman, Editors. *New Bible Dictionary*, pp. 1116-1120.

[92] Ferguson, Sinclair B., David F. Wright, J. I. Packer. *New Dictionary of Theology*, pp. 641-643.

tion to change its ways which were displeasing to the Holy One.[93] The Psalms give us a vocabulary that teaches us about our separation from God. They use descriptive words such as rebel, wanderer, lawless, evildoer, guilty, liar, fool, wicked, and more.

Sin is both simple and complicated at the same time. Sin is a failure to be what God wants us to be and to do what God wants us to do. A wonderful reflection of sin is found in *Addiction and Grace*, written by Dr. Gerry May. As a practicing psychiatrist and contemplative prayer leader, Dr. May observes this about sin, sin is whatever blocks us from the love of God, love of neighbor, and love of self. [94]

Sin blurs our connections with God. Webster's dictionary defines sin as the breaking of religious laws or moral principles. God gives sin its fullest meaning. God is righteous, holy, and utterly good. Sin is the opposite of God's goodness, love, and intention.

The sin solution in an oversimplified statement, is to offer our broken and contrite hearts to God for cleansing. We each need God's love and mercy in our life. The Bible offers many gracious assurances of forgiveness (Psalm 103:8-14; Isaiah 1:18; and Isaiah 55:6-7 are only a few examples). The Psalms offer us many prayers useful for confession of sin, repentance, inner cleansing, and beginning a new life with God (Psalms 6, 32, 38, 51, 102, 130, and 143). Restoration is part of our soul care. When we confess to God, we are lifted up and cleansed from sin.

Perhaps Psalm 51 would be a good place to linger. God promises to scrub our sins away and clean our souls. God promises to restore our joy.

The simplest explanation I know for confession is to admit personal and corporate wrongdoings in word, thought, and deed to God, while asking for help to live a better life.

God, help me stop doing wrong and learn to do good. Help me seek justice and encourage the oppressed. Hear my prayers. Amen.

---

[93] Barker, Kenneth, General Editor. *The New International Study Bible*, p. 1015.

[94] May, Gerry. *Addiction and Grace*, p. 2.

† November 22 †

God's flashlight

Psalm 119:105

All of life contains the possibility of meeting God, and God's self-revelation occurs in many forms, according to teachers at the world famous, ecumenical Shalem Institute for Spiritual Formation (www.shalem.org). Scripture is one way of meeting God in human terms. By reading sacred words, we are spiritually empowered.

The Psalmist reminds us that God's word is a lamp to our feet. The Psalms can serve as brilliant flashlights, lighting the path ahead of us. These wonderful words can help get us back on our feet and on our knees, when our lives are chaotic and in upheaval, when we feel overwhelmed by feelings of helplessness and hopelessness.

The Psalms can help us get through one moment at a time, when one day at a time is overwhelming. God is deeply concerned with our pain. The Psalms help us remember that God sees. God cares. God listens and responds with generous spiritual light when we call out for help.

These Psalm-prayers are time tested and true. People of faith across the ages have found help through them during their deepest moments of need.

When we contemplate sin and the dark side of our lives, the Psalms can serve as a bright light for cleansing our souls. They offer us lifelines to prayer. If we do not know how to pray, chances are that the Psalms can help.

God, shine brightly in my life. Let your words remove all darkness within me. Let the Psalms be a lamp to my feet and a light to my path. Amen.

† November 23 †
Lessons from a desperate parent
Mark 5:22-24

St. Augustine was famous for saying, *Solvitur ambulando,* ("It is solved by walking"). We can figuratively walk through the Gospel stories and find many answers to our questions. These stories are powerful life-lines, offering us inner strength during our lowest and darkest moments. Through them, we experience God's light and love.

True, television newscasters were not covering today's Gospel story. We may never know what is fact and what is myth. But there is remarkable power in story telling. Every life has a story. And the desperate father in today's Gospel reading has a great story worth telling about walking in the light of God.

Albert Schweitzer once said, "Sometimes our light goes out, but is blown into flame by another human being. Each of us owes our deepest thanks to those who have rekindled this light." Jesus can rekindle our inner light and bring us hope when life seems at its darkest hour.

Today's verses speak of an emergency situation. A desperate father of considerable social influence falls on his knees before Jesus and repeatedly begs the Healer to save his beloved little daughter. She is near death. Minutes are precious. Will he come? Jesus stops and listens carefully to his desperate call for help. He compassionately agrees to the request.

Everyone has a story to tell. Each of us has struggled to walk in the light of God, as we understand Divine Presence. Every human being sooner or later encounters moments of hopelessness and helplessness. We realize life is fragile and wonder if our prayers are being heard.

This desperate father teaches us how to walk in the light of God and pray. He begs Jesus again and again, in meaningful repetition for divine help. We have much to learn from him and will linger in this story for the next six days.

God, rekindle the light of hope within us with today's story. Amen.

† November 24 †

A desperately ill woman

Mark 5:25-28

The desperate father and Jesus pushed through the crowd towards his home when Jesus suddenly stopped and asked, "Who touched my clothes?" He had immediately felt the touch of yet another desperate person reaching for help. Healing power had poured out of his body. He refused to leave until the newly healed person publicly identified herself. With fear and trembling, a woman stepped forward and began telling her story of twelve years of suffering and loneliness.

To most fully appreciate her circumstances, we need to understand her cultural background. First century Israel was much different from twenty-first century North America. This woman acted in an extremely unconventional manner. That a Jewish woman, without a male protector, should dare to touch a strange man without his consent was an extraordinary event. Either she was desperate or had great faith.

Her situation is relevant for us. Her story is our story. She once had some financial means, which she spent in futile efforts towards healing. The care she experienced under many physicians resulted in much suffering. They actually made her condition worse. Anyone who has been ill can sympathize with her situation. There, but for the grace of God, are we.

In her first century Jewish context (Leviticus 15:25-30), her religion classified her condition as unpure. These ancient and revered religious laws prevented her from participating in social, religious, and community activities. People avoided her for fear of infection. They could not sit on her chairs or even touch her, or they too, would have to be isolated from others until prescribed cleanliness rituals were completed over a period of time. Her illness placed her outside the religious and social human community.

How lonely that must have been. Can you imagine going twelve years without tender, meaningful, and loving touch? What would it be like to go that long without a hug? Through her illness, she probably felt fear, shame, self-loathing, and social ostracism.

There are many like this woman who are shunned. Some are shunned because of illness, while others are shunned because of sexual orientation, race, religion, and many other reasons. Diseases and perceived differences might have different names, but the resulting loneliness and isolation is universal.

We need meaningful and tender touch in order to thrive. We need meaningful community and companionship. Like this unnamed woman, we might also feel fear, shame, self-loathing, and social ostracism because of well-intentioned religious rules.

Where are we in this story? What do we need from Jesus today?

God, like this anonymous woman, we need to reach out and touch Jesus to heal and thrive. Show us where oppressive religious rules cause damaging self-loathing and ostracism. Bring us into meaningful community, we pray. Amen.

† November 25 †
Jesus stopped for one person
Mark 5:29-34

Even as the eager crowd pressed about him, Jesus felt his remarkable power reach out and heal someone. He stopped in his tracks while the excited crowd breathlessly awaited his words. Slowly surveying the crowd, Jesus asked them, "who touched my clothes?" His baffled inner circle of disciples were impatient at what they felt was a needless delay. Time was of the essence. "But Jesus," they probably responded, "with this enormous crowd, many people have been pressing against you. Perhaps we should hurry, for the sick little girl is near death and awaiting your healing touch."

In fear and trembling, the formerly ill and desperate woman came forward. It was obvious to her that Jesus would not move on until she identified herself. Although it was considered highly improper for a Jewish woman to speak publicly to a man not her husband, she mustered every ounce of courage, and reluctantly came forward. While all eyes were riveted on her, she quietly shared the whole truth of her illness and suffering to Jesus and the gaping crowd. For a moment, time seemed to stand still as the pathos of her life touched their hearts.

Jesus listened intently. He then kindly and publicly blessed her act of faith and restored the tremulous woman back into meaningful community. "Daughter," said Jesus, "your faith has healed you. Go in peace and be freed from your suffering." By saying this, he spoke with an authority his listeners and critics alike would honor.

Jesus respected the desperate woman's courage and gladly affirmed her healing, thus restoring her status as a religiously clean and healthy person to her local religious and social community. Her neighbors, friends, and family would no longer fear being near her. The healed woman could now entertain, experience meaningful touch by the people who loved her, and attend public functions in town and her synagogue. She was an outcast no longer. Jesus healed much more than her physical illness. He had healed the deepest needs of her soul.

What can we take from this story and apply to our own lives? There are many lessons here. Perhaps the most important is that when one person reaches out to Jesus, he stops and compassionately listens. As he healed the deepest needs of this sick woman's soul, so he can heal our hurts and loneliness. Jesus continues even to this day, to bring isolated people into affirming community and deeper relationship with God. But first we must reach out in faith.

Heal us, O Christ, as you have healed the deepest needs of this sick woman. May we too, experience healing faith and your peace, and experience freedom from our human sufferings. Amen.

✝   **November 26**   ✝

Just believe

Mark 5:35-36

It is every parent's worse nightmare – to lose a child through death. Parents should not outlive their children, parents should not bury them. Jairus had experienced such high hopes when Jesus had earlier agreed to accompany him to his home. The synagogue ruler had hoped against hope that they would arrive in time for a miracle. Now it was too late. Crushed in spirit and teary eyed, he listened to his advisors who suggested he not bother Jesus any longer.

Jesus seemed to read Jairus' chaotic and grief stricken thoughts. He quietly ignored the advice of Jairus' servants and spoke with holy boldness, "Do not be afraid, Jairus, just believe."

Jairus was heartbroken. How could this be happening? Jairus was one of the few religious Jewish leaders open to the teachings of Jesus. What was Jairus, or anybody, for that matter, supposed to believe? Was he to believe that Jesus would perform his greatest miracle yet and bring his cherished daughter back from the dead? This was humanly impossible.

Or was it divinely possible? In the midst of this grieving father's broken heart, a faint glimmer of hope refused to be extinguished. All he had to do was just believe without fear, that Jesus would do something remarkable and supernatural. Jairus had just seen with his own eyes how Jesus had miraculously healed a chronically ill woman. He comforted himself with the memory of Jesus' earlier promise to come to his house and heal his beloved daughter. Obviously, Jesus was a wonder worker with amazing powers to cure the sick. But could this remarkable healer overcome death itself?

It seemed too much to believe yet hope grew with every step towards his home. This concerned father did not know what Jesus was going to do, but he obeyed the best he could while trying to control his fear. Jairus placed his trust and confidence in the remarkable Healer, while fervently praying for a miracle. He knew Jesus possessed remarkable powers that could only come from God.

Faith does not occur in a vacuum. Although we know very little about Jairus, we do know he was a ruler in a synagogue. He was well acquainted with theology and the Jewish hope for a future coming Messiah. Could Jesus be the long awaited Messiah? Being steeped in the Jewish scriptures since birth, Jairus was familiar with the encouraging words from the psalmists and prophets from so long ago. During the long walk back to his home, it is possible that he was even comforting himself by reciting sacred words he had memorized from childhood. *"Even though I walk through the valley of the shadow of death, I will fear no evil, for you are with me; your rod and your staff, they comfort me"* (Psalm 23:4). *"The Sovereign LORD will wipe away the tears from all faces; [God] will remove the disgrace of [God's] people from all the earth. The LORD has spoken"* (Isaiah 25:8).

By using our holy imaginations, we become part of these sacred stories. If you were Jairus, what would you be hoping and praying for? Would you be afraid or could you place your full confidence and trust in this remarkable Healer, named Jesus? In your own life faith journey, has faith in Jesus empowered you to overcome fear in the face of overwhelming troubles? Can you, with Jairus, just believe?

Oh God, help our unbelief. Give us faith and courage to overcome the fears we face in our lives. Amen.

†   **November 27**   †

Faith in the face of death

Mark 5:37-40

While there is life, there is hope. Hope and faith are closely intertwined. But hopeful faith is not always easy. While faith in Jesus can personally sustain and uplift us, it can also bring us into experiences of public contempt and ridicule. This was the situation of Jesus and Jairus as they arrived at the home of the synagogue ruler.

The Bible mentions that upon his arrival, Jesus was greeted with the sight and sounds of many grieving people. The bad news had traveled fast. Concerned relatives, friends, and neighbors quickly came to mourn when Jairus' little girl died. Their custom was to gather for several days and nights of noisy lamentations. Comforting the bereaved was sincerely practiced in Judaism as a sacred duty.

The air was filled with crying and loud wailing. Even though their religion taught the mourners their deaths were precious in the sight of God (Psalm 116:15), the cruel finality of death could not be denied. The loud lamentations were a way of honoring their sacred dead and paying final respects. Truly, death is universally our feared, dreaded, and even hated foe.

In the midst of all this commotion, Jesus calmly told the gathered crowd to stop grieving. The child, he said, was not dead. The little girl was only sleeping. The mourners laughed in unbelief and ridicule. Jesus must be crazy. The little girl's corpse was lying in her bedroom in full view. Already her small body was growing cold. According to their custom, she would need to be quickly buried before her body began decomposing in the Middle Eastern heat.

Their lack of belief and mocking laughter did not faze Jesus. He knew the crowd did not have the eyes of faith to see the miracle he was about to perform. Perhaps they were so blinded by sorrow, they could not see with the eyes of faith.

Whatever reason for their disbelief, Jesus quietly but firmly shooed them away. When the scoffing mourners had left, only then would Jesus enter the room where the little girl's body was located, accompanied only by three of his faithful disciples and the bereaved parents. The disciples and grieving parents breathlessly waited to see what Jesus would do next.

Put yourself in this story. Do you find yourself with the mocking crowd or with Jesus by the little girl's body? Take a moment to examine your beliefs about death and life after death. Do you believe Jesus can raise someone from the dead? Is this story just another timeless tragedy of parents outliving a child? Figuratively walk in the sandals of these bereaved parents and tell this story in your own words. Let it become part of your prayer.

Could it be possible, O God, that someone could miraculously be raised from the dead? Is it possible that Jesus is more than a miraculous healer? Is it true that there is hope beyond the grave? Give us the eyes of faith needed to find divine hope in the face of death. Amen.

† November 28 †
Life after death
Mark 5:41-43

I love stories with a happy ending. When the disbelieving crowd of mourners departed to another area, only then would Jesus perform his astonishing miracle. He did it in relative seclusion, away from the prying eyes of those who ridiculed him. In the presence of the little girl's parents, and Peter, James, and John, Jesus gently took the little girl's hand and said in Aramaic, "Little girl, I say to you, get up!" The Bible tells us the twelve-year-old girl awoke from the dead, stood up, and walked. She who had once been dead was now alive.

It is impossible to know who was most astonished. We can only imagine the tears of joy running down the parents' faces. Even the seasoned disciples, so accustomed to Jesus' amazing powers, were flabbergasted. They had seen Jesus do incredible things but to raise someone from the dead! They were speechless. Perhaps even the little girl was surprised at all the fuss being made about her. She was not only very much alive, but even hungry. Jesus, grinning with delight, reunited the living child to her forever-grateful parents. The little bedroom formerly filled with such sorrow and despair, was now full of happy laughter and celebration. Jesus had to gently remind the ecstatic parents to give their daughter something to eat.

So why would Jesus then hush the joyful parents and disciples, admonishing them to be silent about this miracle? As Jesus' popularity among the common people of that area grew, so did his opposition from religious leaders. It would only be a matter of time before the religious authorities would plot and scheme for his death. But as much as the grateful parents wanted to keep this miracle secret, the word of this amazing event would immediately fly around the Galilean countryside the moment the little girl walked out of her bedroom.

What can we learn from this amazing story about faith, hope, and love? In my opinion, Jesus is more than a miracle worker – he can raise the dead. For the believer, death is not the end. We can have hope beyond the grave and look forward to reuniting with loved ones in eternity. This is what I believe. What do you believe about this amazing story?

O God, thank you for this amazing story of faith, hope, and love. Give us the eyes of faith to see this miracle of life after death. Bless us with hope beyond the grave. We pray for these things in the powerful name of Jesus Christ, who can raise the dead. Amen.

† November 29 †

A Holocaust Museum reflection

Psalm 3:1

We know racism and anti-Semitism kills, but did you know homophobia is just as deadly? Years ago, I toured the Holocaust museum in

Washington D.C. Throughout the museum, Nazi concentration camp survivors proudly wore their yellow Star of David while interacting with visitors. More than six million Jews had been exterminated in Hitler's death camps in World War Two. These survivors were rightfully determined to tell their stories to the world, so the horrific lessons of history would never again be repeated.

The museum honored other concentration camp victims as well, including numerous exhibits honoring the many thousands of homosexuals forced to wear the pink triangle by Hitler. They were also brutally tortured and annihilated. The Holocaust museum has wisely acknowledged that the world must know homophobia is as deadly as anti-Semitism and racism. The museum presents the stories of gay and lesbian victims with respect and dignity.

I am deeply grateful for the Holocaust's museum efforts to present these stories, for many history books are often silenced by overt, legalized secular and religious homophobia. In some countries even today, gay and lesbian citizens are arrested, brutalized, tortured, executed, or murdered while the authorities look the other way.

Gay or straight, Jewish or Gentile, we share a common God who delights in human diversity. We are one family on earth. God grieves when people hate and kill others who are different. Whatever our sexual orientation and religious background, today's Psalm offers us God's comfort in the face of hatred, danger, and overwhelming odds against our survival. Psalm 3 offers us a stepping stone to God when enemies outnumber us and when they gleefully insist God will not hear or answer our prayers. Whether we are gay or straight, with the psalmist we are assured God will forever be our shield. God will answer us.

So have a good night's rest, pray for justice, and whenever possible, use your voice to raise public awareness of the deadly effects homophobia has on the world.

God, we praise you who made all people different, yet alike. We pray for the day when homophobia will be globally recognized as the deadly evil it is. We pray for the day when the lives and deaths of gay and lesbian victims, murdered in Hitler's concentration camps, will be honorably recorded in all history books. Hasten the day when the pink triangle will be universally recognized as a sign of courage and honor. Amen.

* On April 28, 2000, the United States Holocaust Memorial Museum's Center for Advanced Holocaust Studies sponsored a specific symposium on the persecution of homosexuals during the Nazi period. A brief synopsis is available at http://www.ushmm.org/museum/press/archive/cahs/mmarch.htm

† **November 30** †

Faith and works

James 2:17

Faith without works is a dead faith. Yes, we are saved by faith alone. But talk is cheap and we must put our words into action. God expects us to change the world. We must both walk the walk, and talk the talk of faith. As followers of Jesus, we are to bring a bit of heaven on earth against the forces of hell. We are not allowed the luxury of indifference or passivity. This holy activism is for all Christians, gay and straight.

Historically, critics such as Frederick Nietzsche (1844-1900) and Karl Marx (1818-1883) have had a very low opinion of Christianity. Nietzsche believed Christian faith made people act in a cowardly manner, by teaching them to passively accept whatever happened in their world as God's will. This discouraged efforts by religious people to change the world. Marx was no kinder in his criticism. He went so far as to say religion was the "opiate of the people." In his opinion, the Christian faith drugged people into passivity and escapism, thereby preventing them from rising against their oppressors.

I disagree strongly with Nietzsche and Marx. I believe faith inspires ordinary people to live extraordinary lives. There are many heroes among us, serving as activists against poverty and injustice, fighting indifference and hatred, as they walk their walk of faith. Throughout history, many people of faith have even suffered harsh consequences of following their conscience. But they joyfully chose to live their faith, even when and if it brought them into harm's way.

As contemporary followers of Christ, we are not allowed the luxury of looking the other way when we see evil and the face of suffering. Our silence and lack of activism condones physical and spiritual violence of all kinds. We have a holy obligation to stop prejudice and oppression, as well as to feed the hungry.

Whether we are gay or straight, Christian faith should motivate us to make a difference in our world. If you are not making a difference, take time to reexamine your faith today. Ask God for a new heart of compassion, a renewed passion for justice, and the courage to live out your faith. May your blessed faith be a stimulus for action, rather than a religious drug lulling you into passivity and escapism, when encountering the world around you.

God, renew and revive our faith in Jesus Christ. Inspire us to make a difference in the world for Jesus' sake. Bless our holy activism through the power of your Holy Spirit. Amen.

† **December 1** †

Walk in integrity

Proverbs 10:9

Godly integrity cannot be bought, bartered, or bribed. Gay or straight, integrity is a virtue of excellence worth pursuing. Our reputations depend on it.

I found myself musing about integrity while reading a newspaper article about a crisis in Zimbabwe. The country was in great turmoil. Millions faced starvation due to a deadly combination of drought, famine, economic mismanagement, and a corrupt government in power. Their president, Robert Mugabe, was forcing the white farmers to give up their homes and lands without compensation to Zimbabwean war veterans. The news article described how several countries publicly supported the original idea, until the international community realized choice farmland was being distributed primarily to Mugabe's favored political allies. The global community immediately withdrew their support of his land redistribution plan when they realized the President's motives were tainted with self-interest and greed. In the meantime, Zimbabwe languished, as a result of their controversial leader's lack of integrity.

God expects us to live with integrity. Personal integrity should be our signature in a world full of dishonesty, deceit, and hidden agendas for profit and gain at the expense of innocent victims.

Today's proverb is refreshing. We are reminded that people of integrity will walk securely with God, but the ones who take crooked paths will always be found out. Sooner or later, truth will prevail over falsehood. Honesty will win over dishonesty. God cannot be fooled.

So ask God for help when tempted to negotiate and concede principles and morals. Do your best and trust God for the rest. When in error, ask for both human and divine forgiveness. Be willing to make restitution for past compromises. If you have previously betrayed the trust of others, be patient with those who no longer trust you. It will take time to regain their trust.

Now walk securely. Let God guide your path one step at a time. Make every day a fresh start and you will be transformed.

Show me, God, where I have compromised my integrity at the expense of others. Forgive me where I have failed to live with honesty and sincerity. Help me live a better life. Amen.

✝ **December 2** ✝

Choose your companions carefully

Proverbs 13:20

Many scripture readers overlook the book of Proverbs to their detriment. These pithy Middle Eastern sayings of wisdom are refreshingly timeless. It does not matter if we are gay or straight, young or old, male or female. There is something for everyone in the wisdom of these teachings.

Today's proverb reminds us friends have great influence in our lives. We must choose our companions carefully. If we walk with the wise, we will become wise. Fools on the other hand, will eventually come to harm.

What is a fool? Fools are people who have little to no judgment or common sense. Perhaps they act in rash and reckless ways, without good sense or wisdom. A fool's paradise is always a deceptive happiness based on illusions.

We jokingly speak of God watching over children and fools. But if our companions are foolish, sooner or later, they will bring us to harm through their irresponsible behavior and life choices. Actions have consequences. Only fools go where the prudent and intelligent fear to tread.

I remember one family whose youngest child drifted into the influence of foolish friends. Through the friends' foolish peer influence, their son dropped out of high school and became involved with drugs and alcohol. Before he knew it, the impressionable teenager was selling drugs to support his growing drug and alcohol addiction. Many of his friends stole from their own parents to support their drug habits. As a drug dealer, this young man hanged out with a rough crowd and thought he was invincible.

Reality eventually caught up with him. He was beaten and left for dead in a drug deal that went badly. His life went downhill from there. By his thirties, he was sleeping on a couch in a gas station. His foolish friends were always ready to party, but none encouraged him to face his problems and turn his life around.

Through God's grace, he met someone who saw his potential even when he hit rock bottom. With this person's encouragement and friendship, he now has a job, makes an honest wage, owns a modest home, has a lover and a bright drug-free future.

I had a memorable conversation with him on his fortieth birthday. By this time, the majority of his former friends were either in prison or dead. He felt lucky to be alive and regretted those wasted years. He now chooses his friends with great care and strives to make every day a fresh start.

Many people come to misfortune and grief through foolish friends. They care not for your welfare or best interests. Their thoughtless risk-taking can bring you into harm's way. So choose your friends with care. Search for wise friends with good judgment, understanding, and prudence. Do not suffer fools gladly.

God, I thank you for the wisdom and caring of good friends who care deeply for my welfare. Help me reciprocate and be a wise, caring, and encouraging friend. Amen.

✝   December 3   ✝

Solved by Walking

Isaiah 40:31

Walking is good for our souls. Many walk for love and wisdom. A local hospice program owns a large portable labyrinth and calls their ministry, "walking the trail of wisdom." By facilitating a number of my own labyrinth walks and retreats, I have learned walking helps us break old patterns of thinking, doing, and being. Walking helps us honor body and spirit. Everything instructs as we slow down and see, listen, taste, feel, pause, and grow.

Walking helps release hurtful and negative feelings. Walking is known as the perfect total-body exercise. Here are four great reasons to walk: it brightens your mood; it strengthens your body; it energizes your mind; it burns calories.[95] Oprah Winfrey has often said, "I've been through every diet under the sun, and I can tell you that getting up, getting out, and walking is always the first goal."

Age-old wisdom reveals that aging people who remain active maintain the vigor and strength of someone ten to fifteen years younger. I looked at a walking journal the other day, and it specifically mentioned that we use more of our body's 650 muscles and 208 bones when we walk, than when we run. Walking also helps prevent osteoporosis (age-related bone loss).

Step by step, we can breathe peace with every step. By breathing a little slower and deeper, we enjoy placing one step in front of the other. People walk for all kinds of reasons. We walk for peace, justice, civil rights, health and wellness, and many other social causes. We walk and talk, walk and meditate. We walk for our physical health, so why not walk for our spiritual health?

The venerable Thich Nhat Hanh reminds us that "everything depends on our steps. We struggle in our mind and body, and don't touch the peace and joy that are available right now – the blue sky, the green leaves, the eyes of our beloved." [96] He calls us to be deeply mindful and in touch with the present moment. Our understanding of what is going on will deepen, and we can begin to be filled with acceptance, joy, peace, and love. Thich Nhat Hanh encourages everyone to begin to practice walking meditation. Because it might be new, we may feel unbalanced, like a baby learning to walk. He says this, "Follow your breathing, dwell mindfully on your steps, and soon you will find your balance. Visualize a tiger walking slowly, and you will find that your steps become as majestic as his." [97]

Walk and find strength with God.

God, help us build our strength by walking, walking with You. Amen.

---

95 Fenton, Mark and the Editors. *Walking: The New Walker's Logbook*, p. 67.
96 Hanh, Thich Nhat. *The Long Road Turns to Joy*, p. 5.
97 Ibid., p. 49.

† December 4 †
Walking Wisdom
Proverbs 3:23

Confucius offers us some fifth century wisdom worth reclaiming in the twenty-first century through his five excellent practices of pilgrimage. Perhaps his practices could help us be better people of faith. His five practices are brilliantly simple. First, Confucius encourages us to practice the arts of attention and listening. Secondly, practice the art of renewing yourself daily. Third, he encourages meandering walking to the center of every place. Fourth, practice reading sacred texts. Finally, he encourages praise and singing.

Thich Nhat Hanh also encourages us to walk with gratitude. Gratitude reminds us how wonderful life is. He teaches young people a simple verse to practice while walking. *"Oui, oui, oui,"* he recommends people say to themselves as they breathe in, and *"Merci, merci, merci,"* as they breathe out. [98] "Yes, yes, yes. Thanks, thanks, thanks." It helps people respond to life, to society, and to the Earth in a positive way.

Walking is good for our spirits. Confucius and Thich Nhat Hanh are not alone with their encouragement to walk in gratitude while singing. Many other spiritual traditions also understand life is a journey and we are all on a sacred path. Walk tall, walk faithfully, walk music in your hearts.

A Navaho song calls us to, "Walk on a rainbow trail; walk on a trail of song, and all about you will be beauty. There is a way out of every dark mist, over a rainbow trail."

Walking is good for our souls and Epicurus, a Greek philosopher who lived 341 to 270 B.C., reminds us that, "It is never too early or too late to care for the well-being of your soul." Seneca, a Roman philosopher, dramatist and statesman who lived 4 B.C. to 64 A.D., encourages us to "find a path or make one." Anaxagoras, another Greek philosopher who lived 500 to 428 B.C., taught in Athens that "life is a journey." An ancient Ilocano saying from the Northern Luzon Island in the Philippines wisely reminds us to go slowly if we are going a long way.

We can experience powerful meditative experiences through the use of finger labyrinths as well, slowly tracing the grooved path of the labyrinth with the fingers of our dominant and non-dominant hands. Or

[98] Hanh, Thich Nhat. *The Long Road Turns to Joy*, p. 36.

watch other walkers and let their movements become part of your meditation.

Many of us who are Christians have much to learn from other spiritual traditions. We will walk life better, because we have cared enough to learn from other faiths in an attitude of respect. Confucius and the other wise sages have been a great blessing for me today.

How are your spiritual practices? Are they as excellent as the ones suggested by the masters?

God, bless our souls with walking wisdom. As we journey through life, help us be more mindful of our breath and body movements. Empower our prayers with this awareness. Amen.

† December 5 †

Envy versus contentment

Proverbs 14:30

True contentment is characterized by God's deep peace within our hearts. Wealth cannot buy this priceless treasure. Envy on the other hand, destroys inner serenity.

Deep-seated jealousies rob people of deep contentment and can take years off their lives. Envy consumes and destroys peace of mind and happiness.

Over the years, I have known many individuals whose consuming envy literally destroyed their health along with the well being of their families. Such toxic and life-draining envy is worse than poison. Envying another person's lover, family, career, achievements, possessions, and money only brings discontentment with great potential for destruction.

To find personal deep abiding contentment, individuals must learn to take responsibility for their life choices and actions. Their blame games must stop. Otherwise they will be as forever restless as a breaking wave on the ocean, constantly searching for an ever-illusive contentment. In the process, toxic perspectives spill over and contaminate the lives of others.

There is a transforming cure for such life-draining, toxic envy and discontent. Begin a lifestyle of counting your blessings. Daily offer heartfelt prayers of gratitude for the little things in your life. Develop your own personal theology of enough. As you learn to be satisfied with what you have, be grateful and express your appreciation through prayer. Be courageous enough to look deep within your heart for sources of your discontent. Humbly ask God for a change of heart. Reach out for help. The life you save may be your own.

God, you are my ultimate source of satisfaction and contentment. Transform my heart and mind with a fresh attitude of gratitude and deep peace. Heal me from envy. Give me courage when needed to change destructive, bitter, and jealous attitudes wherever they may exist. Make me a source of blessing in the process. Amen.

† December 6 †

Strength for the weary and weak
Isaiah 40:28-31

Cleaning my files the other day I came across a sermon I preached at the naval hospital more than five years ago. It was titled, "Amazing Strength." Powerful memories flooded my mind of a courageous, quiet, bald headed woman who came to the chapel for that Sunday morning service.

She came alone with her intravenous bottle swaying with every step. Her eyes never left me during the message. The chapel service had a time for special blessing and anointing for those who wanted healing prayers. She was too weak to come forward for prayer and so I went to her. The woman was undergoing massive chemotherapy and radiation for a vicious metastatic cancer. Her prognosis was very poor. Only God could help her at this stage of her disease. We were not the only ones in the congregation with tears in our eyes.

After the service was over, I visited this frail woman in her hospital room and found her resting in bed with an open Bible on her lap. Sure enough, it was opened to these verses on which I had preached. She labored for breath as she told of her struggle with pain and pending death.

The scripture had greatly encouraged her to hold on for another day. She had imagined herself soaring with the eagles in power and strength.

Her great faith was humbling. Her courage and dignity was profound. These words helped her continue to live with strength and hope. The illness was wasting her body away, but her faith in God was vibrant and deep. She was not afraid.

I will always remember her courage and faith. I will remember the look in her eyes as she listened to these words. I will remember her open Bible during her time of great need and physical suffering. She found that God was enough. In putting her hope in God, she received the strength needed for living one day at a time.

God, strengthen my faith in whatever my circumstances may be. Let these lovely words of courage help me. Amen.

✝   December 7   ✝
Remember Pearl Harbor
Habakkuk 3:19

Remember Pearl Harbor! How could I forget? My beloved Grandmother's birthday was December 7. She and my grandfather had been celebrating her birthday at their home with a circle of new American friends. The radio happened to be on and one of the guests heard the horrible news of the Japanese attack on Pearl Harbor in Hawai'i. The party celebrations stopped as everyone gathered around the radio in horror and dismay. All of the party guests were immigrants to this new country. Many had sons who would soon be drafted and go to war. Some would not return. My uncle was one of those lucky enough to come home with minimal war wounds. He also came back from England with a lovely bride.

I remember both the Pearl Harbor stories and my dearly beloved Grandmother. She left a wonderful legacy for all her grandchildren. She taught us about life. We get sick, have accidents, and lose people we love through death. She encouraged us to live our dreams. It was her own dream for a better life in the United States of America, which gave her the courage to leave her beloved Norway, her family, and friends. Through her courageous living, she showed us how to live with strength and hope in the darkest of times.

Sooner or later, all of us will feel powerless, faint, fatigued, and weary. Old and young, male and female, we all become exhausted and may be too tired to even move. Sometimes life brings too many obstacles, difficulties, and heartaches. There are times when we are doing far too much, for too long, with too little rest.

Yet, my Grandmother taught me that God wants to give us amazing strength. In adversity and prosperity, let God be your strength.

Be my amazing strength in adversity and prosperity, God. Help me remember that when I feel weakest, your strength will always be sufficient for me. Amen.

† December 8 †

Pray for others

Philippians 1:3-8

Like many other great thinkers and activists, the apostle Paul did some of his best writing and praying behind bars. Rather than wallow in depression, despair, and discouragement, Paul chose to write his thoughts down when imprisoned. His prison letters (Galatians, Ephesians, Philippians, and Colossians) offer valuable insights on persevering faith. These jailhouse writings can empower, energize, equip, and encourage us. Paul takes us beyond basic survival and shows us how to live with a spiritual maturity that can never be chained.

Paul begins the letter to the church in Philippi by thanking God for his dear companions in the faith who heroically shared his passion for spreading the gospel message of hope. Paul cared enough for his friends to pray for them with joy and gratitude. He carried them in his heart, confident that God was completing a good work in their lives. Quite honestly, he missed seeing his cherished friends and longed for their companionship. But his faith and love was so great that he could comfort himself through memories. Jail could not break his spirit or destroy his love for his valued friends.

A Nazi concentration camp survivor named Corrie ten Boom once wrote, "The greatest thing one person can do for another is to pray for them." Learn to pray for the people for whom you are thankful. Pray for those you love. Pray for friends, colleagues, neighbors, and family members. Pray in love and appreciation and you will find your heart overflowing with gratitude. They will be immensely strengthened through your prayers.

God, we are so often self-centered and forgetful of others. Teach us to pray for others frequently with an attitude of love and gratitude. Use our prayers to bless their lives. Amen.

✝   December 9   ✝

Always pray for more love

Philippians 1:9-11

Whenever in doubt about how to pray, always pray for more love. The world needs it and so do we. Our loving prayers are the greatest gift we can give another person.

Today's verses are a prayer written in prison by the apostle Paul for his cherished friends. His prayer continues to offer many insights centuries later. Praying for others is hard work and quite frankly, sometimes we struggle for words. If you are like me, there are times when I do not know how to pray for someone about whom I care deeply.

With Christmas fast approaching, consider a prayerful experiment with Paul's prayer. Pray this prayer for everyone on your Christmas card and shopping list as your secret gift. Trust me in this. Your life will never be the same and you will experience a more fulfilling Christmas season. Your prayer just might be the best Christmas gift your friends will ever receive.

How does Paul pray for his friends? He prays for their love to abound, flourish, and overflow in growing knowledge and discernment, wisdom and purity. As a loving friend and spiritual teacher, he asks God to help his friends every day of their lives, until the day of Jesus Christ's return. Paul concludes his prayer by confidently requesting God to motivate his friends to bring loving justice and righteousness to the world. He knew their lifestyles of loving activism and devotion would bring great glory and praise to God. This is holy boldness at its best.

Gay or straight, young or old, male or female, we are created to praise God through our lives. So consider using this prayer for your own use as well. But pray it with great care. It is revolutionary and radical, with the potential to change the world. This is the kind of prayer that could heal racism and homophobia, poverty and world hunger. It could heal broken relationships and bring reconciliation to both individuals and nations. A prayer like this could help us experience the mind and heart of Christ.

God's love in our lives is the most powerful life force on earth. It is a love that can motivate us to live heroic lives, to overthrow injustice, and overcome impossible odds, while living sacrificially for the greater good of others and the world.

May your love abound and flourish daily. May your love be a source of blessing for the world, while transforming and energizing your own life and the lives of others.

Wise and loving God, I pray for more love in my own life as well as for my friends. I want your loving wisdom to characterize my life and guide my steps. I want your love to influence all my decision making and to empower my desire to see justice served without partiality. May you be praised and honored as I strive to live a lover's life with your help. Amen.

✝ **December 10** ✝

Soul Water

1 Corinthians 9:24-27

Years ago, I had the crazy idea of running a marathon in honor of my fortieth birthday. My neighbor, Joe, had successfully run five marathons and offered many valuable insights and suggestions that I followed carefully during the rigorous training schedule.

"Joe," I asked on our way to the starting line, "what do I have to do to finish the race? What is the one most important thing?"

"Well . . . hmm . . . there is only one thing," he said. "If you do this, you will finish the marathon. If not, you won't. Drink water. Stop at every water station and drink deep. Drink whether you feel like it or not. If you do, you'll be OK."

Joe was well in the lead when I lost sight of him. I ran with thousands of runners and stopped at every water station, drinking glasses of water whether I was thirsty or not. At mile 23, I was hurting and wanted to quit. I found myself singing the doxology. I refused to quit and determined to crawl to the finish line if necessary. And I finished the race! Receiving a medal, hugs, and congratulations was a joyful experience.

After coming home and showering, I called my friend Joe. His worried wife answered the phone. She had not seen him finish the race and had hoped he was with me. Hours later, she found Joe in a nearby hospital. He was seriously dehydrated. You see, he had not followed his own advice. He had decided during the thrill of the race to run for speed and neglected to drink water at the numerous water stations along the course. He collapsed at mile 23 and needed emergency intravenous fluids. He was unable to complete the race.

The church is our water station. If we are to thrive and serve God, we need water stations with other people of faith to encourage and cheer us on. And we will encourage and cheer them. It goes both ways. God calls us to run as a community of faith. We need regular worship as part of our race training, whether we feel like it or not. We need to slow down weekly, and drink deeply from the word of God, praying and caring for others, before returning to our busy lives.

As Christmas draws near, consider going to church for a long drink of water. Search for a church that welcomes people of all sexual orientations. Help each other run the marathon of life. Enjoy remembering the reason for the season. And praise God when the going gets difficult.

Praise God from whom all blessings flow; Praise Christ, all creatures here below; Praise Holy Spirit, Comforter; One God, Triune, whom we adore.[99] *Amen. Amen.*

---

[99] Doxology prayer attributed to Thomas Ken, 1674. Thomas Ken was an Anglican priest, author, chaplain, bishop, poet, and hymn writer who lived from 1637-1711. Some of his works can be enjoyed at http://www.cyberhymnal.org/bio/k/e/ken_t.htm

†   December 11   †

"I'm home, thank you."
Isaiah 25:8a; 35:10b

While cleaning out my files, I discovered an old reflection that I wrote when my mother died years ago. Such dear memories! Love never dies as long as there is someone who remembers.

Perhaps some family background would be helpful. My beloved maternal grandparents were simple folks. Neither had much formal schooling. When they arrived in America, they quickly found a worshipping Norwegian-American community and settled into their new country. Together they loved the church and God's people. They often opened their humble home to missionaries, pastors, and youth groups. They sang in the church choir and served as Sunday school teachers. My grandparents outlived all their children with dignity and courage.

My maternal grandparents eventually lost their physical independence as they aged and were gladly welcomed into my parent's home where they resided for ten years. When my grandfather had several progressively debilitating strokes, Grandma lovingly insisted she would care for him at home and not resort to a nursing home. She was a determined soul who stubbornly refused to be separated from her life mate of more than seventy years. My parents were wonderful in assisting them in their daily care. While caring for her aging parents, my mother was diagnosed with terminal cancer. Even though I had been on my own in another state for years, it seemed the most natural decision in the world to move back home. We now had three generations of adults living under one roof. Together Grandma, Dad, and I jointly cared for our dear ones. We helped them eat, wash, and take care of basic bodily needs. We nursed them day and night and were blessed with caring home nursing assistants and hospice volunteers, without whose help the situation would have been overwhelming. Our neighbors were wonderfully supportive and helpful. A local seminary was only twenty minutes away from the house and I enrolled in its masters of divinity program. I did much of my homework in hospital emergency rooms. Somehow we found strength for one day at a time.

My mother was a born again Christian. She knew she was "going home to be with the Lord." And for her homecoming she wished to die at home. Mom wanted to be home with family and not in a hospital with strangers. Many were the nights that we would rush to the emergency room because of her medical complications. One night the emergency room doctor insisted on admitting my mother.

When I saw her the next day, I realized she had only hours to live. Together as a family, against medical advice, we brought Mom home to die. The hospital sent us home with plenty of morphine and instructions to keep her pain free. We rushed home in an ambulance, racing the clock for the inevitable. Our dear friends and close neighbors had everything prepared. Fresh cut tulips were in a vase. The hospital bed and oxygen tank was waiting in the living room under Mom's cherished wall clock. A thoughtfully prepared dinner was warming in the oven. Our friends gently hugged Mom, softly murmuring their good-byes while saying, "I love you." One by one, they quietly left us to dinner.

The joy on my mother's face was beautiful to behold as we sat around the table. She kept saying through her oxygen mask, "I'm home, thank you!" She died at that dinner table, held in Dad's strong arms, surrounded by those she loved. Just before she died, she clearly said, "I can hear God! He is calling my name! And I have no pain and am not afraid." Then she breathed her last. She was home with God. Her pain was gone forever.

With tears streaming down her face, Grandma burst into this song, "When we all get to heaven, what a day of rejoicing that will be! When we all see Jesus, we'll sing and shout the victory." Then she quietly went upstairs where Grandpa was in his wheelchair and told him the news. Together they wept and prayed. Their faith comforted them in their time of deep need.

Here is Christian hope for living one day at a time. Even when we have tears streaming down our faces, we can sing as my grandmother did.

God, thank you for so gently wiping away the tears from our faces. Thank you for hope beyond the grave. Amen.

† **December 12** †

Teddy bears and caring friends

Psalm 116:15

Months before Grandpa's death, Grandma had asked me to perform his funeral. That funeral was one of the hardest things I have ever done in my life. I will always remember Grandma sitting in front of me, surrounded by their numerous grandchildren, great grandchildren, and great great grandchildren, as I preached the homily. They had been married for seventy-two years. The funeral home was overflowing with visitors. Many had traveled great distances to comfort Grandma in her grief and bereavement.

Before the casket was closed, many people gravely walked to the casket for a final viewing. One of the great great grandchildren quietly placed her cherished teddy bear in the casket so her beloved Grandpapa would have a toy to play with in heaven.

In that moment, a little child taught us a great truth about God's love and concern for grieving people. We are precious to God. God cares when our hearts are sorrowing. Someday there will be a heavenly reunion with loved ones. Death is not the end, only a transition into another life. So pack your teddy bears for an eternity of playtime with God. Sorrow will someday be turned into joy.

The Christmas season sometimes brings overpowering memories of grief over the loss of loved ones. Be gentle and considerate of people in grief while honoring your own feelings of sadness. Perhaps a bereaved friend needs a teddy bear for comfort, a hug, and your companionship. A great gift for people in sorrow is our time and compassion long after the funeral is over. Although sharing old photos and memories may not fit into a Christmas stocking, your holiday visit might promote healing and some relief from loneliness. Be especially sensitive to closeted gay and lesbian friends who lack sympathetic and loving public recognition of their losses of life partners and friends. Our world does not always honor such loving relationships. Who knows – they might need a teddy bear from a caring friend.

Compassionate God, thank you for the comfort of teddy bears and caring friends. As Christmas approaches, help me be sensitive to those in public and private sorrow. Bring to my attention those in need of a hug, a visit, and my listening ear this holiday season. In Jesus' name I pray, Amen.

✝   **December 13**   ✝

Friends and family

Proverbs 17:17

Today's proverb reminds us of the enduring value of friends and family. A true friend loves at all times. Kinfolk are born to share adversity. Cherish these special people in your life.

When my grandfather died, Grandma was numb with grief. I had the privilege of taking her to their summer home for the first week after Grandpa's funeral. All through that week, I cooked for Grandma and took her out for leisurely drives in the car. We sat in the yard and talked about her life with Grandpa for hours. In the evenings we went to the lake and watched the boats. She took long, undisturbed naps in the sunshine. I remember watching her sleep while my heart ached for her. Grandma had nursed Grandpa devotedly around the clock for the past ten years. She was weary and worn out. Gradually the reality of her loss began to sink in. We became very close. I cherish every memory of that difficult and blessed week.

All too soon, it was time to close up their summer cottage and go home. Grandma turned to me and said, "Thank you for being such a wonderful friend." I thanked her for being such a wonderful grandmother.

When she died the following year, many family friends and relatives came to pay their final respects. During the funeral, we laughed and cried while sharing Alf and Inga stories. I realized some of these beloved friends had become a part of my own extended family. These faithful friends had loved my grandparents and family through prosperity and adversity, health and illness, joy and sorrow. We had danced at each other's weddings, celebrated birthdays and anniversaries, and seen each others' children grow up, sharing comfort at funerals over the years. I felt closer to some of these friends than my own kin.

Loving families of choice are not limited to marriage and blood relatives. This is especially important to acknowledge during the holiday season. Cherish those near and dear to your heart. Let them know how much you love and care for them. Nurture these relationships with pro-found gratitude. Be the best friend you can, love at all times, and share in adversity.

O God, help me value families of all kinds. Open my heart to friends and family alike. I ask that you bring each reader into meaningful, loving cir-cles of friends through this holiday season. I pray for families to be rec-onciled, friendships affirmed, and love to abound. Amen.

† December 14 †

In Jesus' name, Amen.
John 16:24

Christmas is fast approaching. In the busyness of this festive sea-son, consider this prayer experiment. While hustling and bustling to sea-sonal parties and shopping for presents, give the gift of many secret prayers. Look at people from your heart, then briefly and silently pray for them in Jesus' name. Ask God to bless them with a special peace and joy that only the holy babe in the manger can offer.

Notice the excited lines of children eagerly waiting their turn to sit on Santa Claus' knee in the malls. Some of them have never heard the Christmas story of baby Jesus. Pray for them. While praying, do not for-get the many children in homes too poor to afford Christmas gifts. Ask God to provide for their needs.

Pray for nearby shoppers and strangers as you wait in line to pur-chase gifts or return merchandise. In the midst of your own seasonal joy, pray for the homeless, the helpless, and those without hope. Try these very simple prayers when aware of the elderly, the lonely, and the shut-ins. Do not forget those struggling with illness and grief, despair, suicide idea-tion, and domestic violence.

Remember our military service members. Many are far away from loved ones and they routinely serve in harm's way. Duty prevents some from being home for Christmas. Pray with compassion for closeted gay and lesbian military members who must live secret lives, unable to publicly acknowledge lovers and life partners, while they serve our homo-phobic military with courage, honor, and integrity. Pray for the day to hasten when homophobia is recognized as the great evil it is, so our gay and lesbian American citizens can serve openly in uniform with pride and without fear of violence from homophobic fellow soldiers.

Pray for people who have suffered painful rejection from their families and friends because of their real or perceived sexual orientations. In the name of Jesus, ask God to bless them with circles of caring and loving friends.

Our potential to uplift and encourage numerous people through our heartfelt prayers in the name of Jesus is unlimited. Such prayers are not limited to the Christmas season. Pray daily and ask God's blessings and protections for people in every conceivable situation. The world will be a better place because you cared enough to pray.

Dearest God, we pray for all these things in the holy, powerful, and transforming name of Jesus Christ. Amen.

✝ **December 15** ✝

Ten days before Christmas

1 Thessalonians 3:12, 13

The Christmas season has long been profaned by commercialism. Every year it seems we are bombarded earlier and earlier with advertising, urging us to buy more and not less. By now, most people are shopping in earnest. Great shopping sprees often make it easy to forget the true meaning of Christmas. As we dash about buying gifts, we often forget the babe born in a manger had no crib for his bed.

Not everyone is in the shopping frame of mind however. Surrounding us are many families who routinely lack food and clothing. Homeless and domestic violence shelters are full of people who understand the deeper meaning of Christmas better than the more affluent. They understand the first Christmas was one borne out of desperation and poverty.

The birth of Jesus occurred in urgent and physically dirty circumstances. There was no room in the inn, the old beloved Christmas story tells us. Mary's labor could not be ignored. The unborn child was going to be born without the able assistance of midwives or an attending physician. Joseph did the best he could and found a crude and drafty shelter for his laboring wife.

The sweet baby Jesus was born among the animals in the manger, among manure and straw. There was no profaning commercialism that first Christmas. God's most enriching gift to the world was born among the poor and the homeless and the dumb animals.

For this Christmas, do not get caught up in the commercialism and obsess about finding expensive gifts. The best gifts cannot be bought. The best gifts are love, time together, and deep caring relationships. In other words, the best gifts come from the heart.

Imagine your own pilgrimage to Bethlehem for that first Christmas so long ago. Linger in the wonderful Bible stories about this amazing child who came to be God among us, Emmanuel.

Consider sharing the true joy of Christmas with the lonely ones around us, people without families, forgotten people in nursing homes and homeless shelters. Reach out with a strong sense of caring and community.

Through the remainder of the holiday season, pray for your love to increase and overflow for others. Give many gifts from your heart this year. As you do, you will discover the message of the Holy Child of Bethlehem still resonates throughout the world.

Yes, God, increase my love, let it overflow to others around me this Christmas. Amen.

† December 16 †

Keep looking up

Luke 21:35

Each season of Advent is a reminder for Christians to wake up spiritually and be alert for the Second Coming of Christ. The Bible tells us that some day he will return to earth. Dramatic and terrifying signs, as some believe, will mark the end times. Everyone will see these signs. The sun, moon, stars, and tides will be deeply affected. The world will be convulsed. There will be worldwide political, social, and physical upheavals. There will be much terror, anguish, and dismay. Heaven will shake and we are told that fire will destroy the earth. Jesus' return will be marked with power, glory, brilliance, majesty, holiness, and love.

The Christian can respond to these events with joy and courage. We are to stand up and lift our heads high. Jesus will return for us. Until that day, we are to guard our heart with God's values of holiness and godliness. We are to live honorably, without carousing, drunkenness, and debauchery, while avoiding jealousy and fighting. The Bible reminds us to constantly be on our guard and give our anxieties and worries to God.

When this Second Advent occurs, we need to pray for exceptional strength and endurance for our loved ones and ourselves. So live in a state of daily readiness. The babe in a manger will someday return in power and glory.

Will we be ready and waiting for him? My beloved grandmother had a favorite saying. She would often say, "Keep looking up. Jesus is coming. Maybe even today."

Help us be ready and live alertly for that day, dear God. Amen.

† December 17 †
God has a big eraser
Luke 3:4-6

Is it a bit odd to think about God's judgment on the world so soon before Christmas? Yet Advent (the four weeks preceding Christmas) is historically a time where Christians are called to prepare for Christ's second return. Since the beginning of the Christian Church, people have been urged to turn from their sins in repentance, and live better lives in preparation for that great and terrible future day of divine judgment.

Repentance is an unpopular word, but it is important for our spiritual health. We need to turn away from what is offensive to God, and turn to God in contrition and humility. Repentance involves an inner change in attitude. It is when we repent that we submit to God without excuse. We need to call sin, sin. Sin is offensive to God. The Bible tells us the effects of sin are deadly.

Repentance takes courage. Honesty is always the best policy with God. Remember that repentance turns us towards God. It is a continuous, daily lifestyle. We are to be like Jesus in word and deed. New life in Christ calls us to daily holiness. We are to be new creations in Christ (2 Corinthians 5:17-21). God wishes to transform us from the inside out (Romans 12:1, 2).

God is eager to forgive when we admit our failings. Forgiveness is a wonderful gift through Jesus Christ. What a wonderful Christmas gift!

The babe in the manger came to erase our sins. Here is the meaning of Christmas. Christ came to destroy sin and the power of sin in the world. This is why the baby grew up and died on the cross. Someday he will return in power and glory. Until that day, cultivate the mind and heart of Christ in daily living. Err on the side of human kindness and compassion. Confess sin and call it what God calls it.

God is in the business of helping sinners become saints. God is eager to erase sin from our lives.

Lord, make me more like Yourself, less like myself. Amen.

✝ December 18 ✝

Courage in your Christmas stocking

Psalm 31:24

Usually Christmas stockings are full of small stocking stuffers such as candy and fruit, inexpensive presents and fun items. But if I could put one word in your stocking, it would be the gift of courage. Please write this word on a small card and place it in your Christmas stocking. Look at it often throughout the upcoming year and let the word be your inspiration when facing overwhelming odds.

While writing spiritual meditations for my friends in Zimbabwe, as they struggled with starvation, economic collapse, and many legalized acts of injustice from corrupt government officials, as Internet pastor and friend, I wrote this courage reflection for them on August 16, 2002. I offer these simple thoughts to you as a special Christmas gift. Please share your courage with others and freely distribute it among your friends. In this way, the gift goes on and on.

Courage helps us look problems in the eye, rather than look the other way. God wants us to live heroically and bravely. Courage is like a muscle. The more we use it, the stronger we will become. If we cower in fear, our courage muscle will atrophy and waste away from disuse. To know what to do and not to do it is the worst cowardice, Confucius taught. An old Italian proverb reminds us it is better to live one day as a lion than a hundred years as a sheep.

Great courage is needed by citizens in every country to confront injustice and familiar patterns of racism and destructive ways of doing things. It takes courage to feed your enemies, rather than use food as a political weapon. Only the brave will change old ways of thinking and being, while learning how to live with mutuality, respect, equality, and dignity. It takes courage to stop death threats, while only cowards commit acts of random violence. Courage is needed to stand up and speak truth, and needed to sit down and listen. Great strength and courage are needed when working together for finding peaceable, nonviolent ways to seek reconciliation, forgiveness, and restoration.

The specific Hebrew word used for strength and courage in to-day's verse is *chazaq*. *Chazaq* is found here and in Psalm 27:14. God is our source of *chazaq*. *Chazaq* does not carry a passive grin and bear it attitude. Here it is being used as a verb, encouraging the one praying to be strong and confident while waiting alertly for God. It is the total opposite of cowardice. *Chazaq* is a bold word describing the believer's confident courage that is only perfected while waiting for God. People of faith from every racial and ethnic background need this bold yet humble quality of mind and heart.

In the mighty power of God, be brave. Be strong. Take courage. Do not give up. God is in the chaos and storms of life, generously giving each seeker the courage, strength, stamina, endurance, perseverance, and fortitude needed for every situation.

God, hear my humble prayer. Bless those I love and myself with chazaq *courage and strength. May my courage make the world a better place. Amen.*

† December 19 †

A praise hymn of liberation theology

Luke 1:46-48

I could easily listen to Christmas music year round, never tiring of the wonderful carols of faith, hope, and love. One of the great seasonal joys is the many lessons and carols offered by various churches, and attending the marvelous Christmas concerts. Who has not thrilled to *Ave Maria* and the *Magnificat*, inspired by Mary, the holy mother of God, the revered *theotokos* (God-bearer)?

The Virgin Mary is the most beloved woman in the entire Bible. Her faith journey has inspired millions throughout the centuries. While living in obscurity, the young teenager was literally touched by the angel Gabriel, with a very special message from God. When Mary said "yes" to God's plan for her life, world history changed forever. The young woman became pregnant with God.

After her angelic visit, the miraculously pregnant teenager hastened to seek the companionship of Elizabeth. Elizabeth was an aged relative well beyond childbearing years. Somehow she too had conceived and was miraculously pregnant with the child who would become known as John the Baptist.

Young Mary and elderly Elizabeth spent three encouraging months together (Luke 1:56). Both understood God had divinely chosen them to birth remarkable children for a holy purpose beyond their comprehension.

Upon Mary's arrival, while overcome with emotion the younger woman burst into a hymn of praise, now known as the *Magnificat* (Luke 1:46-56). Mary understood all generations would call her blessed. Her glorious hymn is among the most cherished in all of scripture, possibly inspired by an earlier hymn of praise by a woman named Hannah (1 Samuel 2:1-10).

Mary joyously sings of the amazing spiritual revolution God has called her to participate in, through the birth of her remarkable child. She sings of liberation theology, worship, and of God's remarkable compassion for the outcast, downtrodden, oppressed, and forgotten people in the world.

If you have never heard the *Magnificat* sung before, I urge you to do so this year. Consider memorizing parts of her hymn through the lovely words in Luke's gospel. Your soul and spirit will rejoice.

With Mary, my soul glorifies and rejoices in you, God my Savior. You are as mindful of my humble state, as you were with young Mary. Blessed be your name forever and ever. Amen.

✝ December 20 ✝

More about Mary

Luke 1:49-50

Mary was a remarkable teenager. She understood God's holiness and might. God was her awesome God! This youthful woman of faith has something else to teach us. She understood God is merciful and personal. God sees us. God does great things for us as we worship.

Mary's words offer us insight into her personal life of faith. She had no idea of what was ahead, but she knew God was in control and held her future. This humble, poverty stricken woman offers us her experience in God. God had done great things in her life. She was willing to do the humanly impossible for God.

Perhaps for Christmas, we could follow her example of praise and worship. Her testimony can be ours. God is willing and eager to do great things in our lives. Praising God is a good way to begin. Through praise, we experience the tender mercies of God in everyday life. Mary knew that God's mercies are new every morning. God would provide everything she would need. Great is God's faithfulness.

Holy, merciful, mighty, and deeply personal God, do great things for us too! Amen.

† December 21 †

Depend on God

Luke 1:51-56

We can depend on God. God is enough. God is generous. God's ways are certainly not our ways, but God's faithfulness extends from generation to generation. Mary spoke with timeless wisdom. God will never leave or forsake us.

Her thoughtful and spiritually mature reflection helps us remember that God cares, sees, and listens. God responds and gets personally involved in our lives. God scatters the arrogant and lifts up the lowly. God fills the hungry and sends the rich away empty. God is a God who keeps divine promises.

As Christmas draws closer, remember Mary's words while shopping for gifts or taking our children to see Santa Claus. Christmas is so much more than trees and presents. Christmas is about God's mighty deeds through Jesus Christ, the babe in the manger. Christmas invites us to linger in Bethlehem and be with this remarkable child, God in a diaper.

Reflect on today's verses and let the Spirit of God bless your meditations. Listen to the still, often very quiet voice of God in your heart. As you do, you will better hear the outside voices clamoring for your attention. Center on Christ alone. You will be deeply blessed.

God, thank you for caring for the poor, the humble, and the hungry. Thank you for being dependable and just. Thank you for being our God. Amen.

† December 22 †

A favorite Christmas tree ornament

Isaiah 65:25

I once had a roommate who kept her artificial Christmas tree up year round. The inexpensive tree was prominently displayed in the front window for the entire neighborhood to see and enjoy. Our neighbors thought we were a bit eccentric but harmless. That inexpensive tree provided good natured entertainment for many and a few sarcastic comments by others.

Each month had a different and distinctly seasonal ornamental theme. July was easy with patriotic red, white, and blue. November decorations had turkey ornaments and autumn colors. Easter brought the tree festive little toy bunnies, colored eggs, and ceramic chicks. Christmas however, was a marvelous hodgepodge of ornaments. I am convinced Martha Stewart would have shaked her head in dismay at our little tree.

Christmas ornaments can beautifully reflect the meaning of the season. One of my all time favorites is a cheap ceramic little lamb lying peacefully next to a lion, inspired by today's verse found in Isaiah.

This simple ornament brings each viewer into the rest of the Christ child story. The holy child of Bethlehem was born with a divine mission, to conquer sin and death. The babe in the manger grew up to be the greatest spiritual leader world history would ever know, who promised to return to earth again, in great power and heavenly glory.

When that great and wonderful day occurs, a new heaven and earth will be ushered in, bringing into existence a world where the lion and lamb peacefully coexist, and God will dwell permanently in our midst. There will be no more sin, crying, pain, or death in that new creation. All this theology is reflected in my simple little Christmas ornament.

What ornaments hang on your own tree this year? Do any of them tell the Christmas story? If not, consider adding some that reflect the spiritual meaning of the season. A nativity scene, star of David, the three kings from the Orient, and the lion with the lamb complement Santa Claus, and bring us powerful reminders of the real meaning of this holiday season.

Dear God, I thank you for the simple lessons Christmas ornaments bring. Through ornaments on my own tree, and the trees of others, bless my Christmas season prayers today. Amen.

† **December 23** †

The census

Luke 2:1-4

The U.S. government recently completed a national census. Many gay- and lesbian-affirming Christian churches even preached on the vital need to be seen, heard, counted, and identified in order to change the many unjust, cruel, and homophobic laws that promote bigotry and deny sexual minorities basic human rights. Some citizens received different forms in the mail for the census, asking for very personal information. Other people angrily refused to answer the census based on their distrust of the government and their desire for privacy. The government hired temporary employees to go door to door, to find citizens who had refused to answer the census. Those people refusing to cooperate were issued financial fines.

The census Joseph experienced in first century Israel was a much different experience. He had no choice but to travel an arduous and dangerous road to his hometown to register. There was no other alternative but to bring Mary, who was almost nine months pregnant and ready to give birth. Joseph obeyed the Roman census law. The consequences were severe for those refusing to cooperate. The Roman government did not make exceptions for hardship cases among the peasant class.

Joseph's obedience to civil law fulfilled ancient prophecy. Bethlehem was both the town where King David was born (1 Samuel 17:12; 20:6), and it was where the ancient prophets expected the long awaited Messiah to be born. "But you, Bethlehem of Ephrathah, who are one of the little clans of Judah, from you shall come forth for me one who is to rule in Israel, whose origin is from old, from ancient days" (Micah 5:2, NRSV).

Remember that God has already counted and included each of us as dearly loved people. Let us prepare for Christmas with joyful celebration, secure in knowing we are valued, precious, cherished, and beloved in God's sight.

God, not only have you counted us by name, but you even know our deepest concerns and needs. Thank you for being so wonderful and loving. Amen.

† December 24 – Christmas Eve †

God in a diaper

Luke 2:5-7

The most powerful Christmas Eve service over the past forty years for me took place on a U.S. Navy ammunition ship in the Persian Gulf. I was the ship's chaplain. For many of the young men and women on board this would be the first Christmas away from home.

Several of us secretly labored to make it a memorable evening for them. We worked months in advance, thoughtfully preparing for Christmas. Every sailor would be included and would receive a Christmas stocking as his or her gift when they awoke on Christmas Day.

Several U.S. churches had mailed us cookies and fudge for the sailors. Each piece had to be individually wrapped before we stuffed Christmas stockings. Before the shipboard service, we carefully hung the Christmas stockings by each sailor's sleeping area.

I will always remember that particular Christmas Eve. We were thousands of miles away from our loved ones in unfriendly waters. It was a time before e-mail and cellular phones. All we had was each other. We gathered in the ship's cafeteria for a time of Christmas caroling. I had written a simple play and the commanding officer had a major part in it. The young sailors sang, laughed, and seemed to enjoy everything. I remember the looks on their faces as they crowded into the area. Suddenly Santa Claus arrived with gifts. The sailors were delighted. Then we lit candles and listened to the timeless and beloved Christmas story. We closed the Christmas Eve service with singing. Years later, I received a letter from one of those sailors. He wrote, "Dear Chaplain, I should have thanked you then, but didn't. I want you to know that you gave me one of the best Christmases in my life. Thank you for all your hard work."

Compared to Mary and Joseph, my Christmas Eve was quite easy. Mary labored for hours in a small and dirty stable without even a midwife. All she had was anxious Joseph who refused to abandon her. You had to be there to appreciate poor Joseph's stress level. Here baby Jesus was born.

The Prince of peace and light to the nations was born in obscurity and poverty. God's show and tell was then wrapped in swaddling cloths. Mary was no longer great with child. She now had a great child, God in a diaper. Perhaps we should enjoy a pregnant pause and linger with the idea, both funny and serious, of God in a diaper. How like God to dwell among us as a newborn baby.

God, bless us with Christmas joy as we remember the first Christmas with gratitude. Amen.

† **December 25 – Christmas Day** †

Peace on earth

Luke 2:8-14a

Christmas is a time of joyous gatherings and celebrations. Perhaps by now the Christmas gifts have been opened. Or perhaps we are preparing dinners and entertaining guests. Many have traveled huge distances to be with family and friends. Merry Christmas!

The first Christmas was celebrated by an angelic host singing "glory to God in the highest, and on earth peace." The festive angels appeared to a startled group of humble shepherds watching their sheep at night. The shepherds were terrified at first. Who among us would not be afraid of such a sight?

The angels reassured them and encouraged them to be brave. They had good news of great joy for all the peoples of the earth. These simple shepherds were the first to hear it! Truly, God's ways are not ours. The first Christmas was for the humble, the poor, and the lowly, among peasant shift workers.

God blessed them with an angelic praise concert, singing alleluias.

Alleluia! Glory to God in the highest, with peace on earth and goodwill towards all. Amen.

† December 26 †

Holding God in your arms
Luke 2:15-20

God comes to us with every birth. All parents can appreciate a sense of the divine as they hold new life in their arms. My beloved grandmother always used to say there is something wonderful about holding a baby. It is like holding God in your arms. Up to her dying day, she always loved holding a newborn child. Babies helped her feel closest to God.

As Mary and Joseph tenderly cradled the Christ child, they knew they were holding God in their arms. Together they proudly showed their sweet baby to the excited shepherds who crowded about them.

The rough shepherds, who never tired of tending their own little lambs, quickly spread the news about this amazing child from God throughout the countryside. They spoke to anyone who would listen to their incredible story of the awesome angelic concert under the stars, and the little baby who had been born in a stable.

Their astonishing story continues to amaze every generation.

Now with the shepherds, it is time to return to our daily lives, after having experienced the extraordinary through the Christmas story. With the young virgin mother, we too can treasure this wonderful tale of divine mercy and love, while pondering the deeper meanings of holding God in our arms through a newborn child.

Thank God for babies. Every baby is a reminder of divine love, mercy, and grace. How like God to bless the world through infant innocence and purity. Learn to love holding babies and hold them at every opportunity. You will feel closer to God. Every time you hold a baby in your arms, you are seeing Jesus in human form.

God, I thank you for babies and for the Christmas story. As the Christmas season winds down, help me feel closer to you every time I see and hold a baby. Amen.

† December 27 †

Prevailing, persevering prayer wisdom from an elder
Luke 2:21-32

We can join elderly Simeon in praising God today as he eagerly reached out and held the tiny baby, Jesus. Through Holy Spirit inspiration, Simeon realized God had graciously answered his prevailing, persevering prayers. His feeble old eyes, dimmed with age and cataracts, had finally seen the salvation of the world. Simeon had spent his entire life waiting and praying for the promised Messiah. With Jesus in his frail arms, he knew his prayers had been answered. Now he could die in peace.

In this brief story, Simeon brings every generation of Bible readers a wealth of spiritual insight and wisdom, seasoned by decades of faithful praying. Gay or straight, we are called to pray. Prayer is not only our life-line to God, but also our means of making the world a better place to live. History has always belonged to the intercessors, those who care enough to pray patiently throughout a lifetime.

If you wish to change the world, make a commitment to pray. Pray for needs, causes, people, and places near and dear to your heart throughout your lifetime. Pray daily, pray often, and pray privately and publicly. Pray until something happens and then pray more for even greater miracles of grace and mercy.

Consider keeping a prayer journal and marvel at God's answers. As you keep track of God's gracious response to your intercessory prayers, you will be greatly blessed. Sometimes God answers immediately and in remarkable ways. Then there are times when God seems silent for days, weeks, months, or even years before clear answers are seen. But pray boldly, patiently, passionately, and with joyful expectation. In doing so, someday you too, might find yourself holding God's answers in your arms.

In the process, you will also be transformed and energized, blessed and encouraged through the power of prayer. Through your prayers, you can make the world a better place. Why not begin today?

Teach me how to pray, O God, with the joyful and faithful dedication of Simeon. Amen.

† December 28 †

Growing in wisdom and grace

Luke 2:33-40

Today's passage provides a glimmer of insight about the child-hood of Jesus. From the first moments of his conception and birth, his parents marveled at what was said about him. From birth, complete and total strangers blessed their baby boy publicly. People excitedly told others about this remarkable child, such as the shepherds, the foreign and strange Magi from afar (Matthew 2:1-12), and the very old devout Simeon and Anna in the temple. Jesus was blessed, affirmed, celebrated, and marveled at by all patiently awaiting the long expected Messiah. The grace of God was clearly upon him.

Simeon both blessed and prophesied about this amazing child. He specifically told Mary that one day a sword would pierce her heart. In other words, Jesus would break her heart. Anna, who was also a very old and wise prophetess, immediately identified the Christ child as an historic and revolutionary person sent from God. Both elders spoke to many worshippers in the temple about the child, Jesus.

We do know that Mary and Joseph returned to their hometown, Nazareth. There they raised Jesus as a devout, orthodox Jewish son. Jesus grew up and became strong, filled with wisdom, and God's grace was evident upon him. He was blessed from conception, birth, child dedication, and childhood. He could reach his full potential because he was loved, blessed, valued, and cherished.

Many people live in search of their blessing. Often their parents have never given it to them. As a result, their children often spend their lives seeking affirmation and belonging, sometimes in the wrong places. Families are not easy to live with. Sometimes we break each other's hearts. All children need parental blessing to thrive.

Perhaps you have never felt parental blessing. Some parents are incapable of blessing their children. I have noticed over the years that the most painful thing a parent can say is, "I wish you had never been born." I have seen tears come to people's eyes when I have said, "God bless you."

Out of the same mouth comes blessings and cursing. Choose to bless. Blessings beget blessings. God bless you.

God, bless us, each and every one. Bless us daily. Bless our loved ones.
Teach us how to bless others and grow in the wisdom and grace of young
Jesus. Amen.

† December 29 †

Amazing spiritual insights

Luke 2:41-47

Jesus grew up with God-power. His parents were devout and loving people of faith. They were determined to raise their children with the
benefits of a religious education and upbringing. Their children would
learn how to pray, study sacred words, worship regularly, practicing and
honoring daily, weekly, and annual religious rituals and observances. This
would empower their children when life became difficult.

As a result, Jesus had a rich spiritual upbringing. He loved learning about God and was full of questions as only a twelve-year-old can be.
He so hungered for God-knowledge that he lingered in Jerusalem to be
with the religious teachers of the temple. While his parents were frantic
with worry over his welfare, Jesus astonished the religious teachers with
his spiritual understandings. His worried parents found their remarkable
child in the temple courts.

Many parents chose not to raise their children within a church. As
a result, their little ones grow up without hearing wonderful Sunday school
stories about Jesus. I have found over the years, that when those children
become adults, they lack a spiritual foundation that helps them cry out to
God in their deepest moments of human need. Many do not know how to
pray.

On the other side of the spectrum, there are abusive and intolerant
religious institutions that teach bigotry, condemnation, and hate towards
those different from themselves. Much grief has resulted and many wars
have been fought in the name of God. Religious intolerance always ends
in human tragedies. Fortunately there are some people who are reluctant
to perpetuate that kind of religion to the next generation.

Yet children and adults alike need a healthy spiritual foundation
that is personal, sustaining, dignifying, uplifting. No matter what age we
are, we need God, even when religious institutions fail us. We are never

too old to approach God, as blessed and cherished children. So with child-like curiosity, be open to learning more about God and you will find great healing and strength for your soul. Study the amazing spiritual insights as revealed by the inquisitive twelve-year-old Jesus and you will be empowered for life.

God, help us reclaim childhood innocence and eagerly learn about you. Bless us as we raise our children with some basic spiritual foundations to equip them for life. Amen.

† December 30 †

Spiritual insight and priorities

Luke 2:48-50

At age twelve, Jesus already had established some of his spiritual priorities. His love for God's house was profound. He was already spiritually mature. As a preteen, Jesus had a tender, intimate, loving, and trusting name for God that most of his peers and certainly his parents did not use. His prayer life was radical. Jesus believed in prayer and having special places to worship and pray.

Jesus grew up in a religious atmosphere. He enjoyed regular worship in the local synagogue including periodic pilgrimages to Jerusalem. He grew up with a distinct rhythm of daily worship and hours of prayer. These influenced him as he grew into manhood. From birth, Jesus was taught the Torah (the first five books in the Old Testament). As a child, he was taught to memorize many Old Testament prayers. Regular worship habits were part of his society and culture. The memory and oral traditions were engraved in his heart.

As a Jewish son, his religious education began at birth. It began in the home before he was introduced to formal teaching. It was seen and heard, before book learning. Jewish parents had very high regard for their children. The relationship with the father and mother is intimate and tender. The fifth commandment is to honor our parents. Jesus did that. When his worried parents found him in the temple, he obediently came home with them.

The New Testament reminds us that we are positively influenced by a knowledge of Holy Scripture (2 Timothy 1:5; 3:15). Sacred words are empowering when taken in context. Consider reading the Bible from cover to cover. It is a big book and takes some time and discipline. The Bible is full of wonderful words of life. Like Jesus, consider visiting a local place of worship. Find one that welcomes and affirms you as a valued, precious, child of God. Consider praying a tender, intimate, loving name for God. Your life will never again be the same.

Teach your children about God through the Jesus stories, and they too, will be empowered.

God, help us seek and find you, while learning to love your houses of worship. Amen.

†   December 31 – New Year's Eve   †

Let this child teach us on New Year's Eve

Luke 2:51-52

It is New Year's Eve. For many this is a time for celebrating the New Year. Some will party, others attend retreats, church prayer vigils, and worship services while many will chose to stay home and avoid the drunk drivers. I usually enjoy this particular evening at home with friends and loved ones. It is an enjoyable way to reflect on the old year and anticipate the new with good food and friends.

This used to be a very painful evening for me. Many years ago, a very dear friend of mine was killed on New Year's Eve. He was my best friend and I had almost married him. His death was sudden and totally unexpected. He died doing what he loved when his parachute never opened. He crashed into the earth and never regained consciousness. I was paralyzed with grief, along with his many friends and family. As a result, I live in keen awareness of the frailty and preciousness of life. Each day is a gift. I frequently tell my beloved friends and family members that I love them. I often say, "God bless you." I try and live each day as if it might be my last, asking forgiveness when needed, making peace when possible and not letting the sun go down on my anger. Yes, I go dancing, clogging, at every opportunity.

My beloved grandmother taught me to honor the memories of dear departed ones by thanking the good Lord for all the good memories while living one day at a time. I treasure cherished memories of my deceased friend, Bob. As long as we remember, we honor the lives, lived with love, and they still live on within our hearts.

A bookmark of mine shows a little girl at life's crossroad. The road signs point in different directions. One sign points to "Your life." The other sign points to another path significantly named, "No longer an option." The old year is almost finished. This is a great time to reflect on your life and what is no longer an option. It is a wonderful opportunity to reflect inward, upward, and outward. What kind of year has it been for you? Do you have any treasured memories? What was good, bad, beautiful, and ugly? How have you grown? Where has God been present in your life? What are your resolutions, hopes, and dreams for the New Year?

For next year, consider letting the teachings of Jesus help you in the days, weeks, and months ahead. Jesus grew from a remarkable child into the greatest spiritual teacher our world has ever known. His words are full of wisdom, helpful for walking with God and our neighbors, one step at a time when one day feels overwhelming. The Gospels offer many wonderful words of life. Never underestimate their power to help you and those you love. Jesus will always be God's show and tell. Through the Gospel stories, we experience God's loving heartbeat.

Live as God's beloved people. Have a happy New Year. As we close the year, an old Gaelic blessing comes to mind, "And may the LORD hold you in the hollow of God's hand." God bless you.

God, accept our gratitude for this past year. Bless us in the New Year. Help us be loved all our days. Amen.

† Bibliography †

Bible Translations Used:

Unless otherwise noted, all Bible translations used are from the New Revised Standard Version, Copyright of the New Revised Standard Version, 1989 by the Division of Christian Education of the National Council of the Churches of Christ in the United States of America.

The Amplified Bible, New Testament. Grand Rapids: Zondervan Publishing Company. 1987.

Barker, Kenneth, General Editor. *The NIV Study Bible.* New International Version. Grand Rapids: Zondervan. 1985.

Gold, Victor Roland, Thomas L. Hoyt, Jr., Sharon H. Ringe, Susan Brooks Thistlethwaite, Burton H. Throckmorton, Jr., Barbara A. Withers, Editors. *The New Testament and Psalms: An Inclusive Version.* New York: Oxford University Press. 1995.

The Life Recovery Bible: The Living Bible. Wheaton: Tyndale House. 1992. (Notes and Bible helps, copyright 1992 by David A. Stoop and Stephen F. Arterburn, Executive Editors.)

Meeks, Wayne E., General Editor. *The Harper Collins Study Bible: New Revised Standard Version with the Apocryphal/Deuterocanonical Books.* New York: Harper Collins. 1989. (Copyright of the New Revised Standard Version, 1989 by the Division of Christian Education of the National Council of the Churches of Christ in the United States of America.)

Other Resources Quoted:

á Kempis, Thomas. *The Imitation of Christ.* Grand Rapids: Zondervan Publishing Company. 1983.

Ayo, Nicholas, James Flanigan, Joseph Ross, and J. Massynghaerde Ford. *Where Joy and Sorrow Meet: A Way of the Cross.* Notre Dame: Ave Maria Press. 1999.

Barna, George. "New Study Predicts a Cyberchurch," *Internet for Christians Newsletter.* Issue 57, 12 May 1998.

Bauer, Walter, William F. Arndt, and F. Wilbur Gingrich. *A Greek-English Lexicon of the New Testament and Other Early Christian Literature*. Revised and augmented, fifth edition. Chicago and London: University of Chicago Press. 1958.

Beuchner, Frederick. *Listening to Your Life: Daily Meditations with Frederick Beuchner*. San Francisco: HarperSanFrancisco. 1992

Bennett, William J. *The Book of Virtues: A Treasury of Great Moral Stories*. New York: Simon & Schuster. 1993.

Blackmore, James H. *Reflections on the Temptations of Christ*. Nashville: Thomas Nelson Publishers. 1992.

Bonhoeffer, Dietrich. *The Cost of Discipleship*. New York: Collier Books Publishing, Macmillan Publishing Company, revised and unabridged edition. 1938.

The Book of Common Prayer and the Administration of the Sacraments and Other Rites and Ceremonies of the Church, According to the Episcopal Church. New York: Seabury Press. 1979.

Bounds, E. M. *Power Through Prayer*. Chicago: Moody Press. 1982.

Breathnach, Sara Ban. *The Simple Abundance Journal of Gratitude*. New York: Warner Books. 1990.

Bretall, Robert, Editor. *A Kierkegaard Anthology*. Princeton, NJ: Princeton University Press. 1946.

Bromiley, Geoffrey W. *Theological Dictionary of the New Testament*. Abridged in one volume. Grand Rapids: Eerdmans. 1985.

Brown, Colin, Editor. *The New International Dictionary of New Testament Theology, Vol. 3*. Grand Rapids: Regency Zondervan. 1986.

Broyles, Anne. *Journaling: A Spirit Journey*. Nashville: The Upper Room. 1998.

Bruce, F. F. *The Hard Sayings of Jesus*. Downers Grove: InterVarsity Press. 1983.

---------- Editor. *The International Bible Commentary with the New International Version.* Grand Rapids: Zondervan. 1999.

Callahan, William R. *Noisy Contemplation: Deep Prayer for Busy People.* Hyattsville, MD: Quixote Center. 1982.

Capon, Robert Farrar. *The Parables of the Kingdom.* Grand Rapids: Eerdmans. 1985.

Chambers, Oswald. *My Utmost for His Highest.* New York: Dodd Mead & Co., renewed 1963 by the Oswald Chambers Publications Assn., Ltd. 1935.

Continuum Publishing Group. *The Complete Book of Christian Prayer.* New York: Continuum Press. 1997.

Damiano, Celestina J., and Tomas T. Goodey. *The Way of the Cross, with Text from Scripture.* Baltimore: Barton-Cotton, Inc. 1965.

Davies, Horton, Editor. *The Communion of Saints: Prayers of the Famous.* Grand Rapids: Eerdmans. 1990.

Davis, Kathy. *Proverbs from Around the World: A Mile Walked with a Friend Contains Only a Hundred Steps, Vol. II.* Glendale Heights: Great Quotations. 1992.

De Mello, Anthony. *Sadhana, A Way to God: Christian Exercises in Eastern Form.* New York: Image Books. 1984.

Douglas, J. D., F. F. Bruce, J. I. Packer, N. Hillyer, D. Guthrie, A. R. Millard, and D. J. Wiseman, Editors. *New Bible Dictionary.* Second edition. Wheaton: Tyndale. 1962.

Duck, Ruth. *Everflowing Streams: Songs for Worship.* New York: The Pilgrim Press. 1981.

Earle, Mary. "Reading the Text of an Illness." *Presence: The Journal of Spiritual Directors International.* Volume 6, No. 1. January 2000.

Edwards, Tilden. *Living in the Presence: Spiritual Exercises to Open Our Lives to the Awareness of God.* San Francisco: Harper Collins. 1987, 1995.

---------- *Sabbath Time*. Nashville: Upper Room Books. 1992.

Fenton, Mark, and the Editors of *Walking. The New Walker's Logbook*. Boston: Walking Magazine. 1995.

Foster, Richard J. *Celebration of Discipline: The Path to Spiritual Growth*. Revised and expanded. San Francisco: Harper Collins. 1978, 1988.

---------- *The Challenge of the Disciplined Life: Christian Reflections on Money, Sex, and Power*. New York: Harper Collins. 1985.

---------- *Prayer: Finding the Heart's True Home*. New York: Harper-SanFrancisco. 1992.

Ferguson, Sinclair B., David F. Wright, J. I. Packer. *New Dictionary of Theology*. Downers Grove: InterVarsity Press. 1988.

Gaebelein, Frank E., General Editor. *The Expositor's Bible Commentary*. Volume 9. Grand Rapids: Zondervan. 1984.

Gaines Lane, Gretchen. *My Memory Book: A Journal for Grieving Children*. Second Edition. Gaithersburg, MD: Chi Rho Press. 1995.

Guthrie, D., and J. A. Motyer, Editors. *The New Bible Commentary*. Grand Rapids: Eerdmans. 1970.

Hall, Thelma. *Too Deep for Words: Rediscovering Lectio Divina with 500 Scripture Texts for Prayer*. New York: Paulist Press. 1988.

Hanh, Thich Nhat. *The Long Road Turns to Joy: A Guide to Walking Meditation*. Berkley: Parallax Press. 1996.

---------- *Being Peace*. Berkeley: Parallax Press. 1987.

Harris, R. Laird, Gleason L. Archer, Jr., and Bruce K. Waltke. *Theological Wordbook of the Old Testament*. Volume. 1. Chicago: Moody Press. 1980.

Hendriksen, William. *New Testament Commentary: The Gospel of Matthew*. Grand Rapids: Baker House. 1973.

Hickman, Hoyt L., Don E. Saliers, Lawrence Hall Stookey, and James F. White. *Handbook of the Christian Year*. Nashville: Abingdon. 1986.

Hinson, E. Glenn. Editor. *Spirituality in Ecumenical Perspective*. Louisville: Westminster/John Knox Press. 1993.

Hunter III, George G. *How to Reach Secular People*. Nashville: Abingdon. 1992.

Huston, Sterling W. *Crusade Evangelism and the Local Church*. Minneapolis: World Wide Publishing. Rev. 1996.

Jesdanum, Anick. "Working Netless...by Choice." *The Sun*. 22 September 2000, p. A8.

Job, Rueben P., and Norman Shawchuck. *A Guide to Prayer for All God's People*. Nashville: The Upper Room. 1994. (Especially *Picturing God*, by Ann Belford Ulanov.)

---------- *A Guide to Prayer for Ministers and Other Servants*. Nashville: The Upper Room. 1993.

L'Engle, Madeleine and Carole F. Chase. *Glimpses of Grace: Daily Thoughts and Reflections*. San Francisco: HarperSanFrancisco. 1996.

Lockyer, Herbert. *All the Prayers of the Bible: A Devotional and Expositional Classic*. Grand Rapids: Lamplighter Books. 1959.

May, Gerald G. *Addiction and Grace*. New York: Harper and Row. 1988.

Muggeridge, Malcolm. *Something Beautiful for God*. New York: Harper and Row. 1971.

Muto, Susan. *John of the Cross for Today: The Dark Night*. Notre Dame: Ave Marie Press. 1994.

Norris, Kathleen. *Dakota: A Spiritual Geography*. New York: Ticknor and Fields. 1993.

Nouwen, Henri J. M. *Can You Drink the Cup?* Notre Dame: Ave Maria Press. 1996.

---------- *Behold the Beauty of the LORD*. Notre Dame: Ave Marie Press. 1987.

---------- *Life of the Beloved: Spiritual Living in a Secular World*. New York: Crossroad Press. 1992.

O'Donohue, John. *Anam Cara: A Book of Celtic Wisdom*. New York: Harper Collins. 1997.

Osbeck, Kenneth W. *Amazing Grace: 366 Inspiring Hymn Stories for Daily Devotions*. Grand Rapids: Kregel Publishers. 1990.

Peterson, Eugene. *The Message: The New Testament in Contemporary Language*. Colorado Springs: NavPress. 1993.

---------- *Answering God*. San Francisco: Harper and Row. 1989.

Ruiz, Alphonse. *The Prayers of St. John of the Cross*. New York: New City Press. 1991.

Sanford, John A. *The Kingdom Within: The Inner Meaning of Jesus' Sayings*. Revised edition. New York: Harper Collins Publishers. 1987.

Satterfield, Carrolle E., and William Donald Borders. *My Daily Way of the Cross*. Baltimore: Barton-Cotton, Inc. 1980.

Smalley, Gary and John Trent. *The Blessing*. Nashville: Thomas Nelson Publishers. 1986.

Simcox, Carroll E. *3000 Quotations on Christian Themes*. Grand Rapids: Baker Book House, 2nd reprint. 1988.

Stein, Joseph. *Fiddler on the Roof*. Pocket Books: New York. 1965.

Strong, James. *The Exhaustive Concordance of the Bible*. Nashville: Holmen Bible Publishers.

Sweeting, George. *More Than 2,000 Great Quotes and Illustrations*. Waco: Word Books. 1985.

Thomas, Dylan. *The Poems of Dylan Thomas*, published by New Directions. Copyright © 1952, 1953 Dylan Thomas. Copyright © 1937, 1945, 1955, 1962, 1966, 1967 the Trustees for the Copyrights of Dylan Thomas.

Thoreau, Henry David. *Walden: Life in the Woods.* (Especially chapter 2, "Where I Lived and What I Lived For.") Originally published in 1854. Boston: Houghton Mifflin Co. 1995

Truluck, Rembert. *Steps to Recovery from Bible Abuse.* Gaithersburg: Chi Rho Press, Inc. 2000.

Vardey, Lucinda, Editor. *The Flowering of the Soul: A Book of Prayers by Women.* Boston: Beacon Press. 2002.

Vine, W. E., Merrill F. Unger, and William White, Jr. *Vine Expository Dictionary of Biblical Words.* Nashville: Thomas Nelson Publishers. 1985.

Wuellner, Flora Slosson. *Prayer and Our Bodies.* Nashville: The Upper Room. 1987.